THE WORLD SPORTS RECORD ATLAS

THE WORLD SPORTS RECORD ATLAS

COMPILED BY DAVID EMERY AND STAN GREENBERG
FOREWORD BY SEBASTIAN COE

Facts On File Publications
New York, New York ● Oxford, England

World Sports Record Atlas
compiled by David Emery and Stan
Greenberg

Copyright © First Editions 1986

First published in the United States by
Facts on File Inc.
460 Park Avenue South,
New York, NY 10016

Emery, David.
   The World Sports Record Atlas.

   1.   Sports – Records.
   I. Greenberg, Stan.   II. Title.
GV741.E54 1986
796'.021   86-9008

ISBN 0-8160-1378-0
ISBN 0-8160-1579-1 (Pbk.)

Designed, edited and produced by
First Editions
27 Palmeira Mansions, Church Road,
Hove, East Sussex, England

Printed in England by
Redwood Burn, Trowbridge
Phototypeset in England by
Presentia Art, Horsham

FOREWORD BY SEBASTIAN COE

Worthwhile world records do not get broken accidentally. It should be remembered that even the attempts that fail are the work of only the most dedicated toilers in their field.

It is beyond the scope of a foreword or even this book to analyse the intense motivation needed, but some idea of how strong this drive to succeed is can be gained by considering the arduousness of the regimes which record breakers submit themselves to in order to achieve their goals.

I know the resolution needed in midwinter to turn once more into a wet and icy wind for yet another repetition run up a long steep hill, when I can hardly see through frozen eyelashes. Being continually bent over the insides of a complex, highly stressed racing machine, trying to resolve difficult technical problems in the small hours of the morning also has its own draining demands.

These unique people — the record breakers — drive themselves remorselessly to a common but unachievable goal in whatever is their chosen medium, be it on land or sea or in the air. Unachievable? Yes, because it is not just a record they are after — that they may well get — they are pursuing the ultimate in excellence which can never be reached and all this is done in the certain knowledge that the record will be only borrowed, it is not theirs to *keep*.

My Olympic gold medals are mine for always, my records are not. This is because there is no limit to human aspirations, mental or physical. Someone, somewhere will always be reaching out for a yet more distant star. This book helps us to remember the previous holders of the records, it is they who have defined the present. In a sense we record breakers are only building on the foundations laid by those who preceded us.

There is another important aspect of record breaking that must be mentioned, a special ability of so many of these supermen and superwomen. It is the gift of inspiring others to share their dream and work selflessly almost to exploitation in the pursuit of the goal, so that it becomes a great team effort.

Bullying and cajoling seldom work, not more than once anyway, without the personal example which must be shown. Above all it takes courage, some may have to cope with total exhaustion, while others risk even death.

A man's dreams may be his own business, but in the glare of modern media exposure he is very often carrying the added burden of a whole nation's expectations. All may share in the victory, but he has to carry the weight of failure alone. Despite all the genuine sympathy, in the end it is always a case of "we win — he loses".

So why do they go on? If we could answer this question simply and neatly then we would have a better answer as to why the human species is supreme: a better answer than merely walking upright, or having fingers and thumb, or being labelled a tool-making animal. It is not that we just think, but it is the how and why of it that is so fascinating.

In memory of all those brave people in this book who have succeeded for that brief but wonderful moment, and to all the unrecorded and unknown who also tried but failed, I wish this book of records great success.

Sebastian Coe

CONTENTS

SEBASTIAN COE'S WORLD RECORDS

Outdoors

800m	1:42.33	Oslo	5/7/79
Mile	3:49.0	Oslo	17/7/79
1500m	3:32.1	Zurich	15/8/79
1000m	2:13.40	Oslo	1/7/80
800m	1:41.73	Florence	10/6/81*
1000m	2:12.18	Oslo	11/7/81*
Mile	3:48.53	Zurich	19/8/81
Mile	3:47.33	Brussels	28/8/81
4 x 800m Relay	7:03.89	London	30/8/82*

Indoors

800m	1:46.0	Cosford	11/2/81
800m	1:44.91	Cosford	12/3/83*
1000m	2:18.58	Oslo	19/3/83*

*unbroken at time of writing

INTRODUCTION
BY DAVID EMERY

The substance of this book can be simply told: it is about the human spirit. Yes, that same complex, wondrous, maddening, soaring subject which has inspired the greatest artists, musicians and authors for a thousand years.

So who are Stan Greenberg and I to ponder such elusive metaphysics? Well, for a start we had two great allies: the tape measure and the stop watch. Mundane appliances, perhaps, when appraised alongside micro-surgery or nuclear fission, but in their own humble way they give a clearer evaluation of human spirit than a roomful of highly sophisticated equipment.

Each generation throws forward its great men and women, the pioneers of thought and fashion, the leaders of industry and church, the rulers and the rebels. But only in sport can their achievements be measured so precisely, their ability compared so exactly.

That is not to suggest, of course, that sport's importance compares with any of the above. In most forms it is a mere sideshow, albeit a gloriously spectacular sideshow, when considered together with the real business of living. But it is in sport as with nothing else that we see year by year, month by month, human beings pushing back the frontiers of the possible, proving unarguably our advancement and improvement.

In this revue we have sought not only to highlight the great world record breakers in more than 30 sports, we have also attempted to underline trends and, where valid, to analyse their origins and movements.

For instance, it is no coincidence that America's huge upsurge in black sprinting power coincided with the battle for Human Rights and Martin Luther King. Suddenly more and more negroes were winning places at American Universities, where their naturally rhythmic, loose-limbed running ability and burning sense of grievance were channelled by top class coaching.

We have considered, too, the geographical implications. How, of the world's heavyweight boxing champions, 32 have come from the United States. How East Germany have come from nowhere to dominate women's swimming. How Britain have consistently produced kings of speed in cars and boats as well as establishing a tradition of brilliant milers, culminating in the golden triumvirate of Seb Coe, Steve Ovett and Steve Cram.

Nowhere do these national quirks surface more dramatically than in the world of squash where the tiny area of Peshawar has produced a dynasty of world beating squash players, including the currently invincible Jahangir Khan.

Natural advantages are also a factor. It helps to have the sun on your back if you are going to be a water skier (even though Britain's cold water heroes have tried their best to prove differently). And if you want to be a middle or long distance runner you should find a mother and father living some way above sea level — preferably no less than 5,000 feet (1515m). The consequent thinness of the air will then force your body to produce more oxygen-carrying haemoglobin in your blood and therefore develop you into a far more efficient racing machine . . . as the Kenyans and the other high altitude Africans proved at the 1968 Mexico City Olympics and thereafter.

Thin air, of course, also helps sprinters (up to 400m) to move faster because it offers less resistance. And here it is interesting to note the comparisons between the world record and the best non-altitude mark. (See also 400m, pp24-25).

Event	World rec	Best non altitude	Date	Athlete
100m	9.93 secs	9.96 secs	Mel Lattany, (USA)	1984
200m	19.72	19.75	Carl Lewis, (USA)	1983
400m	43.86	44.26	Alberto Juantorena, (CUB)	1976
Long jump	8.90m (29ft 2½in)	8.79m (28ft 10¼in)	Carl Lewis, (USA)	1983

Without becoming over-technical we have also examined physiological factors with particular reference to the battle of the sexes. Certain sports doctors in recent years have attempted to prove that women will one day catch the men and overtake them in endurance events such as marathon running. That, we believe, is untrue. The one area where women do carry an advantage over men is in long distance swimming – such as cross Channel – where their higher ratio of body fat offers greater flotation, as well as superior insulation against cold.

But in running events they lag a fairly consistent 10 per cent behind men, even in the Marathon where they have made such enormous strides in the past decade. (See also Marathon, pp54-55).

MARATHON WORLD RECORD PROGRESSION

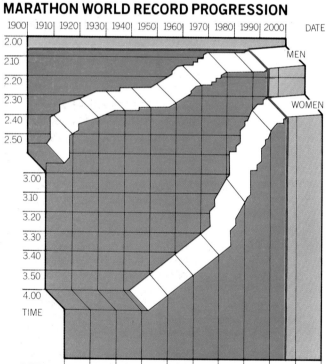

1,500m WORLD RECORD PROGRESSION

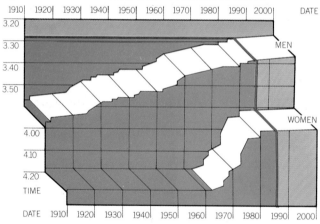

100m WORLD RECORD PROGRESSION

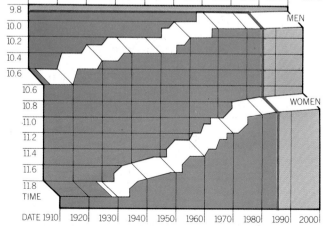

PERCENTAGE DIFFERENCE BETWEEN MEN'S AND WOMEN'S RUNNING RECORDS

Event	Men's record	Women's record	Percentage difference
100m	9.93	10.76	7.71
200m	19.72	21.71	9.17
400m	43.86	47.99	8.61
800m	1:41.73	1.53.28	10.20
1,500m	3:29.67	3:52.47	9.81
Mile	3:46.31	4:16.71	11.84
3,000m	7:32.01	8:22.62	10.05
5,000m	13:00.40	14:48.07	12.13
10,000m	27:13.81	30:59.42	12.13
Marathon	2:07:12	2:21:06	9.86
Relays			
4 x 100m	37.83	41.53	8.91
4 x 200m	1:20.26	1:28.15	8.95
4 x 400m	2:56.16	3:15.92	10.09
4 x 800m	7:03.89	7:50.17	9.84

The average percentage difference over these 14 events is 9.95. Theorists who claim women are better suited to distance running are not supported by the figures — the smallest gap between the sexes is over the 100m sprint

The rarely run (for women) 5,000m has the biggest gap (12.13 per cent) and with the 10,000m, now accepted into the full Olympic programme of events, still has some way to go.

We have touched, but not dwelled, on the subject of drugs. Every record included in the statistical lists in this book has been ratified by the international ruling body of that particular sport. It would be naive to believe that all are beyond reproach. But we have to accept the internal policing of the federation involved, a policing which, thankfully, seems to be strengthening year by year.

By that same token, there are many records which we have discarded because of doubt, even though they appear on other lists. But where they hold special significance, such as the astonishing run of North Korea's Sin Kim Dan in 1963, when she reportedly recorded 1 min 59.1 sec for the 800m and thus became the first woman through the two minute barrier, they are included in the text.

There is no suggestion that Sin Kim Dan's performance was artifically aided, just that North Korea were not part of the International Amateur Athletic Federation at the time and there were question marks over the competence of the time-keepers.

Certainly, though, the legendary Miss Dan ran with the aid of one drug which has helped create every page of this book. The self-induced adrenalin. It is the athlete's greatest weapon and worth understanding.

Our bodies have an amazing mechanism to help us deal with those things which threaten our safety, or with those tasks which demand supreme effort. It can be triggered by fear itself or by conscious recruitment. So a sudden movement in the shadows can bring the mechanism into play just as effectively as the learned deliberate building up of controlled aggression prior to a competition.

Scientists call this mechanism the "fight or flight" reaction.

Once a situation is "read" as requiring this reaction, rapid messages are passed from the brain through the autonomic system to two small glands which sit above (*supra*) the kidneys (*renals*).

These *Suprarenal Glands* might be thought of as resembling two tiny fruits. The "skin" and the "flesh" have quite separate functions. The "skin" — or *Cortex* produces the *Cortico-Steroids*. The "flesh" or *Medulla* produces *Adrenalin* (or *Epinephrine*) and *Noradrenaline* (or *Noredinephrine*). It is the medulla which is the primary target of the "emergency" message. As soon as it is received, the hormones adrenalin and noradrenalin are released from the two glands and carried in the blood to all parts of the body.

Adrenalin has highly specific effects as it spreads through the body. The most significant are the releasing of fuel — *glucose* from storage as *glycogen* in the liver; and selective blood flow. It diverts blood from skin and intestine by constricting relevant blood vessels. On the other hand, blood vessels in brain, lungs and muscle dilate. This selective blood flow and increased blood pressure and extra fuel ensures that blood rich in oxygen and fuel is brought rapidly to the sites where it is most needed in an emergency — the "mission control" of the brain, and the "engine rooms" — the muscles. By the same token, waste is rapidly removed. Breathing is, however, shallow and fast, so many athletes work to control breathing in the pre-start moments. While perception of fatigue is delayed, a substantial oxygen debt is established. This aspect of the mechanism alone helps take athletes beyond previous limits.

Without doubt, the learned ability to control and use this mechanism is of immense advantage to an athlete. As understanding and application of sports psychology grow, athletes will develop specific skills in this direction.

Some of the finest sports, of course, are immeasurable. Golf. Boxing. Tennis. Here we can relate only the happenings and leave you to draw your own conclusions as to who was the greatest.

The stopwatch tells us that Sebastian Coe would have beaten Roger Bannister by 80 yards over the mile. What it can't tell us is how Bannister would have fared with Coe's modern training regime.

In the boxing ring would Joe Louis have prevailed over Muhammad Ali? On golf's fairways would Jack Nicklaus have dominated Bobby Jones? Would Rod Laver have outmanoeuvered John McEnroe at Wimbledon? These imponderables can never be answered, but inside these pages we hope you find a mountain of fuel to fire your own arguments.

Where performances are measurable by that stop watch and tape we have tried to illustrate the improvements by a graphic stairway, showing the size of step taken by each generation. And we have added a prediction for the Year 2,000.

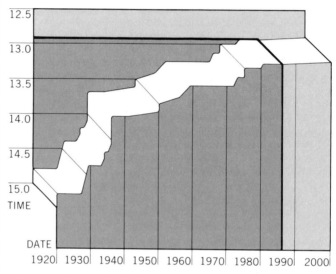

● The record progression in the 110m hurdles

The full list of Year 2,000 predictions is:

MEN
Predicted Records for the Year 2000

	Current	Year 2000
100m	9.93	9.89
200m	19.72	19.66
400m	43.86	43.70
800m	1:41.73	1:40.50
1500m	3:29.46	3:27.00
1 mile	3:46.32	3:44.00
3000m	7:32.1	7:28.00
5000m	13:00.40	12:50.00
10,000m	27:13.81	26:50.00
Marathon	2:07.12	2:05.00
110mH	12.93	12.89
400mH	47.02	46.80
300mSt	8:05.4	8:03.00
High Jump	2.41m (7ft 10½in)	2.46m (8ft 0½in)
Pole Vault	6.00m (19ft 8¼in)	6.20m (20ft 4¼in)
Long Jump	8.90m (29ft 2½in)	8.90m (29ft 2½in)
Triple Jump	17.97m (58ft 11½in)	18.20m (59ft 8½in)
Shot	22.62m (74ft 2¼in)	23.00m (75ft 5in)
Discus	71.86m (235ft 9in)	74.00m (242ft 9in)
Hammer	86.34m (283ft 3in)	87.50m (287ft 1in)
Javelin (old)	104.80m (343ft 9in)	100.00m (328ft) (new)
Decathlon (new)	8847pts	9100pts

WOMEN

	Current	Year 2000
100m	10.76	10.70
200m	21.71	21.50
400m	47.60	47.20
800m	1:53.28	1:52.00
1500m	3:52.47	3:51.00
1 mile	4:16.71	4:10.00
3000m	8:22.62	8:19.00
5000m	14:48.07	14:30.00
10,000m	30:59.42	30:30.00
Marathon	2:21.06	2:18.00
100mH	12.36	12.30
400mH	53.56	52.90
High Jump	2.07m (6ft 9½in)	2.10m (6ft 10½in)
Long Jump	7.44m (24ft 5in)	7.55m (24ft 9¼in)
Shot	22.53m (73ft 11in)	23.00m (75ft 5in)
Discus	74.56m (244ft 7in)	75.50m (247ft 8in)
Javelin	75.40m (247ft 4in)	77.00m (252ft 7in)
Heptathlon (new)	6946pts	7100pts

It will be fascinating to discover just how these forecasts match up in 14 years' time. We can be sure of one thing: no matter how fantastic they seem to us now, they will be commonplace to a future batch of record breakers. For that is the nature of the human spirit, reaching out for the ultimate performance while realising it is unobtainable.

Or as Robert Browning said so much more eloquently:

A man's reach should exceed his grasp,
Or what's a Heaven for?

CONVERSION FACTORS

To convert measurements from the metric system to the Imperial system, or vice versa, the following conversion factors apply.

Speed	Mph to Km/h	multiply by	1.609344
	Km/h to mph	multiply by	0.621371
	Mph to knots	multiply by	0.8684
	Knots to mph	multiply by	1.1515
Length	Miles to kilometres	multiply by	1.609344
	Kilometres to miles	multiply by	0.621371
	Metres to yards	multiply by	1.093613
	Yards to metres	multiply by	0.9144
	Metres to feet	multiply by	3.280843
	Feet to metres	multiply by	0.3048
Weight	Kilograms to pounds	multiply by	2.204622
	Pounds to kilograms	multiply by	0.453592

CONVERSION TABLES

Conversions from metric system to Imperial do not always exactly agree with conversions from Imperial system to metric as figures are rounded up to the nearest one inch or 2cm respectively for distances in the longer throwing events. Similarly in the jumps and shot, distances/heights are measured to the nearest quarter inch or 1cm.

Imperial to metric

High Jump

5ft 0in	1.52m
5ft 1in	1.55m
5ft 2in	1.57m
5ft 3in	1.60m
5ft 4in	1.62m
5ft 5in	1.65m
5ft 6in	1.67m
5ft 7in	1.70m
5ft 8in	1.72m
5ft 9in	1.75m
5ft 10in	1.78m
5ft 11in	1.80m
6ft 0in	1.83m
6ft 1in	1.85m
6ft 2in	1.88m
6ft 3in	1.90m
6ft 4in	1.93m
6ft 5in	1.95m
6ft 6in	1.98m
6ft 7in	2.00m
6ft 8in	2.03m
6ft 9in	2.05m
6ft 10in	2.08m
6ft 11in	2.11m
7ft 0in	2.13m
7ft 1in	2.16m
7ft 2in	2.18m
7ft 3in	2.21m
7ft 4in	2.23m
7ft 5in	2.26m
7ft 6in	2.28m
7ft 7in	2.31m
7ft 8in	2.33m
7ft 9in	2.36m
7ft 10in	2.39m
7ft 11in	2.41m
8ft 0in	2.44m

Pole Vault

13ft 0in	3.96m
13ft 3in	4.04m
13ft 6in	4.11m
13ft 9in	4.19m
14ft 0in	4.26m
14ft 3in	4.34m
14ft 6in	4.42m
14ft 9in	4.49m
15ft 0in	4.57m
15ft 3in	4.65m
15ft 6in	4.72m
15ft 9in	4.80m
16ft 0in	4.87m
16ft 3in	4.95m
16ft 6in	5.03m
16ft 9in	5.10m
17ft 0in	5.18m
17ft 3in	5.26m
17ft 6in	5.33m
17ft 9in	5.41m
18ft 0in	5.48m
18ft 3in	5.56m
18ft 6in	5.64m
18ft 9in	5.71m
19ft 0in	5.79m
19ft 3in	5.86m
19ft 6in	5.94m
19ft 9in	6.02m
20ft 0in	6.09m

Long Jump

16ft 0in	4.87m
16ft 6in	5.03m
17ft 0in	5.18m
17ft 6in	5.33m
18ft 0in	5.48m
18ft 6in	5.64m
19ft 0in	5.79m
19ft 6in	5.94m
20ft 0in	6.09m
20ft 6in	6.25m
21ft 0in	6.40m
21ft 6in	6.55m
22ft 0in	6.70m
22ft 6in	6.86m
23ft 0in	7.01m
23ft 6in	7.16m
24ft 0in	7.31m
24ft 6in	7.47m
25ft 0in	7.62m
25ft 6in	7.77m
26ft 0in	7.92m
26ft 6in	8.08m
27ft 0in	8.23m
27ft 6in	8.38m
28ft 0in	8.53m
28ft 6in	8.68m
29ft 0in	8.84m
29ft 3in	8.91m
29ft 6in	8.99m
29ft 9in	9.07m
30ft 0in	9.14m

Triple Jump/Shot

40ft 0in	12.19m
40ft 6in	12.34m
41ft 0in	12.49m
41ft 6in	12.65m
42ft 0in	12.80m
42ft 6in	12.95m
43ft 0in	13.10m
43ft 6in	13.26m
44ft 0in	13.41m
44ft 6in	13.56m
45ft 0in	13.71m
45ft 6in	13.87m
46ft 0in	14.02m
46ft 6in	14.17m
47ft 0in	14.32m
47ft 6in	14.48m
48ft 0in	14.63m
48ft 6in	14.78m
49ft 0in	14.93m
49ft 6in	15.09m
50ft 0in	15.24m
50ft 6in	15.39m
51ft 0in	15.54m
51ft 6in	15.70m
52ft 0in	15.85m
52ft 6in	16.00m
53ft 0in	16.15m
53ft 6in	16.30m
54ft 0in	16.46m
54ft 6in	16.61m
55ft 0in	16.76m
55ft 6in	16.91m
56ft 0in	17.07m
56ft 6in	17.22m
57ft 0in	17.37m
57ft 6in	17.52m
58ft 0in	17.68m
58ft 6in	17.83m
59ft 0in	17.98m
59ft 6in	18.13m
60ft 0in	18.29m
60ft 6in	18.44m
61ft 0in	18.59m
61ft 6in	18.74m
62ft 0in	18.90m
62ft 6in	19.05m
63ft 0in	19.20m
63ft 6in	19.35m
64ft 0in	19.51m
64ft 6in	19.66m
65ft 0in	19.81m
65ft 6in	19.96m
66ft 0in	20.11m
66ft 6in	20.27m
67ft 0in	20.42m
67ft 6in	20.57m
68ft 0in	20.72m
68ft 6in	20.88m
69ft 0in	21.03m
69ft 6in	21.18m
70ft 0in	21.33m
70ft 6in	21.49m
71ft 0in	21.64m
71ft 6in	21.79m
72ft 0in	21.94m
72ft 6in	22.10m
73ft 0in	22.25m
73ft 6in	22.40m
74ft 0in	22.55m
74ft 6in	22.71m
75ft 0in	22.86m
75ft 6in	23.01m
76ft 0in	23.16m

Discus/Hammer/Javelin

130ft	39.62m
135ft	41.16m
140ft	42.68m
145ft	44.20m
150ft	45.72m
155ft	47.24m
160ft	48.78m
165ft	50.30m
170ft	51.82m
175ft	53.34m
180ft	54.86m
185ft	56.40m
190ft	57.92m
195ft	59.44m
200ft	60.96m
205ft	62.48m
210ft	64.02m
215ft	65.54m
220ft	67.06m
225ft	68.58m
230ft	70.10m
235ft	71.64m
240ft	73.16m
245ft	74.68m
250ft	76.20m
255ft	77.72m
260ft	79.26m
265ft	80.78m
270ft	82.30m
275ft	83.82m
280ft	85.34m
285ft	86.88m
290ft	88.40m
295ft	89.92m
300ft	91.44m
305ft	92.96m
310ft	94.50m
315ft	96.02m
320ft	97.54m
325ft	99.06m
330ft	100.58m
335ft	102.10m
340ft	103.64m
345ft	105.16m
350ft	106.68m

Weightlifting

100lb	45.5kg
125lb	57kg
150lb	68kg
175lb	79.5kg
200lb	91kg
225lb	102.5kg
250lb	113.5kg
275lb	125kg
300lb	136.5kg
325lb	147.5kg
350lb	159kg
375lb	170.5kg
400lb	181.5kg
425lb	193kg
450lb	204.5kg
475lb	215.5kg
500lb	227kg
525lb	238.5kg
550lb	249.5kg
575lb	261kg
600lb	272.5kg
625lb	283.5kg
650lb	295kg
675lb	306.5kg
700lb	317.5kg
725lb	329kg
750lb	340.5kg
775lb	352kg
800lb	363kg
825lb	374.5kg
850lb	385.5kg
875lb	397kg
900lb	408.5kg
925lb	420kg
950lb	431kg
975lb	442.5kg
1000lb	453.5kg
1025lb	465kg
1050lb	476.5kg
1075lb	488kg
1100lb	499kg
1125lb	510.5kg
1150lb	522kg

Metric to Imperial

High Jump

1.50m	4ft 11in
1.55m	5ft 1in
1.60m	5ft 3in
1.65m	5ft 5in
1.70m	5ft 7in
1.75m	5ft 8¾in
1.80m	5ft 10¾in
1.83m	6ft 0in
1.85m	6ft 0¾in
1.90m	6ft 2¾in
1.95m	6ft 4¾in
1.98m	6ft 6in
2.00m	6ft 6¾in
2.05m	6ft 8¾in
2.10m	6ft 10¾in
2.13m	7ft 0in
2.15m	7ft 0½in
2.20m	7ft 2½in
2.25m	7ft 4½in
2.29m	7ft 6in
2.30m	7ft 6½in
2.35m	7ft 8½in
2.40m	7ft 10½in
2.44m	8ft 0in
2.45m	8ft 0½in

Pole Vault

4.00m	13ft 1½in
4.25m	13ft 11¼in
4.27m	14ft 0in
4.50m	14ft 9in
4.57m	15ft 0in
4.75m	15ft 7in
4.88m	16ft 0in
5.00m	16ft 4¾in
5.10m	16ft 8¾in
5.18m	17ft 0in
5.20m	17ft 0¾in
5.30m	17ft 4½in
5.40m	17ft 8½in
5.49m	18ft 0in
5.50m	18ft 0½in
5.60m	18ft 4½in
5.70m	18ft 8¼in
5.79m	19ft 0in
5.80m	19ft 0¼in
5.90m	19ft 4¼in
6.00m	19ft 8¼in
6.09m	20ft 0in
6.10m	20ft 0¼in

Long Jump

5.00m	16ft 4in
5.20m	17ft 0¾in
5.40m	17ft 8½in
5.60m	18ft 4½in
5.80m	19ft 0¼in
6.00m	19ft 8¼in
6.20m	20ft 4¼in
6.40m	21ft 0in
6.60m	21ft 8in
6.70m	22ft 0in
6.80m	22ft 3¾in
7.00m	22ft 11¾in
7.01m	23ft 0in
7.20m	23ft 7½in
7.31m	24ft 0in
7.40m	24ft 3½in
7.60m	24ft 11¼in
7.62m	25ft 0in
7.80m	25ft 7¼in
7.92m	26ft 0in
8.00m	26ft 3in
8.20m	26ft 11in
8.23m	27ft 0in
8.40m	27ft 6¾in
8.53m	28ft 0in
8.60m	28ft 2¾in
8.70m	28ft 6½in
8.80m	28ft 10½in
8.84m	29ft 0in
8.90m	29ft 2½in
9.00m	29ft 6½in

Triple Jump/Shot

13.00m	42ft 8in
13.50m	44ft 3½in
14.00m	45ft 11¼in
14.20m	46ft 7¼in
14.40m	47ft 3in
14.60m	47ft 10¾in
14.63m	48ft 0in
14.80m	48ft 6¾in
14.93m	49ft 0in
15.00m	49ft 2½in
15.20m	49ft 10½in
15.24m	50ft 0in
15.40m	50ft 6¼in
15.54m	51ft 0in
15.60m	51ft 2¼in
15.80m	51ft 10in
15.85m	52ft 0in
16.00m	52ft 6in
16.15m	53ft 0in
16.20m	53ft 1¾in
16.40m	53ft 9¾in
16.46m	54ft 0in
16.60m	54ft 5½in
16.76m	55ft 0in
16.80m	55ft 1½in
17.00m	55ft 9¼in
17.07m	56ft 0in
17.20m	56ft 5¼in
17.37m	57ft 0in
17.40m	57ft 1in
17.60m	57.9in
17.68m	58ft 0in
17.80m	58ft 4¾in
17.98m	59ft 0in
18.00m	59ft 0¾in
18.20m	59ft 8½in
18.29m	60ft 0in
18.40m	60ft 4½in
18.59m	61ft 0in
18.60m	61ft 0¼in
18.80m	61ft 8¼in
18.90m	62ft 0in
19.00m	62ft 4in
19.20m	63ft 0in
19.40m	63ft 7¾in
19.51m	64ft 0in
19.60m	64ft 4¾in
19.80m	64ft 11½in
19.81m	65ft 0in
20.00m	65ft 7½in
20.11m	66ft 0in
20.20m	66ft 3¼in
20.40m	66ft 11¼in
20.42m	67ft 0in
20.60m	67ft 7in
20.72m	68ft 0in
20.80m	68ft 3in
21.00m	68ft 10¾in
21.03m	69ft 0in
21.20m	69ft 6¾in
21.33m	70ft 0in
21.40m	70ft 2½in
21.60m	70ft 10½in
21.64m	71ft 0in
21.80m	71ft 6¼in
21.94m	72ft 0in
22.00m	72ft 2¼in
22.20m	72ft 10in
22.25m	73ft 0in
22.40m	73ft 6in
22.55m	74ft 0in
22.60m	74ft 1¾in
22.80m	74ft 9¾in
22.86m	75ft 0in
23.00m	75ft 5½in

Discus/Hammer/Javelin

40.00m	131ft 3in
41.00m	134ft 6in
42.00m	137ft 9in
42.68m	140ft 0in
43.00m	141ft 1in
44.00m	144ft 4in
45.00m	147ft 8in
45.72m	150ft 0in
46.00m	150ft 11in
47.00m	154ft 2in
48.00m	157ft 6in
48.76m	160ft 0in
49.00m	160ft 9in
50.00m	164ft 0in
51.00m	167ft 4in
51.82m	170ft 0in
52.00m	170ft 7in
53.00m	173ft 11in
54.00m	177ft 2in
54.86m	180ft 0in
55.00m	180ft 5in
56.00m	183ft 9in
57.00m	187ft 0in
57.92m	190ft 0in
58.00m	190ft 3in
59.00m	193ft 7in
60.00m	196ft 10in
60.96m	200ft 0in
61.00m	200ft 1in
62.00m	203ft 5in
63.00m	206ft 8in
64.00m	210ft 0in
65.00m	213ft 3in
66.00m	216ft 6in
67.00m	219ft 10in
67.06m	220ft 0in
68.00m	223ft 1in
69.00m	226ft 4in
70.00m	229ft 8in
70.10m	230ft 0in
71.00m	232ft 11in
72.00m	236ft 3in
73.00m	239ft 6in
73.16m	240ft 0in
74.00m	242ft 9in
75.00m	245ft 1in
76.00m	249ft 4in
76.20m	250ft 0in
77.00m	252ft 7in
78.00m	255ft 11in
79.00m	259ft 2in
79.24m	260ft 0in
80.00m	262ft 5in
81.00m	265ft 9in
82.00m	269ft 0in
82.30m	270ft 0in
83.00m	272ft 4in
84.00m	275ft 7in
85.00m	278ft 10in
85.04m	280ft 0in
86.00m	282ft 2in
87.00m	285ft 5in
88.00m	288ft 8in
88.40m	290ft 0in
89.00m	292ft 0in
90.00m	295ft 3in
91.00m	298ft 7ft
91.44m	300ft 0in
92.00m	301ft 10in
93.00m	305ft 1in
94.00m	308ft 5in
94.48m	310ft 0in
95.00m	311ft 8in
96.00m	314ft 11in
97.00m	318ft 3in
97.54m	320ft 0in
98.00m	321ft 6in
99.00m	324ft 10in
100.00m	328ft 1in
100.58m	330ft 0in
101.00m	331ft 4in
102.00m	334ft 8in
103.00m	337ft 11in
103.64m	340ft 0in
104.00m	341ft 3in
105.00m	344ft 6in

Weightlifting

100kg	220¼lb
110kg	242½lb
113.5kg	250lb
120kg	264½lb
130kg	286½lb
136.5kg	300lb
140kg	308½lb
150kg	330½lb
159kg	350lb
160kg	353½lb
170kg	374¾lb
180kg	396¾lb
181.5kg	400lb
190kg	418¾lb
200kg	440¾lb
204.5kg	450lb
210kg	462¾lb
220kg	485lb
227kg	500lb
230kg	507lb
240kg	529lb
249.5kg	550lb
250kg	551lb
260kg	573lb
270kg	595lb
272.5kg	600lb
280kg	617¼lb
290kg	639¼lb
295kg	650lb
300kg	661¼lb
310kg	683¼lb
317.5kg	700lb
320kg	705¼lb
330kg	727½lb
340kg	749½lb
340.5kg	750lb
350kg	771½lb
360kg	793½lb
363kg	800lb
370kg	815½lb
380kg	837¾lb
385.5kg	850lb
390kg	859¾lb
400kg	881¾lb
408.5kg	900lb
410kg	903¾lb
420kg	925¾lb
430kg	947¾lb
431kg	950lb
440kg	970lb
450kg	992lb
453.5kg	1000lb
460kg	1014lb
470kg	1036lb
476.5kg	1050lb
480kg	1058lb
490kg	1080¼lb
499kg	1100lb
500kg	1102¼lb

100m (MEN)

The 100m is considered by many as the purest of all athletic events; no need for tactical considerations or concern about conserving energy here. It is just one mighty explosion of speed from gun to finish, with time perhaps for only three huge lungfuls of air along the way.

It is an event that, apart from a few notable exceptions, black Americans have made their own. The Olympic title and the world record have become part of their culture and a symbol of their battle for recognition, particularly in the Sixties era of Civil Rights and Martin Luther King.

The peerless Jesse Owens struck the first mighty blow for the negro with his performances in the 1936 Nazi Olympics where, before the horrified gaze of Adolf Hitler, he rubbished the theory of Aryan supremacy with four gold medals, including the 100m.

That year, too, Owens produced a 100m time of 10.2 seconds during the American College Championships. That mark was equalled ten times but not beaten for 20 years – the longest stretch ever.

But even Owens is overshadowed by one extraordinary human speed machine in the battle for the title of "Fastest Man in the World" . . . another American negro, Bob Hayes.

Hayes, a muscle-packed bullet of a sprinter seemed to pick himself up and hurl himself bodily down the track. His surging, rolling style had the purists shuddering, yet in 1963 during a sprint relay leg he was reportedly clocked at over 27 miles per hour, the fastest human speed ever recorded – although experts have since doubted this *(see panel)*. Hayes, a product of those turbulent Sixties in America, went on to win the 1964 Olympic title in Tokyo by a margin of 2m. It was the widest ever until 1984, in an event usually measured in centimetres. At 22 he retired from the track to become an outstanding professional footballer with the Dallas Cowboys.

Hayes, who claimed a share of the world record with 10. in that Tokyo final, is one of 25 Americans to appear on th record list since Donald Lippincott ran 10.6 in 1912 . . . com pared to only 13 non-Americans.

Why? It is partly due to the climate, especially on the We coast of America, because sprinters do need sun to war their muscles and reduce the threat of injury. And it is als because the negro's physiological make-up is suited to explo sive activities like sprinting.

But mainly it is because of the American high school an college system which searches for athletic excellence an then provides saturation coaching. The lure of capitalist fam and fortune is another factor of course. Not only fighters ar black and hungry; many athletes are too.

Of the non-Americans to hold the 100m world recor since 1912 a mere three have come from Europe. But they d include the brilliant Armin Hary of West Germany wh became the first to run 10.0 in Zurich, 1960.

The progression of the record has been aided b improvements in footwear and track surfaces – and also i start techniques. The crouch start used by all sprinters wa popularised by Charles Sherrill, later General Sherrill the U Ambassador to Turkey, in 1887. But it was not until 1927 tha starting blocks were introduced by another American, Georg Bresnahan.

Until then, sprinters dug toe holds in the cinders (this wa seen in the film *Chariots of Fire* about the 1924 Olympi

The average speed attained by the four Americans who set the 4 x 100m relay mark of 37.83 at the Los Angeles Olympics was 38.06km/h (23.65mph). In that relay it is reasonably estimated that Carl Lewis, on the last leg, exceeded 40km/h (25mph).

The fastest average speed attained in an individual world record is 36.92km/h (22.94mph) when Tommie Smith (USA) ran 19.5 sec for 220 yds straight at San Jose, California on 7 May 1966.

Man: 40km/h (25mph)

Soon after he turned professional in 1937 Jesse Owens ran against horses in exhibition races before baseball matches. In his first race over 100 yards he beat the horse by about a yard. In 1964 the then fastest African sprinter, Serafino Antao of Kenya, ran against a cheetah over the same distance. He was beaten by about the same margin, a yard, but it was obvious that the cheetah was not at full speed.

100m champion Harold Abrahams). The difference between blocks and holes has been gauged at one thirtieth of a second, about a foot (30cm) in distance. Blocks were not allowed in the Olympic Games until 1948.

The first sub 11 second time for 100m was run by Luther Cary (USA) in Paris on 4 July 1891. It was recorded as 10¾ secs, now written as 10.8. The first electronically-timed sub 10 seconds came from Jim Hines (USA) with 9.95 during the Mexico Olympics of 1968. It stood until 1983 when yet another American speedster, Calvin Smith, clipped it by two hundredths of a second at Colorado Springs.

Smith, like Hines, was competing at altitude where the thin air gives sprinters less resistance and so permits them to run faster. The best at sea level is the 9.96 clocked by Mel Lattany (USA) on 5 May 1984 at Athens, Georgia.

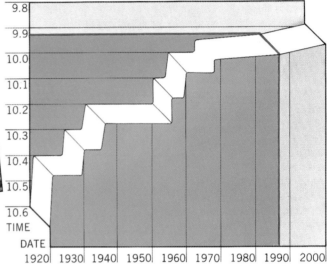

While it has been estimated that the greatest speed attained by a man is just in excess of 40km/h (25mph), compared to the animals he is quite a slow-coach. The fastest animal, the cheetah, has been reliably timed at 101km/h (63mph), and less reliable claims of 145km/h (90mph) have been made. The average speed of the holder of the quarter-mile record for a racehorse, "Big Racket", is 69.62km/h (43.26mph) achieved when clocking 20.8 sec for the distance in Mexico in 1945. The fastest known greyhound was "The Shoe", who was timed at 20.1 sec for 410 yds in Australia in 1968, achieving an average speed of 67.14km/h (41.72mph). Its top speed was estimated at more than 71km/h (45mph).

Horse: 69.62km/h (43.26mph)

Cheetah: 101km/h (63mph)

100m (Men)

Time	Competitor	Venue	Date
10.6	Donald Lippincott (USA)	Stockholm	6/7/12
10.6	Jackson Scholz (USA)	Stockholm	16/9/20
10.4	Charles Paddock (USA)	Redlands	23/4/21
10.4	Eddie Tolan (USA)	Stockholm	8/8/29
10.4	Eddie Tolan (USA)	Copenhagen	25/8/29
10.3	Percy Williams (CAN)	Toronto	9/8/30
10.3	Eddie Tolan (USA)	Los Angeles	1/8/32
10.3	Ralph Metcalfe (USA)	Budapest	12/8/33
10.3	Eulace Peacock (USA)	Oslo	6/8/34
10.3	Christian Berger (HOL)	Amsterdam	26/8/34
10.3	Ralph Metcalfe (USA)	Osaka	15/9/34
10.3	Ralph Metcalfe (USA)	Dairen	23/9/34
10.3	Takayoshi Yoshioka (JAP)	Tokyo	15/6/35
10.2	Jesse Owens (USA)	Chicago	20/6/36
10.2	Harold Davis (USA)	Compton	6/6/41
10.2	Lloyd La Beach (PAN)	Fresno	15/5/48
10.2	Barney Ewell (USA)	Evanston	9/7/48
10.2	Emmanuel Mcdonald Bailey (GBR)	Belgrade	25/8/51
10.2	Heinz Fütterer (GER)	Yokohama	31/10/54
10.2	Bobby Morrow (USA)	Houston	19/5/56
10.2	Ira Murchison (USA)	Compton	1/6/56
10.2	Bobby Morrow (USA)	Bakersfield	22/6/56
10.2	Ira Murchison (USA)	Los Angeles	29/6/56
10.2	Bobby Morrow (USA)	Los Angeles	29/6/56
10.1	Willie Williams (USA)	Berlin	3/8/56
10.1	Ira Murchison (USA)	Berlin	4/8/56
10.1	Leamon King (USA)	Ontario, Calif.	20/10/56
10.1	Leamon King (USA)	Santa Ana	27/10/56
10.1	Ray Norton (USA)	San Jose	18/4/59
10.0	Armin Hary (GER)	Zurich	21/6/60
10.0	Harry Jerome (CAN)	Saskatoon	15/7/60
10.0	Horacio Esteves (VEN)	Caracas	15/8/64
10.0	Bob Hayes (USA)	Tokyo	15/10/64
10.0	Jim Hines (USA)	Modesto	27/5/67
10.0	Paul Nash (SA)	Krugersdorp	2/4/68
10.0	Oliver Ford (USA)	Albuquerque	31/5/68
10.0	Charles Greene (USA)	Sacramento	20/6/68
10.0	Roger Bambuck (FRA)	Sacramento	20/6/68
9.9	Jim Hines (USA)	Sacramento	20/6/68
9.9	Ronnie Ray Smith (USA)	Sacramento	20/6/68
9.9	Charles Greene (USA)	Sacramento	20/6/68
9.9	Jim Hines (USA)	Mexico City	14/10/68
9.9	Eddie Hart (USA)	Eugene	1/7/72
9.9	Reynard Robinson (USA)	Eugene	1/7/72
9.9	Steve Williams (USA)	Los Angeles	21/6/74
9.9	Silvio Leonard (CUB)	Ostrava	5/6/75
9.9	Steve Williams (USA)	Siena	16/7/75
9.9	Steve Williams (USA)	Berlin	22/8/75
9.9	Steve Williams (USA)	Gainsville	27/3/76
9.9	Harvey Glance (USA)	Columbia	3/4/76
9.9	Harvey Glance (USA)	Baton Rouge	1/5/76
9.9	Donald Quarrie (JAM)	Modesto	22/5/76
9.95	Jim Hines (USA)	Mexico City	14/10/68
9.93	Calvin Smith (USA)	Colorado Springs	3/7/83

*automatic timing

The graphic grid shows the difference between the 100m record breakers. One square equals one metre or 0.1 secs. So Lippincott in 1912 would finish some seven metres or 0.7 secs behind current world record holder Calvin Smith

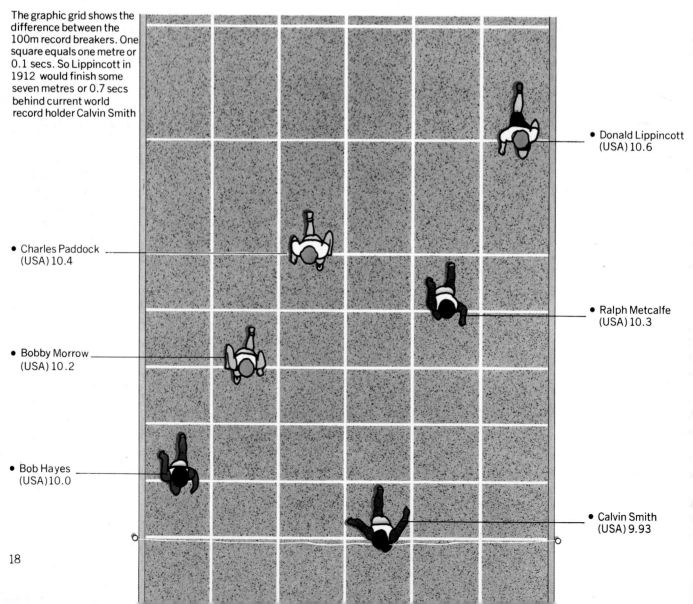

• Charles Paddock (USA) 10.4

• Bobby Morrow (USA) 10.2

• Bob Hayes (USA) 10.0

• Donald Lippincott (USA) 10.6

• Ralph Metcalfe (USA) 10.3

• Calvin Smith (USA) 9.93

• Calvin Smith (left) breaks the world 100m record

• Olympic champion Carl Lewis

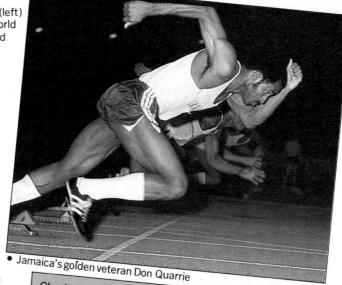

• Jamaica's golden veteran Don Quarrie

HOW THE RECORD FELL

Calvin Smith looks anything but the conventional conception of a crack sprinter . . . just 5ft 9in tall (1.75m) and weighing 144lb (66kg). And when he runs his head rolls from side to side like a man in torment. Yet on 3 July 1983 at Colorado Springs, the slender, God-fearing man from Mississippi became the fastest human on earth with a 100m time of 9.93 secs.

The historic run came during the Olympic Sports Festival staged by the US Olympic Committee at the US Air Force Academy some 2,195m above sea level. Smith's event occurred 15 minutes after Evelyn Ashford had broken the women's 100m world record. "That has really inspired me," he told friends. "If I can get a good start the 'ol Jim Hines' record could go."

In the event, his start was better than he could have dreamt – "probably my best ever," he said later – and he had taken a commanding advantage by the 60m mark. Driving his slim arms more intensely than usual, he maintained his power

Charley Paddock, the fair-haired, bouncy American featured in *Chariots of Fire*, might have held the world 100m record for 35 years . . . but his performance was never put forward for ratification! Competing over 110 yds in Pasadena in 1921, Paddock was timed at 10.2 secs. Even though 110 yds is 0.58m *more* than 100m, the American Athletic Union refused to accept it. The time was not bettered until Willie Williams (USA) ran 10.1 in the Berlin Olympic Stadium in 1956.

over the final 40m. It was a performance made even more praiseworthy in that he had no-one to push him as both his leading rivals Carl Lewis and Emmit King had declined to take part.

100m (WOMEN)

Recent world record holders like Marlies Göhr (GDR) and Evelyn Ashford (USA) are known to have exceeded speeds of 22.5mph (36.2km/h) during those runs. But the only leading woman to have been scientifically timed was American double Olympic champion Wyomia Tyus who reportedly touched more than 23mph (37km/h) in Kiev, USSR on 31 July 1965.

Wyomia, the only sprinter, male or female, to win successive Olympic 100m titles (1964 and 1968) was also the first woman to record 11.0 seconds exactly. Born in Griffin, Georgia, she was the second great American negress of the track. The first had been Wilma Rudolph, born in Clarksville, Tennessee, the 20th of a family of 22 children. "I had to be fast," she joked, "otherwise there was nothing left to eat on the dining table."

Wilma, who was born with polio and could not dispense with a brace on her right leg until the age of 12, was America's female Jesse Owens. Through her athletic prowess – three Olympic golds at Rome in 1960 and two 100m world records – she improved the standing of blacks throughout the United States.

But above all others in the record books for the women's 100m stands the name of Poland's Stanislawa Walasiewicz, or Stella Walsh as she was known in the United States where she was taken at the age of two. She broke or equalled the world record 11 times with a best of 11.6 in 1937. It was astonishing running at a time when women's athletics was struggling to be accepted. Old ideals still prevailed, although less rigorously than during the Ancient Olympics when women were barred on pain of death.

Stanislawa, who became Mrs Olson, an American citizen, in 1947, was certainly ahead of her time. Even in 1945, at the age of 34, she was credited with a 100m time of 11.2 seconds at Cleveland, Ohio. Stunned officials declared it impossible and invalid. "They couldn't believe anyone could run that fast," said Stella. "The years have proved it right." Sadly, other factors were revealed after Stella was found shot dead in a discount store car park in December 1980. The post mortem report suggested she had predominantly male characteristics.

● Wilma Rudolph

100m (Women)

Time	Competitor	Venue	Date
11.7	Stanislawa Walasiewicz (POL)	Warsaw	26/8/34
11.6	Stanislawa Walasiewicz (POL)	Berlin	1/8/37
11.5	Fanny Blankers-Koen (HOL)	Amsterdam	13/6/48
11.5	Marjorie Jackson (AUS)	Helsinki	22/7/52
11.4	Marjorie Jackson (AUS)	Gifu	4/10/52
11.3	Shirley de la Hunty (AUS)	Warsaw	4/8/55
11.3	Vera Krepkina (URS)	Kiev	13/9/58
11.3	Wilma Rudolph (USA)	Rome	2/9/60
11.2	Wilma Rudolph (USA)	Stuttgart	19/7/61
11.2	Wyomia Tyus (USA)	Tokyo	15/10/64
11.1	Irena Kirszenstein (POL)	Prague	9/7/65
11.1	Wyomia Tyus (USA)	Kiev	31/7/65
11.1	Barbara Ferrell (USA)	Santa Barbara	2/7/67
11.1	Ludmilla Samotyosova (URS)	Leninakin	15/8/68
11.1	Irena Szewinska (POL)	Mexico City	14/10/68
11.0	Wyomia Tyus (USA)	Mexico City	15/10/68
11.0	Chi Cheng (ROC)	Sudstadt	18/7/70
11.0	Renate Meissner (GDR)	Berlin	2/8/70
11.0	Renate Stecher (GDR)	Berlin	31/7/71
11.0	Renate Stecher (GDR)	Potsdam	3/6/72
11.0	Ellen Stropahl (GDR)	Potsdam	15/6/72
11.0	Eva Gleskova (TCH)	Budapest	1/7/72
10.9	Renate Stecher (GDR)	Ostrava	7/6/73
10.8	Renate Stecher (GDR)	Dresden	20/7/73
		*	
11.08	Wyomia Tyus (USA)	Mexico City	15/10/68
11.07	Renate Stecher (GDR)	Munich	2/9/72
11.04	Inge Helten (GER)	Furth	13/6/76
11.01	Annegret Richter (FRG)	Montreal	25/7/76
10.88	Marlies Oelsner (GDR)	Dresden	1/7/77
10.88	Marlies Göhr (GDR)	Karl-Marx-Stadt	9/7/82
10.81	Marlies Göhr (GDR)	Berlin	8/6/83
10.79	Evelyn Ashford (USA)	Colorado Springs	3/7/83
10.76	Evelyn Ashford (USA)	Zurich	22/8/84

* automatic timing

The greatest average speed recorded for a world individual record is 33.45km/h (20.79mph) by Evelyn Ashford (USA) at Zurich, Switzerland, in 1984 when she ran 100m in 10.76 sec. The average speed attained by the GDR foursome when they clocked 41.37 sec in the World Cup 4 x 100m relay at Canberra in 1985 was 34.80km/h (21.63mph). It is reasonably estimated that Marlies Göhr, on the last leg, and Evelyn Ashford on the last leg of the winning American team at the Los Angeles Olympic Games both exeeded 37km/h (23mph).

Even so, Stella's ratified mark of 11.6 stood for 11 years, until the flying Dutch housewife Fanny Blankers-Koen warmed up for her four golds display at the 1948 London Olympics by lowering the barrier by a tenth in Amsterdam. The first 11.2 to be ratified came from Wilma Rudolph. Then, suddenly, the era of East Europe was upon the world. The German Democratic Republic had entered its own team at the 1968 Olympics for the first time; now athletic standards in that relatively small country rocketed.

Renate Meissner-Stecher was their first great woman sprinter. Between 1970 and 1972 she four times equalled the world record of 11.0. Then, in the space of five weeks in 1973, she lowered it comprehensively, first to 10.9, then to 10.8. Both were hand-timed, however, and subsequent records have been ratified only on automatic equipment.

AMERICA v EASTERN EUROPE

In no other athletic event is the battle beween East and West more clearly defined than in the women's 100m world record. Since 1977 the record has fallen five times — to just two women: Marlies Göhr of East Germany and Evelyn Ashford of the United States. In her maiden name of Marlies Oelsner, Frau Göhr became the first woman to smash the automatically-timed 11 seconds barrier with 10.88 at Dresden in 1977. It was a staggering performance, slicing 13/100ths of a second off the previous best – or nearly a metre and a half on the track. And she was just 19.

From then until 1983 the pretty psychology student with the short pattering stride produced a string of other sub 11 runs, equalling her own record in 1982 and lowering it to 10.81 in 1983. In that spell she collected two European Championships (1978 and 1982) and the World Championship of 1983. Surprisingly, though, she was beaten into second place in the Moscow Olympics by Russia's Lyudmila Kondratyeva.

Ashford, of the unorthodox, heel-flicking style, had missed those Games through Jimmy Carter's boycott. And a hamstring injury caused her to break down in the middle of the World Championship 100m final. But she had beaten Göhr in the 1979 and 1981 World Cups. The conclusive leg of

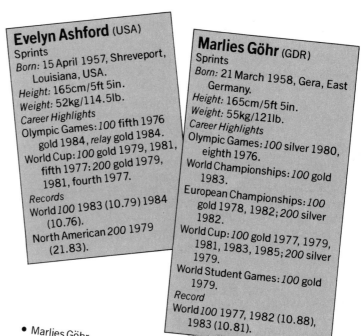

Evelyn Ashford (USA)
Sprints
Born: 15 April 1957, Shreveport, Louisiana, USA.
Height: 165cm/5ft 5in.
Weight: 52kg/114.5lb.
Career Highlights
Olympic Games: 100 fifth 1976 gold 1984, relay gold 1984.
World Cup: 100 gold 1979, 1981, fifth 1977; 200 gold 1979, 1981, fourth 1977.
Records
World 100 1983 (10.79) 1984 (10.76).
North American 200 1979 (21.83).

Marlies Göhr (GDR)
Sprints
Born: 21 March 1958, Gera, East Germany.
Height: 165cm/5ft 5in.
Weight: 55kg/121lb.
Career Highlights
Olympic Games: 100 silver 1980, eighth 1976.
World Championships: 100 gold 1983.
European Championships: 100 gold 1978, 1982; 200 silver 1982.
World Cup: 100 gold 1977, 1979, 1981, 1983, 1985; 200 silver 1979.
World Student Games: 100 gold 1979.
Record
World 100 1977, 1982 (10.88), 1983 (10.81).

• Marlies Göhr

Evelyn Ashford

• Göhr (left) heads Ashford (right)

their thrilling duel was expected to be fought at the Los Angeles Games of 1984. Instead came the East European boycott. Ashford took the crown... and then jetted out to Zurich where Göhr waited for the greatest ever women's 100m race.

Together Göhr and Ashford took their blocks for the Weltklasse 100m on a breathless Zurich night. From the gun, Göhr blasted her more muscular frame into a narrow lead. By 20m she was a metre ahead. But Ashford held her form magnificently under the pressure to produce a superb final 40m as Göhr tightened. At the finish she held the new world record... 10.76 to Göhr's 10.84 in second place. "I have the utmost respect for Marlies," said Evelyn, "but this surely establishes me as the best. I may have won the Olympic title, but this run meant as much if not more to me."

110m HURDLES (MEN)

As Ed Moses has dominated the 400m hurdles, so Renaldo 'Skeets' Nehemiah seemed destined to dominate the 110m hurdles. Instead the wonderfully talented black American with the physique of a middleweight boxer and the balance of a gymnast waited only long enough to break the apparently impossible 13 seconds barrier and then switched his talents to the more lucrative arena of American gridiron football as a wide receiver with the San Francisco 49ers. He made a small fortune with his signing on fee, but with athletics becoming progressively more open and professional, and his apparent inability to catch an American football while moving at top speed, 'Skeets' may well be tempted back if eligibility allows.

At the end of 1985, when he was still only 26, Nehemiah still held five of the top six times ever recorded. And he had been retired for four years. In his heyday through 1980 and 81 he could claim 11 of the 15 fastest times and was generally accepted even by his fiercest rivals as holding a two metre advantage in the event, a huge margin in such a short, explosive contest.

Nehemiah, a sensation as a schoolboy, clocked 13.6 secs over the junior 3ft 3in (99cm) hurdles at the age of 14 and 14.2 secs in his debut over the senior 3ft 6in (1.07m) hurdles.

In 1978, aged 18, he improved the world junior record five times, ending with 13.23 secs. Skeets was clearly ready to take on the biggest of big boys and he did so as early as the following April with his first senior world record of 13.16 secs.

One month later – and that already remarkable record had been trimmed to 13.00 secs, right on the edge of the high hurdlers' toughest barrier. For two seasons Nehemiah flirted with it. He ran 12.91 secs to win the Collegiate title – but the wind was +3.5 metres per second, way above the legal limit for records. At the same time he had to stomach his bitter disappointment over America's boycott of the Moscow Olympics and watch East Germany's Thomas Munkelt take the gold in 13.39, a training run performance for Skeets.

But then on 19 August 1981 at Zurich's fabulous Weltklasse spectacular, it all came right for Nehemiah. On a glorious night when Sebastian Coe was to smash the world mile record for the second time, the truly outstanding achievement belonged to the cool, immaculately turned out American. Nehemiah was once again lined up alongside Greg Foster, his perennial rival who must have been experiencing similar emo-

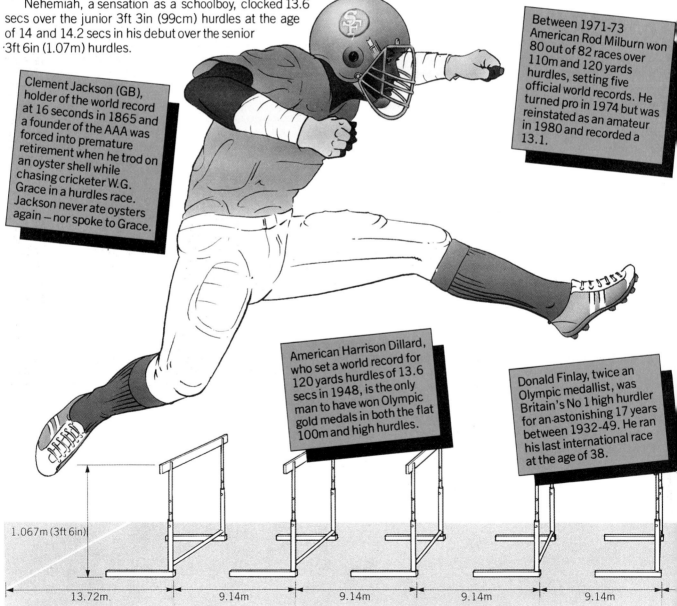

Clement Jackson (GB), holder of the world record at 16 seconds in 1865 and a founder of the AAA was forced into premature retirement when he trod on an oyster shell while chasing cricketer W.G. Grace in a hurdles race. Jackson never ate oysters again – nor spoke to Grace.

Between 1971-73 American Rod Milburn won 80 out of 82 races over 110m and 120 yards hurdles, setting five official world records. He turned pro in 1974 but was reinstated as an amateur in 1980 and recorded a 13.1.

American Harrison Dillard, who set a world record for 120 yards hurdles of 13.6 secs in 1948, is the only man to have won Olympic gold medals in both the flat 100m and high hurdles.

Donald Finlay, twice an Olympic medallist, was Britain's No 1 high hurdler for an astonishing 17 years between 1932-49. He ran his last international race at the age of 38.

1.067m (3ft 6in)

13.72m.   9.14m   9.14m   9.14m   9.14m

tions as Harald Schmidt in the 400m hurdles: the second best athlete in his event in the world, yet a complete also-ran.

From the gun Foster launched a supreme effort. He was level with Nehemiah for the first two hurdles and maintained his form superbly. At the end he had clocked 13.03 secs, by far the best time of his life and only three hundredths of a second outside Nehemiah's world record. What a run . . . but he was still a clear metre behind the man who tormented him. Nehemiah, celebrating as soon as he crossed the line, had recorded 12.93 secs. The barrier had gone.

It had been another American with a catchy nickname who had revolutionised high hurdling back in the Thirties — Forrest "Spec" Towns who produced the first sub 14 seconds time at Oslo's Bislett Stadium on 27 August 1936. Towns clocked 13.7 to clip 0.4 secs off his own world record, the largest improvement ever made in the 110m hurdles.

● Rod Milburn

cantabrian

Hurdle racing, introduced at Oxford University in 1860, began with heavy, rigid sheep hurdles staked into the ground. Not surprisingly, athletes were most careful not to hit them! In 1866 the height was standardised at 3ft 6in (1.07m) and the obstacles themselves slowly refined. The modern hurdle, with its weighted feet and natural toppling motion when bumped, was introduced in 1935 by American Harry Hillman, a gold medallist at the 1904 Olympics. Because of the heaviness of the early barriers, the pioneer hurdlers used a jumping action to clear them. It was not until a quarter of a century later, around 1886, that Oxford student Arthur Croome is thought to have been the first to develop a straight lead leg.

110m Hurdles

Time	Competitor	Venue	Date
15.0	Forrest Smithson (USA)	London	25/7/08
14.8	Earl Thomson (CAN)	Antwerp	18/8/20
14.8	Sten Pettersson (SWE)	Stockholm	18/9/27
14.6	George Weightman-Smith (RSA)	Amsterdam	31/7/28
14.4	Eric Wennstrom (SWE)	Stockholm	25/8/29
14.4	Bengt Sjostedt (FIN)	Helsinki	5/9/31
14.4	Percy Beard (USA)	Cambridge, Mass.	23/6/32
14.4	Jack Keller (USA)	Palo Alto	16/7/32
14.4	George Saling (USA)	Los Angeles	2/8/32
14.4	John Morriss (USA)	Budapest	12/8/33
14.4	John Morriss (USA)	Turin	8/9/33
14.3	Percy Beard (USA)	Stockholm	26/7/34
14.2	Percy Beard (USA)	Oslo	6/8/34
14.2	Al Moreau (USA)	Oslo	2/8/35
14.1	Forrest Towns (USA)	Chicago	19/6/36
14.1	Forrest Towns (USA)	Berlin	6/8/36
13.7	Forrest Towns (USA)	Oslo	27/8/36
13.7	Fred Wolcott (USA)	Philadelphia	29/6/41
13.6	Dick Attlesey (USA)	College Park	24/6/50
13.5	Dick Attlesey (USA)	Helsinki	10/7/50
13.4	Jack Davis (USA)	Bakersfield	22/6/56
13.2	Martin Lauer (GER)	Zurich	7/7/59
13.2	Lee Calhoun (USA)	Berne	21/8/60
13.2	Earl McCullouch (USA)	Minneapolis	16/7/67
13.2	Willie Davenport (USA)	Zurich	4/7/69
13.2	Rodney Milburn (USA)	Munich	7/9/72
13.1	Rodney Milburn (USA)	Zurich	6/7/73
13.1	Rodney Milburn (USA)	Siena	22/7/73
13.1	Guy Drut (FRA)	St Maur	23/7/75
13.0	Guy Drut (FRA)	Berlin	22/8/75
		*	
13.24	Rodney Milburn (USA)	Munich	7/9/72
13.21	Alejandro Casanas (CUB)	Sofia	21/8/77
13.16	Renaldo Nehemiah (USA)	San Jose	14/4/79
13.00	Renaldo Nehemiah (USA)	Westwood	6/5/79
12.93	Renaldo Nehemiah (USA)	Zurich	19/8/81

*automatic timing

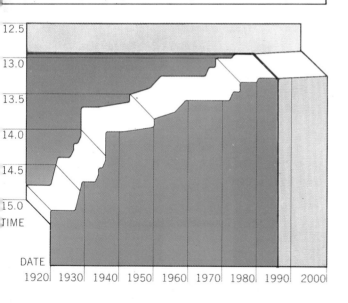

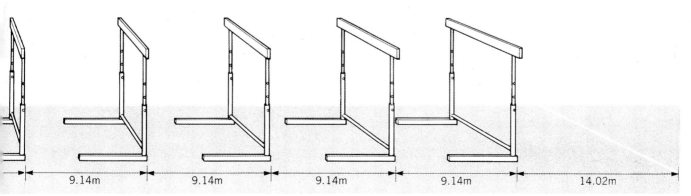

400m (MEN)

The closest finish in an Olympic 400m final came in 1960 when Otis Davis (USA) and Carl Kaufmann (GER) both set a new world record of 44.9. Eventually, the automatic timing decided the winner – Davis had clocked 45.07 against Kaufmann's 45.08 and so took the gold by one hundredth of a second.

Britain's Edward Colbeck produced a world amateur best for the 440 yards of 50.4 in 1868 despite having run into a sheep and broken its leg on the way round.

The men's 400m, like no other event, has been aided by altitude. Of the top ten best times ever, *seven* have been achieved with the advantage of thin air. Such is the influence, in fact, that it will surely need another major Games to be held at altitude before Lee Evans' 1968 mark – along with Bob Beamon's long jump the oldest record on the books – is erased.

Mexico City stands 2240m (7347ft) above sea level and the 21-year-old Evans from Madera, California, made full use of the atmospheric conditions on that Friday of 18 October. For once he ignored his reputation as a head waiter who paced himself and then beat the opposition with a last desperate spurt, and instead went hard from the start. On any other occasion Evans' time of 43.86 would have been sensational enough for a massive margin of victory. But at that altitude he was less than a metre ahead of American second string Larry James, who clocked 43.97, still the second fastest of all time.

With Ron Freeman finishing third in 44.41, it was America's first and only clean sweep of the one lap race since the largely meaningless 1904 Olympics when 95 per cent of the competitors were Americans.

Evans, who was to turn professional in 1972 after failing to gain selection to defend his Olympic title, said later: "I ran the race exactly according to plan. I hit the first bend hard and then thought about form and relaxation on the back straight. After that I ran the second turn hard and mustered up some kind of kick to hold on. When I heard the time I was delighted. I know the altitude helps but to go sub 44 was a real ambition."

Evans was never to achieve such a goal again. His second best time – and the third best of all time – was 44.06, achieved at the 2249m altitude of Echo Summit, California. It was there, also, that Larry James supplied the fourth fastest time ever of 44.19.

The fastest at low altitude, or sea level, are the 44.1 of Wayne Collett (USA) at Eugene, Oregon in 1972 and the 44.26 by Cuba's Alberto Juantorena which won the 1976 Olympic gold in Montreal.

The origins of the 400m record are over 440 yds, a slightly longer distance of 402.34m. A generally accepted conversion is 0.3 sec, and thus the barrier breakers become:

Below 50 secs, Robert Philpot (GBR) who ran 49.6 (440 yds) on 7 March 1871;

Below 49 secs, Lon Myers (USA) with 48.6 (440 yds) at Birmingham on 16 July 1881;

Below 48 secs, Maxie Long (USA) with 47.8 (440 yds) in New York on 29 September 1900;

Below 47 secs, Ben Eastman (USA) with 46.4 (440 yds) at Stanford on 26 March 1932;

Below 46 secs, Herb McKenley (JAM) with 46.2 (440 yds) in Champagne, Illinois on 1 June 1946; and

Below 45 secs, Otis Davis (USA) with 44.9 in Rome on 6 September 1960.

400m (Men)

Time	Competitor	Venue	Date
47.8	Maxie Long (USA)	New York	29/9/00
47.4	Ted Meredith (USA)	Cambridge, Mass.	27/5/16
47.0	Emerson Spencer (USA)	Palo Alto	12/5/28
46.4	Ben Eastman (USA)	Palo Alto	26/3/32
46.2	Bill Carr (USA)	Los Angeles	5/8/32
46.1	Archie Williams (USA)	Chicago	19/6/36
46.0	Rudolph Harbig (GER)	Frankfurt/Main	12/8/39
46.0	Grover Klemmer (USA)	Philadelphia	29/6/41
46.0	Herb McKenley (JAM)	Berkley	5/6/48
45.9	Herb McKenley (JAM)	Milwaukee	2/7/48
45.8	George Rhoden (JAM)	Eskitstuna	22/8/50
45.4	Lou Jones (USA)	Mexico City	18/3/55
45.2	Lou Jones (USA)	Los Angeles	30/6/56
44.9	Otis Davis (USA)	Rome	6/9/60
44.9	Carl Kaufmann (GER)	Rome	6/9/60
44.9	Adolph Plummer (USA)	Tempe	25/5/63
44.9	Mike Larrabee (USA)	Los Angeles	12/9/64
44.5	Tommie Smith (USA)	San Jose	20/5/67
44.1	Larry James (USA)	S. Lake Tahoe	14/9/68
*			
43.86	Lee Evans (USA)	Mexico City	18/10/68

*automatic timing

Lee Evans sets his long-standing record

The affects of altitude on athletic performances were first realised in 1955 when the Pan American Games were held in Mexico City, which stands 7,347ft (2226m) above sea level. America's Lou Jones smashed the world 400m record with 45.4 secs and Brazil's Adhemar da Silva broke the world triple jump record with 16.56m (54ft 4in), a massive improvement. All the explosive events showed marked improvement, in fact, while the endurance events were unusually slow. Star American miler Wes Santee was beaten by an unknown South American who had experience of such conditions.

It started the sports doctors seriously considering the phenomenon. First, they discovered, not unreasonably, that the 20 per cent thinner air of Mexico City gave proportionally less resistance and so aided sprinters and jumpers. And that the shortage of oxygen handicapped the endurance event athletes.

But second, they discovered the physiological make up of athletes who had been born at altitude differed: namely that their bodies contained more oxygen-carrying red blood corpuscles and were therefore more efficient as running machines, not only at altitude but also at sea level.

These findings were underlined in sensational fashion at the 1968 Olympics at Mexico City. First and second in the 10,000m lived at high altitude – Naftali Temu (KEN) and Mamo Wolde (ETH); second and third in the 5,000m were men from the mountains – Kip Keino (KEN) and Temu. And so it went on. First in the 1500m – Keino; first in the marathon – Wolde; first and second in the steeplechase – Amos Biwott (KEN) and Benjamin Kogo (KEN).

400m (WOMEN)

While the men's 400m record has stood still since 1968, the women's equivalent has experienced a monumental battering from the tall, elegant, East German medical student Marita Koch. Czechoslovakia's wonder woman Jarmila Kratochvilova has also aided and abetted the assault, becoming the first female to go sub 48 seconds while winning the World Championship in Helsinki in 1983.

But it is the 5ft 7¼in (171cm), 143lb (65kg) Miss Koch who has made the event her own, lowering the record on seven occasions from 1978 to 1985.

Her most stunning contribution thus far came in the World Cup in Canberra on 6 October 1985 when she recorded 47.60, the same time as the one that earned flying Scotsman Eric Liddell his famed Olympic gold medal in 1924. To fully appreciate Miss Koch's achievement, it should be emphasised that her 200m time en route was 22.4, good enough to have won the women's 200m Olympic title every year up to and including 1972. It was her 16th world record in all, when added to four she has set over 200m and five in relays.

Miss Koch's predecessor as queen of the 400m was the seemingly indestructable Pole, the regal Irena Szewinska (nee Kirzenstein). As an 18-year-old she won a sprint gold in Tokyo 1964; as a married woman she won gold in Mexico City

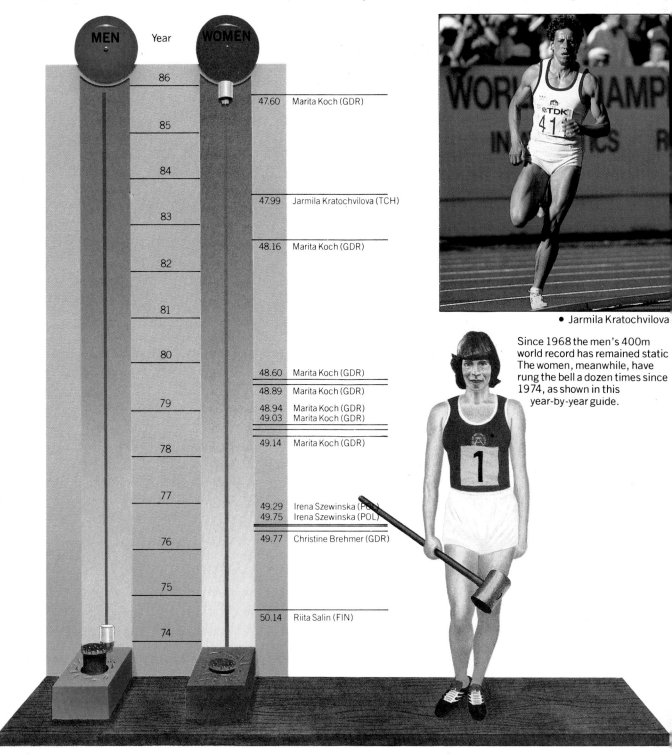

• Jarmila Kratochvilova

Since 1968 the men's 400m world record has remained static. The women, meanwhile, have rung the bell a dozen times since 1974, as shown in this year-by-year guide.

Year		
47.60	Marita Koch (GDR)
47.99	Jarmila Kratochvilova (TCH)
48.16	Marita Koch (GDR)
48.60	Marita Koch (GDR)
48.89	Marita Koch (GDR)
48.94	Marita Koch (GDR)
49.03	Marita Koch (GDR)
49.14	Marita Koch (GDR)
49.29	Irena Szewinska (POL)
49.75	Irena Szewinska (POL)
49.77	Christine Brehmer (GDR)
50.14	Riita Salin (FIN)

• Marita Koch

• Irena Szewinska

over 200m in 1968; and as a mother and a 30-year-old veteran she won gold again in Montreal 1976 . . . with a world record 49.29 over 400m.

Her 400m run at Montreal, quite simply, was one of the finest performances ever seen from a woman. Irena had travelled there with some concern over the form of East German *wunderkind* Christina Brehmer, the 18-year-old who had taken her world record earlier in the year. The Olympic final was expected to provide a titanic battle. In the event, Irena's only opponent was the clock as she raced away unopposed to win by more than a second.

Irena Szewinska was certainly the first woman to dip below 50 secs for the event, but other barrier breakers are more difficult to establish as the IAAF did not accept official records until 1957. However, unofficial records suggest these firsts:

---

70 secs: Lidia Charushnikova (URS) with 65.0 in Viatka on 12 July 1921

65 secs: Mary Lines (GBR) with 64.4 (over 440 yds) in London on 18 July 1922

60 secs: Kinue Hitomi (JAP) with 59.0 in Myashino on 5 August 1928.

55 secs: Zinaida Safronova (URS) with 54.8 in Leningrad on 21 July 1955.

The official IAAF records then show that Russia's Maria Itkina progressively lowered the mark from 54.0 to 53.4. But meanwhile, over in North Korea, the mysterious Sin Kim Dan (see also 800m), was producing far faster times with five runs moving down from 53.0 to 51.2. But only one of them, her 51.9 in Pyongyang in 1962, was ratified by the IAAF. North Korea were not affiliated to the IAAF until 1962 and the other times were treated with suspicion.

400m (Women)

Time	Competitor	Venue	Date
57.0	Marlene Matthews (AUS)	Sydney	6/1/57
57.0	Marise Chamberlain (NZL)	Christchurch	16/2/57
56.3	Nancy Boyle (AUS)	Sydney	24/2/57
55.2	Polina Lazareva (URS)	Moscow	10/5/57
54.0	Maria Itkina (URS)	Minsk	8/6/57
53.6	Maria Itkina (URS)	Moscow	6/7/57
53.4	Maria Itkina (URS)	Krasnodar	12/9/59
53.4	Maria Itkina (URS)	Belgrade	14/9/62
51.9	Sin Kim Dan (PRK)	Pyongyang	23/10/62
51.7	Nicole Duclos (FRA)	Athens	18/9/69
51.7	Colette Besson (FRA)	Athens	18/9/69
51.0	Marilyn Neufville (JAM)	Edinburgh	23/7/70
51.0	Monika Zehrt (GDR)	Paris	4/7/72
49.9	Irena Szewinska (POL)	Warsaw	22/6/74
50.14	Riita Salin (FIN)	Rome	4/9/74
49.77	Christine Brehmer (GDR)	Dresden	9/5/76
49.75	Irena Szewinska (POL)	Bydgoszcz	29/7/76
49.29	Irena Szewinska (POL)	Montreal	29/7/76
49.14	Marita Koch (GDR)	Leipzig	2/7/78
49.03	Marita Koch (GDR)	Potsdam	19/8/78
48.94	Marita Koch (GDR)	Prague	31/8/78
48.89	Marita Koch (GDR)	Potsdam	29/7/79
48.60	Marita Koch (GDR)	Turin	4/8/79
48.16	Marita Koch (GDR)	Athens	8/9/82
47.99	Jarmila Kratochvilova (TCH)	Helsinki	10/8/83
47.60	Marita Koch (GDR)	Canberra	6/10/85

automatic timing

400m HURDLES (MEN)

No athlete has ever dominated his event the way Ed Moses has dominated the 400m hurdles. Not Emil Zatopek. Nor Paavo Nurmi. Moses and his perfectly proportioned 6ft 1¼in (186cm), 161lb (73kg) physique towers above all others. Since 1977 he has been unbeaten in 109 successive races, including heats, and of the top 20 times posted in his event, 18 are his. The top ten are his exclusive property.

Moses' unrivalled speed over this man-killer of a distance stems from his unique ability to hold a 13 stride pattern between all ten flights of hurdles. This requires huge strength to maintain the rhythm in the closing 60m when oxygen debt has begun to bite hard.

His predecessors as world record holders, John Akii-Bua (UGA) and David Hemery (GBR) each started with 13 strides, but then had to change eventually to 14 or even 15 strides.

Moses, born in Dayton, Ohio, on 31 August 1955 was a latecomer to athletics. He achieved little at high school and it was only as a 20-year-old engineering student at Morehouse College, Georgia that he attempted his first 440 yards hurdles and recorded 52.0. By the following year he had improved by such a vast degree that he won the Montreal Olympic title in a shattering world record of 47.64 that put him a gaping 8m ahead of the field.

The following year Moses lost for the last time, in Berlin against West Germany's Harald Schmid, who at any other time would have ranked as the world's outstanding 400m hurdler.

Moses took 1982 and 1985 off to recharge his batteries. He could afford to. *USA Today* estimated his earnings from sponsorship, appearance money, shoe and clothing contracts to be 457,500 dollars in 1983. In 1984 they were nearer 600,000 dollars. Both are also world records for track and field athletes.

Moses' current 400m hurdle best came on his 28th birthday in the German city of Koblenz, seven years after his first world record and three years after his last reduction. Moses, in lane five, was only a metre up on fellow American Andre Phillips as they reached the eighth hurdle, but the power of his finish was such that he was 10m clear at the end. His 20 strides to the first hurdle took 5.9 secs from the blocks and thereafter his touchdown times (with the time between each

hurdle in brackets) were: 9.7 (3.8), 13.3 (3.6), 17.1 (3.8), 21.0 (3.9), 24.9 (3.9), 28.9 (4.0), 33.2 (4.3), 37.5 (4.3), 41.9 (4.4) . . . plus 16 strides to the finish in 5.1 for his overall 47.02.

Like Moses in 1976, the 400m hurdles has attracted other startling novices. Ireland's Bob Tisdall arrived at the 1932 Los Angeles Olympics with a very moderate best time of 54.2 sec – and ran away with the gold in 51.8 sec. That would have been a world record except that Tisdall knocked down a hurdle – then against the rules for records – and the world best was absurdly credited to runner up Glenn Hardin (USA) with 52.0. Then in 1956, in his inaugural year of quarter mile hurdling, America's Glenn Davis became the first to beat 50 secs with 49.5 *and* went on to win the Melbourne Olympics.

The standards of the 400m hurdles were transformed when first Geoff Vanderstock (USA), then David Hemery (GBR) went sub 49, a respectable time for good club athletes over a *flat* 400. But both their performances were in the thin air of altitude: Vanderstock at South Lake Tahoe, California, and Hemery at Mexico City.

Hemery's mark was unchallenged until John Akii-Bua, one of 48 children from his father's eight wives, destroyed it *at sea level* in the Munich Olympics of 1972 with one of the most devastating single runs of all time. The clash between Akii-Bua and Moses was eagerly awaited at the Montreal Games four years later, but like so many great duels of recent times, it was rendered impotent by politics as the Africans boycotted the competition.

• David Hemery in Mexico 1968
• Ed Moses maintains his winning streak

The Ed Moses Top Ten

Moses' amazing superiority is confirmed by the fact that he holds all ten of the world's fastest ever 400m hurdle times. Here, hurdle by hurdle, is the Moses genius:

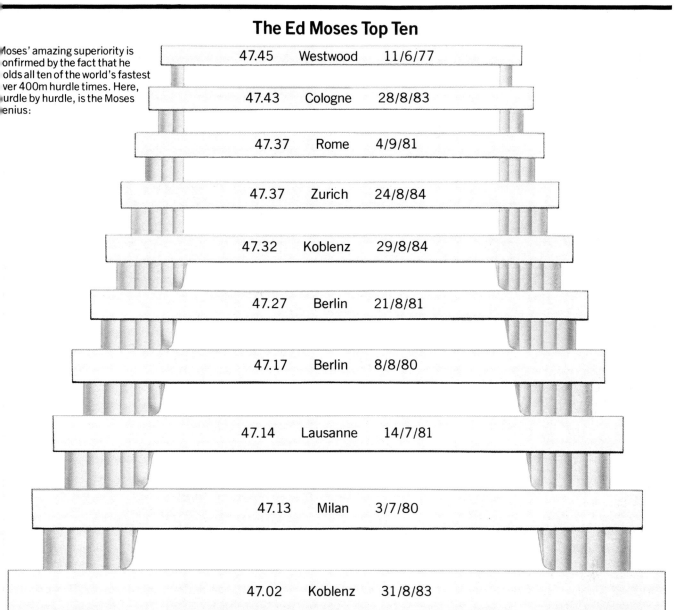

47.45	Westwood	11/6/77
47.43	Cologne	28/8/83
47.37	Rome	4/9/81
47.37	Zurich	24/8/84
47.32	Koblenz	29/8/84
47.27	Berlin	21/8/81
47.17	Berlin	8/8/80
47.14	Lausanne	14/7/81
47.13	Milan	3/7/80
47.02	Koblenz	31/8/83

400m Hurdles

Time	Competitor	Venue	Date
55.0	Charles Bacon (USA)	London	22/7/08
54.2	John Norton (USA)/	Pasadena	26/6/20
54.0	Frank Loomis (USA)	Antwerp	16/8/20
53.8	Sten Pettersson (SWE)	Paris	4/10/25
52.6	John Gibson (USA)	Lincoln	2/7/27
52.0	Morgan Taylor (USA)	Philadelphia	4/7/28
52.0	Glenn Hardin (USA)	Los Angeles	1/8/32
51.8	Glenn Hardin (USA)	Milwaukee	30/6/34
50.6	Glenn Hardin (USA)	Stockholm	26/7/34
50.4	Yuriy Lituyev (URS)	Budapest	29/8/53
49.5	Glenn Davis (USA)	Los Angeles	29/6/56
49.2	Glenn Davis (USA)	Budapest	6/8/58
49.2	Salvatore Morale (ITA)	Belgrade	14/9/62
49.1	Rex Cawley (USA) ·	Los Angeles	13/9/64
48.8	Geoff Vanderstock (USA)	S. Lake Tahoe	11/9/68
		*	
48.12	David Hemery (GBR)	Mexico City	15/10/68
47.82	John Akii-Bua (UGA)	Munich	2/9/72
47.64	Edwin Moses (USA)	Montreal	25/7/76
47.45	Edwin Moses (USA)	Westwood	11/6/77
47.13	Edwin Moses (USA)	Milan	3/7/80
47.02	Edwin Moses (USA)	Koblenz	31/8/83

*automatic timing

HURDLES
(WOMEN)

• Fanny Blankers-Koen, the Flying Dutchwoman

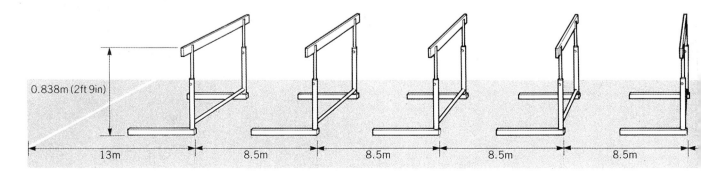

• Grazyna Rabsztyn leads Morgulina (URS)

The standard women's hurdles distance used to be 80m, contested over seven flights of 2ft 6in (76cm) hurdles. This was introduced in 1927 and lasted until 1969 when it was replaced by the 100m hurdles, contested over eight flights of 2ft 9in (84cm) obstacles.

Russia's legendary Irina Press, who dropped from sight at the onset of sex tests, held most records over 80m hurdles with five world bests – from 10.6 down to 10.3 – in 1968.

Holland's fabulous Fanny Blankers-Koen had produced the largest ever improvement in that record when she recorded 11.0 exactly, a reduction of 0.3 seconds at Amsterdam on 20 June 1948.

After the switch to 100m, the first ratified record of 13.3 was set jointly by East Germany's Karin Balzer and Poland's Teresa Sukniewicz at the Kusocinski Memorial meeting in Warsaw in 1969. Balzer went on to claim four more world records over the distance and in the process became the first woman to go below the 13 second barrier with 12.9 in Berlin on 5 September 1969. That mantle of greatness has been passed to another Pole, Grazyna Rabsztyn, born in Wroclaw on 20 September 1952. She set her first world record of 12.48 in 1978, duplicated that a year later and reduced it to 12.36 in 1980. But, prone to big day nerves, she never justified her talent in the major competitions and could finish no better than fifth in three Olympics. Away from those pressures, however, her hurdling technique was superb, as can be judged from the fact that her best flat 100m time was only 11.42. Grazyna's sister Elzbieta is married to West Germany's great hurdler Harald Schmid.

The 400m hurdles, too, has become an Eastern European event since its inception in 1971. Then Britain's Sandra Dyson produced 61.1 during an experimental race in Bonn. Three years later it was added to the IAAF list, came under the scrutiny of some rather more powerful athletes, and the inaugural world record of 56.51 was soon posted by Poland's Krystyna Kacperczyk at Augsburg in July 1974.

That record has been progressively hardened, especially as the event was handed Olympic status at the 1984 Games. There it was won by Morocco's virtually unknown Nawal El Moutawakil who became the first Arabic woman to win an Olympic medal. Just how much she had benefitted from the East European boycott was evidenced the following year.

Sabine Busch, an East German in her first season of competition over 400m hurdles rocketed to a world record 53.55 in East Berlin . . . more than a second faster than the lovely, but decidedly lucky, Nawal.

0.838m (2ft 9in)

13m   8.5m   8.5m   8.5m   8.5m

Chi Cheng

• Sabine Busch

100m Hurdles

Time	Competitor	Venue	Date
13.3	Karin Balzer (GDR)	Warsaw	20/6/69
13.3	Teresa Sukniewicz (POL)	Warsaw	20/6/69
13.0	Karin Balzer (GDR)	Leipzig	27/7/69
12.9	Karin Balzer (GDR)	Berlin	5/9/69
12.8	Teresa Sukniewicz (POL)	Warsaw	20/6/70
12.8	Chi Cheng (ROC)	Munich	12/7/70
12.7	Karin Balzer (GDR)	Berlin	26/7/70
12.7	Teresa Sukniewicz (POL)	Warsaw	29/9/70
12.7	Karin Balzer (GDR)	Berlin	25/7/71
12.6	Karin Balzer (GDR)	Berlin	31/7/71
12.5	Annelie Ehrhardt (GDR)	Potsdam	15/6/72
12.5	Pamela Ryan (AUS)	Warsaw	28/6/72
12.3	Annelie Ehrhardt (GDR)	Dresden	22/7/73
			*
12.59	Annelie Ehrhardt (GPA)	Munich	8/9/72
12.48	Grazyna Rabsztyn (POL)	Furth	10/6/78
12.36	Grazyna Rabsztyn (POL)	Warsaw	12/6/80

automatic timing

400m Hurdles

Time	Competitor	Venue	Date
56.51	Krystyna Kacperczyk (POL)	Augsburg	13/7/74
55.74	Tatyana Storozheva (URS)	Karl-Marx-Stadt	26/6/77
55.63	Karin Rossley (GDR)	Helsinki	14/8/77
55.44	Krystyna Kacperczyk (POL)	Berlin	18/8/78
55.31	Tatyana Zelentsova (URS)	Podolsk	19/8/78
54.89	Tatyana Zelentsova (URS)	Prague	2/9/78
54.78	Marina Makeyeva (URS)	Moscow	27/7/79
54.28	Karin Rossley (GDR)	Jena	17/5/80
54.02	Anna Ambraziene (URS)	Moscow	10/6/83
53.55	Margarita Ponomaryova (URS)	Kiev	22/6/84
53.55	Sabine Busch (GDR)	Berlin	22/9/85

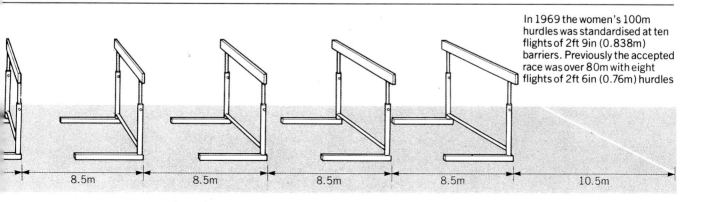

In 1969 the women's 100m hurdles was standardised at ten flights of 2ft 9in (0.838m) barriers. Previously the accepted race was over 80m with eight flights of 2ft 6in (0.76m) hurdles

8.5m   8.5m   8.5m   8.5m   10.5m

31

800m (MEN)

Conditions were perfect when Coe's world record run began at 11pm in Florence on 10 June 1981. Kenya's Billy Konchellah carried them through the first lap in 49.7 (Coe 49.9) before Coe, in a characteristic power glide, took it up on the entrance to the back straight. He reached 600m in 75.0, leaving him 27.2 to break the world record over the final 200m. He needed only 26.7, finishing half the length of the straight ahead of Dragan Zivotic of Yugoslavia. A fault in the electronic timing kept Coe waiting ten minutes for confirmation that he had become the first to dip below 1:42. "That was my goal," he said. "I was beginning to tie up in the last 30m. If it's going to be run faster I believe the improvement must come on the first lap."

Sebastian Coe

Coe broke two minutes at the age of 15 with 1:59.9 in 1972. From then to his second world record his times went like this:

1:56.6	Stretford	1/5/73
1:56.0	Crystal Palace	13/5/73
1:53.8	Cleckheaton	8/6/75
1:53.0	Loughborough	12/5/76
1:50.7	Loughborough	17/6/76
1:47.7	Stretford	8/8/76
1:46.3	Brussels	16/8/77
1:44.95	Crystal Palace	9/9/77
1:44.26	Brussels	18/8/78
1:43.97	Crystal Palace	15/9/78
1:42.33	Oslo	3/7/79
1:41.73	Florence	10/6/81

perts around the world watched the emergence of the giant
berto Juantorena from Cuba in 1976 and predicted a new
a for middle distance running. This was the shape of things
come, they decided, huge men with sprinting power who
uld turn the 800m into an extended 400m. Then up
pped little Sebastian Coe, all 5ft 9½in (177cm) and 123lb
6kg) of him, and they were forced to reconsider.

History would have shown them the error of their thinking,
back in the 1880's the two lap race was dominated by
nerican Laurence 'Lon' Myers who was only 5ft 8in (173cm)
d weighed a mere 114lb (52kg). In those days the event was
er 880yds and in the five years between 1880 and 1885
yers set seven world records for the distance, from 1:56.2
wn to 1:55.4. At one stage he held the best ten times ever.

Official world records, ratified by the International
nateur Athletic Federation (IAAF), were introduced in 1912.
nce then, there have been fewer over 800m than any of the
her men's Olympic events, with only 18 from American Ted
eredith's 1:51.9 in 1912 to Coe's 1:41.73 in Florence in 1981.

Coe follows a fine British tradition. Albert Hill was Olympic
ampion in 1920, Douglas Lowe in 1924 and 1928 and Tom
ampson in 1932. Hampson, in the process, became the first
go below 1:50 with 1:49.8. Another Briton, Sydney Wooder-
n, also claimed the record in 1938, but within a year he had
en ousted by German Rudolph Harbig and his controver-
l coach Woldemar Gerschler.

Gerschler was a pioneer of interval training – hard track
ssions of repetition runs with little recovery time between
ch. Such training is now an essential element of every
hlete's schedule. Then it was revolutionary, and the results
flected it. On 15 July 1939 Harbig recorded an astounding
46.6, a time that would be internationally respectable even
day, to clip almost two seconds off the world's best. The
cord stood for 16 years and Gerschler insisted that but for
e war Harbig would have run even faster.

Harbig was as far ahead of his contemporaries as Coe was
en he set his world record in Florence. Since then 1984
ympic champion Joaquim Cruz has also dipped inside 1:42,
e only man other than Coe to do so. Cruz stands 6ft 1½
37cm) and weighs 161lb (73kg). Is he the shape of things to
me? Or does another little big man wait around
e corner?

800m

Time	Competitor	Venue	Date
1:51.9	Ted Meredith (USA)	Stockholm	8/7/12
1:51.6	Otto Peltzer (GER)	London	3/7/26
1:50.6	Sera Martin (FRA)	Paris	14/7/28
1:49.8	Tom Hampson (GBR)	Los Angeles	2/8/32
1:49.8	Ben Eastman (USA)	Princeton	16/6/34
1:49.7	Glenn Cunningham (USA)	Stockholm	20/8/36
1:49.6	Elroy Robinson (USA)	New York	11.7.37
1:48.4	Sydney Wooderson (GBR)	Motspur Park	20/8/38
1:46.6	Rudolf Harbig (GER)	Milan	15/7/39
1:45.7	Roger Moens (BEL)	Oslo	3/8/55
1:44.3	Peter Snell (NZL)	Christchurch	3/2/62
1:44.3	Ralph Doubell (AUS)	Mexico City	15/10/68
1:44.3	David Wottle (USA)	Eugene	1/7/72
1:43.7	Marcello Fiasconaro (ITA)	Milan	27/6/73
1:43.50	Alberto Juantorena (CUB)	Montreal	25/7/76
1:43.44	Alberto Juantorena (CUB)	Sofia	21/8/77
1:42.33	Sebastian Coe (GBR)	Oslo	5/7/79
1:41.73	Sebastian Coe (GBR)	Florence	10/6/81

automatic timing

● Alberto Juantorena wins Montreal Olympics

● Peter Snell

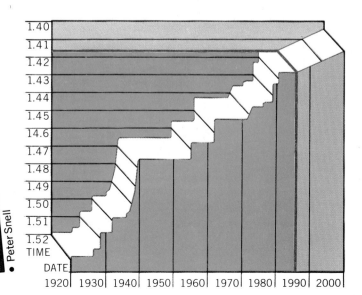

800m (WOMEN)

The two-minute barrier for the women's 800m used to be akin to the four-minute mile for men; and, in the same way, once the barrier was down the floodgates opened. Since blonde West German Hildegard Falck destroyed the mystique with a record-smashing run of 1:58.5 in 1973, six other women have helped reduce the world best to a once unimaginable 1:53.28.

Two-minute 800m have become as commonplace as four-minute miles. Indeed, Miss Falck's achievement no longer rates even in the top 100 times for the distance. For that we have to thank the Red Revolution in women's middle distance running, a phenomenon that has left the rest of the world, as well as the rest of Europe, trailing breathlessly in its wake. At the start of the 1986 track season you had to go down to 35th place in the All-Time Best list for the women's 800m to find an athlete who did not come from Eastern Europe. Then you discovered Mary Slaney with her American record of 1:56.90, set in 1985.

> The first woman to crack the two-minute barrier unofficially was North Korea's Sin Kim Dan who was credited with 1:59.1 in Djakarta on 12 November 1963 during the Games of the New Emerging Forces (GANEFO). This time was not recognised by the IAAF, and nor was her reported 1:58.0 at Pyongyang on 30 August 1964.

One of the reasons for this is the sheer number of women being encouraged to tackle middle distances in Iron Curtain countries; the other is that their coaches know their business. They recognise that women, more than men, mature as athletes with age; that their best performances often do not arrive until they are in their thirties.

Consequently their middle distance women athletes are encouraged to take a gradual build up, to wait until their bodies are strong enough to tackle the enormous burden of training needed for specialised 800m running. In the West, too often, young, promising athletes are allowed to tear into terrifying schedules and suffer debilitating consequences. Even the redoubtable Mrs Slaney had to wait until her late twenties to discover her full potential after being sidelined with serious leg injuries earlier on.

The fore-runner of these formidable platoons from Eastern Europe was Russia's Nina Otkalenko (née Pletnyova) who set five official IAAF records and another two unofficial ones as she took the 800m mark from 2:12.0 in 1951 to 2:05.0 in 1955. Before her the barrier breakers had been far more sedate. Britain's Mary Lines was the first below 2:30 with 2:26.6 (over 880 yds) in London on 30 August 1922; Gladys Lane, another Briton, cracked 2:25 with 2:24.8 (880 yds) in London on 25 July 1925 and Sweden's Inga Gentzel went sub 2:20 with 2:19.2 in Amsterdam on 1 July 1928.

800m (Women)

Time	Competitor	Venue	Date
2:16.8	Lina Radke (GER)	Amsterdam	2/8/28
2:15.9	Anna Larsson (SWE)	Stockholm	28/8/44
2:14.8	Anna Larsson (SWE)	Halsingborg	19/8/45
2:13.8	Anna Larsson (SWE)	Stockholm	30/8/45
2:13.0	Yevdokiya Vasilyeva (URS)	Moscow	17/7/50
2:12.2	Valentina Pomogayeva (URS)	Moscow	26/8/51
2:12.0	Nina Pletnyova (URS)	Minsk	26/8/51
2:08.5	Nina Pletnyova (URS)	Kiev	15/6/52
2:07.3	Nina Otkalenko (URS)	Moscow	27/8/53
2:06.6	Nina Otkalenko (URS)	Kiev	16/9/54
2:05.0	Nina Otkalenko (URS)	Zagreb	24/9/55
2:04.3	Lyudmilla Shevtsova (URS)	Moscow	3/7/60
2:04.3	Lyudmilla Shevtsova (URS)	Rome	7/9/60
2:01.2	Dixie Willis (AUS)	Perth	3/3/62
2:01.1	Ann Packer (GBR)	Tokyo	20/10/64
2:01.0	Judy Pollock (AUS)	Helsinki	28/6/67
2:00.5	Vera Nikolic (YUG)	London	20/7/68
1:58.5	Hildegard Falck (FRG)	Stuttgart	11/7/71
1:57.5	Svetla Zlateva (BUL)	Athens	24/8/73
1:56.0	Valentina Gerasimova (URS)	Kiev	12/6/76
1:54.94	Tatyana Kazankina (URS)	Montreal	16/7/76
1:54.85	Nadyezhda Olizarenko (URS)	Moscow	12/6/80
1:53.43	Nadyezhda Olizarenko (URS)	Moscow	27/7/80
1:53.28	Jarmila Kratochvilova (TCH)	Munich	26/7/83

*automatic timing

Five out of seven
The Olympic Games of 1928 were the first to include women's events and the 800m produced a world record of 2:16.8 for Germany's Lina Radke. But, because of protests over the supposed severity of the distance for women, the 800m was then dropped from the timetable until the 1960 Games in Rome. Russia's Lyudmila Shevtsova demonstrated the upsurge in class by winning in a world record equalling 2:04.3. Four years later in Tokyo Britain's Ann Packer also set a world best of 2:01.1 when taking the 800m gold and in 1976 at Montreal all the first four were inside the then world record of 1:56.0. The winner, Tatyana Kazankina of Russia, returned 1:54.94. The record fell for the fifth time in seven Games in 1980 when another Russian, Nadyezhda Olizarenko, led all the way to finish in 1:53.43.

Jarmila Kratochvilova, the current record holder, is most certainly one of Eastern Europe's late developers. The muscular Czech did not compete over 800m seriously until 1982 when she was 31 and was timed at 1:56.69 compared to her previous best of 2:11.4 in 1975. In her third crack at the event, in Munich on 26 July 1983, she set her world record, covering the first lap in 56.28 and the second in 57.00 to win by almost 50m.

● World champion . . . Jarmila Kratochvilova at Helsinki 1983

● Ann Packer . . . heroine of the 1964 Tokyo Olympics

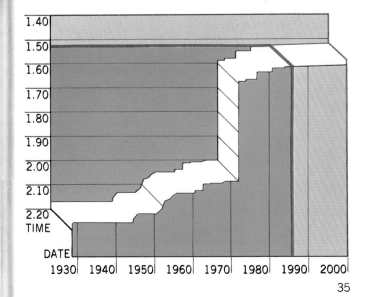

1.40
1.50
1.60
1.70
1.80
1.90
2.00
2.10
2.20

TIME

DATE 1930 1940 1950 1960 1970 1980 1990 2000

1500m (MEN)

Fifty years from now, when the track historians look back on the Eighties, they will marvel at the glorious golden triumvirate then possessed by Great Britain over 1500m: double Olympic champion Sebastian Coe, three times world record holder Steve Ovett and world champion Steve Cram.

In the same fashion that others now look at the Super Swedes of the Forties: Gunder Haegg, Arne Andersson and Lennart Strand, so will they then view Coe, Ovett and Cram. And surely they will pronounce them the most outstanding trio of all time?

Moroccan Said Aouita poses the most potent threat to Britain's dominance over 1500m. The slightly-built "Kid from the Casbah" won the Olympic 5,000m title in Los Angeles and claimed he would have beaten Sebastian Coe in the 1500m had he chosen to run that distance. Aouita was defeated by Steve Cram, Olympic silver medallist, the following year over 1500m and a mile, but then strengthened his argument by setting a world record for the 1500m of 3:29.46 in Oslo.

• Steve Ovett

• Said Aouita

From 1979 to 1985 – and onwards – they dominated 1500m running, setting five world records and taking a clean sweep of all major titles open to them, Commonwealth, European, World and Olympic. Those great Swedish athletes also set five world records, but four of them came when the rest of Europe was engaged in the slightly more pressing event of the Second World War.

The three great Britons twice lined up against each other in Olympic 1500m finals. In Moscow in 1980, Coe, occasionally criticised for tactical frailties, produced one of the most acutely judged races of his life to take the gold. Ovett, who had won the 800m a few days earlier, was third with Cram, then only 19, finishing eighth.

Four years later, in Los Angeles, they were back together again for the first time since Moscow. In the meantime Coe had suffered bouts of the debilitating glandular disorder toxoplasmosis, Ovett had severely injured his right knee in a horrifying collision with a church railing while on a morning training run, and Cram had assumed the crown with consumate victories in Commonwealth, European and World Championships. But in the build up to Los Angeles Cram had suffered a string of injuries, deciding only a week before the Games began that he would definitely take part. Coe had also endured a fairly wretched preparation with a series of surprising defeats. Ovett, though, looked lean and hungry, reportedly in the best form of his life at the age of 28.

• Sebastian Coe

• Britain's golden trio from the right:
Coe, Cram and Ovett

1500m

Time	Competitor	Venue	Date
3:55.8	Abel Kiviat (USA)	Cambridge, Mass.	8/6/12
3:54.7	John Zander (SWE)	Stockholm	5/8/17
3:52.6	Paavo Nurmi (FIN)	Helsinki	19/6/24
3:51.0	Otto Peltzer (GER)	Berlin	11/9/26
3:49.2	Jules Ladoumegue (FRA)	Paris	5/10/30
3:49.2	Luigi Beccali (ITA)	Turin	9/9/33
3:49.0	Luigi Beccali (ITA)	Milan	17/9/33
3:48.8	Bill Bonthron (USA)	Milwaukee	30/6/34
3:47.8	Jack Lovelock (NZL)	Berlin	10/8/41
3:47.6	Gunder Haegg (SWE)	Stockholm	10/8/41
3:45.8	Gunder Haegg (SWE)	Stockholm	17/7/42
3:45.0	Arne Andersson (SWE)	Gothenburg	17/8/43
3:43.0	Gunder Haegg (SWE)	Gothenburg	7/7/44
3:43.0	Lennart Strand (SWE)	Malmo	15/7/47
3:43.0	Werner Lueg (GER)	Berlin	29/6/52
3:42.8	Wes Santee (USA)	Compton	4/6/54
3:41.8	John Landy (AUS)	Turku	21/6/54
3:40.8	Sandor Iharos (HUN)	Helsinki	28/7/55
3:40.8	Laslo Tabori (HUN)	Oslo	6/9/55
3:40.8	Gunnar Nielsen (DEN)	Oslo	6/9/55
3:40.6	Istvan Rozsavolgyi (HUN)	Tata	3/8/56
3:40.2	Olavi Salsola (FIN)	Turku	11/7/57
3:40.2	Olavi Salonen (FIN)	Turku	11/7/57
3:38.1	Stanislav Jungwirth (TCH)	Stara Boleslav	12/7/57
3:36.0	Herb Elliott (AUS)	Gothenburg	28/8/58
3:35.6	Herb Elliott (AUS)	Rome	6/9/60
3:33.1	Jim Ryun (USA)	Los Angeles	8/7/67
3:32.2	Filbert Bayi (TAN)	Christchurch	2/2/74
3:32.1	Sebastian Coe (GBR)	Zurich	15/8/79
3:32.1	Steve Ovett (GBR)	Oslo	15/7/80
3:31.36	Steve Ovett (GBR)	Koblenz	27/8/80
3:31.24	Sydney Maree (USA)	Cologne	28/8/83
3:30.77	Steve Ovett (GBR)	Rieti	4/9/83
3:29.67	Steve Cram (GBR)	Nice	16/7/85
3:29.46	Said Aouita (MOR)	Oslo	23/8/85

• Steve Cram leads Aouita in his
1500m world record

In the event, the apparently strongest weakened first. Ovett, his lungs clogged by the Los Angeles smog after a bout of bronchitis, collapsed at the end of his semi-final. Courageously and against the wishes of some team officials, he insisted on taking his hard-earned place in the final. With a lap to go the three Englishmen were in a line: Olympic champion, world champion, world record holder. Then Ovett staggered and sank semi-conscious onto the track side grass, fighting for breath. As the remaining two reached the final 200m Cram lengthened that once irresistible stride for his characteristic long haul to the line. But Coe had already gone with the killer spurt of acceleration that had hallmarked his finest hour four years earlier.

Only 11 months later Cram was back on top, becoming the first to dip below 3:30 over the metric mile with 3:29.67 in Nice. The era lived on.

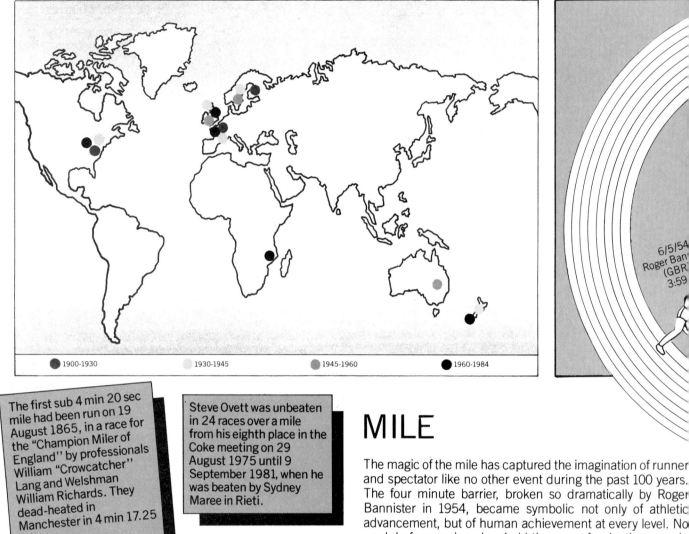

1900-1930   1930-1945   1945-1960   1960-1984

6/5/54
Roger Ban'
(GBR'
3:59

The first sub 4 min 20 sec mile had been run on 19 August 1865, in a race for the "Champion Miler of England" by professionals William "Crowcatcher" Lang and Welshman William Richards. They dead-heated in Manchester in 4 min 17.25 sec.

Steve Ovett was unbeaten in 24 races over a mile from his eighth place in the Coke meeting on 29 August 1975 until 9 September 1981, when he was beaten by Sydney Maree in Rieti.

There had been professional records before 1913. Britain's Walter George ran 4 min 12.75 sec during a match with William Cummings (GBR) at Lillie Bridge on 23 August 1886. George had run even faster in a time-trial – 4 min 10.2 sec at Surbiton in 1885, a time not bettered until 1931.

MILE

The magic of the mile has captured the imagination of runner and spectator like no other event during the past 100 years. The four minute barrier, broken so dramatically by Roger Bannister in 1954, became symbolic not only of athletic advancement, but of human achievement at every level. No mark before or since has held the same fascination even in this metric age where the 1500m has ousted the mile from all major Games.

Despite the rarity of mile races, the finest middle distance runners still seek to test themselves over the time honoured distance – derived from the ancient Roman measure of 1,000 paces – determined to edge ever nearer the ultimate performance.

In the past 100 years, as master milers have emerged from all parts of the globe, the world record has been slashed from Walter George's 4:19.4 in 1982 to Steve Cram's, 3:46.32 in Oslo in July, 1985. A similar improvement over the next 100 years would mean a superman running 3:13.22, or four equal laps of 48.3 sec.

Englishman George was the first great miler on record. He was reliably reported to have clocked 4:10.2 in a training run, which put him so far ahead of his contemporaries that it was not until 1932 that Frenchman Jules Ladoumegue became the first man to go sub 4:10 with 4:09.2.

The next great improvement came from Swedish pair Gunder Haegg and Arne Anderson who, between them, bettered 4min 3sec five times between 1943-45. The four minute mile was becoming tantalisingly closer but with Haegg and Anderson both disqualified for professionalism in 1945 it fell to a new generation of runners to supply it.

By 1954 two athletes, Britain's elegant Roger Bannister and Australia's wiry John Landy, were ready for the ultimate assault. Bannister gained the first blow, at Iffley Road, Oxford,

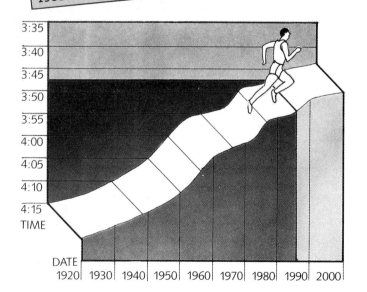

31/5/13
John Paul Jones (USA)
4:14.4

of the record has gone like this:

Competitor	Venue	Date	Time	Competitor	Venue	Date
...Paul Jones (USA)	Cambridge	31/5/13	3:57.2	Derek Ibbotson (GBR)	White City	19/7/57
...man Taber (USA)	Cambridge	16/7/15	3:54.5	Herb Elliott (AUS)	Dublin	6/8/58
...avo Nurmi (FIN)	Stockholm	23/8/23	3:54.4	Peter Snell (NZL)	Wanganui	27/1/62
...les Ladoumegue (FRA)	Paris	4/10/31	3:54.1	Peter Snell (NZL)	Auckland	17/11/64
...ohn Lovelock (NZL)	Princeton	15/7/33	3:53.6	Michel Jazy (FRA)	Rennes	9/6/65
...lenn Cunningham (USA)	Princeton	16/6/34	3:51.3	Jim Ryun (USA)	Berkeley	17/6/66
Sydney Wooderson (GBR)	Motspur Park	28/8/37	3:51.1	Jim Ryun (USA)	Bakersfield	23/6/67
Gunder Haegg (SWE)	Gothenburg	1/7/42	3:51.0	Filbert Bayi (TAN)	Kingston	17/5/75
Arne Andersson (SWE)	Stockholm	10/7/42	3:49.4	John Walker (NZL)	Gothenburg	12/8/75
Gunder Haegg (SWE)	Stockholm	4/8/42	3:49.0	Sebastian Coe (GBR)	Oslo	17/7/79
Arne Andersson (SWE)	Gothenburg	1/7/43	3:48.8	Steve Ovett (GBR)	Oslo	1/7/80
Arne Andersson (SWE)	Malmo	18/7/44	3:48.53	Sebastian Coe (GBR)	Zurich	19/8/81
Gunder Haegg (SWE)	Malmo	17/7/45	3:48.40	Steve Ovett (GBR)	Koblenz	26/8/81
Roger Bannister (GBR)	Oxford	6/5/54	3:47.33	Sebastian Coe (GBR)	Brussels	28/8/81
John Landy (AUS)	Turku	21/6/54	3:46.32	Steve Cram (GBR)	Oslo	27/7/85

27/7/85
Steve Cram (GBR)
3:46.32

on 6 May 1954... and earned immortality in 3:59.4. The lap times were: 57.5, 60.7, 62.3 and 58.9.

Forty six days later in Turku, Finland, an understandably frustrated Landy took the record from Bannister with 3:57.9, an immense improvement. Who was the better? The public were about to find out in the Empire Games that year in Vancouver. Landy was installed as the favourite, but Bannister's powerful finish carried him to victory by five yards in 3:58.8 the fastest he ever ran. Landy's time was 3:59.6 and for the first time two men had beaten four minutes in the same race.

The courageous, barrel-chested Derek Ibbotson of England succeeded Landy as world record holder. But it was left to Australian Herb Elliott, arguably the greatest mile competitor of them all, to bring the next major advance with the first sub 3:55 run. Elliott, Olympic 1500m champion in Rome, 1960, was never beaten over either distance in his career.

Peter Snell (NZ) and Michel Jazy (France) trimmed a few tenths before 19-year-old sensation Jim Ryun (USA) brought the 3:50 barrier within range with a time of 3:51.3 in 1966. A year later Ryun, "The Kansas Express" improved that to 3:51.1 and there it stopped until the first great African miler, Filbert Bayi of Tanzania, announced himself with 3:51.0 in 1975.

Less than three months later New Zealand's flying Kiwi, John Walker, ushered in the sub 3:50 era with 3:49.4, a time which was considered super human until Britain's amazing trio of Steve Ovett, Sebastian Coe and Steve Cram set about it. From 1979 they bettered the record six times between them, ending with Cram's spectacular run at Bislett Stadium.

The metric distance of 1500m is a fraction under 120 yds short of the mile and the accepted conversion factor for top class athletes is 17.5 secs. So Said Aouita's 1500m world record of 3:29.46 is marginally inferior to Cram's mile run of 3:46.32.

Steve Cram's world record came during the aptly titled "Dream Mile" at Oslo's Bislett Stadium on 27 July 1985. The field included Seb Coe, the man who had beaten him a year earlier for Olympic 1500m gold, former world mile record holder John Walker and American Steve Scott, second fastest miler ever. In all there were eight men who had bettered 3:50 for the mile.

American James Mays was the hare and he set a fine pace of 56.01 for the opening lap and 1:53.82 at the halfway stage. Cram, after a cautious start, was soon in a handy position, but when Mike Hillardt of Australia took over the pacing duties and produced a lethargic third lap of 59.32 it seemed all chance of the world record had gone. But an explosive final 220 yd in 25.4 during a last lap of 53.0 not only gave Cram the record, it also recorded his first win over the distance against Coe, who finished third in 3:49.22, ten yards behind Spain's Jose-Luis Gonzalez (3:47.79).

● Steve Cram

● Roger Bannister

1500m & MILE (WOMEN)

Just 23 days after Roger Bannister's apocalyptic four minute run, another tall, elegant Briton was striding to a world mile record . . . Diane Leather, who became the first woman to break the five minute barrier with 4:59.6 at Birmingham on 29 May 1954.

But while the men have driven themselves to the limit to scratch and claw off less than 13 seconds in the following three decades, the women have hacked away almost 44 seconds until the record stands at 4:16.71, set by America's Mary Decker in Zurich on 21 August 1985. And even that is by no means outside the reach of other women right now, when you consider that Decker's time is equivalent to a 1500m run of about 3:58 and that the women's 1500m world record is six seconds faster than that.

It is another illustration of the huge advances made in women's athletics during the past 20 years thanks to a changing, enlightened society. The IAAF first recognised women's records for the mile in 1967 when another Briton, Anne Smith, recorded 4:37.0 at Chiswick, London. En route in that run, Anne also set the first official 1500m mark of 4:17.3.

Since then, like so many other areas of women's athletics, the twin distances of mile and 1500m have become the province of the Eastern European, with the occasional, brilliant outbreak of Mary Decker.

The Soviet influence was never better illustrated than in the 1972 Olympics at Munich, the first occasion the 1500m was added to the programme. Lyudmila Bragina beat her own world record in all three rounds; heat, semi-finals and final. On 4 September she clocked 4:06.5, three days later that was reduced to 4:05.1 and two days after that she finished with an astounding 4:01.38 . . . a time faster than Albert Hill's gold medal performance of 1920.

Another Soviet, Tatyana Kazankina, inherited her crown, becoming the first to go below four minutes with 3:56.0 in 1976. Four years and two Olympic titles later, Kazankina reduced that to 3:52.47 . . . faster than the great Paavo Nurmi's world record of 3:52.6 in 1924. That 56 year gap between men's and women's world records is the shortest for any track or field event. Finishing way back in second that day, Mary Decker still managed an American best of 3:59.43.

Mary was to reduce that to 3:57.12 in Stockholm in 1983, the same year she completed a wonderful 1500m, 3,000m double at the inaugural World Championships in Helsinki.

As ever Decker, who had captivated the world as a pig-tailed 14-year-old ten years earlier, cut out the pace from the start. In the 1500m she reached 400m in 64.04, faster even than the men's race, and remained in front until the final 200m. Then Soviet Zamira Zaitseva, the fastest performer in the race on paper, accelerated away on the bend and opened a substantial five metre lead. Decker's lack of a kick had been exposed, it seemed. This was to be another storming Soviet triumph. Instead, with 60m to go and Zaitseva tiring agonisingly, Mary's relentless stride began to eat into the lead. Just 10m from the finish, the American forged fractionally ahead and Zaitseva, in her desperation, flung herself bodily at the line . . . to end up literally down and out in second place.

The first sub 4:30 time for the women's mile was Paola Cacchi's 4:29.5 at Viareggio in 1973. The Italian took 5.8 secs off Ellen Tittel's mark, the biggest ever improvement.

The first major championships to stage a women's 1500m was the 1969 European meeting in Athens.

• Mary Decker leads Maricica Puica

Two flags fly over the women's middle distances: America's and the USSR's. Who can lower them?

• Lyudmilla Bragina out in front in Munich Olympics

Four days earlier Decker had defeated the might of the ~~S~~oviet Union in even more comprehensive fashion in the ~~3~~,000m. Her opponents: the legendary Kazankina and the ~~th~~en world record holder, Svetlana Ulmasova. At the bell, ~~D~~ecker and Britain's Wendy Sly were virtually level with ~~K~~azankina and Ulmasova a shoestring away. Again Decker's ~~le~~ngthening, elegant stride was to carry the day as she ~~co~~vered the last 200 metres in 30 seconds. It was too much ~~e~~ven for Kazankina who crumpled close to the finish, allowing ~~W~~est Germany's Brigitte Kraus to sneak through for the silver. ~~T~~he world eagerly awaited the rematch in the Los Angeles ~~G~~ames, a prospect destroyed like so many others by the East~~e~~rn European boycott.

Tantalisingly, a fortnight after the Games which had wit~~n~~essed Decker's tear-stained, hysterical stumble, Kazankina now the mother of two children and aged 32 – was back to ~~h~~er best, claiming the world 3,000m record with 8:22.62, almost seven seconds faster than Decker's best and 13 seconds inside the winning time in Los Angeles.

USSR's Natalya Artemova clocked 4:15.8 for the mile in Moscow on 6 August 1984 – a world record. But the Soviets, with no explanation, declined to put it forward for ratification.

The best time for the "in-between" distance of: 2,000m is: 5:28.72 by Tatyana Kazankina of the Soviet Union in 1984.

3000m (WOMEN)

Who can halt the Soviet bloc? Rumania's Maricica Puica claimed the Olympic 3,000m title, profiting perhaps from Decker's controversial exit. But Puica is now into her mid-thirties. With Decker dedicating 1986 to motherhood, the expectations fall on the slender shoulders of Zola Budd, inno-cent party in Decker's Olympic debacle, and rapidly maturing into a distance runner of the highest possible class. In Febru-ary 1986 the little South African-born athlete, who took British citizenship in such a spotlight of publicity, claimed the world's best indoors mark for the distance during a British interna-tional at RAF Cosford, near Wolverhampton.

It was clear indication that, at the age of 19, the once frail Budd is blossoming towards her full, exciting potential. Perhaps, though, her true ability lies in the longer distances; 5,000m, 10,000m, even the marathon. That would seem to leave only Decker, Britain's Olympic silver medallist Wendy Sly and West Germany's Brigitte Kraus to stem this particular Red Sea swamping all in sight from 1,500m to 3,000m.

3000m (Women)

Time	Competitor	Venue	Date
8:53.0	Lyudmilla Bragina (URS)	Moscow	12/8/72
8:52.8	Lyudmilla Bragina (URS)	Durham, N.C.	6/7/74
8:46.6	Grete Waitz (NOR)	Oslo	24/6/75
8:45.4	Grete Waitz (NOR)	Oslo	21/6/76
8:27.12	Lyudmilla Bragina (URS)	College Park	7/8/76
8:26.78	Syvetlana Ulmasova (URS)	Kiev	25/7/82
8:22.62	Tatyana Kazankina (URS)	Leningrad	26/8/84

● Tatyana Kazankina

1500m (Women)

Time	Competitor	Venue	Date
4:17.3	Anne Smith (GBR)	London	3/6/67
4:15.6	Maria Gommers (HOL)	Sittard	24/10/67
4:12.4	Paola Pigni (ITA)	Milan	2/7/69
4:10.7	Jaroslava Jehlickova (TCH)	Athens	20/9/69
4:09.6	Karin Burneleit (GDR)	Helsinki	15/8/71
4:06.9	Lyudmilla Bragina (URS)	Moscow	18/7/72
4:06.5	Lyudmilla Bragina (URS)	Munich	4/9/72
4:05.1	Lyudmilla Bragina (URS)	Munich	7/9/72
4:01.4	Lyudmilla Bragina (URS)	Munich	9/9/72
3:56.0	Tatyana Kazankina (URS)	Podolsk	28/6/76
3:55.0	Tatyana Kazankina (URS)	Moscow	6/7/80
3:52.47	Tatyana Kazankina (URS)	Zurich	13/8/80

1 Mile (Women)

Time	Competitor	Venue	Date
4:37.0	Anne Smith (GBR)	London	3/6/67
4:36.8	Maria Gommers (HOL)	Leicester	14/6/69
4:35.3	Ellen Tittel (FRG)	Sittard	20/8/73
4:29.5	Paola Pigni-Cacchi (ITA)	Viareggio	8/8/73
4:23.8	Natalia Marasescu (ROM)	Bucharest	21/5/77
4:22.1	Natalia Marasescu (ROM)	Auckland	27/1/79
4:21.7	Mary Decker (USA)	Auckland	26/1/80
4:20.89	Lyudmilla Vesalkova (URS)	Bologna	12/9/81
4:18.08	Mary Decker (USA)	Paris	9/7/82
4:17.44	Maricica Puica (ROM)	Rieti	16/9/82
4:16.71	Mary Decker (USA)	Zurich	21/8/85

5,000/10,000m (MEN)

No other area of athletics, save perhaps the 1500m and mile, has been so graced with celebrated, evocative names as the long distance events of 5,000m and 10,000m. Paavo Nurmi, Emil Zatopek, Vladimir Kuts, Ron Clarke, Lasse Viren, Miruts Yifter . . . all of them as fabulously famous in their own way as any other group of sportsmen.

The sympatico between long distance runner and trackside viewer is an intangible the sprinter could never hope to capture. To watch someone like Zatopek, shoulders rolling in apparent agony, mouth creased in torment, repeatedly circling in front of you, forges a lifelong affiliation.

Although Africans like Yifter and, earlier, Henry Rono have been pre-eminent at the events, it is perhaps no surprise to find the champions evolving mainly from the stoic, icy worlds of Scandinavia and Eastern Europe. You need a certain bloody-mindedness to churn out mile after endless mile i training, a strength of spirit tempered by adversity.

Anglo-Saxons such as Walter George and Alf Shrubb ha given Britain supremacy in the 19th century, but their reig was ended by the first of the great Finns, Hanne Kolehmainen with his 5,000/10,000m double at the 191 Olympics. (From then until 1948 each title would only onc escape from Finnish hands).

Kolehmainen's time in winning that 5,000m race i Stockholm was 14:36.6, the first sub 15 min mark, the firs official IAAF record and 24.6 secs inside the previous best the greatest margin of improvement ever for the record.

After Kolehmainen came the incomparable Nurmi wh set more than 20 world records, two of them over 5,000m an two more over 10,000m.

Ville Ritola, Lauri Lehtinen, Taisto Maki, Ilmari Salmine and Viljo Heino all contributed world records at one or bot

• Hannes Kolehmainen, first of the Flying Finns, leads in the 1912 Olympic 5000m

• The maestro Paavo Nurmi

● Emil Zatopek (left) battles with Britain's Chataway

distances to continue this golden era of Finnish athletics before the advent of the mighty Zatopek.

In world record terms, the Czech was irresistible over the longer 10,000m, breaking the best mark five times. But Zatopek, who was to set that unique treble of 5,000m, 10,000m and marathon titles at the 1952 Olympics, was also devastating over the shorter event.

He had made his Olympic debut in London in 1948 when he won the 10,000m only two months after first attempting the event, and finished second in the 5,000. In 1952 he was simply unbeatable.

He took the 10,000m by a yawning 100m margin, the 5,000m four days later by five metres and the marathon three days later by 700m. Zatopek was among the pioneers of interval training, regularly running sessions of up to 40x400m with minimum recovery times. His dedication helped transform the events (he was the first to go sub 29 mins for 10,000m in 1956) and paved the way for the surging, iron-willed Russian Vladimir Kuts.

Kuts set his first 5,000m record of 13:56.6 in the 1954 European Games at Berne. Britain's Chris Chataway, one of Bannister's pacemakers in the four minute mile, took it from him later that year in October, in an enthralling duel before 40,000 at White City. But he held the record for only ten days before Kuts claimed it back.

Between 1923 and 1931 the great Finnish runner Paavo Nurmi broke a total of 29 world records at distances from 1500m to 20,000m. In 1924, at Helsinki on 19 June he broke the 1500m and 5000m marks with only an hour's rest between. The following month, on the same afternoon he won both events at the Paris Olympic Games.

Both Gunder Haegg (SWE) and Ron Clarke (AUS) broke ten world records in a single year, Haegg in 1942, and the Australian in 1965.

Kuts' fourth and final 5,000m record of 13:35.0 stood for more than seven years before Australia's Ron Clarke lowered it by almost ten seconds in three bites during 1965.

Clarke was to go on to set world records at eight distances: two miles, three miles, 5,000m, six miles, 10,000m, ten miles, 20,000m and one hour. He held the last seven simultaneously for several months. Even the great Nurmi, who had broken the same seven, could not claim that distinction.

Clarke brought an amazing upsurge of class to long distance running in the Sixties, progressively lowering the 5,000m best from 13:35.0 to 13:16.6 and the 10,000m from 28:18.2 to 27:39.4. But Clarke, unlike those great names before him – Nurmi, Zatopek, Kuts – was unable to translate such supremacy into gold medals at major Games. Favourite

• Ron Clarke

• Lasse Viren (301) wins 1976 Olympic 5000m

to win the Olympic 10,000m in 1964, he could finish only third. Along with four Commonwealth Games silvers, it was to be his only reward ... scant return for such an illustrious career.

After Clarke came Viren, the astonishing, slim Finn who claimed an Olympic double at Munich, all but disappeared for the following four years, and then re-appeared in Montreal to repeat the feat. There were dark mutterings about blood doping – pumping oxygenated blood into an already replete body to aid respiration – but whatever the truth Viren was a revelation.

In the 1972 5,000m Viren covered the last four laps in 3:59.8 to win by a clear five metres from Tunisia's Mohamed Gammoudi. And even more astonishing was his performance in the 10,000m. Viren fell just before the halfway stage, yet clambered back to his feet to storm through the final 800m in 1:56.6 and smash Clarke's existing world record by a full second.

Four years later Viren became the first athlete to retain both the 5,000 and 10,000m crowns – and one day after the 5,000 final finished fifth in the marathon, his first attempt at the distance.

Viren's 10,000m mark was broken less than a year later by Britain's moustacheoed, swashbuckling David Bedford, who almost single-handedly was to revive interest in the sport in a country that had fallen dormant since the golden days of Bannister, Chataway, Ibbotson, Pirie and Hewson. On a warm night at Crystal Palace Bedford clipped almost eight seconds from the record, just as he had predicted he would to friends during a private lunch the day before.

Viren's 5,000m best was to be assailed by Belgium's small but gutsy Emiel Puttemans and New Zealand's tall, long striding Dick Quax. Then, in quick succession, both distances fell under the spell of the remarkable Henry Rono.

Rono – real name Kipwambok but known as Henry – was a member of the Nandi – a sub group of the Kalenjin tribe from Kenya's Rift Valley. The great Kip Keino, Olympic 1500m and steeplechase champion, was a member of the same tribe, domiciled at 6,000 feet above sea level and thus with an inbuilt advantage for distance running.

Rono began running at the age of 19 in 1972. In the space of three months in 1978 he was to rock world athletics by shattering records for the 3,000m, 3,000m steeplechase, 5,000m and 10,000m. His 5,000m best was the first of them when, competing for Washington State University at Berkeley on 8 April he recorded 13:08.4 to take 4.5 secs off Quax's best. His kilometre splits were 2:41.4; 2:37.4; 2:36.5; 2:39.4 and 2:33.7.

Two months later in Europe he added the 10,000m with 27:22.5, covering the second 5,000m in a staggering 13:33.5, a time which would have been a world record for that shorter distance only 13 years earlier.

That mark was to survive for six years until Portugal's Fernando Mamede, who had three times previously gone sub 27:30, sliced off a huge chunk.

Mamede, then 32 and seemingly close to retirement after a career noted mainly for its unpredictability, became Portugal's first ever world record breaker with a storming 27:13.81 in Stockholm. Behind him his 34-year-old countryman Carlos Lopes also smashed Rono's record with 27:17.48, a portent of the marathon best Lopes was to set a year later.

The pair, running together early on, were led through the first four kilometres by another Portuguese athlete, Aluez, and then briefly by American Ed Eyestone. They reached halfway in 13:45.40, hardly sensational. But then a final lap of 57.45 saw Mamede complete the second 5,000m in an incredible 13:28.41.

The explosion of African talent in distance running came at the 1968 Mexico Olympics when athletes from the Dark Continent took a clean sweep of medals in both the 5,000m and 10,000m. Tunisia's Mohamed Gammoudi won the 5,000m, followed by Kenyans Kip Keino and Naftali Tamu. The 10,000 went to Temu with Mamo Wolde of Ethiopia second and Gammoudi third.

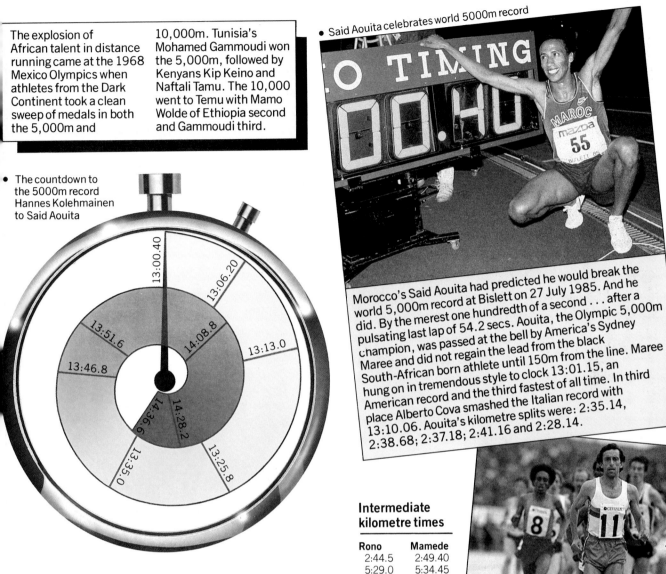

• Said Aouita celebrates world 5000m record

• The countdown to the 5000m record Hannes Kolehmainen to Said Aouita

Morocco's Said Aouita had predicted he would break the world 5,000m record at Bislett on 27 July 1985. And he did. By the merest one hundredth of a second . . . after a pulsating last lap of 54.2 secs. Aouita, the Olympic 5,000m champion, was passed at the bell by America's Sydney Maree and did not regain the lead from the black South-African born athlete until 150m from the line. Maree hung on in tremendous style to clock 13:01.15, an American record and the third fastest of all time. In third place Alberto Cova smashed the Italian record with 13:10.06. Aouita's kilometre splits were: 2:35.14, 2:38.68; 2:37.18; 2:41.16 and 2:28.14.

Intermediate kilometre times

Rono	Mamede
2:44.5	2:49.40
5:29.0	5:34.45
8:14.2	8:16.41
11:04.0	11:00.47
13:48.2	13:45.40
16:35.7	16:30.08
19:17.4	19:16.62
22:02.0	21:58.26
24:48.4	24:41.09
27:22.5	27:13.81

• Fernando Mamede

5000

Time	Competitor	Venue	Date
14:36.6	Hannes Kolehmainen (FIN)	Stockholm	10/7/12
14:35.4	Paavo Nurmi (FIN)	Stockholm	12/9/22
14:28.2	Paavo Nurmi (FIN)	Helsinki	19/6/24
14:17.0	Lauri Lehtinen (FIN)	Helsinki	19/6/32
14:08.8	Taisto Maki (FIN)	Helsinki	16/6/39
13:58.2	Gunder Haegg (SWE)	Gothenburg	20/9/42
13:57.2	Emil Zatopek (TCH)	Paris	30/5/54
13:56.6	Vladimir Kuts (URS)	Berne	29/8/54
13:51.6	Christopher Chataway (GBR)	London	13/10/54
13:51.2	Vladimir Kuts (URS)	Prague	23/10/54
13:50.8	Sandor Iharos (HUN)	Budapest	10/9/55
13:46.8	Vladimir Kuts (URS)	Belgrade	18/9/56
13:40.6	Sandor Iharos (HUN)	Budapest	23/10/56
13:36.8	Gordon Pirie (GBR)	Bergen	19/6/56
13:35.0	Vladimir Kuts (URS)	Rome	13/10/57
13:34.8	Ron Clarke (AUS)	Hobart	16/1/65
13:33.6	Ron Clarke (AUS)	Auckland	1/2/65
13:25.8	Ron Clarke (AUS)	Los Angeles	4/6/65
13:24.2	Kipchoge Keino (KEN)	Auckland	30/11/65
13:16.6	Ron Clarke (AUS)	Stockholm	5/7/66
13:16.4	Lasse Viren (FIN)	Helsinki	14/9/72
13:13.0	Emiel Puttemans (BEL)	Brussels	20/9/72
13:12.9	Dick Quax (NZL)	Stockholm	5/7/77
13:08.4	Henry Rono (KEN)	Berkeley	8/4/78
13:06.20	Henry Rono (KEN)	Knarvik	13/9/81
13:00.41	David Moorcroft (GBR)	Oslo	7/7/82
13:00.40	Said Aouita (MOR)	Oslo	27/7/85

In the meantime Rono's 5,000m mark had also been blown away by another athlete who, like Mamede, had promised so much yet apparently failed to reach fulfilment . . . Britain's David Moorcroft. The Coventry social worker had switched to the 5,000m to escape the genius of Sebastian Coe and Steve Ovett over 1500m and, almost unobtrusively, came within a heartbeat of becoming the first man to go sub 13 mins at the famous Bislett Stadium in Oslo. With most of England's attention focused on the Soccer World Cup in Spain, Moorcroft began his race with no intention of tackling Rono's record. Yet by halfway he felt so good that he simply maintained an extraordinary pace to slash six seconds off Rono's time.

Three years later, at the same venue, Morocco's Said Aouita, Olympic champion, was to shave that by the merest one hundredth of a second. Even with such slender progress no-one doubted the 12 minute era was upon the 5,000m, just as 26 minutes was beckoning the 10,000.

- The countdown to the 10,000m record Alfred Shrubb to Fernando Mamede

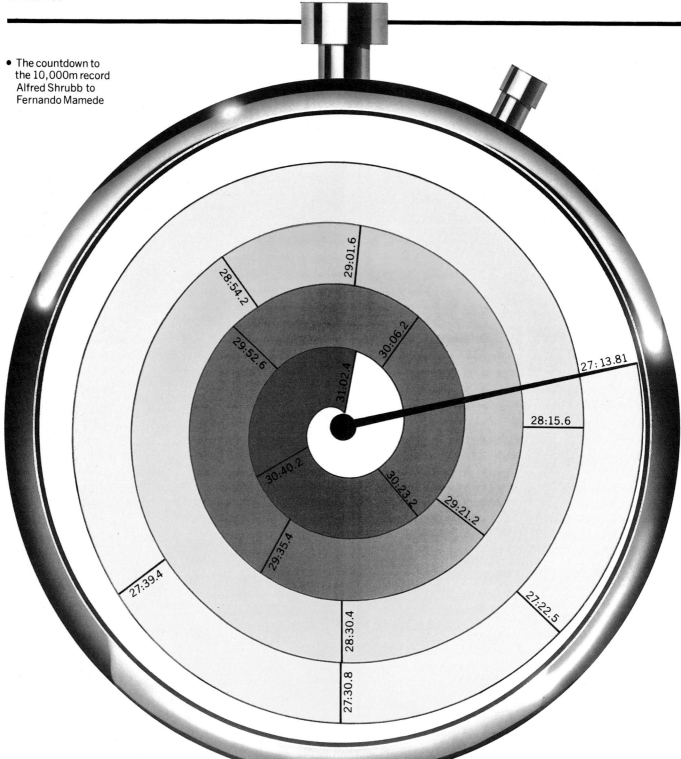

10,000 Metres

Time	Competitor	Venue	Date
31:02.4	Alfred Shrubb (GBR)	Glasgow	5/11/04
30:58.8	Jean Bouin (FRA)	Paris	16/11/11
30:40.2	Paavo Nurmi (FIN)	Stockholm	22/6/21
30:35.4	Ville Ritola (FIN)	Helsinki	25/5/24
30:23.2	Ville Ritola (FIN)	Paris	6/7/24
30:06.2	Paavo Nurmi (FIN)	Kuopio	31/8/24
30:05.6	Ilmari Salminen (FIN)	Kouvola	18/7/37
30:02.0	Taisto Maki (FIN)	Tampere	29/9/38
29:52.6	Taisto Maki (FIN)	Helsinki	17/9/39
29:35.4	Viljo Heino (FIN)	Helsinki	25/8/44
29:28.2	Emil Zatopek (TCH)	Ostrava	11/6/49
29:27.2	Viljo Heino (FIN)	Kouvola	1/9/49
29:21.2	Emil Zatopek (TCH)	Ostrava	22/10/49
29:02.6	Emil Zatopek (TCH)	Turku	4/8/50

Time	Competitor	Venue	Date
29:01.6	Emil Zatopek (TCH)	Stara Boleslav	1/11/53
28:54.2	Emil Zatopek (TCH)	Brussels	1/6/54
28:42.8	Sandor Iharos (HUN)	Budapest	15/7/56
28:30.4	Vladimir Kuts (URS)	Moscow	11/9/56
28:18.8	Pyotr Bolotnikov (URS)	Kiev	15/10/60
28:18.2	Pytor Bolotnikov (URS)	Moscow	11/8/62
28:15.6	Ron Clarke (AUS)	Melbourne	18/12/63
27:39.4	Ron Clarke (AUS)	Oslo	14/7/65
27:38.4	Lasse Viren (FIN)	Munich	3/9/72
27:30.8	David Bedford (GBR)	London	13/7/73
27:30.5	Samson Kimobwa (KEN)	Helsinki	30/6/77
27:22.5	Henry Rono (KEN)	Vienna	11/7/78
27:13.81	Fernando Mamede (POR)	Stockholm	2/7/84

*Automatic timing

5,000/10,000m (WOMEN)

he report from the Associated Press that day of October 19, 83 said simply: "A white South African woman athlete, Zola dd, who runs barefoot, has come within 2.39 seconds of e women's world record for the 5,000 m."

Less than three months later Reuter were reporting: "Zola dd of South Africa clipped more than six seconds off the merican Mary Decker's women's 5,000m world record in ellenbosch, near Cape Town. Zola clocked a time of 15mins 83 secs against Miss Decker's 15:8.26." All round the world shed pictures of an astonished timekeeper gawping at his atch. A star – and a deep seated rivalry between Miss Budd d Miss Decker – had been born.

Zola's effort, so incredible for a 17-year-old, focused orldwide attention on an event which, along with the omen's 10,000m, had been considered a mere athletics deshow. True, great runners like Soviet Tatyana Kazankina d Grete Waitz of Norway had produced highly respectable nes, but neither distance was included in a major Games d so was raced only occasionally. (That is about to change; e 10,000m is on the programme for the 1988 Olympics in eoul.)

Suddenly, the 5,000m was a glamour distance. And five months after Zola's great run (a record not officially ratified as South Africa had been expelled from the IAAF), Norway's flying housewife and mother Ingrid Kristiansen clipped her time by almost three seconds with 14:58.89 during the Bislett Games in Oslo.

Mary Decker, such a supreme athlete from any distance between 800m and 10,000m, set a world best of 31:35.3 for the 10,000m at Eugene in 1982. But two years later, Soviets Olga Bondarenko and Galina Zakharova, running in tandem at Kiev changed the face of the event, Bondarenko clocking 31:13.78 and Zakharova 31:15.00. Again it was to be Norway's Ingrid Kristiansen who broke the magical barrier. Just as she had been the first to dip below 15 minutes in the 5,000m, she now cracked 31 minutes for the 10,000m in front of a sell-out crowd of 19,231 at Bislett on 27 July 1985. Her time of 30:59.42 gave her world records for three events: 5,000m, 10,000m and marathon, a distinction way beyond any male athlete . . . even Zatopek.

But a year later in London the wire services were again buzzing with news of that slender, barefoot girl from Bloemfontein as Zola Budd cut a full ten seconds from Kristiansen's 5,000m time with an astonishing 14:48.07.

• Ingrid Kristiansen

Zola Budd breaks world 5000m record. Ratified later at 14:48.07

ola Budd's 5,000m world record in London came as mething of a surprise. The race at Crystal Palace during e McVitie's Challenge had been set up specially for Ingrid istiansen (NOR) to improve her own existing world best. stead, after swapping the early lead, Zola powered to the nt at 3,000m to win by a clear 50m with a storming last of 68.15 secs. "The record will soon drop to 14:40," she dicted.

5000m (Women)

ime	Competitor	Venue	Date
5:30.6	Jan Merrill (USA)	Palo Alto	22/3/80
5:24.6	Yelena Sipatova (URS)	Podolsk	6/9/81
5:14.51	Paula Fudge (GBR)	Knarvik	13/9/81
5:13.22	Ann Audain (NZL)	Auckland	17/3/82
5:08.26	Mary Decker (USA)	Eugene	5/6/82
4:58.89	Ingrid Kristiansen (NOR)	Oslo	28/6/84
4:48.07	Zola Budd (GBR)	London	26/8/85

10,000m (Women)

Time	Competitor	Venue	Date
31:45.4	Loa Olofsson (DEN)	Copenhagen	6/4/78
31:35.3	Mary Decker (USA)	Eugene	17/7/82
31:35.01	Ludmila Baranova (URS)	Krasnodar	29/5/83
31:27.58	Raisa Sadreydinova (URS)	Odessa	7/9/83
31:13.78	Olga Bondarenko (URS)	Kiev	24/6/84
30:59.42	Ingrid Kristiansen (NOR)	Oslo	27/7/85

THE STEEPLECHASE

World records were not recognised for the steeplechase until 1954 because of variations in the placing, and number, of barriers. At one time the province of Slavic countries, particularly the Poles, the steeplechase has more recently been dominated by Kenyans. They have provided three of the past five Olympic champions – Amos Biwott (1968), Kip Keino (1972) and Julius Korir (1984). In between Ben Jipcho (twice) and Henry Rono have decimated the world record.

Jipcho became the first to dip under eight minutes 20 seconds in 1973 but little could he have suspected that that record would crash by almost 15 seconds in the next five years. First Anders Garderud, the brilliant Swedish Olympic champion, took three successive chunks from it. Then came the amazing assault of Henry Rono in 1978.

By his own admission Rono was a very mediocre hurdler and he had only just recovered from a cold. But in that month of May 1978 he had already set a world record for the 5,000m (13:08.4) and run the fastest 3,000 and 10,000m of the season. He was a man inspired.

He had recorded his best ever steeplechase – a time of 8:14.8 a month earlier and conditions in Seattle hardly seemed ideal for him to better that, with winds gusting up to 8m per second and a temperature of 14° centigrade. Within half a lap, though, he was in front and stayed there unchallenged. His lap times were 63.8, 66.2, 64.0, 65.5, 65.3, 65.1 . . . and a lung bursting 61.4 to hack 2.6 secs off Garderud's world record set in the Montreal Olympics.

Jim Johnson, a distant runner up in 8:36.1, could only gasp: "With better hurdling that guy is going to go close to eight minutes." Instead Rono was struck by illness and injury and never recovered that dazzling form which at one time

threatened to rewrite every record from 3,000m to 10,000m. But of the four he set in the first three months of 197 – 3,000m, 3,000m steeplechase, 5,000m and 10,000m two remain. His 3,000m time of 7:32.1 and that amazin steeplechase.

● Henry Rono

The first known steeplechase was held over open country near Oxford in 1850 with a two mile course and 24 obstacles. Two races, over 2,500m and 4,000m were staged at the 1900 Olympics. The distance was standardised at 3,000m in 1920 when Britain's Percy Hodge took the title.

• Anders Garderud

American Horace Ashenfelter who set a world record of 8:45.4 while winning the 1952 Olympic steeplechase title, was an agent for the Federal Bureau of Investigation. The silver medal went to Vladimir Kazantsev (URS) and one paper reported, "it was the first time an FBI man had deliberately let himself be followed by a Russian."

3,000m Steeplechase

Time	Competitor	Venue	Date
8:49.6	Sandor Rozsnyoi (HUN)	Berne	28/8/54
8:47.8	Pentti Karvonen (FIN)	Helsinki	1/7/55
8:45.4	Pentti Karvonen (FIN)	Oslo	15/7/55
8:45.4	Vasiliy Vlasenko (URS)	Moscow	18/8/55
8:41.2	Jerzy Chromik (POL)	Brno	31/8/55
8:40.2	Jerzy Chromik (POL)	Budapest	11/9/55
8:39.8	Semyon Rzhishchin (URS)	Moscow	14/8/56
8:35.6	Sandor Rozsnyoi (HUN)	Budapest	16/9/56
8:35.6	Semyon Rzhishchin (URS)	Tallinn	21/7/58
8:32.0	Jerzy Chromik (POL)	Warsaw	2/8/58
8:31.4	Zdzislaw Krzyszkowiak (POL)	Tula	26/6/60
8:31.2	Grigoriy Taran (URS)	Kiev	28/5/61
8:30.4	Zdzislaw Krzyszkowiak (POL)	Walcz	10/8/61
8:29.6	Gaston Roelants (BEL)	Leuven	7/9/63
8:26.4	Gaston Roelants (BEL)	Brussels	7/8/65
8:24.2	Jouko Kuha (FIN)	Stockholm	17/7/68
8:22.2	Vladimir Dudin (URS)	Kiev	19/8/69
8:22.0	Kerry O'Brien (AUS)	Berlin	4/7/70
8:20.8	Anders Garderud (SWE)	Helsinki	14/9/72
8:19.8	Benjamin Jipcho (KEN)	Helsinki	19/6/73
8:14.0	Benjamin Jipcho (KEN)	Helsinki	2/6/73
8:10.4	Anders Garderud (SWE)	Oslo	25/6/75
8:09.8	Anders Garderud (SWE)	Stockholm	1/7/75
8:08.02	Anders Garderud (SWE)	Montreal	28/7/76
8:05.4	Henry Rono (KEN)	Seattle	13/5/78

The 3,000 m steeplechase is the track's equivalent of the Grand National with 28 hurdles and seven water jumps — all 3ft (91.4cm) high. The obstacles are solid, weighing between 80-100kg with a width at the top of 5in (12.7cm). The water jump is 12ft (3.66m) in width and length and the water is 2ft 3½in (70cm) deep at the hurdle end.

THE MARATHON (MEN)

The origins of The Marathon are as romantic as the modern history of the event itself. Popular legend holds that it commemorates an Athenian soldier named Pheidippedes who ran from Marathon to Athens with news of victory over the invading Persians and then dropped dead in 490BC.

But the war correspondent of that day, Herodotus, says Pheidippides ran from Athens to Sparta, some 136 miles (219km) in two days. It was only 500 years later that Plutarch wrote about an unnamed soldier who carried news from Marathon to Athens, saying: "Hail! We are victorious" and then gave up the ghost.

Elsewhere, in the Holy Land, around 1080BC, a messenger ran 35km from Even-Heazer to Shiloh to tell of a battle between the Philistines and the Israelites.

You pay your money and take your choice . . . Frenchman Michel Breal certainly did in 1894 when he wrote to Baron Pierre de Coubertin suggesting the inaugural 1896 Olympic Games in Greece should include a long distance race from Marathon to Athens (40 kilometres/24.85 miles) and be called The Marathon.

Fittingly, victory went to a Greek – Spiridon Louis, a shepherd from Amaroussi, who covered the course in 2hrs 58mins 50secs and was personally escorted over the line by Crown Prince Constantine and his brother Prince George. Louis, who never ran competitively again, was given presents

Dorando Pietri collapses over the line in 1908

of a horse and cart and gained free clothing and free shaves for the rest of his life.

The classic marathon distance of 26 miles 385 yards (42.195km) was introduced at the London Olympics of 1908 at the request of Princess Mary, who was starting the race. She wanted the start at Windsor Castle to be directly under the windows of the royal nursery so that her children could watch.

In the race itself Italian Dorando Pietri, stimulated by draughts of alcohol, arrived first at the White City stadium on the verge of collapse. He fell five times before sympathetic officials helped him over the line. He was disqualified for receiving aid and the gold medal awarded to American Johnny Hayes who crossed the line 32 seconds later. But Queen Alexandra had been so taken by the Italian's courage that she insisted on presenting him with a specially inscribed gold cup. They got his name round the wrong way . . . but the Italian just smiled, turned professional and made a small fortune under the single title, Dorando.

The massive interest created by these early races had made organisers throughout the world realise the potential of marathons. New York's Knickerbocker Athletic Club intro-

| 2:55 | 2:52.50 | 2:50 | 2:47.50 | 2:45 |

◁ HAYES (1908)   FOWLER ▷   CLARK ▷ RAINES ▷   BAF

...uced one in September 1896, five months after the Athens ...ympics, and then the following year Boston launched theirs ...n Patriot's Day, 19 April, to commemorate Paul Revere's his-...ric ride in the same fashion as the Greeks had honoured ...heidippedes.

In England, one promoter persuaded Dorando to race ...ound the Albert Hall where each mile needed 20 laps. And ...er in San Francisco a marathon was staged around the ...ecks of the warship *Wyoming*.

The actual distance of the race was still a matter for each ...ganising committee, however, with 25 miles being much ...voured and it was not until 1924 that the International Oly-...pic Committee decreed the "English" distance of 26 miles

One man has died during the Olympic marathon, Portuguese champion Francisco Lazaro (21), who collapsed in the closing stages of the 1912 event in Stockholm.

When Basil Heatley won the silver medal for Britain in the 1964 Tokyo Olympics he sprinted past Japan's Kokichi Tsuburaya off the last bend inside the stadium. Tsuburaya never recovered from this supposed humiliation and four years later committed suicide.

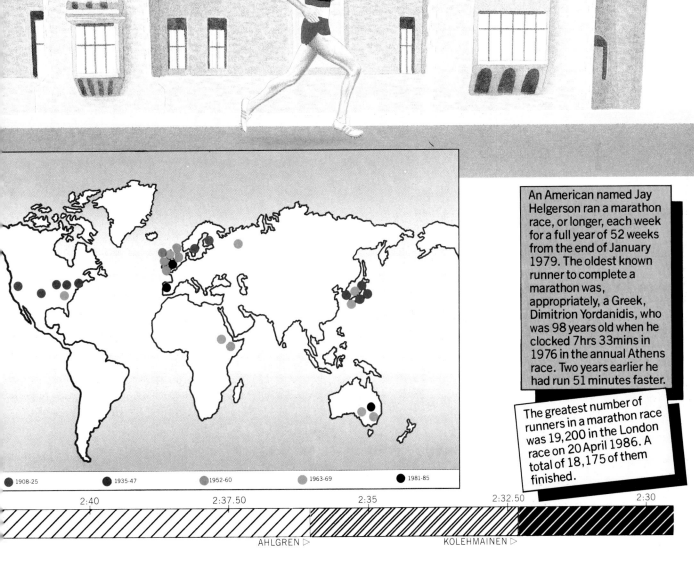

An American named Jay Helgerson ran a marathon race, or longer, each week for a full year of 52 weeks from the end of January 1979. The oldest known runner to complete a marathon was, appropriately, a Greek, Dimitrion Yordanidis, who was 98 years old when he clocked 7hrs 33mins in 1976 in the annual Athens race. Two years earlier he had run 51 minutes faster.

The greatest number of runners in a marathon race was 19,200 in the London race on 20 April 1986. A total of 18,175 of them finished.

● 1908-25   ● 1935-47   ● 1952-60   ● 1963-69   ● 1981-85

2:40	2:37.50	2:35	2:32.50	2:30

AHLGREN ▷   KOLEHMAINEN ▷

385 yards would be the official one. Gradually the other internationally established races fell into line, although it took New York until 1935, and marathon running moved slowly from a quirky happening to a highly respected, competitive event.

No one, though, could have predicted the boom of the Seventies. It started, like so many modern fads, in America where a nation of armchair sports fans suddenly decided they would live longer and more happily if they swapped their slippers for jogging shoes. At the same time Frank Shorter won the Munich Olympic title, the first American to take the marathon gold since 1908.

With Shorter and later Bill Rodgers as the figureheads, the awakening enthusiasm became an explosion. In the land where only the winner normally took all, ordinary men and women discovered the joy of beating their own personal barriers, the satisfaction of simply taking part.

By 1981 the New York Marathon organised by the New York Road Runners' Club, was attracting 16,000 starters with another 30,000 turned down and more than a million spectators on the streets.

London, too, began its own marathon in 1981 with 7,055 official starters and 6,418 finishers. Four years later that figure had swollen to more than 17,500 from four times as many would-be entrants. But that inaugural 1981 race from Greenwich to Constitutional Hill will be remembered for the dead heat between American Dick Beardsley and Norwegian Inge Simonsen. As they crossed the line hand in hand it symbolised the togetherness that had been engendered among the participants by such a desperately individual event.

• Steve Jones

• Abebe Bikila

Finland's Hannes Kolehmainen is recognised as the first of the great marathon runners, with his world record time of 2hrs 32mins 36secs on an over-distance course at the 1920 Antwerp Olympics. But it was Britain's Jim Peters who revolutionised the event.

Between 1952 and 1954 Peters lowered the world best time of 2hrs 25mins 39secs by eight minutes, crashing through the 2-20 barrier, and finishing with a marathon of 2:17:39.4, an average of five and a quarter minutes per mile which had previously been considered good speed for a 10 mile race.

Peters, who had retired as a track athlete in 1948 after finishing ninth in the Olympic 10,000m, returned as a marathon runner in 1951 with an entirely new concept of training and racing. Previously the marathon had been treated as an ultra distance event needing hundreds of long, slow miles in training and strict, sensible pacing in competition.

Peters changed that. He treated it as an extended track race, used speed work in his training and set off in races at a seemingly killer pace.

Sadly, despite all his achievements, Peters will be remembered for his stunning failure in the Commonwealth Games at Vancouver in 1954. Then, having pulverised a field which had ludicrously been told to race at 12 noon on a steaming hot afternoon and entering the stadium with a 17 minute lead, he was unable to complete the race.

In a state of utter exhaustion, due primarily to the excessive heat, Peters fell a dozen times in the final 400m. Finally, he reached a white line and fell over it . . . but it was the finish for the track events, not the marathon. Doctors grabbed him, causing immediate disqualification and for two days he fought for his life inside an oxygen tent.

He retired the same year, with a special gold medal from the Duke of Edinburgh: "To J. Peters as a token of admiration for a most gallant marathon runner."

After Peters came perhaps the most remarkable marathon man of them all, the bare-footed, spindly, iron-willed Abebe Bikila of Ethiopia.

Unheard of outside his own country, Bikila, a bodyguard

2:30   2:27.50   2:25   2:22.50   2:20

MICHELSON ▷   SUZUKI ▷   IKENAKA ▷
KITEI SON ▷
YUK BOK SUH ▷

• Carlos Lopes

Carlos Lopes' world record of 2:07:12 represents 4:51 miling pace and an average speed of 19.9km/h (12.36mph). He was paced through the half distance in 1:03:25 and ran the second half in 1:03:46. His splits included an amazing 29:28 10km section between 15 and 25km. The average speed for the women's best mark of 2:21:06 by Ingrid Kristiansen is 17.94km/h (11.15mph).

below 2:10 was to improve the record by almost four and a half minutes in four years. A decade on and he would have been an exceedingly rich athlete. As it was his most abiding memory of his years of domination is the utter agony he felt after recording a then amazing 2:08:33.6 at Antwerp in 1969. "For days I felt as if my insides were falling out," he says. He was never to run as well again.

The Antwerp course was not re-measured and some claim it was short. But Clayton, who emigrated to Australia via Lancashire and Dublin in 1963, has always insisted the run was genuine. When Clayton set his first world record of 2:09:36.4 in Fukuoka, Japan, in 1967, he became the first athlete to average under five minutes per mile.

Clayton, who ran 200 miles a week in training, was dogged by repeated leg injuries and retired after failing to finish in the 1974 Commonwealth Games.

By now marathon running was becoming a highly specialised business. The competition was fierce, the time at the top limited.

America's Alberto Salazar, with his cramped, crab-like shuffle ruled for three years between 1980 and 1983, setting a world record of 2:08:12.7 in New York. (The course was later found somewhat short.) But then he was destroyed by Australia's Rob de Castella in Rotterdam and it seemed the tall man from Down Under was set to hold the crown for years.

Instead along came Britain's Steve Jones with a world record run of 2:08:05 in his second ever marathon, at Chicago in 1984. And then 36-year-old Carlos Lopes, Olympic champion, sensationally went sub 2:08 with 2:07:12 at Rotterdam six months later. Suddenly that magical 2:05 seemed much, much nearer.

Marathon (Men)

Time	Competitor	Venue	Date
2:55:18.4	Johnny Hayes (USA)	London	24/7/08
2:52:45.4	Robert Fowler (USA)	Yonkers	1/1/09
2:46:52.6	James Clark (USA)	New York	12/2/09
2:46:04.6	Albert Raines (USA)	New York	8/5/09
2:42:31	Harry Barrett (GBR)	London	26/5/09
2:36:06.6	Alexis Ahlgren (SWE)	London	31/5/13
2:32:35.8	Hannes Kolehmainen (FIN)	Antwerp	22/8/20
2:29:01.8	Al Michelsen (USA)	Port Chester	12/10/25
2:27:49	Fusashige Suzuki (JPN)	Tokyo	31/3/35
2:26:44	Yasuo Ikenaka (JPN)	Tokyo	3/4/35
2:26:42	Kitei Son (JPN)	Tokyo	3/11/35
2:25:39	Yun Bok Suh (KOR)	Boston	19/4/47
2:20:42.2	Jim Peters (GBR)	London	14/6/52
2:18:40.2	Jim Peters (GBR)	London	13/6/53
2:18:34.8	Jim Peters (GBR)	Turku	4/10/53
2:17:39.4	Jim Peters (GBR)	London	26/6/54
2:15:17	Sergei Popov (URS)	Stockholm	24/8/58
2:15:16.2	Abebe Bikila (ETH)	Rome	10/9/60
2:15:15.8	Toru Terasawa (JPN)	Beppu	17/2/63
2:14:28	Buddy Edelen (USA)	London	15/6/63
2:13:55	Basil Heatley (GBR)	London	13/6/64
2:12:11.2	Abebe Bikila (ETH)	Tokyo	21/10/64
2:12:00	Morio Shigematsu (JPN)	London	12/6/65
2:09:36.4	Derek Clayton (AUS)	Fukuoka	3/12/67
2:08:33.6	Derek Clayton (AUS)	Antwerp	30/5/69
2:08:18	Rob de Castella (AUS)	Fukuoka	6/12/81
2:08:05	Steve Jones (GBR)	Chicago	21/10/84
2:07:12	Carlos Lopes (POR)	Rotterdam	20/4/85

of Haile Selassie, was the sensation of the 1960 Olympics, winning in a world best time of 2:15:16.2 to collect the first gold medal won by a black African at the Games. Four years later, and wearing shoes, he became the first man to successfully defend the Olympic marathon title, crushing the rest of the world by a margin of three quarters of a mile with another record time of 2:12:11.2. He had undergone an appendix operation only five weeks earlier, yet he appeared as fresh as when he had started and celebrated victory with a series of callisthenics on the grass infield.

In 1969, at the age of 37, he was tragically paralysed from the waist down in a car accident and died from a brain haemorrhage four years later.

Bikila's era gave way to Australian Derek Clayton, a man born a few, tantalising years too early. Clayton, first to dip

| 2:15 | 2:12.50 | 2:10 | 2:07.50 | 2:05 |

POPOV ▷ EDELEN ▷   BIKILA ▷   CLAYTON ▷   LOPES ▷
BIKILA ▷   HEATLEY ▷ SHIGEMATSU ▷   CASTELLA ▷
TERASAWA ▷   SALAZAR ▷
                                              JONES ▷

A Greek woman called Melopene is reported to have run unof-ficially in the 1896 Olympic marathon, recording about four and a half hours, but the first official world best was the 3:40:22 set by Britain's Violet Piercy in London in 1926.

It is only in comparatively recent times, however, that women have broken down the barriers of prejudice and earned equal footing with men. The first all-women marathon was not staged until 1973, for example, and it was only in 1975 that the Women's AAA in Britain allowed women to compete in long distance road races. Women were barred from the famous Boston race, too, until 1972.

Once their case had been won, women such as Britain's Joyce Smith, America's Joan Benoit and Norway's Grete Waitz and Ingrid Kristiansen set about pursuing the men in no uncertain terms.

Mrs Smith had run in the 1972 Munich Olympics over 1500m and was 41 before she took up marathons. In 1981 over her home track in the London Marathon she became the first woman officially to go sub 2:30 with a time of 2:29:57.

Mrs Smith's record lasted barely a month before New Zea-land's Allison Roe trimmed it by more than three minutes with an amazing run in the Boston Marathon, clocking 2:26:46. Allison followed up in New York six months later with the biggest blow yet for women's marathon running . . . beating 1972 Olympic champion Frank Shorter. Shorter was 117th in 2:25:45 Roe 113th in 2:25:29. It was hailed as a world record until the course was found to be fractionally short.

Roe, though, dropped away stricken by injury and the world scene became increasingly dominated by three women: Waitz, Kristiansen and Benoit. The small, gutsy American claimed her first world record in Eugene in 1982 with 2:26:11, a time decimated by Waitz in London the follow-ing April with 2:25:29. But the very next day in Boston Joan defied even Heartbreak Hill to bring almost a three minute improvement with 2:22:43, a time which would have won her Olympic gold in every *men's* marathon up to 1956.

No-one was making jokes about women runners any more . . . and male faces became even grimmer in 1985 when Ingrid Kristiansen proved what a flat, fast course London is by pushing the women's record ever closer to that magic 2:20 barrier with 2:21:06.

Marathon (Women)

Time	Competitor	Venue	Date
3:40:22	Violet Piercy (GBR)	London	3/10/26
3:27:45	Dale Greig (GBR)	Ryde	23/5/64
3:19:33	Mildred Sampson (NZL)	Auckland	21/7/64
3:15:22	Maureen Wilton (CAN)	Toronto	6/5/67
3:07:26	Anni Pede-Erdkamp (FRG)	Waldniel	16/9/67
3:02:53	Caroline Walker (USA)	Seaside	28/2/70
3:01:42	Beth Bonner (USA)	Philadelphia	9/5/71
2:46:30	Adrienne Beames (AUS)	Werribee	31/8/71
2:46:24	Chantal Langlace (FRA)	Neuf Brisach	27/10/74
2:43:54.5	Jackie Hansen (USA)	Culver City	1/12/74
2:42:24	Liane Winter (FRG)	Boston	21/4/75
2:40:15.8	Christa Vahlensieck (FRG)	Dulmen	3/5/75
2:38:19	Jackie Hansen (USA)	Eugene	12/10/75
2:35:15.4	Chantal Langlace (FRA)	Oyarzun	1/5/77
2:34:47.5	Christa Vahlensieck (FRG)	Berlin	10/9/77
2:31:23	Joan Benoit (USA)	Auckland	3/2/80
2:30:58	Patti Catalano (USA)	Montreal	6/9/80
2:30:27	Joyce Smith (GBR)	Tokyo	16/11/80
2:29:57	Joyce Smith (GBR)	London	29/3/81
2:26:46	Allison Roe (NZL)	Boston	20/4/81
2:26:11	Joan Benoit (USA)	Eugene	12/9/82
2:25:29	Grete Waitz (NOR)	London	17/4/83
2:22:43	Joan Benoit (USA)	Boston	18/4/83
2:21:06	Ingrid Kristiansen (NOR)	London	21/4/85

• Joan Benoit

• Ingrid Kristiansen

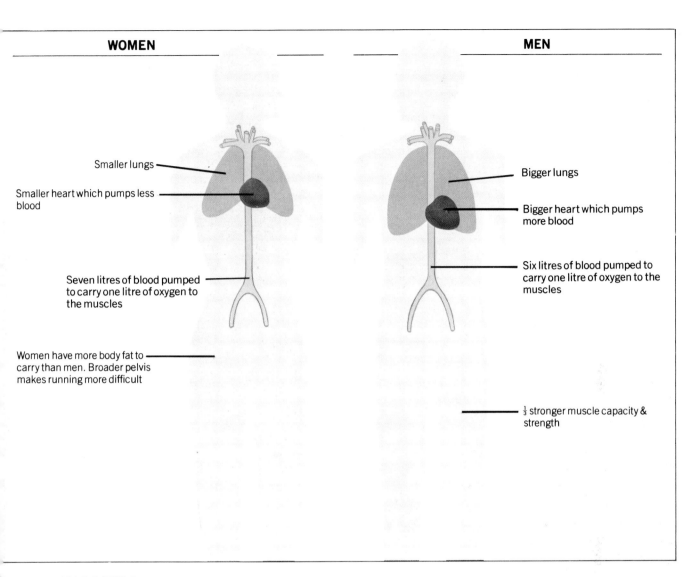

WOMEN	MEN
Smaller lungs	Bigger lungs
Smaller heart which pumps less blood	Bigger heart which pumps more blood
Seven litres of blood pumped to carry one litre of oxygen to the muscles	Six litres of blood pumped to carry one litre of oxygen to the muscles
Women have more body fat to carry than men. Broader pelvis makes running more difficult	$\frac{1}{3}$ stronger muscle capacity & strength

MEN v WOMEN

Since 1969 the women's world record has improved by some 46 minutes while the men's has fallen by less than one and a half minutes. In marathon running, more than any other athletic event, the women seem to have a chance of one day catching the men. Or do they?

In almost every other event men hold a ten per cent advantage over women. And physiologists believe the same will hold true in the marathon that the women's record has been "hardened up".

There are unalterable differences which count against women.

1. Men have bigger hearts and so pump out more blood per beat. Men also have a higher blood/weight ratio: in general five to six litres of blood compared to a woman's four to four and a half. And men have more oxygen-carrying haemoglobin in their blood than women. During marathon running a man needs to pump out six litres of blood to carry one litre of oxygen to his muscles, a woman needs to pump out seven.

2. Women carry a far greater percentage of body fat than men. This helps them in long distance swimming since it makes them buoyant (eight of the ten fastest English Channel swims are by women) but it is dead weight for running.

On average men have 17 per cent fat in their body weight, women have 30. When Ireland's John Treacy finished second in the Los Angeles Olympics marathon he was said to have only four per cent body fat.

A low percentage of body fat is clearly an advantage for marathon runners, who have to haul their mass over 26.2 miles. But women do score on one point: studies have shown that women convert fat to energy quicker than men. This means that they do not burn up their stores of carbohydrate (glycogen) as quickly as the men because their bodies are fuelled by the fat instead. So women probably feel more comfortable than men in the final stages of a marathon.

A woman's shape is also against her as a runner. She is far broader in the pelvis and this tends to make her running style less mechanically efficient. She tends to kick out her heels as she runs, which dissipates energy.

Nor can women deal with hot weather running as efficiently as men. Their skin has greater insulating properties; fine in Channel swimming where heat conservation is vital, but a handicap when heat dissipation is wanted.

Overall, females have a lighter and weaker build and an inferior capacity for physical performance than males. Their bones are lighter and smaller and their muscles are smaller in proportion to their total body weight. Usually the female is one third less strong than the male in either individual muscle or total strength capacity.

DECATHLON

The decathlon is the search for the perfectly balanced all-round athlete. The man who can combine speed and strength, agility and athleticism . . . and maintain a punishing level of excellence throughout the ten-event, two-day competition.

There have been those who have attempted to demean the decathlon, to label its participants as Jacks of all trades with diversified, moderate talent. Steve Ovett, Britain's world record breaking middle distance runner, once described it as "nine Mickey Mouse events and the 1500m."

That is to misunderstand the nature of a competition which, as well as outstanding athletic ability, also calls for protracted willpower and tactical conservation of energies. It also misrepresents the superb calibre of athletes such as Jim Thorpe, Bob Mathias and Britain's double Olympic champion Daley Thompson.

In the past four years Thompson has faced only one serious rival to his world crown as the supreme, all-round athlete – West Germany's mighty Jurgen Hingsen, who has held the world record three times, the same as Daley.

Physically they are quite different. Hingsen, born 25 June 1958, stands 200cm (6ft 6½in) and weighs 97kg (220lb). Thompson, born a month later on 30 July, is far shorter, 185cm (6ft 1in) and much lighter, 86kg (189½lb).

It would seem to be a simple case, in fight parlance, of the fighter against the boxer. Of the German's power against the Briton's skill. In fact, they are marvellously matched opponents: Hingsen usually dominates the shot and discus and his extra height tells in the high jump, but Thompson can match him at javelin.

Paradoxically, too, Hingsen hauls his far larger frame over the final 1500m faster than Thompson who would seem to hold a natural advantage in such a stamina event.

In order, the ten decathlon events are: *first day*: 100m, long jump, shot, high jump, 400m; *second day*: 110m hurdles, discus, pole vault, javelin, 1500m.

This, step by step, is how the two great rivals, Hingsen and Thompson, ended up with their identical world records. Hingsen's was set in Mannheim on 8-9 June 1984, Thompson's came exactly two months later at the Los Angeles Olympics:

Daley Thompson world record
at Los Angeles 8-9 August 1984

Event	Time/dist	Points
100m	10.44 secs	948
Long jump	8.01m (26ft 3½in)	1022
Shot put	15.72m (51ft 7in)	831
High jump	2.03m (6ft 8in)	882
400m	46.97 secs	950
		4633
110m hurdles	14.33 secs*	923
Discus	46.56m (152ft 9in)	810
Pole vault	5.00m (16ft 4¾in)	1052
Javelin	65.24m (214ft 0in)	824
1500m	4:35.00	556
		8798

*time given originally as 14.34 secs, worth 922 points

Jurgen Hingsen world record
at Mannheim 8-9 June 1984

Event	Time/dist	Points
100m	10.70 secs	880
Long jump	7.76m (25ft 5½in)	972
Shot put	16.42m (53ft 10½in)	871
High jump	2.07m (6ft 9½in)	917
400m	48.05 secs	896
		4536
110m hurdles	14.07 secs	954
Discus	49.36m (161ft 11in)	860
Pole vault	4.90m (16ft 0½in)	1028
Javelin	59.86m (196ft 5in)	759
1500m	4:19.75	661
		8798

• Three of the finest (from left): Bob Mathias, Bill Toomey and Bruce Jenner

The decathlon dates back to the 19th century, and in 1884 the AAU held a multi-event competition comprising 100 yards, shot, high jump, 880 yards walk, hammer, pole vault, 120 yards hurdles, 56lb weight, long jump and one mile . . . all in one day. But the first decathlon to contain the modern events was staged at the 1912 Stockholm Olympics — and immediately ran into controversy.

The title went to the outstanding American Indian Jim Thorpe who crushed his rivals but was later stripped of his gold medal because he had infringed amateur status by accepting token payments for playing baseball. The 1912 event was held over three days. Even so Thorpe's points score of 6756 (computed on the 1962 tables) was a fine one and not beaten for 15 years.

First over the 7,000 pts mark was Finland's Akilles Jarvinen whose brother Matti was a world record holder in the javelin. Then came the era of Glenn Morris (USA), a future screen Tarzan whose 7,421 pts set while winning the 1936 Olympic title stood until the arrival of the young Bob Mathias in 1950. Mathias had been only 17½ when he took the 1948 Olympic gold — the youngest male track and field gold medallist ever. He went on to retain that title, and to set another world record. But it was his countryman Rafer Johnson — who lit the flame in the 1984 Los Angeles Olympics stadium — who was first through the 8,000 pts barrier in 1960.

Another American, Bruce Jenner brought astonishing improvement in the space of one year. Then, after winning the Montreal Olympics with a superb 8617 pts he retired to make a small fortune as a male model and clear the arena for the onset of the gladiatorial battle between Thompson and Hingsen.

• One man stands among the fallen . . . Thompson after his 1982 European triumph

Thompson's Olympic triumph confirmed his superiority in competition over the German. This is how he performed, event by event:

1. 100m

Thompson exploded from his blocks to set his best ever legal time for a 100m during a decathlon, clocking 10.44 into a one metre per second head wind. Hingsen, drawn in the same heat, finished almost five metres down in 10.91 and 122 points adrift. Thompson's best ever 100m time in a one-off individual race was 10.36 secs, although he had recorded a windy 10.28.

2. LONG JUMP

The long jump is Thompson's best event. But going into the Olympics, Hingsen's personal record of 8.04m (26ft 4in) was ahead of Thompson's legal best of 8.00m (26ft 3in), although the Briton had jumped a wind-assisted 8.11m (26ft 7¼in). Hingsen got progressively better in Los Angeles with 7.50, 7.70 and 7.80. But Thompson topped him on each occasion with 7.83, 7.84 and a final round 8.01 (26ft 3½in) to not only crack his lifetime best but also add another 46 points to his lead. A reproduction of such a jump would have given Thompson fifth place in the individual long jump event won by American superstar Carl Lewis only two days earlier.

3. SHOT

Hingsen stepped into the shot put circle with the air of a man bent on swatting a fly. During his world record in June he had put the shot 16.42m (53ft 10½in). Thompson's lifetime best was a relatively puny 16.10 (52ft 10in) in open competition and he had never bettered 15.66m (51ft 4½in) in a decathlon. Hingsen won OK. But with a disappointing 15.87m (52ft 0¾in) against Thompson's 15.72m (51ft 7in). The German's net gain was nine points. Thompson was 155 points ahead and still thundering towards a world record.

4. HIGH JUMP

Thompson had been struggling in the high jump all season. From a personal best of 2.14m (7ft 0¼in) set indoors he had deteriorated to a seasonal best of 1.87m (6ft 1½in). Hingsen had cleared 2.18m (7ft 1¾in). Here, surely, was his chance again. Instead Thompson cleared 2.03m (6ft 8in) at his third attempt and the German, who had received treatment for a knee injury, eventually made 2.12m (6ft 11½in), a fine effort but one which could claw back only 77 points. Thompson led Hingsen by 78 points. Would the strain start to show?

5. 400m

Thompson had been working hard on his 400m in training . . . and it showed as he clocked 46.97 secs, the second fastest time of his career, despite tensing up near the finish. Hingsen also ignored the pain of his knee injury to produce a storming 47.69 secs, only 4/100ths of a second away from his personal best. But Thompson added another 36 points to the gap between the two of them to end the afternoon with 4633, a world record for the first day of a decathlon. Hingsen, on 4519, was 17 points short of the halfway score in his existing world record, which was clearly under threat.

6. 110m HURDLES

Hingsen had a distinct advantage over Thompson in the first event of the second day, holding a personal best of 14.07 secs compared to 14.26. Again, though, Hingsen missed his opportunity, clocking a disappointing 14.29 to finish half a metre clear of Thompson in 14.33. Hingsen had gained a derisory five points. (Thompson's original time of 14.34 has since been amended.)

7. DISCUS

In the end, after all the months of preparation and hours of competition, Thompson's gold medal and share of the world record depended on one turn of the discus wheel of fortune. Hingsen had produced a lifetime best of 50.82m (166ft 9in); Thompson, after two throws, had managed only 41.24m (135ft 4in). The difference, in points, was 176 . . . enough to give the German a commanding lead. Thompson, clearly nervous but supremely competitive, stepped in for his final attempt – and hurled a life-saving 46.56m (152ft 9in). Thompson still led . . . by 33 points.

8. POLE VAULT

Thompson and Hingsen are evenly matched in the pole vault. And with the javelin and 1500m to come – both events in which the German had posted superior performances – Thompson knew he desperately needed to improve his slender 33 point lead. Once again, it would be his competitive temperament which would see him through. Hingsen, troubled now by a stomach upset, went out at 4.70m (15ft 5in) having cleared 4.50m (14ft 9in), well short of his personal best of 5.10m (16ft 8¾in). Thompson went over 4.70m at his second attempt . . . and promptly raised the bar to 4.90m (16ft 0¾in). Twice he failed. Then on the third try, with daylight to spare, he soared clear and celebrated with a backflip in the landing area. Thompson went on to jump 5.00m (16ft 4¾in). His lead was 153 points and a world record looked certain.

9. JAVELIN

Hingsen, beaten by Thompson in European and World Championships, was now reliving his nightmare. Depressed and disconsolate he threw 60.44m (198ft 3in), some seven metres short of his best. Thompson, almost leisurely, recorded 65.24m (214ft 0in), close to his best ever. Already he had scored 8,242 points.

10. 1500m

Thompson needed to run 4:34.8 secs to gain a total of 8799 points and claim the world record. During the world championships a year earlier, when he had been suffering the after-effects of injury, he had clocked 4:29.72. Curiously, in Los Angeles, such an effort proved beyond him. When he reached the bell Thompson needed a last lap of 71.6; this from an athlete who had run 63.5 at a similar stage of the European Championships to break the world record. Now he slumped to 71.8 and a final time of 4:35.00. Enough only for a share of the record. Hingsen, who clocked 4:22.60, finished with 8673 points, the eighth highest in history.

● Daley Thompson puts on record style

Individual world records (1962 tables)

Event	Time/dist	Points
100m	9.93 secs	1094
Long jump	8.90m (29ft 2½ in)	1189
Shot put	22.62m (74ft 2in)	1197
High jump	2.41m (7ft 10¾ in)	1194*
400m	43.86 secs	1119
		5793
110m hurdles	12.93 secs	1104
Discus	71.86m (235ft 9in)	1223*
Pole vault	6.00m (19ft 8¼ in)	1274*
Javelin	104.80m (343ft 9¾ in)	1235*
1500m	3:29.46	1113
		11742

estimated points score: these performances are outside the scale of official decathlon scoring tables.

Thompson's best ever marks (1962 tables)

Event	Time/dist	Points
100m	10.28 secs (w)	992
Long jump	8.11 (26ft 7¼ in) (w)	1041
Shot put	16.10m (52ft 10in)	853
High jump	2.14m (7ft 0¼ in) (indoors)	975
400m	46.86 secs	955
		4816
110m hurdles	14.26 secs	931
Discus	48.62m (159ft 6in)	847
Pole vault	5.20m (17ft 0¾ in)	1098
Javelin	65.38m (214ft 6in)	826
1500m	4:20.3	657
		9175

(w) *wind-assisted performance, which is legitimate for world record purposes in a decathlon competition.*

These scores have all been computed using the 1962 Scoring Tables. During the decathlon's life, six sets of scoring tables have been used. The first were introduced in 1912. Then there were modifications in 1920, 1934, 1950 and, most recently, on 1 April 1985. Each change was made to place different emphasis on certain events and so aid the search for the truly all-round athlete. There are some anomalies in the scores listed below where previous records convert to higher totals than the mark which replaces it.

Points	Competitor	Venue	Date
6270	Aleksander Klumberg (EST)	Helsinki	16-17/9/22
6668	Harold Osborn (USA)	Paris	11-12/7/24
6651	Paavo Yrjola (FIN)	Viipuri	17-18/7/26
6768	Paavo Yrjola (FIN)	Helsinki	16-17/7/27
6774	Paavo Yrjola (FIN)	Amsterdam	3-4/8/28
7036	Akilles Jarvinen (FIN)	Viipuri	19-20/7/30
6896	James Bausch (USA)	Los Angeles	5-6/8/32
6999	Hans-Heinrich Sievert (GER)	Hamburg	22-23/7/33
7292	Hans-Heinrich Sievert (GER)	Hamburg	7-8/7/34
7421	Glenn Morris (USA)	Berlin	7-8/8/36
7453	Bob Mathias (USA)	Tulare	29-30/6/50
7731	Bob Mathias (USA)	Helsinki	25-26/7/52
7758	Rafer Johnson (USA)	Kingsburg	10-11/6/55
7760	Vasiliy Kuznetsov (URS)	Krasnodar	17-18/5/58
7896	Rafer Johnson (USA)	Moscow	27-28/7/58
7957	Vasiliy Kuznetsov (URS)	Moscow	16-17/5/59
8063	Rafer Johnson (USA)	Eugene	8-9/7/60
8089	Yang Chuan-Kwang (TPE)	Walnut	27-28/4/64
8230	Russ Hodge (USA)	Los Angeles	23-24/7/66
8319	Kurt Bendlin (FRG)	Heidelberg	13-14/5/67
8417	Bill Toomey (USA)	Los Angeles	10-11/12/69
8456	Nikolai Avilov (URS)	Munich	7-8/9/72
8524	Bruce Jenner (USA)	Eugene	9-10/8/75
8538	Bruce Jenner (USA)	Eugene	25-26/6/76
8617	Bruce Jenner (USA)	Montreal	29-30/7/76
8622	Daley Thompson (GBR)	Gotzis	17-18/5/80
8649	Guido Kratschmer (FRG)	Bernhausen	13-14/6/80
8704	Daley Thompson (GBR)	Gotzis	22-23/5/82
8723	Jurgen Hingsen (FRG)	Ulm	14-15/8/82
8743	Daley Thompson (GBR)	Athens	7-8/9/82
8779	Jurgen Hingsen (FRG)	Bernhausen	4-5/6/83
8798*	Jurgen Hingsen (FRG)	Mannheim	8-9/6/84
8798*	Daley Thompson (GBR)	Los Angeles	8-9/8/84

Hingsen's total converts to 8832 points on the new 1985 tables, while Thompson's converts to 8847 points.

HEPTATHLON

The heptathlon is a two day competition comprising seven events in this order: *first day:* 100m hurdles, high jump, shot, 200m; *second day:* long jump, javelin, 800m. It was introduced in 1981 to replace the five-event pentathlon which had been held, in varying forms, since 1928.

The pentathlon was dominated by the Soviet Irina Press who set six world records and collected the inaugural Olympic gold medal for the event in 1964. But since the heptathlon was brought in it has become the sole property of the East Germans. Ramona Neubert, a medical student from Pirna, won her first nine competitions and set four world records in the process, three of them being ratified. Her perennial runner up was the year younger Sabine Mobius, a Leipzig sports student.

But Mädchen Mobius became Fräu Paetz in 1983 and the following season was back, snatching away Neubert's world record with a storming performance in Potsdam that amassed 6867 points, 205 more than her previous best. Sabine, tall and powerful (1.74m/5ft 8½in and 68kg/150lb) had collected silver medals behind Neubert in the European and World Championships with an annual progression of: 1981 – 6210 points; 1982 – 6532 pts; 1983 – 6662 pts; 1984 – 6867 pts. But in 1985 she slipped back to 6595 points as Americans Jackie Joyner and Jane Frederick topped the world ranking list with 6718 points and 6666 points respectively.

WORLD RECORD
Set by Sabine Paetz (GDR)
at Potsdam 5-6 May 1984

Event	Time/dist	Points
100m hurdles	12.64 secs	1056
High jump	1.80m (5ft 10¾in)	1031
Shot put	15.37m (50ft 5¼in)	915
200m	23.37 secs	999
Long jump	6.86m (22ft 6¼in)	1089
Javelin	44.62m (146ft 5in)	836
800m	2:08.93	941
		6867

Best ever marks set by
Sabine Paetz

Event	Time/dist	Points
100m hurdles	12.54 secs	1071
High jump	1.83m (6ft 0in)	1059
Shot put	16.16m (53ft 0¼in)	958
200m	23.37secs	999
Long jump	7.12m (23ft 4½in)	1141
Javelin	44.62m (146ft 5in)	836
800m	2:07.03	969
		7033

In the last event – the 800m – of the women's pentathlon at the 1980 Olympic Games in Moscow, Olga Rukavishnikova (URS) finished second in 2min 04.8sec. This gave her an overall points score of 4937, more than the then world record. In third place behind her came teammate Nadyezda Tkachenko in a time of 2min 05.2sec, bringing her total to an even higher 5083 points. So for 0.4sec Rukavishnikova held the world record, the shortest reign ever in any event.

This, in event by event order, is the way Sabine Paetz set her world record:

1. 100m HURDLES
Her time here of 12.64 secs was world class in any terms (it would have comfortably won her the Olympic gold medal three months later in Los Angeles) and clipped 19/100ths of a second off her previous best. In her existing world record, Neubert had clocked 13.42.

2. HIGH JUMP
Sabine's high jump of 1.80m (5ft 10¾in) compared well with her best ever of 1.83m (6ft 0in). Neubert had leapt 1.82m (5ft 11½in) in what was one of her recognised strong events, exactly the same height as achieved by Britain's Mary Peters en route to the world pentathlon record and Olympic gold in Munich 1972.

3. SHOT
Mighty Soviet pentathlete Irina Press was a colossus in the shot put circle, heaving an incredible 17.16m (56ft 3¾in) on the way to her 1964 pentathlon world record and gold medal at the Tokyo Olympics. Paetz was never going to get near that but she did manage an impressive 15.37 (50ft 5¼in), 12cm further than Neubert had thrown, to maintain her world record lead.

4. 200m
Paetz's 23.37 secs was faster than any time needed to win the individual Olympic gold up to and including Wilma Rudolph in 1960 (24.0). Among pentathletes it had been bettered only by East Germany's famed Burglinde Pollak during her world record performance at Bonn in 1973. Neubert had clocked 23.35.

5. LONG JUMP
Again a truly world class performance from Paetz with 6.86m (22ft 6¼in), only four centimetres outside her lifetime best. No other pentathlete had ever got near that in a two-day competition . . . not even West Germany's Heidemarie Rosendahl who had leapt 6.78m (22ft 3in) to win the *individual* long jump at the 1972 Munich Olympics. At the same stage in her world best, Neubert had recorded 6.79m (22ft 3½in).

6. JAVELIN
The javelin, dropped from women's multi-event competition since 1947, was known to be Paetz's weakness. Neubert had hurled an impressive 49.94m (163ft 10in) in her world record. Paetz clung on with 44.62 (146ft 5in), puny compared to the 70m plus being thrown by the world's top line javelin exponents, but still her best ever.

7. 800m
And so to the 800m, the killing final event that tests the last reserves of stamina, just as the 1500m completes the men's decathlon. Paetz had done her calculations. She knew she had to go sub 2:10 to beat Neubert who had finished with 2:07.51. Teeth gritted, and on the verge of collapse she managed 2:08.93. It was enough.

• Mary Peters

• Ramona Neubert

The Germans introduced a set of scoring tables for a pentathlon in the 1930s, but the first 'modern' tables came in 1954. With some adjustments in 1971 these tables lasted until replaced by new compilations as from 1 April 1985. The pentathlon events have changed somewhat over the years – as has the order of events – so progressive records are difficult to compare. The heptathlon was introduced in 1981.

Pentathlon
(Shot, high jump, 200m, 80mH, long jump)

Points	Competitor	Venue	Date
692	Fanny Blankers-Koen (HOL)	Amsterdam	15-16/9/51
704	Aleksandra Chudina (URS)	Bucharest	8-9/8/53
747	Nina Martynenko (URS)	Leningrad	6-7/7/55
750	Aleksandra Chudina (URS)	Moscow	6-7/7/55
767	Nina Vinogradova (URS)	Moscow	11-12/8/56
846	Galina Bystrova (URS)	Odessa	15-16/10/57
872	Galina Bystrova (URS)	Tbilisi	1-2/11/58
880	Irina Press (URS)	Krasnodar	13-14/9/59
902	Irina Press (URS)	Tula	21-22/5/60
959	Irina Press (URS)	Tula	25-26/6/60
972	Irina Press (URS)	Kiev	17-18/10/60
137	Irina Press (URS)	Tbilisi	8-9/10/61
246	Irina Press (URS)	Tokyo	16-17/10/64

(100mH, shot, high jump, long jump, 200m)

Points	Competitor	Venue	Date
4727	Liese Prokop (AUT)	Vienna	4-5/10/69
4775	Burglinde Pollak (GDR)	Erfurt	5-6/9/70
4801	Mary Peters (GBR)	Munich	2-3/9/72
4831	Burglinde Pollak (GDR)	Sofia	12/8/73
4932	Burglinde Pollak (GDR)	Bonn	22/9/73

(100mH, shot, high jump, long jump, 800m)

Points	Competitor	Venue	Date
4765	Eva Wilms (FRG)	Gottingen	24/5/77
4823	Eva Wilms (FRG)	Bernhausen	18/6/77
4839	Nadyezda Tkachenko (URS)	Lille	18/9/77
4856	Olga Kuragina (URS)	Moscow	20/6/80
5083	Nadyezda Tkachenko (URS)	Moscow	24/7/80

Heptathlon

Points	Competitor	Venue	Date
6716	Ramona Neubert (GDR)	Kiev	27-28/6/81
6772	Ramona Neubert (GDR)	Halle	19-20/6/82
6836	Ramona Neubert (GDR)	Moscow	18-19/6/83
6867	Sabine Paetz (GDR)	Potsdam	5-6/5/84

LONG JUMP

It was, quite simply, the most astonishing single exploit in track and field history . . . a giant leap forward for mankind that was generations ahead of its time.

Until that momentous afternoon in Mexico City on Friday, 18 October 1968, the tall, gangling American, Bob Beamon, had been just another good long jumper. In one stupendous, explosive moment he was to set himself apart with a world record that, Carl Lewis apart, could stretch to the 21st century. When Beamon, a 9.5 seconds 100-yds sprinter from New York, lined up on the Olympic runway, the long jump best stood at 27ft 4¾in (8.35m), set by America's Ralph Boston and the Soviet Union's Igor Ter-Ovanesyan.

The dream was of 28ft (8.53m) and it would surely be a gradual process. Why, hadn't the great Jesse Owens' record of 26ft 8¼in (8.13m) lasted for 25 years and been improved upon only by fractions since?

Beamon's was the fourth jump of the competition. He set off with that loose-limbed run aided by a 2m tail wind, the maximum allowed for records, hit the board at optimum speed and launched himself into a mighty upwards parabola through the thin air of altitude. The huge crowd gasped. They had never seen such elevation. As he landed the tumult around the pit confirmed the greatness of the jump. A new world record surely? The officials in charge seemed to be taking an inordinately long time to check the distance. Then uproar! Beamon was dancing everywhere, kissing the track, and fellow competitors were rushing to congratulate him. The electric board flickered into life. Up came an 8 . . . then a 9. Confusion! And then the stunning realisation that the jump was 8.90m or 29ft 2½in.

Beamon had not broken the 28ft (8.53m) barrier – he had obliterated it. (In fact, the first 28ft jump was not posted until 1980 when East Germany's Lutz Dombrowski recorded 28ft ¼in (8.54m) to win the 1980 Olympic title).

In the years to come Beamon never bettered 8.20m (26ft 11in), perhaps partly because of a serious hamstring injury in

1969 which caused him to change his take-off leg. He turne professional in 1973.

In 1981 the emergence of the 19-year-old Carl Lew threatened Beamon's record as Lewis quickly established 2 feet (8.53m) as his regular area of jumping. But Lewis stead fastly refused to travel to altitude to attack the record, prefe ring to pit his ability at sea level, and by the end of 1985 h best ever of 8.79m (28ft 10½in) was still comfortably short o Beamon's incredible mark.

Beamon's first recorded predecessor was Chionis o Sparta who is reported to have leapt 7.05m (23ft 1¾in) i 656 BC. That is a good deal further than the 6.35m (20ft 10i which won the inaugural Olympic title in 1896 for America Ellery Clark. By 1900, though, the world record stood at highly respectable 7.50m (24ft 7¼in), set by America's Mye Prinstein and the mark improved regularly until the event wa revolutionised by Jesse Owens at Ann Arbor, Michigan, i 1935. Then Owens added exactly 6in to the record with a lea of 26ft 8¼in (8.13m), a feat that was to endure for 25 years an 79 days. Will Beamon outlast him?

● Ralph Boston

New Zealander John Delamere used a somersault style of long jumping to reach 7.79m (25ft 6¾in) in 1974. But the method was banned by the International Amateur Athletic Federation the same year.

Long Jump (Men)

Distance	Competitor	Venue	Date
7.61m	Peter O'Connor (GBR)	Dublin	5/8/01
7.69m	Edwin Gourdin (USA)	Cambridge, Mass.	23/7/21
7.76m	Robert LeGendre (USA)	Paris	7/7/24
7.89m	William DeHart Hubbard (USA)	Chicago	13/6/25
7.90m	Edward Hamm (USA)	Cambridge, Mass.	7/7/28
7.93m	Sylvio Cator (HAI)	Paris	9/9/28
7.98m	Chuhei Nambu (JAP)	Tokyo	27/10/31
8.13m	Jesse Owens (USA)	Ann Arbor	25/5/35
8.21m	Ralph Boston (USA)	Walnut	12/8/60
8.24m	Ralph Boston (USA)	Modesto	27/5/61
8.28m	Ralph Boston (USA)	Moscow	16/7/61
8.31m	Igor Ter-Ovanesyan (URS)	Yerevan	10/6/62
8.31m	Ralph Boston (USA)	Kingston	15/8/64
8.34m	Ralph Boston (USA)	Los Angeles	12/9/64
8.35m	Ralph Boston (USA)	Modesto	29/5/65
8.35m	Igor Ter-Ovanesyan (URS)	Mexico City	19/10/67
8.90m	Bob Beamon (USA)	Mexico City	18/10/68

● Carl Lewis

When Jesse Owens broke the world long jump record by jumping 8.13m (26ft 4¼in) at Ann Arbor on 25 May 1935 he set a mark that was to stand for 25 years and 79 days – the longest period for a world record in a standard event to remain unbeaten.

● Bob Beamon leaps into legend

63

● The Willie Banks roadshow takes off to a world record

The triple jump in action. First the hop, *landing on the same foot as take-off*; then t

TRIPLE JUMP

Brazil have always had their Soccer. They now have Joaquim Cruz to strike fear into the middle distance runners of the world. But what else? Well, they have also made one field event virtually their own, that quirky, idiosyncratic contest once known as the hop, step and jump, but now, with more dignity, titled the triple jump.

It all began with the great Adhemar Ferreira da Silva, who won every triple jump championship open to him from 1951 to 1959, including two Olympic titles, and smashed the world record five times. A record in itself for the event.

In that era he took the best from 16m (52ft 6in) to 16.56m (54ft 4in). And when he retired his countryman, Nelson Prudencio, was waiting to take over, claiming one of the five world records which fell during the incredible triple jump competition at the Mexico Olympics in 1968 as the mark was hunted from 17.10m (56ft 1¼in) to the eventual gold medal distance of 17.39 (57ft 0¾in) by Soviet Viktor Saneyev.

But the best was still to come for Brazil in 1975, when, in the thin air of that same Mexico City Olympic Stadium Joao de Oliveira propelled himself to 17.89m (58ft 8¼in), an astonishing 45cm (1ft 5¾in) improvement on Saneyev's then world best.

De Oliveira hopped 6.05m (19ft 10¼in), stepped 5.40m (17ft 8¾in) and jumped 6.44m (21ft 1½in) for a record which stood for almost ten years until America's extrovert Willie Banks set his roadshow down in Indianapolis on 16 June 1985 and leapt 17.97m (58ft 11½in).

It was a prodigious effort, without the aid of altitude, by Banks who had long predicted that he would be the first to break the 18m barrier. Such a distance would have caused apoplexy among the Americans and Irishmen who dominated the event before the First World War. The inaugural Olympic title went to James Connolly (USA) in 1896, but he took two hops and a jump as was the fashion in those days.

By 1908 when Ireland's Tim Ahearne took the gold with a world record of 14.91m (48ft 11in) the event had been stan-

dardised. There was to be one hop (landing on the same foot as take off), one step (landing on the other foot) and one jump (taking off from the foot you landed on in the step).

Tim's younger brother, Daniel Ahearn (he dropped the final 'e' from his name when he emigrated to the USA), extended that record to 15.52m (50ft 11in) in New York three years later.

Triple Jump (Men)

Distance	Competitor	Venue	Date
15.52m	Daniel Ahearn (USA)	New York	30/5/11
15.52m	Anthony Winter (AUS)	Paris	12/7/24
15.58m	Mikio Oda (JAP)	Tokyo	27/10/31
15.72m	Chuhei Nambu (JAP)	Los Angeles	4/8/32
15.78m	Jack Metcalfe (AUS)	Sydney	14/12/35
16.00m	Naoto Tajima (JAP)	Berlin	6/8/36
16.00m	Adhemar da Silva (BRA)	Sao Paulo	3/12/50
16.01m	Adhemar da Silva (BRA)	Rio de Janeiro	30/9/51
16.12m	Adhemar da Silva (BRA)	Helsinki	23/7/52
16.22m	Adhemar da Silva (BRA)	Helsinki	23/7/52
16.23m	Leonid Shcherbakov (URS)	Moscow	19/7/53
16.56m	Adhemar de Silva (BRA)	Mexico City	16/3/55
16.59m	Oleg Ryakhovskiy (URS)	Moscow	27/7/58
16.70m	Oleg Fedoseyev (URS)	Nalchik	3/5/59
17.03m	Jozef Schmidt (POL)	Olsztyn	5/8/60
17.10m	Giuseppe Gentille (ITA)	Mexico City	16/10/68
17.22m	Giuseppe Gentille (ITA)	Mexico City	17/10/68
17.23m	Viktor Saneyev (URS)	Mexico City	17/10/68
17.27m	Nelson Prudencio (BRA)	Mexico City	17/10/68
17.39m	Viktor Saneyev (URS)	Mexico City	17/10/68
17.40m	Pedro Perez (CUB)	Cali	5/8/71
17.44m	Viktor Saneyev (URS)	Sukhumi	17/10/72
17.89m	Joao de Oliveira (BRA)	Mexico City	15/10/75
17.97m	Willie Banks (USA)	Indianapolis	16/6/85

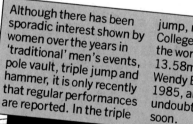

Although there has been sporadic interest shown by women over the years in 'traditional' men's events, pole vault, triple jump and hammer, it is only recently that regular performances are reported. In the triple jump, now an American College event for women, the world best had reached 13.58m (44ft 6¾in) by Wendy Brown (USA) in 1985, and will undoubtedly exceed 14m soon.

on the other foot; finally the jump, *taking off from the foot landed on in the step*

65

HIGH JUMP

The first high jumper to lift himself over 6ft was England Rugby international Marshall Brooks who cat jumped (head-on and hands first) 6ft 0⅛in (1.83m) in 1876.

Since then the world record has been set by four methods:

1. Scissors and Eastern Cut-Off.
2. Western Roll.
3. Straddle.
4. Fosbury Flop.

The simple scissors style – jumping the bar with the lead leg first and flicking the trailing leg over in a scissors motion while the body lays along the bar – evolved into the Eastern Cut-Off.

This was devised by Irish American Mike Sweeney and dubbed "The Sweeney Twist" in its early days. It involved jumping scissors style, but turning the torso to end up facing the bar. Sweeney improved the world best to 1.97m (6ft 5½in) in 1885.

Then along came the Western Roll, courtesy of George Horine . . . and by a quirk of fate. As a young scissors jumper Horine and his family moved house in America to one where the backyard allowed him to approach the high jump only from the left side and not his normal right flank. He still took off from his left foot and gradually devised a style of turning on his side as he crossed the bar. Horine took Sweeney's record to 2.00m (6ft 7in).

Scissors and Eastern Cut-off

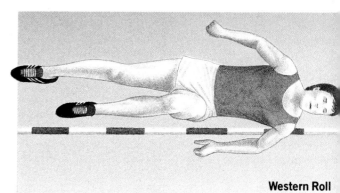

Western Roll

Straddle

The greatest height achieved by a horse under official conditions is 2.47 (8ft 1¼in) by "Huaso" in Chile in 1949. A height of 2.51m (8ft 3in) was claimed for "Heatherbloom" in Australia in 1903.

The best high jump by a man with one leg is the 2.04m (6ft 8¼in) achieved by Arnie Boldt of Canada in 1981. Boldt had lost his leg above the knee in a farm accident at the age of three.

Fosbury Flop

• Igor Paklin

American Franklin Jacobs holds the record for the greatest height jumped over an athlete's own head. Jacobs, 1.73m (5ft 8in) tall, jumped 2.32m (7ft 7¼in) in 1978 . . . or 59cm (1ft 11¼in) over his height.

Watutsi tribesmen of Central Africa reportedly cleared heights of 2.50m (8ft 2½in) during ceremonial displays. The tribe is famed for its tall men, many over 2.13m (7ft), but they achieve these jumps taking off from a small mound. The principle of such jumping was behind the success of the built-up shoe until it was banned by the IAAF in 1958.

Later jumpers improved the technique, sometimes not always within the spirit of the competition: Harold Osborn (USA), who in 1924 became the only man to win an individual event and the decathlon at an Olympic Games, developed the trick of pushing the bar back against the uprights as he jumped. This led to a new international ruling which changed the design of the support pegs of the high jump, allowing the bar to fall off either side.

The Western Roll and Eastern Cut-Off were in general use for years with the Western Roll providing superior results overall. Then both were revolutionised by the Straddle, in which the jumper clears the bar in a prone position, belly down.

First introduced in 1930, the Straddle inexplicably took another decade to catch on and it was not until Les Steers (USA) used it to raise the record to 2.11m (6ft 11in) in 1941 that the method became universally popular. Even so, both the 1948 Olympic title (Eastern Cut-Off) and the 1952 Olympic title (Western Roll) went to old-fashioned techniques.

During the 1950s the Dive Straddle, where the head leads the body, was flirted with, primarily in Europe.

But it was the straightforward Straddle which brought the first 7ft (2.13m) jump from American Charlie Dumas in 1956.

The following year saw the introduction in Europe of the controversial built-up shoe, with its 5cm (2in) thick sole. Standards leapt, including a new world record of 2.16m (7ft ½in) from the Soviet Yuriy Styepanov. But 12 months later the shoe was banned by the International Amateur Athletic Federation and for the next 16 years all world records were set by conventional Straddle jumpers, including six in succession from 1961-63 by the great Soviet Valeriy Brumel.

In 1968 Dick Fosbury (USA) pioneered a new style of clearing the bar, head first on his back. It became known as the Fosbury Flop and swept the world after he had won the Mexico Olympic title. Fellow countryman Dwight Stones broke the world record with the technique in 1973 with 2.30m (7ft ½in) and floppers have since raised it to 2.41m (7ft 10¾in).

High Jump (Men)

Height	Competitor	Venue	Date
2.00m	George Horine (USA)	Palo Alto	18/5/12
2.01m	Edward Beeson (USA)	Berkeley	2/5/14
2.03m	Harold Osborn (USA)	Urbana	27/5/24
2.04m	Walter Marty (USA)	Fresno	13/5/33
2.06m	Walter Marty (USA)	Palo Alto	28/4/34
2.07m	Cornelius Johnson (USA)	New York	12/7/36
2.07m	David Albritton (USA)	New York	12/7/36
2.09m	Mel Walker (USA)	Malmo	12/8/37
2.11m	Lester Steers (USA)	Los Angeles	17/6/41
2.12m	Walter Davis (USA)	Dayton	27/6/53
2.15m	Charles Dumas (USA)	Los Angeles	29/6/56
2.16m*	Yuriy Styepanov (URS)	Leningrad	13/7/57
2.17m	John Thomas (USA)	Philadelphia	30/4/60
2.17m	John Thomas (USA)	Cambridge, Mass.	21/5/60
2.18m	John Thomas (USA)	Bakersfield	24/6/60
2.22m	John Thomas (USA)	Palo Alto	1/7/60
2.23m	Valeriy Brumel (URS)	Moscow	18/6/61
2.24m	Valeriy Brumel (URS)	Moscow	16/7/61
2.25m	Valeriy Brumel (URS)	Sofia	31/8/61
2.26m	Valeriy Brumel (URS)	Palo Alto	22/7/62
2.27m	Valeriy Brumel (URS)	Moscow	29/9/62
2.28m	Valeriy Brumel (URS)	Moscow	21/7/63
2.29m	Patrick Matzdorf (USA)	Berkeley	3/7/71
2.30m	Dwight Stones (USA)	Munich	11/7/73
2.31m	Dwight Stones (USA)	Philadelphia	5/6/76
2.32m	Dwight Stones (USA)	Philadelphia	4/8/76
2.33m	Vladimir Yashchenko (URS)	Richmond	3/7/77
2.34m	Vladimir Yashchenko (URS)	Tbilisi	16/6/78
2.35m	Jacek Wszola (POL)	Eberstadt	25/5/80
2.35m	Dietmar Mogenburg (FRG)	Rehlingen	26/5/80
2.36m	Gerd Wessig (GDR)	Moscow	1/8/80
2.37m	Zhu Jianhua (PRC)	Beijing	11/6/83
2.38m	Zhu Jianhua (PRC)	Shanghai	22/9/83
2.39m	Zhu Jianhua (PRC)	Eberstadt	10/6/84
2.40m	Rudolf Povarnitsin (URS)	Donetsk	11/8/85
2.41m	Igor Paklin (URS)	Kobe	4/9/85

*Made with built-up shoe.

JUMPS (WOMEN)

The Rumanians have made the women's jumping events a speciality of their own. The tall, leggy Iolanda Balas (1.85m/6ft 0¾in) cast an indomitable shadow over the women's high jump from 1958-1966, setting 14 world records, the most for an athlete in any event.

More recently, her countrywoman Anisoara Cusmir, has made the long jump pit her own protected area with four world records and the Los Angeles Olympic title. And all before Anisoara, now Mrs Stanciu, was 23.

No athlete has held such total domination for so long as Iolanda Balas. Consider these statistics: in 80 separate meetings during her prime she had jumped higher than any other woman in history. More specifically, by the end of 1963 when she was 27 Iolanda had jumped 1.80m (5ft 10¾in) or better 72 times. Yet it was not until the following year that Australia's Michelle Brown jumped as high. And by that time Iolanda's world record stood at a massive 1.91m (6ft 3¼in).

On 1 November 1964 Brown followed Balas as the second woman six foot high jumper with 1.83m (6ft 0¼in). By then, though, Balas had cleared that particular barrier in 46 competitions.

● Anisoara Cusmir

Balas finished fifth at the 1956 Olympic Games in Melbourne. It was to be her only defeat until injury finished her career in 1966 with two Olympic and two European Games golds. She married her coach, Ion Soeter, a year later. Because of her long, long legs Balas had to evolve a personalised style of the scissors. It was so effective that her final record of 1.91m (6ft 3¼in) stood for the longest period ever in the event... 10 years 56 days until Austria's Ilona Gusenbauer cleared 1.92m (6ft 3½in) in 1971.

In the long jump, Anisoara Cusmir, with her equally idiosyncratic style of pumping arms and over-striding legs on her run up, carried the record from 7.09m (23ft 3¼in) to mighty 7.43m (24ft 4½in).

But even that 34cm (1ft 1¼in) improvement could not equal the feat of Japan's Kinue Hitomi whose first recognised world record of 5.98m (19ft 7½in) in 1928 was 38cm (1ft 3in) better than the existing, unratified world best. Hitomi is reported to have been the first woman over 20ft (6.09m) as well, but her leap of 20ft 2½in (6.16m) in Seoul, in October 1929, was never ratified. Instead the honour fell to Germany's Christel Schulz with 20ft 1in (6.12m) in Berlin a full ten years later.

Other barrier breakers were: *21ft (6.40m)*: Hildrun Claus (GDR) with exactly 21ft (6.40m) in August 1960; *22ft (6.70m)*: Mary Rand (GB) with 22ft 2½in (6.76m) while winning the Tokyo Olympics gold medal in 1964; *23ft (7.01m)*, Vilma Bardauskiene (USSR) with 23ft 2½in (7.07m) in Kishinyov in August 1978; *24ft (7.31m)*: Anisoara Cusmir with 24ft 4½in (7.43m) in Bucharest in June 1983.

There were dark mutterings immediately after Bulgaria's Lyudmilla Andonova set her shock world high jump record of 2.07m (6ft 9½in) during the 1984 Alternative Olympics in Berlin. The 24-year-old had not registered any kind of jump at all the previous year... and her best before that was only 1.99m (6ft 6¼in). Was she another of the Eastern Europeans who drop out for a year's sabbatical, take treatment in a sanitorium and then return with amazing results? In other words, had she 'changed her drugs'? Lyudmilla had the perfect answer for the East German journalists: "My daughter Jana was born at ten to one on the morning of 18 August 1983," she said. "She measured 51cm and weighed 3.45kg. Any more questions?"

● Tamara Bykova

● Heike Dreschler

High Jump (Women)

Height	Competitor	Venue	Date
1.65m	Jean Shiley (USA)	Los Angeles	7/8/32
1.65m	Mildred Didrikson (USA)	Los Angeles	7/8/32
1.66m	Dorothy Odam (GBR)	Brentwood	29/5/39
1.66m	Esther Van Heerden (RSA)	Stellenbosch	29/3/41
1.66m	Ilsebill Pfenning (SUI)	Lugano	27/7/41
1.71m	Fanny Blankers-Koen (HOL)	Amsterdam	30/5/43
1.72m	Sheila Lerwill (GBR)	London	7/7/51
1.73m	Aleksandra Chudina (URS)	Kiev	22/5/54
1.74m	Thelma Hopkins (GBR)	Belfast	5/5/56
1.75m	Iolanda Balas (ROM)	Bucharest	14/7/56
1.76m	Mildred McDaniel (USA)	Melbourne	1/12/56
1.76m	Iolanda Balas (ROM)	Bucharest	13/10/57
1.77m	Cheng Feng-Jung (CPR)	Peking	17/11/57
1.78m	Iolanda Balas (ROM)	Bucharest	7/6/58
1.80m	Iolanda Balas (ROM)	Cluj	22/6/58
1.81m	Iolanda Balas (ROM)	Poiana Stalin	31/7/58
1.82m	Iolanda Balas (ROM)	Bucharest	4/10/58
1.83m	Iolanda Balas (ROM)	Bucharest	18/10/58
1.84m	Iolanda Balas (ROM)	Bucharest	21/9/59
1.85m	Iolanda Balas (ROM)	Bucharest	6/6/60
1.86m	Iolanda Balas (ROM)	Bucharest	10/7/60
1.87m	Iolanda Balas (ROM)	Bucharest	15/4/61
1.88m	Iolanda Balas (ROM)	Warsaw	18/6/61
1.90m	Iolanda Balas (ROM)	Budapest	8/7/61
1.91m	Iolanda Balas (ROM)	Sofia	16/7/61
1.92m	Ilona Gusenbauer (AUT)	Vienna	4/9/71
1.92m	Ulrike Meyfarth (FRG)	Munich	4/9/72
1.94m	Yordanka Blagoyeva (BUL)	Zagreb	24/9/72
1.94m	Rosemarie Witschas (GDR)	Berlin	24/8/74
1.95m	Rosemarie Witschas (GDR)	Rome	8/9/74
1.96m	Rosemarie Witschas-Ackermann (GDR)	Dresden	8/5/76
1.96m	Rosemarie Ackermann (GDR)	Dresden	3/7/77
1.97m	Rosemarie Ackermann (GDR)	Helsinki	14/8/77
1.97m	Rosemarie Ackermann (GDR)	Berlin	26/8/77
2.00m	Rosemarie Ackermann (GDR)	Berlin	26/8/77
2.01m	Sara Simeoni (ITA)	Brescia	4/8/78
2.01m	Sara Simeoni (ITA)	Prague	31/8/78
2.02m	Ulrike Meyfarth (FRG)	Athens	8/9/82
2.03m	Ulrike Meyfarth (FRG)	London	21/8/83
2.03m	Tamara Bykova (URS)	London	21.8/83
2.04m	Tamara Bykova (URS)	Pisa	25/8/83
2.05m	Tamara Bykova (URS)	Kiev	23/6/84
2.07m	Lyudmilla Andonova (BUL)	Berlin	20/7/84
2.08m	Stefka Kostadinova (BUL)	Sophia	31/5/86

Long Jump (Women)

Distance	Competitor	Venue	Date
5.98m	Kinue Hitomi (JAP)	Osaka	20/5/28
6.12m	Christel Schulz (GER)	Berlin	30/7/39
6.25m	Fanny Blankers-Koen (HOL)	Leiden	19/9/43
6.28m	Yvette Williams (NZL)	Gisborne	20/2/54
6.28m	Galina Vinogradova (URS)	Moscow	11/9/55
6.31m	Galina Vinogradova (URS)	Tbilisi	18/11/55
6.35m	Elzbieta Krzesinska (POL)	Budapest	20/8/56
6.35m	Elzbieta Krzesinska (POL)	Melbourne	27/11/56
6.40m	Hildrun Claus (GDR)	Erfurt	7/8/60
6.42m	Hildrun Claus (GDR)	Berlin	23/6/61
6.48m	Tatyana Shchelkanova (URS)	Moscow	16/7/61
6.53m	Tatyana Shchelkanova (URS)	Leipzig	10/6/62
6.70m	Tatyana Shchelkanova (URS)	Moscow	4/7/64
6.76m	Mary Rand (GBR)	Tokyo	14/10/64
6.82m	Viorica Viscopoleanu (ROM)	Mexico City	14/10/68
6.84m	Heidi Rosendahl (GER)	Turin	3/9/70
6.92m	Angela Voigt (GDR)	Dresden	9/5/76
6.99m	Sigrun Siegl (GDR)	Dresden	19/5/76
7.07m	Vilma Bardauskiene (URS)	Kishinyov	18/8/78
7.09m	Vilma Bardauskiene (URS)	Prague	29/8/78
7.15m	Anisoara Cusmir (ROM)	Bucharest	1/8/82
7.20m	Vali Ionescu (ROM)	Bucharest	1/8/82
7.21m	Anisoara Cusmir (ROM)	Bucharest	15/5/83
7.27m	Anisoara Cusmir (ROM)	Bucharest	4/6/83
7.43m	Anisoara Cusmir (ROM)	Bucharest	4/6/83
7.44m	Heike Drechsler (GDR)	Berlin	22/9/85

● Iolanda Balas

POLE VAULT

The 6m pole vault, one of field athletics greatest barriers, fell in Paris on 14 July 1985 to a man who has revolutionised his event. Sergey Bubka of Russia was only 21 when he performed his mighty leap (19ft 8¼in on the imperial scale or 5ft 6in taller than a London bus) and immediately began to talk of future jumps of 6.20m or even 6.30m.

It would have sounded like heresy to some, but no doubt his spirit of adventure hit a chord in some of the other great names whose courage and agility have meant that the pole vault record has been broken more times than any other field event.

Already Bubka – 6ft 0in (183cm) and 176lb (80kg) – has extended the record five times, more even than the great Cornelius Warmerdam who totally dominated the event in the early Forties, or those two outstanding Americans of the Sixties, John Pennel and Bob Seagren.

Bubka's unbounded confidence is illustrated in the way he achieved his latest, historic record. Having won the competition with a vault of 5.70 he declined to edge towards his target but insisted instead that the bar be immediately raised to 6m, which he cleared on his third attempt. Said Bubka: "Such heights are only unattainable if you believe them to be so. I do not. To me it is just another number on the way through normal progression. I will go higher."

Four days earlier Bubka's 20-year-old wife, a Master of Sport in gymnastics, had given birth to a son. "That inspired me," he said, and promptly named his son Vitaly, after his coach and mentor Vitaly Petrov.

The origins of pole vaulting date back as far as the time of Henry VIII. It is suggested the event was also included in the mythical Tailteann Games in Ireland. By the end of the 19th century two distinct styles had evolved, one similar to today's, the other called the Ulverston style because of its use around the Ulverston area of the Lake District. This system involved climbing up the pole when it was vertical and the greatest exponent was Britain's Thomas Ray who took the world best from 3.42m (11ft 2¾in) in 1879 to 3.57m (11ft 8⅝in) in 1888.

With the Ulverston method banned around the turn of the century, the emphasis fell on light, springy poles and bamboo became the vogue. It was with a bamboo pole that Cornelius Warmerdam achieved more superiority over his peers than even Bubka enjoys today. In 1940 he became the first man to vault above 15ft (4.57m) and went on to repeat the feat 42 times before the next athlete achieved it 11 years later. Warmerdam's 4.79m (15ft 8½in) indoors at Chicago on 20 March 1943 is still the best ever with a bamboo pole.

Bamboo used to break, however, sometimes with alarming results, and steel poles became fashionable in the Fifties. But it was the switch to glass fibre which brought the dramatic upsurge in the Sixties. George Davies (USA) became the first to set a world record with a glass pole in 1961 with 4.83m (15ft 10¾in) and their arrival was truly confirmed when John Uelses, a German-born American, became the first to clear 16ft (4.87m) a year later.

Pole vaulting, like other field events, has always held two sets of frontiers, one imperial, the other metric. At one time the 18ft jump was almost as emotive as the 6m one. This, using each measurement in turn where relevant, is how the barriers fell:

12ft: Norman Dole, with 12ft 1¼in (3.69m) in Oakland, California, on 23 April 1904.

13ft: Robert Gardner (USA) with 13ft 1in (3.99m) in Philadelphia on 1 June 1912.

4m: Marcus Wright (USA) with 4.02m (13ft 2¼in) in Cambridge, Massachussets, on 8 June 1912.

14ft: Sabin Carr (USA) with 14ft 0in (4.26m) in Philadelphia on 27 May 1927.

15ft: Cornelius Warmerdam (USA) 15ft 0in (4.57m) in Berkeley, California, on 13 April 1940.

16ft: John Uelses (USA) with 16ft 0¾in (4.89m) in Santa Barbara, California, on 31 March 1962.

5m: Pentti Nikula (FIN) with 5.10m (16ft 8¾in) indoors in Pajulahti, Finland, on 2 February 1963.

17ft: John Pennel (USA) with 17ft 0¾in (5.20m) in Coral Gables, Florida, on 24 August 1963.

18ft: Christos Papanikolaou (GRE) with 18ft 0¼in (5.49m) in Athens on 24 October 1970.

19ft: Thierry Vigneron (FRA) with 19ft 0¼in (5.80m) in Macon on 20 June 1981.

6m: Sergey Bubka (URS) with 6.0m (19ft 8¼in) in Paris on 13 July 1985.

A foot injury prevented world record holder Charles Hoff (NOR) challenging for the 1924 Olympic title. But he did make the final of the 800m!

World record pole vault 6m (19ft 8¼in)

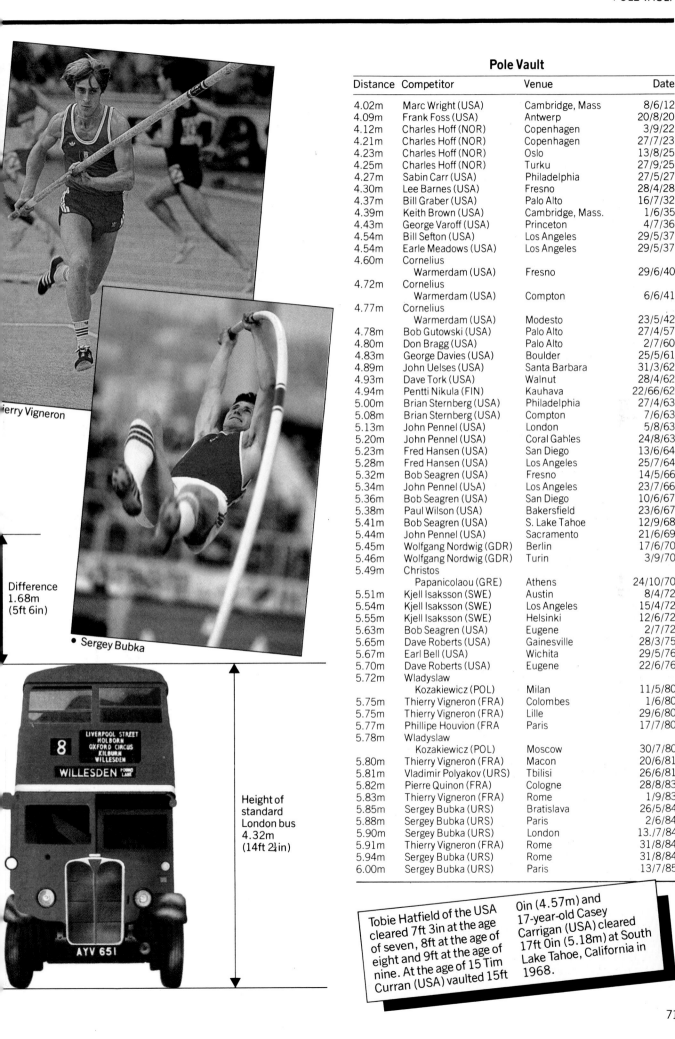

Thierry Vigneron

• Sergey Bubka

Difference
1.68m
(5ft 6in)

LIVERPOOL STREET
HOLBORN
OXFORD CIRCUS
KILBURN
WILLESDEN

8

WILLESDEN

AYV 651

Height of
standard
London bus
4.32m
(14ft 2¼in)

Pole Vault

Distance	Competitor	Venue	Date
4.02m	Marc Wright (USA)	Cambridge, Mass	8/6/12
4.09m	Frank Foss (USA)	Antwerp	20/8/20
4.12m	Charles Hoff (NOR)	Copenhagen	3/9/22
4.21m	Charles Hoff (NOR)	Copenhagen	27/7/23
4.23m	Charles Hoff (NOR)	Oslo	13/8/25
4.25m	Charles Hoff (NOR)	Turku	27/9/25
4.27m	Sabin Carr (USA)	Philadelphia	27/5/27
4.30m	Lee Barnes (USA)	Fresno	28/4/28
4.37m	Bill Graber (USA)	Palo Alto	16/7/32
4.39m	Keith Brown (USA)	Cambridge, Mass.	1/6/35
4.43m	George Varoff (USA)	Princeton	4/7/36
4.54m	Bill Sefton (USA)	Los Angeles	29/5/37
4.54m	Earle Meadows (USA)	Los Angeles	29/5/37
4.60m	Cornelius Warmerdam (USA)	Fresno	29/6/40*
4.72m	Cornelius Warmerdam (USA)	Compton	6/6/41
4.77m	Cornelius Warmerdam (USA)	Modesto	23/5/42
4.78m	Bob Gutowski (USA)	Palo Alto	27/4/57
4.80m	Don Bragg (USA)	Palo Alto	2/7/60
4.83m	George Davies (USA)	Boulder	25/5/61
4.89m	John Uelses (USA)	Santa Barbara	31/3/62
4.93m	Dave Tork (USA)	Walnut	28/4/62
4.94m	Pentti Nikula (FIN)	Kauhava	22/66/62
5.00m	Brian Sternberg (USA)	Philadelphia	27/4/63
5.08m	Brian Sternberg (USA)	Compton	7/6/63
5.13m	John Pennel (USA)	London	5/8/63
5.20m	John Pennel (USA)	Coral Gahles	24/8/63
5.23m	Fred Hansen (USA)	San Diego	13/6/64
5.28m	Fred Hansen (USA)	Los Angeles	25/7/64
5.32m	Bob Seagren (USA)	Fresno	14/5/66
5.34m	John Pennel (USA)	Los Angeles	23/7/66
5.36m	Bob Seagren (USA)	San Diego	10/6/67
5.38m	Paul Wilson (USA)	Bakersfield	23/6/67
5.41m	Bob Seagren (USA)	S. Lake Tahoe	12/9/68
5.44m	John Pennel (USA)	Sacramento	21/6/69
5.45m	Wolfgang Nordwig (GDR)	Berlin	17/6/70
5.46m	Wolfgang Nordwig (GDR)	Turin	3/9/70
5.49m	Christos Papanicolaou (GRE)	Athens	24/10/70
5.51m	Kjell Isaksson (SWE)	Austin	8/4/72
5.54m	Kjell Isaksson (SWE)	Los Angeles	15/4/72
5.55m	Kjell Isaksson (SWE)	Helsinki	12/6/72
5.63m	Bob Seagren (USA)	Eugene	2/7/72
5.65m	Dave Roberts (USA)	Gainesville	28/3/75
5.67m	Earl Bell (USA)	Wichita	29/5/76
5.70m	Dave Roberts (USA)	Eugene	22/6/76
5.72m	Wladyslaw Kozakiewicz (POL)	Milan	11/5/80
5.75m	Thierry Vigneron (FRA)	Colombes	1/6/80
5.75m	Thierry Vigneron (FRA)	Lille	29/6/80
5.77m	Phillipe Houvion (FRA	Paris	17/7/80
5.78m	Wladyslaw Kozakiewicz (POL)	Moscow	30/7/80
5.80m	Thierry Vigneron (FRA)	Macon	20/6/81
5.81m	Vladimir Polyakov (URS)	Tbilisi	26/6/81
5.82m	Pierre Quinon (FRA)	Cologne	28/8/83
5.83m	Thierry Vigneron (FRA)	Rome	1/9/83
5.85m	Sergey Bubka (URS)	Bratislava	26/5/84
5.88m	Sergey Bubka (URS)	Paris	2/6/84
5.90m	Sergey Bubka (URS)	London	13./7/84
5.91m	Thierry Vigneron (FRA)	Rome	31/8/84
5.94m	Sergey Bubka (URS)	Rome	31/8/84
6.00m	Sergey Bubka (URS)	Paris	13/7/85

Tobie Hatfield of the USA cleared 7ft 3in at the age of seven, 8ft at the age of eight and 9ft at the age of nine. At the age of 15 Tim Curran (USA) vaulted 15ft 0in (4.57m) and 17-year-old Casey Carrigan (USA) cleared 17ft 0in (5.18m) at South Lake Tahoe, California in 1968.

THROWING EVENTS (MEN)

Of the men's throwing events, the four tests of massive strength allied to skilful technique, two can be traced back to the Ancient Greek Games: the Discus and the Javelin. The Hammer evolved from the sledgehammer throwing competitions held on 16th century farms in England and Scotland and the Shot began in various Celtic sports days as "Putting the Stone".

The modern discus event dates from the turn of the century when the weight of the implement was fixed at 2kg (4lb 6½oz). In 1912 the inside diameter of the throwing circle was also standardised at 2.50m (8ft 2½in). The throw, to be valid, must land within a 40 degree sector in front of the net-enclosed circle which is known as *the beast's lair*. The discus is made of hardwood or fibreglass with smooth metal rims and metal weights buried in the centreparts.

Until 1985 the javelin, which consists of three parts, a pointed metal head, a shaft and a cord grip, weighed a minimum of 800 grammes (1lb 12½oz) and measured between 2.60m (8ft 6¼in) and 2.70m (8ft 10¼in) in length. But in the hands of increasingly mighty men the sporting spear became a lethal weapon as it hurtled towards 100m, and not always in a straight line. So the International Amateur Athletic Federation introduced new specifications for the men's Javelin, such as moving the centre of gravity, which effectively reduced the distance that it could be thrown.

Henry VIII was said to be a great fan of sledgehammer throwing, but after the Industrial Revolution had weakened the support for rural sports in England the hammer was found mainly in Scotland's Highland Games.

In 1865 an 16lb (7.26kg) round iron ball replaced the sledge head although the shaft remained stiff wood. By 1908 the hammer had been standardised into the implement of today: a spherical metal head, a spring steel wire, and a grip weighing altogether not less than 16lb (7.26kg).

● Ralph Rose, the first shot-put world record h

The field events angles of attack:

shot, 22.62m

Imre Nemeth, hammer world
record holder from 1948-50

The javelin's strong,
Nordic tradition is clear
from the table of Olympic
medals. Finland have by
far the best record with six
gold, six silver and four
bronze medals. Sweden
have four golds, two silvers
and three bronzes, and
Norway one of each.

Originally an unlimited run-up, as in the javelin, was permitted, but after several deaths and many bad accidents the
hammer was thrown from a cage, like the discus.

The shot weighs 16lb (7.26kg), the same as the hammer,
and is seemingly the most straightforward of the field events.
But it is so restrictive in its rules that huge men have to employ
a battle of wits to decide how best to use their massive muscles inside the skimpy 2.13m (7ft) diameter circle. The shot
must not be thrown, but put, that is . . . pushed from above
the shoulder, and it must land in a 40 degree sector.

At one Olympics only, in 1912, a two-handed shot put was
introduced where competitors used first their right hand then
their left and the aggregate total distance was recorded.
America's Ralph Rose won with 27.70m (74ft 5¼in). Just for
fun former world record holder Al Feuerbach (USA) tried it out
in 1974. He put 21.38m (70ft 1¼in) with his right hand and
15.67m (51ft 5in) with his left for a total of 37.05m (121ft 6¾in).

Al Oerter, discus thrower
extraordinary

Irish-American world
record holder Matt
McGrath hurt his knee
during the 1920 Olympics
and was placed only fifth.
But he took the silver
medal in 1924 at the age of
46.

discus 71.86m   hammer 86.34m   javelin 104.80m

SHOT PUT (MEN)

The best shot put ever seen is not recognised by international athletics as a world record because it was set by a professional, the remarkable Brian Oldfield of America.

Oldfield, who turned to the paid ranks in 1973 after finishing sixth in the 1972 Munich Olympics, threw an amazing 22.86m (75ft 0in) at El Paso on 10 May 1975 . . . more than a metre better than the existing amateur record.

Oldfield, re-instated as an amateur in 1980, never recaptured that form – and nor had anyone else up to the end of 1985 – when East Germany's Ulf Timmermann extended the IAAF record to 22.62m (74ft 2½in) in Berlin. Thus far, Oldfield who used a rotational technique copied from one-time world record holder Alexsandr Baryshnikov (URS), is the only professional athlete to have surpassed the amateurs in any event since the inception of official records.

American shot putters have won 15 Olympic gold medals and made a clean sweep of medals seven times.

Three-times world record holder Jack Torrance (USA) was known as "the Elephant Baby". At 1.90m (6ft 2¾in) he weighed a scale-bending 138kg/304lb.

Shot Put (Men)

Distance	Competitor	Venue	Date
15.54m	Ralph Rose (USA)	San Francisco	21/08/09
15.79m	Emil Hirschfield (GER)	Breslau	6/5/28
15.87m	John Kuck (USA)	Amsterdam	29/7/28
16.04m	Emil Hirschfield (GER)	Bochum	26/8/28
16.04m	Frantisek Douda (TCH)	Brno	4/10/31
16.05m	Zygmund Heljasz (POL)	Poznan	29/6/32
16.16m	Leo Sexton (USA)	Freeport	27/8/32
16.20m	Frantisek Douda (TCH)	Prague	24/9/32
16.48m	John Lyman (USA)	Palo Alto	21/4/34
16.80m	Jack Torrance (USA)	Des Moines	27/4/34
16.89m	Jack Torrance (USA)	Milwaukee	30/6/34
17.40m	Jack Torrance (USA)	Oslo	5/8/34
17.68m	Charles Fonville (USA)	Lawrence	17/4/48
17.79m	Jim Fuchs (USA)	Oslo	28/7/49
17.82m	Jim Fuchs (USA)	Los Angeles	29/4/50
17.90m	Jim Fuchs (USA)	Visby	20/8/50
17.95m	Jim Fuchs (USA)	Eskiltuna	22/8/50
18.00m	Parry O'Brien (USA)	Fresno	9/5/53
18.04m	Parry O'Brien (USA)	Compton	5/6/53
18.42m	Parry O'Brien (USA)	Los Angeles	8/5/54
18.43m	Parry O'Brien (USA)	Los Angeles	21/5/54
18.54m	Parry O'Brien (USA)	Los Angeles	11/6/54
18.62m	Parry O'Brien (USA)	Salt Lake City	5/5/56
18.69m	Parry O'Brien (USA)	Los Angeles	15/6/56
19.06m	Parry O'Brien (USA)	Eugene	3/9/56
19.25m	Parry O'Brien (USA)	Los Angeles	1/11/56
19.25m	Dallas Long (USA)	Santa Barbara	28/3/59
19.30m	Parry O'Brien (USA)	Albuquerque	1/8/59
19.38m	Dallas Long (USA)	Los Angeles	5/3/60
19.45m	Bill Nieder (USA)	Palo Alto	19/3/60
19.67m	Dallas Long (USA)	Los Angeles	26/3/60
19.99m	Bill Nieder (USA)	Austin	2/4/60
20.06m	Bill Nieder (USA)	Walnut	12/8/60
20.08m	Dallas Long (USA)	Los Angeles	18/5/62
20.10m	Dallas Long (USA)	Los Angeles	4/4/64
20.20m	Dallas Long (USA)	Los Angeles	29/5/64
20.68m	Dallas Long (USA)	Los Angeles	25/7/64
21.52m	Randy Matson (USA)	College Stn.	8/5/65
21.78m	Randy Matson (USA)	College Stn.	22/4/67
21.82m	Allan Feurbach (USA)	San Jose	5/5/73
21.85m	Terry Albritton (USA)	Honolulu	21/2/76
22.00m	Alexsandr Baryshnikov (URS)	Paris	10/7/76
22.15m	Udo Beyer (GDR)	Gothenburg	6/7/78
22.22m	Udo Beyer (GDR)	Los Angeles	25/7/83
22.62m	Ulf Timmermann (GDR)	Berlin	22/9/85

• Ulf Timmermann

The first record to be ratified for the shot was the 15.54m (51ft 0in) set by the tall (1.98m/6ft 6in) American Ralph Rose, Olympic champion in 1904 and 1908 and runner up in 1912. Rose's record stood for 19 years and progress continued to be slow until the arrival of America's giant Jack Torrance who, during four months of 1934 added almost one full metre to the mark to finish with a prodigious 17.40m (57ft 1in).

For the next 42 years the shot put world record became part of the American way of life. It was broken 29 times, always by USA athletes until Baryshnikov's 22m (72ft 2¼in) throw in Paris in 1976.

Of those 29 improvements, ten belonged to the outstanding Parry O'Brien, twice Olympic champion, and unbeaten in 116 consecutive events between July 1952 and June 1956. O'Brien also pioneered a new style, ridiculed at first, whereby he started his throw with his right foot pointing backwards and made an 180 degree turn before releasing the shot.

DISCUS (MEN)

The discus throw has attracted the most colossal of athletes through the ages, yet all have been dwarfed by one man and his supreme competitive instincts.

Al Oerter, four times Olympic champion and four times world record holder, is the personification of the will to win. As fellow American Jay Silvester once said with considerable feeling: "When you throw against Oerter, you don't expect to win, you just hope." Even at the age of 43 and after a seven year retirement Oerter was back, throwing further than ever and aiming for a place in the 1980 Olympic team. His dream was wrecked only by Jimmy Carter's Moscow boycott.

Oerter claimed his first Olympic title in 1956 at the age of 20 and his second in 1960. But it was not until 1962 that he broke his first world record, becoming the first man through the 200ft barrier with 61.10m (200ft 5in). Oerter's third Olympic victory, in Tokyo 1964, was also his bravest. For a year he had been suffering from the effects of a slipped disc and throwing in a surgical collar. Then, eight days before the final, he slipped in training and tore cartilages in his rib cage as well, the worst possible injury for an event demanding rotational power.

The doctors told him it would be eight weeks, never mind eight days, before he could throw again. But on the morning of the qualifying round he was there, wrapped in strapping and packed in ice, to throw an Olympic record. In the final, crippled by the pain, he was facing world record holder Ludvik Danek of Czechoslovakia. By the fifth round Danek had established a commanding lead and Oerter was back in fourth. He forced himself to slow down, to endure a longer stretch of agony . . . and took the gold medal with a 61.00m (200ft 1in) throw.

Pushed back to fourth that day was Jay Silvester, who four years later would arrive in Mexico City as the world record holder and favourite for the 1968 Olympic title. It made no difference . . . Oerter produced the finest throw of his life so far, 64.78m (212ft 6in), to take his fourth title.

The discus is the only men's event at which a world record has not been set in the Olympics.

● Mac Wilkins

Ben Plucknett (USA) set two world records in 1981 but neither was ratified as he was found to have taken anabolic steroids. During his chequered career Plucknett had been shot twice in the stomach in 1978 while acting as a club bouncer in California.

Three American throwers have each broken the world discus record four times: Fortune Gordien, Al Oerter and Mac Wilkins, who achieved his quartet in the space of one week and two meetings in 1976.

Discus (Men)

Distance	Competitor	Venue	Date
47.58m	James Duncan (USA)	New York	27/5/12
47.61m	Thomas Lieb (USA)	Chicago	14/9/24
47.89m	Glenn Hartranft (USA)	San Francisco	2/5/25
48.20m	Clarence Houser (USA)	Palo Alto	3/4/26
49.90m	Eric Krenz (USA)	Palo Alto	9/3/29
51.03m	Eric Krenz (USA)	Palo Alto	17/5/30
51.73m	Paul Jessup (USA)	Pittsburgh	23/8/30
52.42m	Harald Anderson (SWE)	Oslo	25/8/34
53.10m	Willi Schroder (GER)	Magdeburg	28/4/35
53.26m	Archie Harris (USA)	Palo Alto	20/6/41
53.34m	Adolfo Consolini (ITA)	Milan	26/10/41
54.23m	Adolfo Consolini (ITA)	Milan	14/4/46
54.93m	Robert Fitch (USA)	Minneapolis	8/6/46
55.33m	Adolfo Consolini (ITA)	Milan	10/10/48
56.46m	Fortune Gordien (USA)	Lisbon	9/7/49
56.97m	Fortune Gordien (USA)	Hameenlinna	14/8/49
57.93m	Sim Iness (USA)	Lincoln	20/6/53
53.10m	Fortune Gordien (USA)	Pasadena	11/7/53
59.28m	Fortune Gordien (USA)	Pasadena	22/8/53
59.91m	Edmund Piatkowski (POL)	Warsaw	14/6/59
59.91m	Rink Babka (USA)	Walnut	12/8/60
60.56m	Jay Silvester (USA)	Frankfurt/Main	11/8/61
60.72m	Jay Silvester (USA)	Brussels	20/8/61
61.10m	Al Oerter (USA)	Los Angeles	18/5/62
61.64m	Vladimir Trusenyov (URS)	Leningrad	4/6/62
62.45m	Al Oerter (USA)	Chicago	1/7/62
62.62m	Al Oerter (USA)	Walnut	27/4/63
62.94m	Al Oerter (USA)	Walnut	25/4/64
64.55m	Ludvik Danek (TCH)	Turnov	2/8/64
65.22m	Ludvik Danek (TCH)	Sokolov	12/10/65
66.54m	Jay Silvester (USA)	Modesto	25/5/68
68.40m	Jay Silvester (USA)	Reno	18/9/68
68.40m	Rickard Bruch (SWE)	Stockholm	5/7/72
68.48m	John van Reenen (RSA)	Stellenbosch	14/3/75
69.08m	John Powell (USA)	Long Beach	4/5/75
69.18m	Mac Wilkins (USA)	Walnut	24/4/76
69.80m	Mac Wilkins (USA)	San Jose	1/5/76
70.24m	Mac Wilkins (USA)	San Jose	1/5/76
70.86m	Mac Wilkins (USA)	San Jose	1/5/76
71.16m	Wolfgang Schmidt (GDR)	Berlin	9/8/78
71.86m	Yuriy Dumchev (URS)	Moscow	29/5/83

HAMMER

The round-the-head style of hammer throwing was devised by Highland Games expert Donald Dinnie in the 1860s and he remained virtually unbeaten for 30 years. Then came the dynasty of Irish-born Americans who monopolised the world record from 1885 to 1949.

The first of these so-called "Irish Whales" was John Flanagan, three times Olympic champion, who took the record from a meagre 44.46m (145ft 10in) in 1895 to 56.18m (184ft 4in) in 1909. He was succeeded by Matt McGrath with 57.10m (187ft 4in) in 1911 before Pat Ryan set the first official IAAF record with 57.77m (189ft 6½in) in New York on 17 August 1913. It was to stand for 25 years and ten days.

Officially Ryan's successor was Germany's Erwin Blask with 59.0m (193ft 7in), but a year earlier the last of the great Irishmen, Pat O'Callaghan had thrown 59.55m (195ft 4⅞in) at the Cork County Championships. The performance was never put forward for ratification because the circle was fractionally too small and the hammer a few grammes overweight, factors which, of course, would have hindered rather than helped O'Callaghan. O'Callaghan never did hold the world record, but Olympic gold medals in 1928 and 1932 assured his immortality.

It had taken 43 years for the record to progress from 55 to 60 metres, when Hungary's Jozsef Csermak threw 60.34m (197ft 11in) in 1952. Yet within eight more it had soared through the 70m barrier with America's Harold Connolly, the 1956 Olympic champion. Nine years on and the Soviet Union's Anatoliy Bondarchuk was over 75m and in 1978 another Soviet, Boris Zaichuk, unleashed the 80m era.

As the Irish-Americans had dominated, so now did the Soviets. From 1980 they remorselessly drove the record forwards eight times in four years through three athletes: Yuriy Syedikh, Juri Tamm, and Sergey Litvinov.

Syedikh, 191cm (6ft 3in) and 110kg (242.5lb) had been denied his opportunity of three successive Olympic gold medals by the East European boycott of the 1984 Los Angeles Games. He took a measure of revenge at the unlikely gathering of the Cork City Sports Day on 3 July 1984 when, with his opening throw, he mustered an incredible 86.34m (283ft 3in), an improvement of 2.20m (7ft 2½in) on the previous best.

Germany's Karl-Hans Riehm, a 24-year-old soldier from Trier, beat the existing world record with all six of his throws during a competition at Rehlingen on 19 May 1975. The record stood at 76.66m (251ft 6in) to Aleksey Spiridonov (URS) and Riehm threw 76.70; 77.56; 77.10; 78.50; 77.16; 77.28.

The first reported death caused by hammer throwing was of eight-year-old spectator John Gyfford in 1566.

Hammer (Men)

Distance	Competitor	Venue	Date
57.77m	Patrick Ryan (USA)	New York	17/8/13
59.00m	Erwin Blask (GER)	Stockholm	27/8/38
59.02m	Imre Nemeth (HUN)	Tata	14/7/48
59.57m	Imre Nemeth (HUN)	Katowice	4/9/49
59.88m	Imre Nemeth (HUN)	Budapest	19/5/50
60.34m	Jozsef Csermak (HUN)	Helsinki	24/7/52
61.25m	Sverre Strandli (NOR)	Oslo	14/9/52
62.36m	Sverre Strandli (NOR)	Oslo	5/9/53
63.34m	Stanislaw Nyenashev (URS)	Baku	12/12/54
64.33m	Mikhail Krivonosov (URS)	Warsaw	4/8/55
64.52m	Mikhail Krivonosov (URS)	Belgrade	19/9/55
65.85m	Mikhail Krivonosov (URS)	Nalchik	25/4/56
66.38m	Mikhail Krivonosov (URS)	Minsk	8/7/56
67.32m	Mikhail Krivonosov (URS)	Tashkent	22/10/56
68.54m	Harold Connolly (USA)	Los Angeles	2/11/56
68.68m	Harold Connolly (USA)	Bakersfield	20/6/58
70.33m	Harold Connolly (USA)	Walnut	12/8/60
70.67m	Harold Connolly (USA)	Palo Alto	21/7/62
71.06m	Harold Connolly (USA)	Ceres	29/5/65
71.26m	Harold Connolly (USA)	Walnut	20/6/65
73.74m	Gyula Zsivotzky (HUN)	Debrecen	4/9/65
73.76m	Gyula Zsivotzky (HUN)	Budapest	14/9/68
74.52m	Romauld Klim (URS)	Budapest	15/6/69
74.68m	Anatoliy Bondarchuk (URS)	Athens	20/9/69
75.48m	Anatoliy Bondarchuk (URS)	Rovno	12/10/69
76.40m	Walter Schmidt (FRG)	Lahr	4/9/71
76.60m	Reinhard Thiemer (GDR)	Leipzig	4/7/74
76.66m	Aleksey Spiridonov (URS)	Munich	11/9/74
76.70m	Karl-Hans Riehm (FRG)	Rehlingen	19/5/75
77.56m	Karl-Hans Riehm (FRG)	Rehlingen	19/5/75
78.50m	Karl-Hans Riehm (FRG)	Rehlingen	19/5/75
79.30m	Walter Schmidt (FRG)	Frankfurt/Main	14/8/75
80.14m	Boris Zaichuk (URS)	Moscow	9/7/78
80.32m	Karl-Hans Riehm (FRG)	Heidenheim	6/8/78
80.38m	Yuriy Syedikh (URS)	Leselidze	16/5/80
80.46m	Juri Tamm (URS)	Leselidze	16/5/80
80.64m	Yuriy Syedikh (URS)	Leselidze	16/5/80
81.66m	Sergey Litvinov (URS)	Sochi	24/5/80
81.80m	Yuriy Syedikh (URS)	Moscow	31/7/80
83.98m	Sergey Litvinov (URS)	Moscow	4/6/82
84.14m	Sergey Litvinov (URS)	Moscow	21/6/83
86.54m	Yuriy Syedikh (URS)	Cork	3/7/84

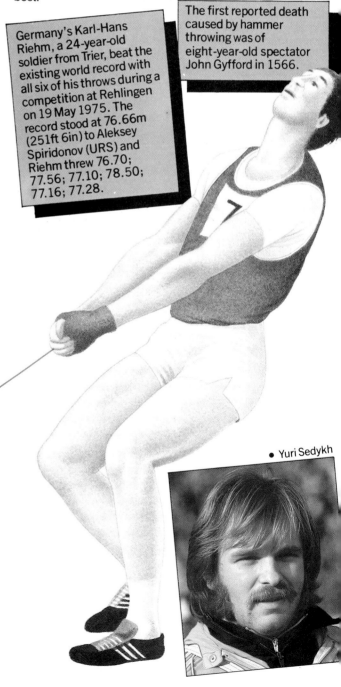

• Yuri Sedykh

JAVELIN (MEN)

Old fashioned stadiums are getting too small for the modern men of the javelin . . . as East Germany's Uwe Hohn proved in frightening fashion in Berlin on 20 July 1984. The mighty Hohn hurled his javelin 104.80m (343ft 10in), way off the metric conversion tables and into the realms of fantasy.

America's Tom Petranoff, a modest 185cm (6ft 1in) and 97kg (215lb), had already petrified athletics officials a year earlier when he nudged the supposedly impossible 100m mark with 99.72m. Now Hohn had gone more than five metres further; soon no track athlete would be safe to run while the javelin was in progress.

A meeting of the International Amateur Athletic Federation recognised the danger and imposed new restrictions on the manufacture of javelins. So Hohn's record could stand for all-time.

It was a far cry from the much lauded Nordic throwers at the turn of the century who had excitedly edged over the 60m mark before Finland's Matti Jarvinen set standards rising sharply in the Thirties, breaking the world record ten times in succession and taking it from 71.57m (234ft 9½in) to 77.23m (253ft 4½in).

British coach and author F.A.M. Webster spent much of his military career in East Africa. He found he could easily out-throw the local natives using his 'scientific' javelin but it was an entirely different story when they switched to their own spears.

Jarvinen's protegee, Yrjo Nikkanen, carried the record to 78.70m (258ft 2in) and there it rested for almost 15 years until America's Franklin "Bud" Held achieved the first 80m plus throw in 1953.

Held's brother Dick had devised a new aerodynamic javelin and it was this, more than anything, which brought the spectacular improvement of the Fifties.

The Finns and Norwegians still held a special love of the event, however, and it was Terje Pedersen of Norway who progressed the next step, taking the record through the 90m mark with a best of 91.72m (300ft 11in) in 1964.

The second man through the 90m and 300ft barrier was Russia's great Janis Lusis, the only man to have won four consecutive European titles (1962-71). Lusis, married to 1960 Olympic javelin champion Elvira Ozolina, collected gold, silver and bronze in three Olympic appearances and twice broke the world record to usher in the era of monster men like Hungary's Petranoff and Hohn. Ferenc Paragi (96.72m/317ft 4in),

• Uwe Hohn

Javelin (Men)

Distance	Competitor	Venue	Date
62.32m	Erik Lemming (SWE)	Stockholm	29/9/12
66.10m	Jonni Myyra (FIN)	Stockholm	25/8/19
66.62m	Gunnar Lindstrom (SWE)	Eksjo	12/10/24
69.88m	Eino Penttila (FIN)	Viipuri	8/10/27
71.01m	Erik Lundqvist (SWE)	Stockholm	15/8/28
71.57m	Matti Jarvinen (FIN)	Viipuri	8/8/30
71.70m	Matti Jarvinen (FIN)	Tampere	17/8/30
71.88m	Matti Jarvinen (FIN)	Vaasa	31/8/30
72.93m	Matti Jarvinen (FIN)	Viipuri	14/9/30
74.02m	Matti Jarvinen (FIN)	Turku	27/6/32
74.28m	Matti Jarvinen (FIN)	Mikkeli	25/5/33
74.61m	Matti Jarvinen (FIN)	Vaasa	7/6/33
76.10m	Matti Jarvinen (FIN)	Helsinki	15/6/33
76.66m	Matti Jarvinen (FIN)	Turin	7/9/34
77.23m	Matti Jarvinen (FIN)	Helsinki	18/6/36
77.87m	Yrjo Nikkanen (FIN)	Karhula	25/8/38
78.70m	Yrjo Nikkanen (FIN)	Kotka	16/10/38
80.41m	Bud Held (USA)	Pasadena	8/8/53
81.75m	Bud Held (USA)	Modesto	21/5/55
83.56m	Soini Nikkanen (FIN)	Kuhmoinen	24/6/56
83.66m	Janusz Sidlo (POL)	Milan	30/6/56
85.71m	Egil Danielsen (NOR)	Melbourne	26/1/56
86.04m	Al Cantello (USA)	Compton	5/6/59
86.74m	Carlo Lievore (ITA)	Milan	1/6/61
87.12m	Terje Pedersen (NOR)	Oslo	1/7/64
91.72m	Terje Pedersen (NOR)	Oslo	2/9/64
91.98m	Janis Lusis (URS)	Saarijarvi	23/6/68
92.70m	Jorma Kinnunen (FIN)	Tampere	18/6/69
93.80m	Janis Lusis (URS)	Stockholm	6/7/72
94.08m	Klaus Wolfermann (FRG)	Leverkusen	5/5/73
94.58m	Miklos Nemeth (HUN)	Montreal	26/7/76
96.72m	Ferenc Paragi (HUN)	Tata	23/4/80
99.72m	Tom Petranoff (USA)	Westwood	15/5/83
104.80m	Uwe Hohn (GDR)	Berlin	20/7/84

THROWING EVENTS (WOMEN)

A glimpse of women shot putting was considered shocking, as the song goes, until the middle of the 1930s. Then in 1934 the International Amateur Athletic Federation agreed to recognise their records. The more genteel javelin had been accepted in 1932, the discus would follow in 1936.

The first women record holders in field events were relatively slim, athletic individuals compared to the elephantine females who now dominate the shot and discus. Germany's Gisela Mauermayer, inaugural pace setter in both the shot and discus was a tall, powerful, but decidedly feminine Fräulein with long, Hollywood legs. Compare her to the current world record holder in the shot, Soviet Natalya Lisovskaya who weighs in at 90kg (198.5lb) or Czechoslovakia's mighty maiden of the discus Zdenka Silhava, 96kg (211.5lb).

Even so, Mauermayer's shot record stood for 14 years and 20 days, the longest period ever. And her discus best survived 12 years. The advent of the heavy weight superwoman carried with it the increasing problem of body building drugs and in 1975 Rumanian shot putter Valentina Cioltan was the first to be found guilty of taking anabolic steroids. A year later, in Montreal, Polish discus thrower Danuta Rosani became the first athlete disqualified at an Olympics for failing a drugs test.

The discus for women of all ages (junior, intermediate, senior) is 1kg (2lb 3oz),

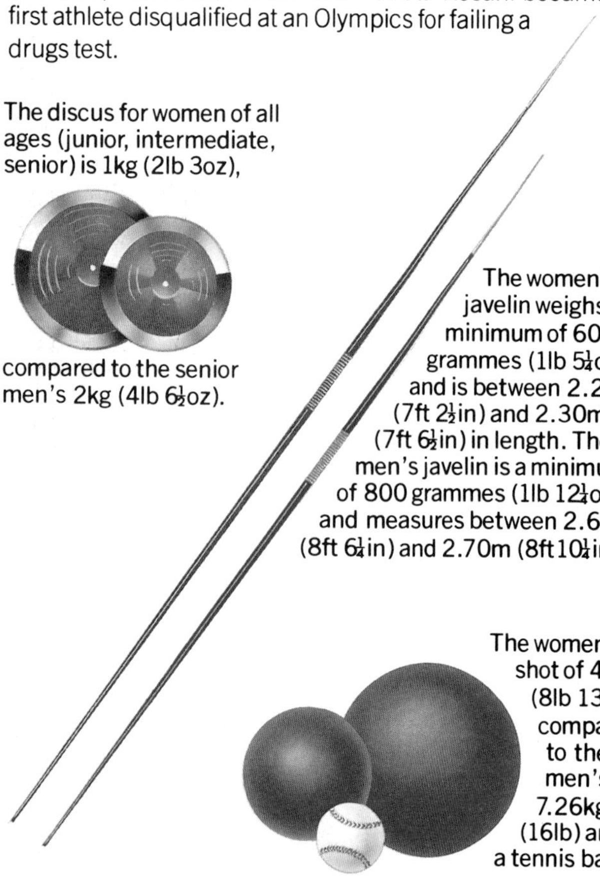

compared to the senior men's 2kg (4lb 6½oz).

The women's javelin weighs a minimum of 600 grammes (1lb 5¼oz) and is between 2.20m (7ft 2½in) and 2.30m (7ft 6½in) in length. The men's javelin is a minimum of 800 grammes (1lb 12¼oz) and measures between 2.60m (8ft 6¼in) and 2.70m (8ft 10¼in).

The women's shot of 4kg (8lb 13oz) compared to the men's 7.26kg (16lb) and a tennis ball.

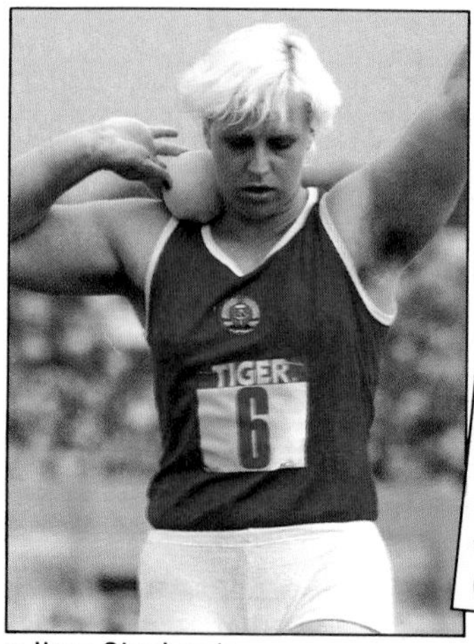

• Ilona Slupianek

Male athletes who have attempted to throw the women's shot (4kg) and discus (1kg) have found themselves at a relative disadvantage compared to throwing their own, heavier implements. This is because they find difficulty getting purchase on the smaller items with their larger hands and fingers. Even so, in training, British record holder Geoff Capes put the women's shot 26.80m (88ft).

Shot (Women)

Distance	Competitor	Venue	Date
14.38m	Gisela Mauermayer (GER)	Warsaw	15/7/34
14.59m	Tatyana Sevryukova (URS)	Moscow	4/8/48
14.86m	Klavdiya Tochonova (URS)	Tbilisi	30/10/49
15.02m	Anna Andreyeva (URS)	Ploesti	9/11/50
15.28m	Galina Zybina (URS)	Helsinki	26/7/52
15.37m	Galina Zybina (URS)	Frunze	20/9/52
15.42m	Galina Zybina (URS)	Frunze	1/10/52
16.20m	Galina Zybina (URS)	Malmo	9/10/53
16.28m	Galina Zybina (URS)	Kiev	14/9/54
16.29m	Galina Zybina (URS)	Leningrad	5/9/55
16.67m	Galina Zybina (URS)	Tbilisi	15/11/55
16.76m	Galina Zybina (URS)	Tashkent	13/10/56
17.25m	Tamara Press (URS)	Nalchik	26/4/59
17.42m	Tamara Press (URS)	Moscow	16/7/60
17.78m	Tamara Press (URS)	Moscow	13/8/60
18.55m	Tamara Press (URS)	Leipzig	10/6/62
18.55m	Tamara Press (URS)	Belgrade	12/9/62
18.59m	Tamara Press (URS)	Kassel	19/9/65
18.67m	Nadyezhda Chizhova (URS)	Sochi	28/4/68
18.87m	Margitta Gummel (GDR)	Frankfurt/Oder	22/9/68
19.07m	Margitta Gummel (GDR)	Mexico City	20/10/68
19.61m	Margitta Gummel (GDR)	Mexico City	20/10/68
19.72m	Nadyezhda Chizhova (URS)	Moscow	30/5/69
20.09m	Nadyezhda Chizhova (URS)	Chorzow	13/7/69
20.10m	Margitta Gummel (GDR)	Berlin	11/9/69
20.10m	Nadyezhda Chizhova (URS)	Athens	16/9/69
20.43m	Nadyezhda Chizhova (URS)	Athens	16/9/69
20.43m	Nadyezhda Chizhova (URS)	Moscow	29/8/71
20.63m	Nadyezhda Chizhova (URS)	Sochi	19/5/72
21.03m	Nadyezhda Chizhova (URS)	Munich	7/9/72
21.20m	Nadyezhda Chizhova (URS)	Lvov	28/8/73
21.60m	Marianne Adam (GDR)	Berlin	6/8/75
21.67m	Marianne Adam (GDR)	Karl-Marx-Stadt	30/5/76
21.87m	Ivanka Khristova (BUL)	Belmeken	3/7/76
21.89m	Ivanka Khristova (BUL)	Belmeken	4/7/76
21.99m	Helena Fibingerova (TCH)	Opava	26/9/76
22.32m	Helena Fibingerova (TCH)	Nitra	20/8/77
22.36m	Ilona Slupianek (GDR)	Celje	2/5/80
22.45m	Ilona Slupianek (GDR)	Potsdam	11/5/80
22.53m	Natalya Lisovskaya (URS)	Sochi	26/5/84

The spectre of drugs haunts the women's field events just as it does the men's and there was first dismay, then outcry over East Germany's Ilona Slupianek. After winning the 1977 European Cup Final the near-six foot (183cm) blonde was found to have taken anabolic steroids and was banned. But only a year later she was re-instated and went on to take the European Championship and, in 1980, the Olympic shot title.

Her victory in those Moscow Games was achieved by a 99cm (3ft 3in) gap over her nearest rival, the largest ever. It underlined her supremacy in a year when she twice broke the world record and topped 22m (72ft 2¼in) some 50 times.

Since Gisela Mauermayer's first world record in 1934, no woman outside Eastern Europe has held the shot world record. The event is dominated by Soviets, such as Galina Zybina who made 15 successive improvements – eight of them ratified – Tamara Press and Nadyezda Chizhova, who won the European title a record four times in a row, took a complete set of Olympic medals and ushered in the 70ft (21.33m) era with an unratified put of 21.45m (70ft 4½in).

After its rather gentle introduction by the elegant Gisela Mauermayer, women's discus throwing was hurled into the second half of the century by the first Russian powerhouse, Nina Dumbadze. By 1952 she had added almost nine metres to Mauermayer's inaugural record with 57.04m (187ft 2 in) before handing over world supremacy to her hulking countrywoman Tamara Press.

The awesome Ms Press, sister of hurdler Irena, swept all fore her in the Sixties, claiming an Olympic title and six world records before fading abruptly from sight at the advent of sex tests.

Briefly the Germans assumed control of the power game . . . until the arrival of perhaps the greatest female discus thrower of them all, another Russian Faina Melnik. In her international debut at the 1971 European Championships she took the gold with her first world record. There were to be ten more world records, an Olympic gold, and the breaking of the 70m (229ft 8in) barrier before she faded at the birth of the Eighties.

• Galina Savinkova

• Faina Melnyk

Discus (Women)

Distance	Competitor	Venue	Date
48.31m	Gisela Mauermayer (GER)	Dresden	11/7/36
53.25m	Nina Dumbadze (URS)	Moscow	8/8/48
53.37m	Nina Dumbadze (URS)	Gori	27/5/51
53.61m	Nina Romashkova (URS)	Odessa	9/8/52
57.04m	Nina Dumbadze (URS)	Tbilisi	18/10/52
57.15m	Tamara Press (URS)	Rome	12/9/60
57.43m	Tamara Press (URS)	Moscow	15/7/61
58.06m	Tamara Press (URS)	Sofia	1/9/61
58.98m	Tamara Press (URS)	London	20/9/61
59.29m	Tamara Press (URS)	Moscow	18/5/63
59.70m	Tamara Press (URS)	Moscow	11/8/65
61.26m	Liesel Westermann (FRG)	Sao Paulo	5/11/67
61.64m	Christine Spielberg (GDR)	Regis Breitingen	26/5/68
62.54m	Liesel Westermann (FRG)	Werdohl	24/7/68
62.70m	Liesel Westermann (FRG)	Berlin	18/6/69
63.96m	Liesel Westermann (FRG)	Hamburg	27/9/69
64.22m	Faina Melnyk (URS)	Helsinki	12/8/71
64.88m	Faina Melnyk (URS)	Munich	4/9/71
65.42m	Faina Melnyk (URS)	Moscow	31/5/72
65.48m	Faina Melnyk (URS)	Augsburg	24/6/72
66.76m	Faina Melnyk (URS)	Luxhniki	4/8/72
67.32m	Argentina Menis (ROM)	Constanza	23/9/72
67.44m	Faina Melnyk (URS)	Riga	25/5/73
67.58m	Faina Melnyk (URS)	Moscow	10/7/73
69.48m	Faina Melnyk (URS)	Edinburgh	7/9/73
69.90m	Faina Melnyk (URS)	Prague	27/5/74
70.20m	Faina Melnyk (URS)	Zurich	20/8/75
70.50m	Faina Melnyk (URS)	Sochi	24/4/76
70.72m	Evelin Jahl (GDR)	Dresden	12/8/78
71.50m	Evelin Jahl (GDR)	Potsdam	10/5/80
71.80m	Maria Vergova (BUL)	Sofia	13/7/80
73.26m	Galina Savinkova (URS)	Leselidze	22/5/83
73.36m	Irena Meszynski (GDR)	Prague	17/8/84
74.56m	Zdenka Silhava (TCH)	Nitra	26/8/84

Javelin (Women)

Distance	Competitor	Venue	Date
46.74m	Nan Gindele (USA)	Chicago	18/6/32
47.24m	Anneliese Steinheuer (GER)	Frankfurt/Main	21/6/42
48.21m	Herma Bauma (AUT)	Vienna	29/6/47
48.63m	Herma Bauma (AUT)	Vienna	12/9/48
49.59m	Natalya Smirnitskaya (URS)	Moscow	25/7/49
53.41m	Natalya Smirnitskaya (URS)	Moscow	5/8/49
53.56m	Nadyezhda Konyayeva (URS)	Leningrad	5/2/54
55.11m	Nadyezhda Konyayeva (URS)	Kiev	22/5/54
55.48m	Nadyezhda Konyayeva (URS)	Kiev	6/8/54
56.73m	Dana Zatopkova (TCH)	Prague	1/6/58
57.40m	Anna Pazera (AUS)	Cardiff	24/7/58
57.49m	Birute Zalogaitite (URS)	Tbilisi	30/10/58
57.92m	Elvira Ozolina (URS)	Leselidze	3/5/60
59.55m	Elvira Ozolina (URS)	Bucharest	4/6/60
59.78m	Elvira Ozolina (URS)	Moscow	3/7/63
62.40m	Yelena Gorchakova (URS)	Tokyo	16/10/64
62.70m	Ewa Gryziecka (POL)	Bucharest	11/6/72
65.06m	Ruth Fuchs (GDR)	Potsdam	11/6/72
66.10m	Ruth Ruchs (GDR)	Edinburgh	7/9/73
67.22m	Ruth Fuchs (GDR)	Rome	3/9/74
69.12m	Ruth Fuchs (GDR)	Berlin	10/7/76
69.32m	Kate Schmidt (USA)	Furth	11/9/77
69.52m	Ruth Fuchs (GDR)	Dresden	13/6/79
69.96m	Ruth Fuchs (GDR)	Split	29/4/80
70.80m	Tatyana Biryulina (URS)	Moscow	12/7/80
71.88m	Antoaneta Todorova (BUL)	Zagreb	15/8/81
72.40m	Tiina Lillak (FIN)	Helsinki	29/7/82
74.20m	Sofia Sakorafa (GRE)	Khania	26/9/82
74.76m	Tiina Lillak (FIN)	Tampere	13/6/83
75.26m	Petra Felke (GDR)	Schwerin	4/6/85
75.40m	Petra Felke (GDR)	Schwerin	4/6/85

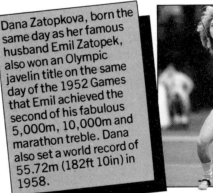

Dana Zatopkova, born the same day as her famous husband Emil Zatopek, also won an Olympic javelin title on the same day of the 1952 Games that Emil achieved the second of his fabulous 5,000m, 10,000m and marathon treble. Dana also set a world record of 55.72m (182ft 10in) in 1958.

• Petra Felke

An American, a Fin and a Greek all figure in the recent improvements in the women's javelin record, but once again, it is the Eastern Europeans who hold overall supremacy.

None more so than Ruth Fuchs (GDR) who set her first world best in 1972 and her sixth in 1980. Amazingly, half an hour before Ruth announced herself to the world in 1972 Poland's Ewa Gryziecka threw 62.70m (205ft 8in) in Bucharest. It was to be one of the shortest world marks on record as over in Potsdam Miss Fuchs annihilated it with 65.06m (213ft 5in).

By contrast, the longest lasting javelin record was the 62.40m (204ft 8in) by Yelena Gorchakova (URS) in the 1964 Olympic qualifying round which stood for 7 years 238 days.

The Iron Curtain domination was interrupted by Finnish World Champion Tiina Lillak, Greece's European champion Anna Verouli, world record holder Sofia Sakarafa and Britain's exciting duo – Tessa Sanderson and Fatima Whitbread. But then, in 1985, up popped East Germany's new wonder girl Petra Felke to comprehensively smash the 75m (246ft 1in) barrier and seem set to reign for a long time.

THE HISTORY OF GOLF

Golf's origins will still be discussed, debated and disputed long after the first course is built on the moon. But there can be no doubt where the home of the game is – St. Andrews in the Kingdom of Fife, Scotland. Written evidence of golf there dates back to the 16th century and, probably before and definitely after, players from all parts of the globe have marvelled at the mystique of the most famous 18 holes in the world.

Such is the wonder of the Old Course that it is also the most copied, although none has come close to capturing the intricacies and subtleties of this flat strip of land with its unseen mountains of problems. And nowhere else on earth can boast one of the course's main features – a wind that can have changed direction by the time a player has reached his drive and reverted back before he addresses his putt.

Many have fallen in love with the town at first sight, but few have offered the same initial affection to the course. Its charm is not immediately apparent, but those who have survived the long courtship have found the marriage to be 'til death do us part.

Bobby Jones tore up his card on his first visit convinced he would not return. He did, many times, and came to admit: "I could take out of my life everything except my experiences at St. Andrews and I would still have a rich, full life."

Champagne Tony Lema defied those who believe that golfers must serve a long and hard apprenticeship at St. Andrews before attempting to tame the Old Lady. He won the Open there in 1964 on his first visit to the town.

James Braid became the first player to break 300 at St Andrews for an Open when he shot 299 in 1910 – a remarkable 19 shots better than when he had won there just five years earlier.

• Tony Lema

• St Andrews, the home of golf

Sevvy Ballesteros

● Bobby Jones

● Tom Morris snr's final bunker

Sevvy Ballesteros returned the best aggregate for an Open at St. Andrews with a 276 four round total in 1984 – two shots better than the previous best by Kel Nagle in 1960.

Ever since Tom Morris jnr won The Open in 1868 at the age of 17 years and five months, golf has been setting records which may never be broken. It is difficult to imagine that a younger player will ever win the world's greatest tournament, or that a son will succeed his father and claim the crown as Morris jnr did that year. It is harder to envisage another equalling the remarkable feat of Bobby Jones, who in 1930 won the Amateur and Open Championships on both sides of the Atlantic.

When Harry Vardon won The Open in 1914 it was the sixth time he had done it – a record which still stands today. And is it conceivable that any player will again win 11 tournaments in succession as Byron Nelson did on the American tour in 1945, when he also claimed another seven titles?

Wherever the game has been played, be it the highest course in the world – the Tuctu Golf Club, Morococha, Peru, (4.369m, 14,335ft above sea level) or the current lowest, Furnace Creek, Death Valley, California (67m, 220ft below sea level) golf has produced amazing facts and records.

At least a dozen players have justifiable claims to having been great ones, but few would argue against Jack Nicklaus as the greatest of them all. The record speaks for itself. A remarkable 20 major championships – six in the US Masters, as many US PGA's, four US Opens, three Opens and two US Amateurs. Few players have had as big an impact on golf as Arnold Palmer, but his record of major title wins still leaves him trailing the Golden Bear by 12.

The Nicklaus record will stand for many years and may never be bettered. Of the current professionals only Sevvy Ballesteros has a realistic chance. The flamboyant, but fiercely determined Spaniard won four majors before he was 28 and has been the most dominant and feared golfer during the Eighties apart from Tom Watson, (who is closest to Vardon's Open record with five wins behind him) but he has not won a major since 1983.

But Nicklaus didn't – and Ballesteros is unlikely – to beat another Tom Morris jnr record of four successive Open wins between 1868 and 1872.

The scores in the first British Open at Royal Liverpool (Hoylake) in 1897 and the last one there, in 1967, were:

Leading Scores (1897)

	1	2	3	4	Total
H.H. Hilton (Royal Liverpool)	80	75	84	75	314
J. Braid (Romford)	80	74	82	79	315
F.G. Tait (Black Watch)	79	79	80	79	317
G. Pulford (Royal Liverpool)	80	79	79	79	317
A. Herd (Huddersfield)	78	81	79	80	318
H. Vardon (Ganton)	84	80	80	76	320

Leading Scores (1967)

	1	2	3	4	Total
R. de Vicenzo (Argentina)	70	71	67	70	278
J. Nicklaus (USA)	71	69	71	69	280
C.A. Clark (Sunningdale)	70	73	69	72	284
G. Player (South Africa)	72	71	67	74	284
A. Jacklin (Potters Bar)	73	69	73	70	285
A. Miguel (Spain)	72	74	68	72	286
H. Henning (South Africa)	74	70	71	71	286

Not one of the 1897 competitors would have qualified for the final 36 holes in 1967.

The lowest round in 1897, 74 by James Braid was regarded as a phenomenal score. The lowest round in 1967 was de Vicenzo's and Player's third round 67.

Roberto de Vicenzo became the oldest player to win the Open Championship Cup at Hoylake in 1967. He was 44 years 93 days – 51 days older than Harry Vardon in 1914. Tom Morris snr was 46 when he won the Championship Belt in 1867.

Tom Watson claimed the record for a 72-hole aggregate in the Open Championship when he shot 268 at Turnberry in 1977. Lowest 18-hole score was carded by Mark Hayes in the same tournament. His 63 was equalled by Isao Aoki at Muirfield in 1980.

Manchester club professional Denis Durnian clipped one shot off the existing record for the lowest nine holes in the Open when he took just 28 shots on his outward half during the second round of Birkdale in 1983.

Jack Nicklaus set or equalled every record in the US Open when winning at Baltusrol in 1980 with a 272 72-hole aggregate. He and Tom Weiskopf shot first round 63's to equal Johnny Miller's score at Oakmont in 1973. Nicklaus led with a record 134 after two rounds while Isao Aoki joined him on the 204 record mark after 54 holes.

Sam Snead's 59 at the Greenbrier Open in 1959 still stands as the lowest round in American professional tournaments. Al Geiberger had the assistance of preferred lies when he equalled it in the 1977 Danny Thomas Memphis Classic.

Sevvy Ballesteros is the youngest winner of the Open Championship Cup this century. The Spaniard was 22 years 103 days when he won at Lytham in 1979.

Roberto de Vicenzo

Harry Vardon (GBR)
Open: 1896, '98, '99, 1903,
'11, '14; US Open: 1900.

Walter Hagen (USA)
Open: 1922, '24, '28, '29;
US Open '14, '19; US PGA: '21,
'24, '25, '26, '27.

Bobby Jones (USA)
Open: 1926, '27, '30; Amateur:
'30; US Open '23, '26, '29, '30;
US Amateur '24, '25, '27, '28,
'30.

Gene Sarazen (USA)
Open: 1932; US Open: 1922,
'32; US Masters '35: US PGA:
'22, '23, '33.

Ben Hogan (USA)
pen: 1953; US Open: '48, '50,
'51, '53; US Masters '51, '53;
US PGA '46, '48.

Sam Snead (USA)
Open: 1946; US Masters: '49,
'52, '54; US PGA: '42, '49, '51.

Peter Thompson (AUS)
Open: 1954, '55, '56, '58, '65.

Arnold Palmer (USA)
Open: '61, '62; US Open: '60;
US Masters: '58, '60, '62, '64.
US Amateur: '54.

Gary Player (SA)
pen: 1959, '68, '74; US Open:
65; US Masters: '61, '74, '78;
US PGA: '62, '72.

Jack Nicklaus (USA)
Open: 1966, '70, '78; US Open:
'62, '67, '72, '80; US Masters:
'63, '65, '66, '72, '75, '86; US
PGA: '63, '71, '73, '75, '80
US Amateur: '59, '61.

Tom Watson (USA)
Open: 1975, '77, '80, '82, '83;
US Open: '82; US Masters: '77,
'81.

Sevvy Ballesteros (ESP)
Open: '79, '84; US Masters: '80,
'83.

THE RYDER CUP

Sam Torrance, unless he wins The Open, will always be known as the man who won the Ryder Cup for Great Britain and Europe.

Nobody at The Belfry on 15 September 1985, nor the millions who watched on television as Torrance scored the decisive point, will ever forget the scenes of jubilation that greeted the triumph.

Not least of all because such occasions of British success in this competition are almost as rare as visits from Halley's Comet. America has had such a grip on the competition that Britain's side has been augmented by Europeans since 1979 – to make a better match of it.

The Cup has rarely been out of American hands since Sam Ryder donated it in 1927.

Britain won it twice in the first four years, but the 1985 victory was only the second success since and the first in 28 years. They did hold it for six months in 1969 when the challenge at Royal Birkdale provided the only tie in the entire series.

America almost completed a greenwash in 1947, but in the last singles match, Sam King registered Britain's only point.

● Walter Hagen accepts the 1937 Ryder Cup

Year	Winners	Scores GB and Ireland (& Europe since 1979)	Scores USA	Year	Winners	Scores GB and Ireland (& Europe since 1979)	Scores USA
1927	USA	2½	9½	1963	USA	9	23
1929	Britain	7	5	1965	USA	12½	19½
1931	USA	3	9	1967	USA	8½	23½
1933	Britain	6½	5½	1969	Tie	16	16
1935	USA	3	9	1971	USA	13½	18½
1937	USA	4	8	1973	USA	13	19
1947	USA	1	11	1975	USA	11	21
1949	USA	5	7	1977	USA	7½	12½
1951	USA	2½	9½	1979	USA	11	17
1953	USA	5½	6½	1981	USA	9½	18½
1955	USA	4	8	1983	USA	13½	14½
1957	Britain	7½	4½	1985	Britain & Europe	16½	11½
1959	USA	3½	8½				
1961	USA	9½	14½				

A MEMORABLE MATCH

Few sports invoke more post-match debate than golf. And fewer rounds can have induced more memories and comment than the one which decided the first Open Championship held at Turnberry in 1977.

It has been hailed as the greatest head-to-head the Open has ever seen. Not surprisingly it featured Jack Nicklaus — widely acknowledged as the best ever golfer. Nicklaus was simply The King with 14 major titles already accumulated. His opponent, for shortly into the third round the tournament was already a two-horse race, was the pretender to his throne, Tom Watson, who had served notice of intent by winning the Open at Carnoustie in 1975 and also The US Masters in 1977.

Lightning stopped play briefly during that third round, but nothing prevented the firework display on the course as both Nicklaus and Watson shot 65 to enter the final day locked in combat.

Watson had earlier in his career been dubbed a "choker" but if there were still any doubters this would be the day when he made his critics choke on their own suspicions.

Nicklaus birdied the first and after another at the short fourth was three shots clear. The vast gallery loved it and the excitement intensified as Watson clawed back with birdies at the fifth, seventh and eighth.

A short delay, while more marshalls were called to control a crowd who did not want to miss one single second of this epic contest, disrupted Watson more than Nicklaus.

By the 13th tee Nicklaus was two ahead again with just six holes left. The engraver was ready to inscribe the Cup.

Watson claimed the 13th with a 12-ft birdie putt and made another at the 15th with a mighty stroke from 20 yd when most were wagering on whether he would get down in two.

Another long putt dropped on the 17th and Watson strode to the last tee ahead for the first time. And still the drama unfolded as Nicklaus refused to surrender even when Watson arrowed his 7-iron approach to just 18 in from the hole.

Nicklaus somehow conjured a 30ft putt from off the green into the hole. "I knew he was going to make it," said Watson. "So I just concentrated my mind on having to hole mine." He did, to win by one stroke.

● Jack Nicklaus

● Nicklaus congratulates Watson at Turnberry

Jack Nicklaus is the greatest record breaker the game of golf has known. Ever since he joined the United States Tour in 1962, golf has been under the spell of that old Jack magic.

Born Jack William Nicklaus on 21 January 1940, in Columbus, Ohio, but known throughout the world as simply The Golden Bear, he served immediate notice of intent when he won the US Open in his first year on the tour.

Since then he has accumulated another 17 Grand Slam title wins and has been American PGA Player of the Year five times. With two US Amateur triumphs, he has collected 20 major titles and has won 70 times on the US Tour alone.

His four US Open wins are a joint record shared with three others, while only Walter Hagen won as many US PGA Championships — five. Nobody has claimed The Masters as many times and when he won his sixth green jacket in April 1986, at the age of 46, he was the oldest ever champion.

After winning his latest crown at the Augusta National he admitted: "It would be the smart thing to quit now . . . but I'm not that smart."

Golf has never known a smarter golfer and who is to say that he will not add to his incredible list of majors — certainly not the American journalist who wrote immediately before Nicklaus's 1986 Masters Triumph, "The Golden Bear is washed up, finished, through."

TRENDS IN WORLD SOCCER

When FIFA President Joao Havelange decided to increase the number of finalists in the 1982 World Cup from 16 to 24, many cynics in Europe saw it as a vote-grabbing exercise, a way to hold onto power by pleasing Latin America and the Third World.

The Europeans, used to keeping a tight grasp of their own on football power, considered that the entry of too many minnows would merely clutter and devalue the World Cup.

Certainly Chile and El Salvador and New Zealand conformed, winning no points at all. But in the north-east of Spain Cameroon were performing remarkably well and Algeria managed to beat West Germany, the eventual losing finalists . . . the explosion of football within Africa was at last reaching a world stage.

Cameroon drew all three games, including 1-1 with the eventual champions, Italy, and finished above Peru. Algeria took four points, beating Chile as well as West Germany and only a dubious 1-1 draw between the Germans and Austria prevented the North Africans from reaching the second stage. It was easily the best showing by any African country at the finals of a World Cup.

Now, far from regretting the opening of the competition, the Europeans ought to be hoping that the dark continent can rescue football from the problems it has created for itself.

For many years the game has been in danger of being destroyed by theorists and narrow-minded coaches, whose rationale is that well trained, ordinary players can stifle, frustrate and nullify better players. The seeds were sewn by Alf Ramsey's wingless wonders in the 1966 World Cup. Since then negative football has triumphed too often.

Even the Brazilians, whose teams had taken the beautiful game onto a different plane in the 1950s, 1960s and early 1970s, became infected. They tried to play "European" football in West Germany in 1974 and the infection stayed with them in 1978 and disappeared only in 1982. The men in the green and gold were the outstanding team in Spain, but they threw away their quarter-final with Italy.

The pendulum of world dominance swings between Europe and South America because, usually, the World Cup alternates between the two continents. No European team has won any of the five World Cups held in South America and only Brazil, of South American countries, has triumphed in Europe. European countries tend to do better in terms of finalists and semi-finalists but that is because the old continent still has the biggest concentration of teams and players.

Perhaps if Havelange develops his ideas to the full and gives the World Cup to Africa, or Asia, or North America the game's power base will crumble even more.

The World Cup is a relative newcomer. It began in 1930 and it was not until 1950 that England, the birthplace of the game and its chief missionary, deigned to join in. England began playing international football in 1872 and considered

● Cameroon Captain Roger with the Africa Cup

themselves to be the best team in the world until the rude awakening of the 1950 tournament when they lost 1-0 to the United States. One British newspaper considered the wire service which sent the shock scoreline from Belo Horizonte had made a mistake and printed it as 10-1!

England did not do well in a World Cup until 1966 when they beat West Germany at Wembley, but then the odds were heavily stacked in their favour. Not surprisingly, the home team usually does well. Thus Sweden reached the 1958 final and Chile the 1962 semi-finals.

In Europe, despite England's early chauvinistic attitude, the power bases are West Germany in the north and Italy in the south. Italy have won the World Cup three times and appeared in the 1970 final, West Germany have won it twice and appeared in two other finals.

In South America the two most powerful teams are Brazil and Uruguay, with the Brazilians being the first to win the trophy three times and the Uruguayans the inaugural champions in 1930 and also the winners in 1950.

But Brazil, apart from when they are flirting with the commando approach of someone like Claudio Coutinho, contain a dimension which evades the others.

The game they show to the outside world is occasionally marred by brutality — the battle of Berne in 1954, the harshness in West Germany in 1974 — but even this can be excused by the knowledge that such tactics are clearly foreign to them.

> The first black player to be picked by England was full-back Viv Anderson, then with Nottingham Forest, now with Arsenal, for the match with Czechoslovakia in 1979. Since then eight other black players have won selection — Laurie Cunningham, Cyrille Regis, Luther Blissett, Ricky Hill, Danny Thomas, John Barnes, Mark Chamberlain and Brian Stein.

The player who has appeared in most World Cup final competitions is Mexican goalkeeper Antonio Carbajal. He played in the 1950 finals and ended with his fifth appearance in England in 1966.

Mario Zagalo, the Brazilian left-winger is the only man to play in and manage a World Cup winning team. He won winner's medals in 1958 and 1962 and managed the 1970 side.

● Viv Anderson

● Algeria's World Cup squad

● Morocco's World Cup qualifying squad

● Nigeria's star Humphrey Ebobor

• Pélé scores

• John Barnes

• Brian Stein shoots

As Brian Glanville wrote of the 1950 tournament in his *The History of the World Cup* "Black players had long since transformed and dominated Brazilian football. Their extraordinary reflexes, at once balletic and explosive, their conception of the game, so radically new, so explosively effective, at one point in the tournament caused a Roman newspaper to cry *'Come resitere'* – How to resist?"

Other countries have assimilated black players, although none to the same extent as Brazil where soccer provides both an emotional release and a way out of misery and poverty. Portugal's Eusebio, that marvellously gifted forward who illuminated the 1966 tournament, was born in Mozambique and even in Britain there are signs of Africa's emergence. Most of the black players have Caribbean roots but their origins are in Africa. The England squad for Mexico 1986 should contain at least two black players, John Barnes and Viv Anderson, but they are just the tip of the iceberg. Teams in the English League frequently contain a percentage of black players well over the national average.

Players from Africa are now beginning to show through Stein of South Africa and now England at Luton, Nwajiobi who plays alongside him, and Chiedozie, of Tottenham who picked Nigeria rather than England.

The veteran Northern Ireland manager Billy Bingham thinks that Nigeria will soon be world beaters. Crowds of 50,000 are commonplace in Nigeria, passions run high and players are treated like gods ... just like in Brazil. Even in South Africa the white men play cricket and rugby and the blacks play football before huge crowds.

If ever poverty and starvation can be held at bay and black Africans can dream of circuses knowing that the bread is safe in the larder, then the world of football may never be the same again.

When their self-confidence is not eroded by the nagging fear that they must match the Europeans at their own physical game, they turn to the style they play at home, inside the Maracana, a style which marries the Latin influence of the Portuguese settlers to the explosive strengths of players whose natural home is Africa.

GREAT TEAMS

World Cup football has been dominated by Brazil and Italy, West Germany and Uruguay, yet there are other teams whose influence on the game has been immense, teams who finished with nothing except the satisfaction of knowing they raised the expectations of spectators all over the world.

Austria in the 1930s, Hungary in the 1950s and Holland in the 1970s transformed the game. All three grew up around great players, but also introduced tactical systems to the world that created the fashion for the next few years.

Austria, managed by Hugo Meisl, were the Wunderteam of the 1930s with Sindelar, a slight, ball-playing centre-forward, and Smistik, an authoritive, attacking centre-half. They just lost 4-3 to England at Stamford Bridge in 1932, lost to the champions Italy in the 1934 World Cup semi-finals and then beat England 2-1 in Vienna in 1936.

Hungary were indebted to Ferenc Puskas, the Galloping Major, whose left foot was both a rapier and a club. But the team also contained the fair-haired Sandor Kocsis, nicknamed Golden Head, the magisterial wing-half Joszef Bozsik and Nandor Hidegkuti, the man who created havoc in Wembley in 1953.

Hidegkuti played as a withdrawn centre-forward, leaving England's centre-half Billy Wright with no one to mark and the England defence in absolute confusion. That 6-3 defeat was England's first by a foreign team at Wembley and helped make the Hungarians favourites for the 1954 World Cup in Switzerland. Ultimately they were to fail, beaten as much as anything by an injury to Puskas which kept him out of the quarter and semi-finals and affected him in the final.

The team broke up after that. The Budapest uprising put down by the Russians in 1956 sent Puskas and Kocsis to Spain where Puskas linked up with Di Stefano to fashion the amazing Real Madrid team. Ironically when coaches sought the secret of that Real Madrid team they bumped up against Puskas's commonsense. "We were just a bunch of good players who came together at the right time," said the Galloping Major, "plus they turned a blind eye to our   smuggling!"

• Johan Cruyff in the 1974 World Cup Final

• The great Puskas

With Johan Cruyff providing the inspiration, Holland were undoubtedly the best team in the 1974 World Cup finals, introducing the concept of Total Football. Cruyff, an athletic gifted conductor who roamed the field, now a striker, now a winger, now an inside forward, sometimes even a full back, was the team's lynch pin, but there were other fine players: Johan Neeskens, who followed Cruyff to Spain, Rudi Krol, whose amazing long range shooting provoked memories of Puskas, and Rensenbrink, who was to be injured in the final, a match which Holland lost despite going ahead with a penalty in the first minute.

Thirteen goals in six games in 1958 made French striker Just Fontaine the highest scorer in a World Cup final tournament. An illustration of how the game has changed is that the leading scorer in the 1982 World Cup was Paolo Rossi of Italy with six in seven matches.

Geoff Hurst of England in 1966 is the only man to have scored a hat trick in a World Cup final, but the record number of goals by an individual in a World Cup final tournament match is four, a feat which has been achieved eight times.

The Dutch also reached the 1978 final in Buenos Aires, but this time there was no Cruyff. He stayed at home, worried by kidnap threats. Who knows what Holland would have achieved with him.

Of course the world's big four nations — West Germany, Italy, Uruguay, and Brazil — also introduced new tactical patterns. Italy perfected *Catenaccio,* refining it to a negative, fear obsessed defensive web but this was in the 1960s. Their greatest teams must be those of the 1930s, which won the World Cup in Italy in 1934 and retained it in France four years later. The first had the Argentinian's Luisito Monti, who won a runners up medal with his native country in 1930, at centre-half, and Raimondo Orsi on the wing who missed that final through injury, plus the inside-forwards Meazza and Ferrari. The influential goalkeeper Giampiero Combi was captain in 1934. By 1938 there were only two men left, Ferrari and Meazza.

West Germany, winners in 1954 and finalists in 1966, produced surely their best team in 1974, although they were hard pressed by the Dutch. This was another total football team. They removed the influential Franz Beckenbauer from the midfield — he had marked Bobby Charlton in the 1970 quarter-final — to libero and created a new style.

This team contained some remarkable talent, expressive players welded together with typical German efficiency . . . interesting how nationalistic clichés show up clearly on the football field: Paul Brietner, who was to take over from Beckenbauer as the *eminence grise* of Bayern Munich, the strong running Uli Hoeness, the elegant Wolfgang Overath and the deadly goalscorer Gerd Muller. No wonder they played so well together . . . six of them had been in the losing semi-final team four years earlier. The team was not to survive until Argentina in 1978, though. Just as Cruyff decided not to participate so did Beckenbauer. He went instead to the New York Cosmos.

Picking the best Brazilian team is difficult. Could it be the 1950 side with Jair, Ademir and Zizinho, at last taking the skills that graced the Copacabana to the Maracana Stadium, or the 1958 which introduced 4-2-4, or the mighty 1970 team which won the Jules Rimet trophy for the third time and kept it?

It has really to be a choice between 1958 and 1970 and there is a linking factor — the incomparable Pelé, recognised as the best player the world has seen. He arrived in the 1958 team as a 17-year-old. The Brazilians already had such players as Didi, a majestic inside-forward who perfected the "falling leaf" shot in which the ball curled and seemed to die in mid-air, the two Santoses, Djalma and Nilton, at full back, plus the hard working Zagalo on the left wing. Then there was Gar-

● Paul Breitner West Germany takes on Scirea of Italy

● Italy 1934

● England 1966

World Cup 1930-82 Final Series

Country	P	W	D	L	F	A	Country	P	W	D	L	F	A	Country	P	W	D	L	F	A
Brazil	57	37	10	10	134	62	Switzerland	18	5	2	11	28	44	North Korea	4	1	1	2	5	9
West Germany	54	31	11	12	122	78	Scotland	14	3	5	6	20	29	Turkey	3	1	0	2	10	11
Italy	43	24	9	10	74	46	Peru	15	4	3	8	19	31	Honduras	3	0	2	1	2	3
Argentina	34	16	5	13	63	50	Portugal	6	5	0	1	17	8	Israel	3	1	0	2	1	3
England	29	13	8	8	40	29	Norway	10	3	4	3	11	17	Kuwait	3	0	1	2	2	6
Uruguay	29	14	5	10	57	39	Mexico	24	3	4	17	21	62	Morocco	3	0	1	2	2	6
Hungary	29	14	3	12	85	48	Belgium	14	3	2	9	15	30	Australia	3	0	1	2	0	5
USSR	24	12	5	7	37	25	East Germany	6	2	2	2	5	5	Colombia	3	0	1	2	5	11
Poland	21	12	4	5	38	22	Paraguay	7	2	2	3	12	19	Iran	3	0	1	2	2	8
Yugoslavia	28	12	4	12	47	36	USA	7	3	0	4	12	21	Norway	1	0	0	1	1	2
Sweden	28	11	6	11	48	46	Wales	5	1	3	1	4	4	Egypt	1	0	0	1	2	4
France	27	11	3	13	59	50	Rumania	8	2	1	5	12	17	South Korea	2	0	0	2	0	16
Austria	23	11	2	10	38	40	Algeria	3	2	0	1	5	5	New Zealand	3	0	0	3	2	12
Spain	23	8	5	10	26	30	Bulgaria	12	0	4	8	9	29	Haiti	3	0	0	3	2	14
Czechoslovakia	25	8	5	12	34	40	Tunisia	3	1	1	1	3	2	Zaire	3	0	0	3	0	14
Holland	16	8	3	5	32	19	Cameroon	3	0	3	0	1	1	Bolivia	3	0	0	3	0	16
Chile	21	7	3	11	26	32	Cuba	3	1	1	1	5	12	El Salvador	6	0	0	6	1	22

ncha, the "little bird", a right-winger who had suffered from olio as a boy.

Pelé was introduced in the quarter-final, and scored the oal which defeated Wales 1-0. In the final Brazil beat Sweden -2 and Pelé scored twice. One was an amazing overhead ck, quick turn and half volley which must be rated as one of e best in a World Cup final. Pelé played only one full match 1962 before pulling a thigh muscle and he was brutally acked out of the 1966 finals by Morais of Portugal. But he as back for the 1970 tournament, and at his physical peak. arrincha's place had been taken by Jairzinho, a strong irres-ible runner, Tostao had shaken off a serious eye injury to ay at centre-forward with high intelligence and deadly fect, Gerson, a balding genius at inside-left, and Rivelino a ooding withdrawn left-winger with a remarkable shot, made the creative unit. The defence was marshalled around the aptain, Carlos Alberto, who was to score the last goal in the -2 win in the Final over Italy.

Hard to choose but the 1958 side must get the vote.

The England team which won the 1966 World Cup is the e best remembered . . . the team with which Alf Ramsey troduced 4-4-2. Bobby Charlton with his exciting running d long range shooting, Bobby Moore, so composed at the ck, Gordon Banks, a goalkeeper par excellence, Geoff urst, the only man to score a hat trick in a World Cup final, e tireless Alan Ball . . . all of them written into the English otball legend.

But no one argues that the golden age of English football was the 1930s and who knows how England would have fared had they not broken with FIFA in 1928. Those 1930s teams were a match for anybody. They beat the Austrian Wunder-team in 1932 and then beat Italy 3-2 in 1934 in the November after the Italians' World Cup victory in Rome.

These were the years of the W formation, the years of goalkeepers like Harry Hibbs and Vic Woodley, of full-backs like George Male and Eddie Hapgood, of centre-halves such as Stan Cullis, wing-halves such as Joe Mercer and Wilf Copping, wingers of the calibre of Joe Hulme, Cliff Bastin and Stanley Matthews, inside-forwards like David Jack and Raich Carter, battering ram centre-forwards like Dixie Dean, Tommy Lawton and Ted Drake.

In those days England ruled the world, but preferred to play against Scotland, Wales and Northern Ireland.

Goalscoring and Attendances in World Cup Finals

Year	Country	Matches	Goals (avge)	Attendance (avge)
1930	Uruguay	18	70 (3.8)	434,500 (24,138)
1934	Italy	17	70 (4.1)	395,000 (23,235)
1938	France	18	84 (4.6)	483,000 (26,833)
1950	Brazil	22	88 (4.0)	1,332,000 (60,772)
1954	Switzerland	26	140 (5.3)	943,000 (36,270)
1958	Sweden	35	126 (3.6)	868,000 (24,800)
1962	Chile	32	89 (2.7)	776,000 (24,250)
1966	England	32	89 (2.7)	1,614,677 (50,458)
1970	Mexico	32	95 (2.9)	1,673,975 (52,311)
1974	West Germany	38	97 (2.5)	1,774,022 (46,684)
1978	Argentina	38	102 (2.6)	1,610,215 (42,374)
1982	Spain	52	146 (2.8)	1,766,277 (33,967)

Brazil 1970

● West Germany 1974

TENNIS

World tennis has known two outstanding eras: the Frenchmen of the Twenties and Thirties and the Australians of the Fifties and Sixties. A third great era seemed to be dawning in 1985, that of the Swedes, a decade after the trail had been blazed for them so spectacularly by Bjorn Borg.

Great Britain, too, had brief years of supremacy thanks to Fred Perry and Bunny Austin. And the Americans, from the time of Big Bill Tilden through to the tempestuous talent of John McEnroe, have launched a ceaseless challenge.

But none of the eras, not even the Australians', burned so brightly as that magnificent period in French tennis history when the world was put to the sword by the Four Musketeers. "All for one and one for all" became the chivalrous, swashbuckling motto of Jacques ("Toto") Brugnon, Jean Borotra, Henri Cochet and Rene Lacoste as, between 1924-32, they collected 19 major titles and held the Davis Cup (the men's world team championship) from 1927-33.

It was a reign never since equalled. The Australians, under their legendary captain and coach Harry Hopman, had a far longer winning period. But they were never quite so consistently supreme, falling occasionally to the American challenge.

The French quartet spanned a decade in their ages, from the eldest Brugnon down to the youngest Lacoste. In 1923 when they conducted their first Davis Cup campaign as a foursome, against Ireland in Dublin, Brugnon was a month past his 28th birthday and Lacoste was still a month short of being 19.

The four emerged from quite different backgrounds. Brugnon and Lacoste were from Paris, Cochet from the industrial city of Lyon and Borotra from the Basque country of the south west.

Brugnon was the least successful in singles, yet he was the cornerstone of the Musketeers' triumphs with his dependable, unifying nature. He was a master of doubles play, brilliant on the volley and return of serve (he was never beaten in mixed doubles with Suzanne Lenglen) but it was his unfailing charm that most impressed and Henri Cochet once remarked: "In all the victories of the French team Toto had a role that surpassed all he had already done with his racquet."

• Bill Tilden

Borotra, the Bounding Basque, was the quintessential Frenchman, hand-kissing, arm-waving, a magnetic extrovert who announced his annual arrival at Wimbledon with gifts of fruit and flowers. Borotra had a natural athleticism which he allied to a flair for tennis in devastating fashion. His antics infuriated players like Tilden, but the crowd were captivated. Once, during a Wimbledon doubles with Toto Brugnon, Borotra chased a wide ball and crashed into the stands, onto the laps of two startled women. He managed to get the ball into play and then graciously kissed the ladies' hands in an extravagant fashion while Brugnon somehow kept the rally going with three shots. Just as Brugnon seemed certain to lose the point, Borotra swept from the stand to smash away the winner.

Cochet, most successful of the four in terms of singles titles with four French Opens, two Wimbledons and one USA championship, was a game, gutsy competitor with the world's finest overhead and a magical half volley. For him the impossible was easy; too often, however, his talent led him to experiment and make potentially simple shots impossible.

Lacoste was the greatest contrast of them all, a pale studious youngster whose father had told him to give up sport at 15 because he was too frail. By the age of 20, however, he was champion of Wimbledon and, a year later, champion of the USA. A machine-like baseliner, Lacoste worked harder in training than any contemporary, spending hours on court and then further hours at home in front of a full length mirror. His health was finally to tell on him. In 1929 he was rushed to hospital with pneumonia and from his sick bed announced his retirement. He was 25.

The Four Musketeers had become Three and they were to need the advantage of their home clay courts to retain the Davis Cup until 1933 when Britain's Fred Perry and Bunny Austin beat them 3-2 to initiate three years of British rule.

Between 1937-49 the USA won the Davis Cup six times with players such as Donald Budge, Bobby Riggs and Jack Kramer. But as the Fifties began, so did the era of the Australians. The first wave was led by Frank Sedgman. Then in 1953 came those teenage tearaways Lew Hoad and Ken Rosewall, followed by Neale Fraser, Rod Laver and Roy Emmerson. Finally, as the incomparable Laver turned professional in 1963, came Fred Stolle, John Newcombe and Tony Roche.

• Henri Cochet

● 1900-1926   ● 1927-1945   ● 1946-1966   ● 1967-1986

● Bobby Riggs

● Newcombe and Roche

The longest set in a men's singles was in the Heart of America Tournament in Kansas City in 1968 when Australia's John Brown beat America's Bill Brown 36-34 6-1.

● Ken Rosewall

Altogether the Australians were to win the Davis Cup 15 years out of 18 between 1950-67. The other three years they were the beaten finalists against America.

In major singles tournaments throughout the world the Australians reigned supreme as well. Between 1950-70 they won Wimbledon 13 times, the US Championship 14 times, the French Open ten times and their own Australian Open 18 times.

These were boom years as the sport gathered worldwide appeal. The advent of Open tennis, with professionals and amateurs classed as one, would come in 1968 and there

> The youngest player to win a match at Wimbledon was America's Kathy Rinaldi who, at 14 years and 92 days, beat South African Sue Rollinson 6-3 2-6 9-7 in the 1981 first round.

> In 1980 a panel of eight eminent judges voted the 1937 Davis Cup match between Don Budge (USA) and Gottfried Von Cramm (Germany) as the finest ever. Budge, trailing 4-1 in the final set, eventually won the deciding rubber 6-8 5-7 6-4 6-2 8-6.

● John McEnroe

would be controversial, highly-paid circuses such as Lamar Hunt's World Championship Tennis, based in Dallas. Yet they were also immensely friendly years with the Australian champions spreading their good natured chumminess over a can of beer.

Suddenly, however, tennis became the province of pop-style hero worship. In 1973 the 17-year-old Bjorn Borg was besieged at Wimbledon and a year later the brash, snarling Jimmy Connors won the title to the accompaniment of girlish screams. Tennis had changed and so had its powerbase.

Sweden, after 50 years of trying, reached the Davis Cup final for the first time in 1975 and promptly beat Czechoslovakia 3-2 thanks to the brilliance of Borg, who won both his singles and the doubles with Ove Bengtson. Between 1973 and 1980, in fact, Borg set the highest sequence of singles victories in the Davis Cup with 33.

But Sweden were a one-man team. Until the early Eighties that is . . . as Mats Wilander, Anders Jarryd, Henrik Sundstrom, Joakim Nystrom and Stefan Edberg emerged to establish them as the premier nation in the world. In 1983 they again reached the Davis Cup final. But Wilander, Nystrom, Jarryd and Hans Simonsson were beaten in Sydney by an unfancied Australian team with a pride in the past.

They were back the next year and this time made no mistake with a resounding 4-1 victory in Gothenburg over America who included John McEnroe, Jimmy Connors and doubles specialist Peter Fleming. Even the heroics of new Wimbledon champion Boris Becker could not halt Sweden the following year as they retained the trophy against West Germany.

> Bjorn Borg won 42 successive singles at Wimbledon

● Bjorn Borg

America's superiority in women's tennis, aided by the immensely powerful Virginia Slims circuit, was clearly illustrated by their seven consecutive victories in the Federatio Cup (the women's world team championship) betwee 1976-82.

It was the time of the veteran Billie Jean King, the ne queen Chris Evert and the emerging Tracy Austin and Andre Jaeger. And in 1982 there arrived the freshly naturalised Ma tina Navratilova.

Had Miss Navratilova chosen to remain a Czech the fac of women's world tennis might well have changed, such ha been her impact throughout the Eighties. Between 1981-8 she dominated Wimbledon, winning the world's premi tournament five times in a row to make it seven times in a The left hander who combines near-masculine power wi all-court, feline grace held all four major titles – Frenc

Wimbledon, USA and Australian – in 1983-84 to accomplish the modern version of the Grand Slam.

Who can argue against her as the supreme women's player of all time?

The French would, for a start. They would point in no uncertain fashion to Suzanne Lenglen, La Grande Suzanne of the egotistical, driving father and the salmon-pink bandeau, who was the first superstar of tennis in the Twenties. Miss Lenglen (1899-1938) survived two match points to beat the 40-year-old Dorothy Lambert Chambers at Wimbledon in 1919 and thereafter was beaten only once until her retirement

• Helen Wills Moody

The most successful Federation Cup player has been Chris Evert Lloyd (USA). In 28 ties from 1977 to 1982 she won 42 out of 43 matches, 28 out of 28 singles and 14 out of 15 doubles.

1926. That one loss came against American Molla Mallory in the 1921 US Championships, when La Lenglen was suffering from the after-effects of bronchitis. In the revenge match, in the 1922 Wimbledon final, Mrs Mallory was despatched 6-2 6-0 in 27 minutes.

Jaundice caused Suzanne to default from the 1924 Wimbledon title. She had realised all was not well when she dropped a set against Elizabeth Ryan (USA), one of only three sets she lost during singles in the seven years of her reign in which she won the Wimbledon singles and doubles (with Elizabeth Ryan) in 1919, 1920, 1921, 1922, 1923, 1925; and the French singles and doubles (with various partners) in 1920, 1921, 1922, 1923, 1925, 1926.

The succession from one great champion to another was immediate. In 1927 Helen Wills Moody, a beautiful woman with a poker face and relentless baseline style, won the first of her eight Wimbledon crowns. In nine attempts from 1927-

1938 she lost only once, to Kitty McKane in 1924, and from 1927-32 won every major singles championship – except the Australian which she never attempted – without losing a set.

The start of the Fifties belonged to the third great woman player, Maureen Connolly who, at the age of 16 won the US singles title in 1951 and thereafter lost only four more matches in a career cut short when she broke her leg in a riding accident and retired in 1954. "Little Mo" was never beaten in singles at Wimbledon, winning in 1952, 1953 and 1954 and her fearsome groundstrokes, hit with stunning power and accuracy, brought her the Grand Slam of all four major titles in 1953 – the first woman to achieve it.

Seventeen years on came the second Grand Slam, from Margaret Smith of Australia, a marvellous athlete, superbly fit and with an unusually heavy serve for a woman. "Big Marge" used her formidable reach on the volley and huge stamina to collect a record number of international titles in singles, doubles and mixed doubles and would surely have won even more but for occasional, inexplicable lapses of confidence. She captured three Wimbledons, five US Opens, five French Opens and 11 Australian Opens.

At the same time as the young Miss Smith, now Mrs Court, was making her way so was a young American, Billie Jean Moffitt, now Mrs King. The fast-talking, fast-volleying, fast-thinking Miss Moffitt went on to reach nine Wimbledon singles finals and win six of them between 1963-75, despite fearsome knee injuries. Her 1979 doubles win with Martina Navratilova gave her a record 20th Wimbledon title, surpassing the 19 held by Elizabeth Ryan. Billie Jean also took four US singles titles and one apiece from France and Australia. The founder of the women's professional tour, she struck the mightiest of blows for women's tennis in 1973 when she beat Bobby Riggs, the 1939 Wimbledon champion and then 55 years of age, 6-4 6-3 6-3 at Houston, Texas in front of the biggest ever crowd for a single match, 30,472. Riggs had previously demolished Margaret Court on one of her crisis of confidence days.

Billie Jean's autumn coincided with the spring of Chris Evert, now Mrs Lloyd, a baseliner like Helen Wills Moody and just as poker faced on court. Mrs Lloyd, first woman to earn a million dollars in tournament prize money, holds the highest winning match streak for women with 56 consecutive successes in 1974. She also holds the record for the most consecutive wins on one surface with 125 on clay and from 1971 until 1983 had reached the semi-final or better of every Grand Slam event she entered, winning three Wimbledons, six US Opens, two French and one Australian singles titles.

Martina Navratilova   • Billie Jean King   • Elizabeth Ryan and Chris Evert Lloyd

SQUASH

The soldiers who guarded the Khyber Pass in the 1920s could never have dreamt of the significant contribution their presence would make to the history of squash. The game then was mostly the preserve of the British public schools and services, a sport to be enjoyed in the tennis off-season or as a pre-sundown relaxation in the colonies.

At an open air court in Peshawar (near India's border with Afghanistan), an eight-year-old called Hashim Khan got a job as a ball boy for five rupees a month. Squash fascinated him, and after the officers retired to the bar he would climb down from the back wall. And under the moonlight he would have his own game, 'Hashim v Hashim.' The racket was too big for him, so he held it well down the handle, an unorthodox grip which he maintained throughout his career.

Hashim saved his rupees to pay for lessons and progressed to become club coach himself. But it was not until 1944 – when the fame of his mastery over all-comers was beginning to spread – that he entered a tournament. At the age of 28 he became champion of All India.

After partition, the 5ft 4in barrel-chested Hashim was sent to London as Pakistan's ambassador at the British Open. From 1950, he won the title seven years out of eight, the last when he was 41.

The game had been known since the 1830s when Harrow School, adapting from a crude version played in courtyards near the City, introduced a softer ball ("squash") to rackets. But it was Hashim, who founded a tradition and a dynasty. Egyptians Amr Bey (first man to win the Open and the Amateur in the same season, 1932) and Mahmoud Karim dominated the sport either side of the Second World War. Now Hashim's style, based on the aggression and survival instincts associated with the Pathan people from the foothills of the Himalayas, blunted the ambition of the touch players. He was the forerunner of the dedicated professionals. And when Hashim wasn't winning, cousin Roshan, nephew Mohibullah or younger brother Azam were.

Hashim's aura began the popularising of the sport which accelerated when the left-handed Cornishman, Jonah Barrington, took up the theme "Anything you Khan do, I can do better."

Jonah was searching for a purpose to his life in 1964, having been sent down after a year at University College, Dublin, where he was reading history and drinking ten pints of Guinness a day. His biggest achievement in squash was to have scraped into the comparatively weak Cornwall team. He was out of work when a friend, who played him only because Jonah's more proficient brother was unavailable, told him there was a clerical post going at the Squash Rackets Association's offices in London.

When Barrington got the job it was the start of a remarkable transformation, an obsession which was to see him rise to British Open champion in two years. He was inspired by the Khans. He persuaded Roshan's brother Nasrullah, pro at the prestigious Lansdowne Club, to coach him. And he practised regularly with Azam, who was working at Shepherd's Bush.

Barrington, always publicity conscious, promised the Press "I'll be world champion" and kept his word. Between 1966, when he was 25, and 1973, he won six Opens. His rivalry with Australian Geoff Hunt is legendary. Hunt, six years younger, eventually succeeded Jonah and won eight Opens, but not before he had followed the Briton's example of gruelling training.

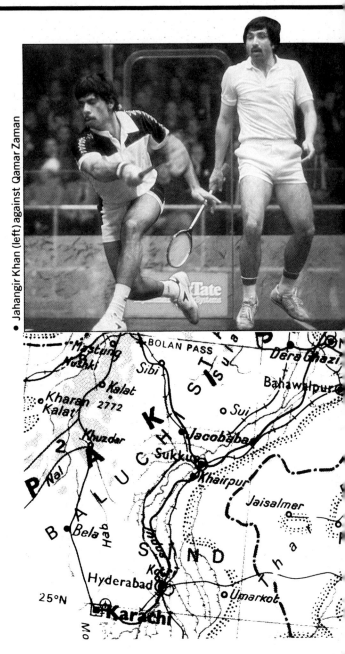

● Jahangir Khan (left) against Qamar Zaman

Hunt's last great achievement, when he won the 1981 British Open to soccer-style roars of encouragement from the spectators, epitomised his strength. At 34, he mentally and physically outlasted the latest of the Khans, Jahangir, then 1... By that time professional squash was on stage – a glass bac... court being mounted at the Churchill Theatre, Bromley. The next development was a transportable Perspex court, allow... ing viewing through all four sides, so that 3,000 were able... see the Open at Wembley Conference Centre in 1985, whe... Jahangir took his fourth title. That year Jahangir also won h... fifth World Open, which had come into being in 1975.

Jahangir, son of Roshan, had then been unbeaten fo... nearly five years. He had been world amateur champion at 1... and is programmed to regain for Pakistan the record of Britis... Open wins. By the end of 1985, Jahangir's dominance wa... restricting his rivals to only a few points per match. The Kha... empire lived on majestically. The women's game grew, too,... the 1980s, although in some respects they could claim... have been the trailblazers. Their first British Open was... 1922, nine years before the men's. The Cave sisters, Nan... and Joyce, were pioneers, winning three times each in t... early years.

• Heather Mckay of Australia, one of the most outstanding champions in any sport who was unbeaten for 16 years

During the 1950s, Surrey's Janet Shardlow, a tennis player good enough to make the Wightman Cup squad and appear at 14 Wimbledons, dominated the scene, winning the British Open ten times. And the finest squash champion of them all, Heather McKay, was also a convertee from tennis.

Heather was one of 11 children of a baker and his wife from Queanbeyan, New South Wales. She took up squash to improve her fitness for tennis and hockey at the age of 17 and three years later, in 1962, travelled to Britain as Australian champion. She lost the final of the Scottish Open to Fran Marshall — and that was the last defeat of her entire career.

She towered over the British Open for 16 seasons, retiring as World Champion to Canada, where she promptly took up racquetball and became their best player within a year.

The women's game in Britain has gained greater depth in the past decade and this was emphasised in 1985 when Martine Le Moignan, Alison Cumings, Lucy Soutter and Lisa Opie won the World Team Championship for England. The New Zealander Susan Devoy confirmed her superiority by taking the individual tournament. However, 18-year-old Miss Soutter promised much for the future, taking the junior world title in the same year as she became British senior champion.

• *Above:* Hashim Khan

• *Above right:* Geoff Hunt

• *Right:* World Champion Sue Devoy (rear) against Lisa Opie

BASEBALL

The New York Yankees won 33 American League championships between 1921 and 1981, going on to win 22 World Series.

Pete Rose, with 4,204 at the end of 1985, had recorded most hits. Ty Cobb made 4,191 and Hank Aaron 3,771.

Hank Aaron hit most homers, 755, and batted in most runs, 2297. Babe Ruth is second in both lists with 714 and 2,211.

● L.A. Dodgers v San Diego

oner Doubleday was credited with inventing baseball at ooperstown, New York, in 1839. But it is now generally ccepted that it evolved from English rounders.

In fact, an early reference to rounders in mid 18th century nglish literature refers to it as base-ball. The development of e game is, however, entirely due to American genius. And e siting of baseball's Hall of Fame at Cooperstown preserves e Doubleday legend.

The early rules were drawn up in 1845 by Alexander Cart-right. His club, the Knickerbockers, lost the first recorded atch the following year by 23-1 to the New York Nine at the ysian Fields, New Jersey. Refinements quickly followed and 1857 the first official rule-book, edited by Henry Chadwick, as published.

The game carried on developing into the elite product of day – the American major leagues who draw talent from all ver the baseball-playing world. Three major evolutionary eps have taken place since the formation of the first major ague, the National in 1876.

The first was the recognition of the American League in 903. The leagues produce a champion club, after a 162-ame season, who then contest the sport's showpiece – the orld Series in October.

The next leap forward came immediately after the First orld War with the emergence of baseball's greatest figure. abe Ruth, the Sultan of Swat, almost single-handedly, hanged the whole emphasis from defence to offence. In 919 he set a seasonal home run record of 29 and within eight ears his prodigious power had lifted that to 60. So popular as he that a chocolate bar – the Baby Ruth – was named fter him. It is still marketed today.

The third change came in 1947 with the lifting of the nwritten colour bar when the Brooklyn Dodgers signed Jac-ie Robinson. This paved the way for a succession of great lack players including Hank Aaron who was to beat Ruth's areer homer record.

Other significant events have included the uprooting of lubs right across the Continent, notably the Dodgers from lew York to Los Angeles and the Giants from New York to San rancisco. But New York still has the greatest of all teams – le Yankees who have been dominant since the Twenties. Vinning has always meant everything to the Yankees, the Best Team Money Can Buy".

The importance of statistics means players are judged on easonal targets. Hitters can be loosely divided into those with echnique and those with power. The technicians are judged n the frequency of hitting safely to reach first base or beyond.

The leading technical hitters achieve this more than three mes for every ten times at-bat, giving an average of .300 or nore. The batting title goes to the man with the best average. le will have hit successfully more than 200 times during the ear.

Power hitters are judged on the number of home runs they it and the number of runs they bat in (RBI's) – advancing layers ahead to score. More than 30 homers and 100 RBI's epresent a fine season.

Hitters have to contend with pitchers who employ a astball of up to 100mph, changes of pace and pitches that urve or slide. Pitchers are either starters or relievers. Starters xpect to pitch between 25 and 40 times a season and their enchmark is to be on the winning side 20 times.

Relievers play in the majority of games and pitch in the losing innings. They are credited with saves if they maintain ne starter's winning position or wins if they reverse a losing

● The Cardinal's Willie McGee (51) reaches base

Joe Jackson, one of the players in the Chicago White Sox bribes scandal of 1919, is the only player to bat .400 but not win the seasonal batting title.

Cy Young pitched most winning games, 511. Walter Johnson, 416, lies second with Grover Alexander and Christy Mathewson sharing third on 373.

Baseball – World Series

Year	Winners	Losers
1946	St Louis Cardinals	Boston Red Sox
1947	New York Yankees	Brooklyn Dodgers
1948	Cleveland Indians	Boston Braves
1949	New York Yankees	Brooklyn Dodgers
1950	New York Yankees	Philadelphia Phillies
1951	New York Yankees	New York Giants
1952	New York Yankees	Brooklyn Dodgers
1953	New York Yankees	Brooklyn Dodgers
1954	New York Giants	Cleveland Indians
1955	Brooklyn Dodgers	New York Yankees
1956	New York Yankees	Brooklyn Dodgers
1957	Milwaukee Braves	New York Yankees
1958	New York Yankees	Milwaukee Braves
1959	Los Angeles Dodgers	Chicago White Sox
1960	Pittsburgh Pirates	New York Yankees
1961	New York Yankees	Cincinnati Reds
1962	New York Yankees	San Francisco Giants
1963	Los Angeles Dodgers	New York Yankees
1964	St Louis Cardinals	New York Yankees
1965	Los Angeles Dodgers	Minnesota Twins
1966	Baltimore Orioles	Los Angeles Dodgers
1967	St Louis Cardinals	Boston Red Sox
1968	Detroit Tigers	St Louis Cardinals
1969	New York Mets	Baltimore Orioles
1970	Baltimore Orioles	Cincinnati Reds
1971	Pittsburgh Pirates	Baltimore Orioles
1972	Oakland Athletics	Cincinnati Reds
1973	Oakland Athletics	New York Mets
1974	Oakland Athletics	Los Angeles Dodgers
1975	Cincinnati Reds	Boston Red Sox
1976	Cincinnati Reds	New York Yankees
1977	New York Yankees	Los Angeles Dodgers
1978	New York Yankees	Los Angeles Dodgers
1979	Pittsburgh Pirates	Baltimore Orioles
1980	Philadelphia Phillies	Kansas City Royals
1981	Los Angeles Dodgers	New York Yankees
1982	St Louis Cardinals	Milwaukee Braves
1983	Baltimore Orioles	Philadelphia Phillies
1984	Detroit Tigers	San Diego Padres
1985	Kansas City Royals	St Louis Cardinals

Babe Ruth hit home runs at a higher percentage than anyone. Ralph Kiner holds second place.

Nolan Ryan tops the strike-out list with 4,083. Steve Carlton, 3,920, and Tom Seaver, 3,537, also campaigning in 1985, are second and third.

• Fernando Valenzuela

The Dodgers play the Cardinals

one. All pitchers are judged on the number of runs they give up – excluding fielding errors – known as the earned run average (ERA).

Ty Cobb, the Georgia Peach, was the batting legend of the early 20th century. He made more than 4,000 hits, a record that stood until 1985. He had the highest lifetime batting average of .367 and headed the American League in that discipline in 12 seasons.

Of the early pitchers, Cy Young won most games, 511, and recorded 16 20-win seasons. Walter Johnson won 416 games and did not concede a run in 113 separate games.

The Murderers' Row Yankees of the Twenties emerged with Ruth and Lou Gehrig dominant. Gehrig, the Iron Horse, hit with great power and remained a durable and influential hitter despite suffering from Parkinson's Disease – subsequently known in America as Gehrig's Disease. Star of the National League was Rogers Hornsby who set the modern season batting record of .424.

From the Forties through to the Sixties, the Yankees had more batting heroes. Joltin' Joe DiMaggio, the Yankee Clipper, hit safely in 56 consecutive games in 1941. He gained further celebrity by marrying screen idol Marilyn Monroe. Mickey Mantle became their leading power hitter. He twice hit homers of more than 550ft (167m) and in 1961 recorded 54. But even this was eclipsed by Roger Maris who beat Ruth's record with 61. Ted Williams at Boston was, perhaps, the leading batsman of his age. He retired in 1961 with six batting titles, 521 homers and was the last man to bat .400, in 1941. He was rivalled by Stan Musial of St Louis who lifted seven National League batting titles. Ralph Kiner won seven successive home run titles with Pittsburgh.

These were followed by Atlanta's Aaron and Willie Mays. Both hit with power and accuracy. Aaron passed Ruth's career homer record in 1973. Mays, also outstanding in the field, hit four homers in one game for the Giants in 1961.

Sandy Koufax, of Los Angeles, and Whitey Ford, of the Yankees, were outstanding pitchers despite all this batting talent.

• Dodgers Stadium

The Cincinatti kid

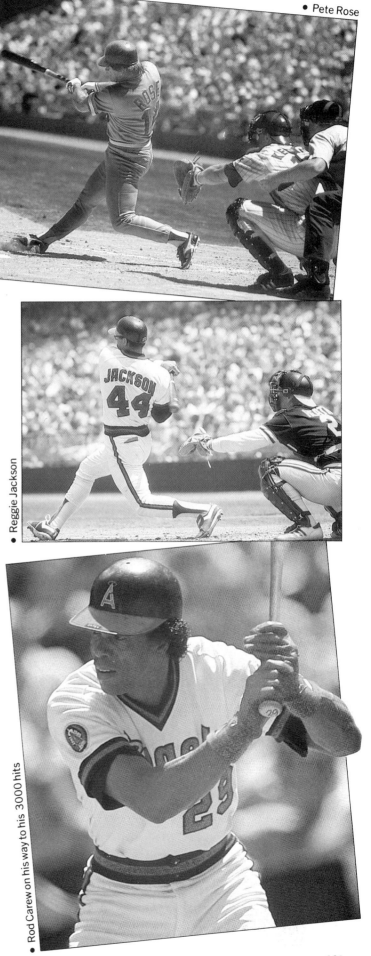

• Pete Rose

• Reggie Jackson

• Rod Carew on his way to his 3000 hits

The most controversial of modern players is power hitter Reggie Jackson, dubbed Mr October for his achievements for the Yankees in the 1977 World Series against the Dodgers. Jackson hit an astonishing four homers from four sucessive swings spread over two games and five homers in all. He achieved even his wish of having a chocolate bar named after himself like Ruth. The Reggie Bar, however, is no longer made.

George Brett of Kansas, with .390 in 1980 and Minnesota's Rod Carew, .388 in 1977, have been close to the .400 season and are certainties for the Hall of Fame.

But in 1985 it was Pete Rose, nicknamed Charley Hustle, who gained baseball immortality by passing Cobb's career hits record of 4,191. President Reagan had a special telephone installed in the Cincinatti dug-out so he could congratulate Rose on setting the new mark. In the same year Nolan Ryan made it to No 1 in the career strike-out list with more than 4,000 to join the pitching greats.

But baseball has a darker side. In 1919 Chicago White Sox players rigged the World Series for gamblers. Maris, and specially Aaron, found much animosity while beating Ruth's home run records. And in the Eighties the sport has been tarnished by pay disputes and even strikes. But it is still a great game. Ernie Harwell described it in his celebrated 1955 homage to the game: "Baseball? It's just a game — as simple as a ball and a bat. Yet as complex as the American spirit it symbolises. It's a sport. Business. And sometimes even religion."

FOOTBALL

• Super Bowl '86, Chicago Bears 46 – New England Patriots 10

The present image of football is that of the 1986 Super Bowl game played by perfectly prepared supermen with intense concentration and dedication to an intricate set of commands, on a carpet inside a stadium fit for the 21st century. It was not always like this. The sport began almost by accident and despite the behemoth strides it has made it still clings to its roots, just as the metaphorical ivy still clings to the walls of the colleges at which it started

Professional football may be about dollars but the game still stubbornly sticks to the past in one respect. It has an ethos that belongs to a different era. It is no coincidence that huge crowds watch fledgling fresh faced boys in college matches, crowds just as big as those that watch the NFL, the sports' most snowbound peak.

Football began when McGill University from Montreal stepped in after the Ivy League fell out over how the game should be played. Harvard's rules were akin to soccer while McGill played rugby as begun by William Webb Ellis at Rugby School more than 50 years before. The two colleges compromised. The first game was played to Harvard's rules, the second to McGill's. Harvard won the first game 3-0, the second was goalless, but no matter. Harvard liked rugby and when Yale and Princeton followed a new game was born.

It evolved quickly, but the next significant move came in 1913 when the Army invited Notre Dame for a match at West Point. Notre Dame were not then the famous 'Irish' who dominated college football for so long. But receiver Knute Rockne, later to be the coach who fashioned the college into one of the totem poles of American life, and his quarter back Gus Dorais perfected the forward pass. The physically inferior college boys sliced the Army into small pieces and the game changed utterly.

The professional game differs slightly from the college game and although it started in 1895 in Latrobe Pennsylvania its main power base before 1920 was in Ohio. Fierce rivalry between towns such as Canton and Massilon led to their football teams employing professionals. Canton signed up the legendary Jim Thorpe who won pentathlon and decathlon medals at the 1912 Olympics only to be stripped of his title when it was realised he had earned money from baseball.

In 1919 a League was formed called the American Professional Football Association including Canton and Massilon and incorporating other mid west towns such as Akron Columbus and Dayton. It was the forerunner of the National Football League which began operation in 1922 and has reigned ever since.

The most dominant team up to the Second World War were from the club which provided the team which crushed the New England Patriots in the New Orleans Super Bowl . . . the mighty Chicago Bears. Originally called the Decatur (Illinois) Staleys they owed their pre-eminence to one man – George Halas, known throughout the football world as Papa Bear.

In 1920 he was manager, coach and a player. His record 98 yd run after catching a fumble cleanly in 1923 stood until 1972, but it was as a coach and innovator that Halas made his greatest mark. He signed the legendary Red Grange, the top college player of the time, and set attendance records in New York for a pro game with 73,000, more than double the best for any other professional game.

While Halas was developing the "T" formation another dynasty was beginning. The Green Bay Packers were on the march. People say the Packers have such fanatical fans because there is little else to do in Green Bay, but they backed

Jim Thorpe

two formidable coaches in Curly Lambeau and Vince Lombardi who brought them glory before and after the second World War. Lambeau's ace was Don Hutson, signed from the University of Alabama in 1935. His first reception as a pro brought a touchdown and in eight of his 11 seasons in the league he was the top pass receiver and in five he scored the highest number of points. With him the Packers won the title in 1936, 1939 and 1944.

Lombardi joined the Packers in 1959 and the Packers won the title in 1961, 1962, 1965, 1966 and 1967 and then took the first two Super Bowls. It was Lombardi who uttered the phrase "Winning isn't everything. It's the only thing." Although on his deathbed in 1970 he said he wished he hadn't said that. What he meant, he claimed, was that striving to win was the important thing. Lombardi's key man was Paul Hornung, who created a record 19 points in a play off game against the New York Giants in 1961.

	Football — Super Bowl Winners	
	Winners	Losers
1967	Green Bay Packers	
1968	Green Bay Packers	Kansas City Chiefs
1969	New York Jets	Oakland Raiders
1970	Kansas City Chiefs	Baltimore Colts
1971	Baltimore Colts	Minnesota Vikings
1972	Dallas Cowboys	Dallas Cowboys
1973	Miami Dolphins	Miami Dolphins
1974	Miami Dolphins	Washington Redskins
1975	Pittsburgh Steelers	Minnesota Vikings
1976	Pittsburgh Steelers	Minnesota Vikings
1977	Oakland Raiders	Dallas Cowboys
1978	Dallas Cowboys	Minnesota Vikings
1979	Pittsburgh Steelers	Denver Broncos
1980	Pittsburgh Steelers	Dallas Cowboys
1981	Oakland Raiders	Los Angeles Rams
1982	San Francisco 49ers	Philadelphia Eagles
1983	Washington Redskins	Cincinnati Bengals
1984	Los Angeles Raiders	Miami Dolphins
1985	San Francisco 49ers	Washington Redskins
1986	Chicago Bears	Miami Dolphins
		New England Patriots

The highest aggregate score in a Super Bowl game was in 1986 when the Chicago Bears beat the New England Patriots by 46-10. Chicago's score was a record for a single team.

• Super Bowl '85, San Francisco 49ers beat the Miami Dolphins 38-16

● A Redskin fan

● Cheerleader in support of the L.A. Raiders

● The gladiators return — Eric Dickerson, Rams

Team Scoring

The greatest number of points accumulated in a single college football game was 222 by Georgia Tech (known as The Rambling Wrecks) against Cumberland University (who did not score a single point) in 1916. The Georgia team score included a remarkable 32 touchdowns.

The National Football League's record is held by the Washington Redskins who beat the New York Giants by 72-41 in 1966. The aggregate score of 113 is also a professional record.

Individual Scoring

The most points scored in a career by a player in the professional ranks is 2,002 by George Blanda between 1949 and 1975. The greatest number of points achieved in a single season is 176 by Paul Hornung of the Green Bay Packers in 1960, when his total included 15 touchdowns. The most points scored in a single game is 40 by Ernie Nevers playing for the Chicago Cardinals against the Chicago Bears in 1929 when he also set a record 6 touchdowns in a game.

In college football, where players have a maximum career of four years, the game record is 43 points by Jim Brown playing for Syracuse against Colgate in 1956. He later went into the movies. The season record is 174 by Lydell Mitchell of Penn State in 1971 and by Mike Rozier of Nebraska in 1983. The career mark of 368 points was set by Luis Zendejas of Arizona State between 1981 and 1984.

Touchdowns

The professional record for the most touchdowns in a career was 126 set by Jim Brown when he played for Cleveland from 1957 to 1965. The most in a season was 24 by John Riggins of Washington Redskins in 1983, while the most in a single game was 6 by Ernie Nevers for Chicago Cardinals v Chicago Bears in 1929; Dub Jones for Cleveland v Chicago Bears in 1951; Gale Sayers for Chicago v San Francisco in 1965.

The most touchdowns in a college game was 7 by Arnold Boykin for Mississippi v Mississippi State in 1951. The season record is 29 by Lydell Mitchell of Penn State in 1971 and Mike Rozier of Nebraska in 1983. The career mark is 59 by Glenn Davis of the Army from 1943 to 1946, and by Tony Dorsett of Pittsburgh from 1973 to 1976.

● John Riggins 24 touchdowns in one season

● The Coliseum, home of the Raiders and two Olympic Games

The National Football League has absorbed two rival leagues. First in 1950 the All-America Football Conference (AAC) merged with the NFL with three teams Cleveland, San Francisco and Baltimore joining. It was Cleveland who were to have the most immediate effect, winning the NFL in their first season. They were led by coach Paul Brown ... but it was another Brown, Jim, who made the Cleveland Browns a national institution. He is regarded as the greatest running back of all time and he set records for rushing which stood until last season.

But it was the challenge of the American Football League in 1960 which was the most vigorous. Launched by Texan millionaire Lamar Hunt, it included such teams as the New York Jets, Miami Dolphins and the Oakland Raiders. It struggled in the early years but was rescued virtually by one man ... the legendary Joe Namath. Broadway Joe, a hero figure in New York's bars and night clubs, signed for the Jets for a then record three year contract worth $427,000.

The two leagues merged in 1966, still run on the same lines but meeting for a Super Bowl. The NFL, through the Packers, swept the first two, but Namath and the Jets gave the AFL its first win. Their opponents, the Baltimore Colts, were overwhelming favourites, but Namath drove the Jets to a 16-7 victory and became part of football folklore.

In 1970 the League was divided into its present form ... two conferences, the National and the American. The National encompassed the NFL teams while three NFL teams, Cleveland, Baltimore and Pittsburgh joined the AFL

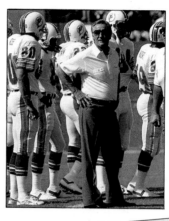

Jim Thorpe, double gold medallist in decathlon and pentathlon in the 1912 Olympics and famed Gridiron exponent with Canton, was voted the outstanding athlete of the first half century.

● Don Shula, Miami

Pittsburgh Steelers have recorded most wins in the Superbowl ... with four in 1975, 1976, 1979 and 1980. The highest aggregate score came in 1979 when Pittsburgh beat Dallas Cowboys 35-31. The record victory margin was in 1986 when Chicago Bears beat New England Patriots 46-10. The Superbowl was first staged in 1967 between the winners of the NFL and AFL. Since 1970 it has been contested by the winners of the National and American Conferences of the NFL.

● Joe Namath, Jets

• Walter Payton, Chicago Bears

• Jim McMahon, Bears

• Dan Marino, Miami

teams. And it was the AFC which was to provide the two out-standing teams of the re-instituted NFL.

The first were the Dolphins in fun-loving Miami. The man who created them is the present coach Don Shula, who joined them aged 32 in 1969. His move from Baltimore caused such a furore that Miami had to give up their number one draft choice for tampering with an employee of another club. Miami were never to regret the move. In 1972 Shula's Dolphins won every game . . . still the only time a perfect record has been achieved. His latest team, led by quarter back Dan Marino, are also threatening to set up another dynasty.

The other team were the Pittsburgh Steelers. They were coached by the laidback Chuck Noll, who played under Paul Brown at Cleveland and clearly learned well. In his opening year the Steelers lost 13 games but things were to change, and how. The Steelers won the Super Bowl for four years on the trot from 1977. With running back Franco Harris, and receiv-ers Lynn Swann and John Stallworth, plus Mean Joe Greene, they were invincible. But the player who pushed them to the heights was balding quarter back Terry Bradshaw, whose agile brain matched the strength of his throwing arm.

Great coaches create great teams, but as in every sport it comes down finally to the players. Would Chicago have won the latest Super Bowl but for the exploits of Walter Payton, who rivals Jim Brown as the greatest running back of all time?

The first great figure was Howard "Red" Grange, a running back for the University of Illinois who ran 36 times with the ball against the University of Pennsylvania for a total of 363 yds and three touchdowns. He signed for the Bears for $3,000 a game and made them a fortune. Jim Thorpe, the man who said "Thanks King" when King Gustav V of Sweden handed him his medals, was voted in 1950 as the best player of the first half of the 20th century. Legend did not attach itself to Ernie Nevers of the Chicago Cardinals as it did to Thorpe, but he was another of the greats, once scoring all 40 points in a victory over the Bears.

O.J. Simpson was another running back to make history. Now a television commentator, O.J. or, as he is sometimes know, the Juice, was the first to run 250 yds in a game and the first to run 2000 yds in a season.

Joe Namath and Terry Bradshaw are the two names that come to mind quickest when quarter backs are mentioned, but now Dan Marino at Miami is challenging Namath for glamour and Jim McMahon of the Bears is outdoing Namath in terms of eccentricity. McMahon was fined $5,000 by NFL Commissioner Pete Rozelle for wearing a headband with the name of a sporting goods firm on it. At the Super Bowl he ran onto the field with a headband with "Rozelle" printed on it!

But one of the greatest of all time was Johnny Unitas, who played 17 years for Baltimore and one for San Diego, leading Baltimore to title wins in 1958 and 1959.

Football is not only about running and passing. It is also about blocking and tackling in order to allow or stop the run-ners and passers from functioning. In this respect linebackers Dick Butkus of the Chicago Bears in the late Sixties, Jack Lambert, of the Super Bowl Steelers, and Ray Nitschke, of the Green Bay Packers, were every bit as valuable as the more glamorous attackers. It is also about defending the quarter back, a job which John Hannah of the New England Patriots does as well, reckon the experts, as anybody ever has. Jim Parker of Baltimore was the first lineman in the Hall of Fame, ten years after it was started. Ron Mix of San Diego Chargers followed, but the massive men of the scrum know they will never be known as "Broadway Joe."

• The Italian bob about to crash in the 1936 winter Olympics

BOBSLEIGH

The sport, which is fearsome, and can be deadly, began in a delightful, amateurish way. An American, Stephen Witney, tied two toboggans together at Davos, Switzerland in 1889 and entered it for an international toboggan race. The authorities didn't like the contraption and banned it.

A year later more bobbers started to use the famous Cresta Run at St. Moritz. By 1898 the first actual race was held there: ten started, seven finished and Lord Hemsley (whose bob was called Rocket) beat Bertie Dwyer (Tortoise) by three seconds.

Five-man bobs were common: the rules said that at least two crewmembers had to be women, although they didn't drive or work the brakes and simply sat in the middle.

By 1906, the bobbers had built their own run at St Moritz next to the Cresta. They used simple 'sleds.' Soon they began to evolve. Women were no longer allowed in them, and even today there are no women bobbers. The International Federation of Bobsleigh and Tobogganing was formed in 1923 and bobbers competed in the first Winter Olympic Games, at Chamonix in 1924.

The 1928 Games were at St. Moritz and a 17-year-old American, Billy Fiske, was the driver as his five-man bob won. Fiske repeated this at Lake Placid in 1932, this time in a more familiar four-man bob. One crewmember, Eddie Eagan, the 1920 Olympic light-heavyweight boxing champion, became the only person to win gold in Winter and Summer Games.

Fiske himself also became a great tobogganer on the Cresta Run in the 1930s.

• The great Swiss driver Eric Schaerer

Billy Fiske, who won medals in two Winter Olympics (1928, 1932) became the first American to join the RAF in 1939. He died from wounds received on a bombing raid and is remembered by a plaque in St. Paul's Cathedral, London.

Meinhard Nehmer, an East German army officer, won his third Olympic medal at Lake Placid in 1980, when, as part of a four-man team, he twice got down in under 60 seconds – the equivalent of Bannister's four-minute mile.

● The East German bob GDR II speeds to gold in the 1984 winter Olympics

The Americans were always strong then. In bobbing – in Olympic Years the Games are regarded as world championships – they took a medal in every Games until 1956. After the War the pace of change increased. But, interestingly, this did not prevent Giacomo Conti, who won the two-man for Italy with Eugenio Monti, becoming the oldest Winter Games gold medallist. He was seven months past his 47th birthday. That same year, Franz Kapus drove the Swiss four-man team to victory. He was 46.

The most significant feature of the previous Games – Oslo, 1952 – had been that the German teams who won both the two and four-man were so heavy that in future there would be a weight-limit. In 1956, something equally significant happened, the Soviet Union entered the Winter Olympics for the first time. By 1976 the East Germans (GDR) would be in, too, competing with – and beating – them.

The only time the bobbers didn't compete was at Squaw Valley, California in the 1960 Games (the organisers wouldn't build a run for only nine competing countries). So they went to Cortina instead.

In 1964 at Innsbruck Conti himself made one of the last great gestures of old-fashioned sportsmanship. He lent his great rivals, Tony Nash and Robin Dixon (GB), a bolt for their two-man bob – and they took the gold, not he.

Bobbing was, in fact, moving towards professionalism in all but name. Athletes – preferably sprinters – were brought in to give a harder, faster push at the crucial running start. Refrigerated tracks allowed training all year round. The East Germans were to profit enormously from just such a track at Oberhof, a custom-built complex in the south of their country.

Bobs were made of fibre glass and shaped, aerodynamically, like small rockets. They had the same potency as rockets, too, reaching speeds in excess of 90mph and, on some corners, putting a force of 4G onto the bobbers. The dimensions had settled to maximum weights (including crew) of 630 kilos for the four-man, 390 for the two-man. A former president of the Federation, Almicare Rotta, was moved to say bobbers need "the qualities of a mountaineer, a parachutist and a deep-sea diver."

The course is approximately 1500 metres long and twists and turns down a slope like a fossilised snake. But the essence of the sport remains unaltered: you must have a fast start, you must select the right line going down. Races are decided over four runs, with the best overall time winning.

To measure the increase in speed, take two examples. At Innsbruck in 1976, the East German two-man team covered a course 1220 metres long (with 14 curves) in a best time of 55.87 seconds. At Sarajevo in 1984, another East German two-man team covered a course 1300 metres long (13 curves) in a best time of 40.98 seconds. By Sarajevo, teams from both Germanies, the Soviet Union, Switzerland, Italy, Great Britain, Austria, Canada, the United States, Holland, Rumania, Sweden, Japan, Yugoslavia and Taiwan were competing.

Eugenio Monti (Italy) won six medals – two gold, two silver, two bronze – between 1956 and 1968.

Wolfgang Hoppe, an East German army engineer who won the Olympic two-man gold at Sarajevo, was previously a decathlete, demonstrating how invaluable athletics training is to bobbers.

SPEED SKATING

Speed skating began in Holland where, on the frozen canals, it was both a pastime and a mode of transport and there are records of 'touring' between towns as far back as 1676. It spread and the first known competition took place on the Fens in Britain in 1763. By the 1880s it was popular in Europe and North America. It evolved into races over four distances – 500m, 1500m, 5000m, 10,000m. The 1000m was incorporated into the Winter Olympic Games at Innsbruck in 1976. Women's events were included for the first time in the 1960 Olympics.

The skates are between 30 and 45cm long and the blade one millimetre wide. The blade is held by the bottom of the boot at an angle to give grip during cornering.

The standard track is 400m and the lanes must be at least 4m wide. In the 500m event, the skaters go down the straight, round a bend, cross over – skaters only compete two at a time, and this prevents either one having the advantage of being on the inside lane – round another bend and into the finishing straight. In the 500, skaters do not use the hands-behind-the-back posture; instead they use them for propulsion. In full flight they cover 100m in seven or eight strides.

Up to the 1970s, the world championship was decided by the overall winner of all the distances although even then some skaters had begun to specialise in the 500 and merely skated the other distances because they had to.

Specialisation was why Erhard Keller was able, in 1968, to get a time of 39.2 seconds, beating the 800m record which had stood for five years.

By the mid-1970s the sprinters had their own championships – over 500m and 1000m – and technique was improving with the skaters being full-timers, chosen for their sheer strength, and maintaining that by ferocious fitness projects. The Dutch developed a deeper blade, enabling skaters to lean over more on the corners – and go faster. Ice improved. And in the mid-1970s a one-piece suit was developed instead of the traditional two piece. Tests in wind tunnels proved it allowed a skater to move faster.

The 500m record has been consistently lowered at Medeo, a sports complex near Alma Ata in the Soviet Republic of Kazakhstan 1500 miles south east of Moscow. It is a mountainous area and the track is 1691m above sea level. Skaters spend time there getting acclimatised to the altitude. The ice is specially prepared using fresh mountain water, and the air is clear.

It is the perfect place to break records, although records can only be established in international competitions. So while the times coming out of Medeo may be artificially produced, they are set in international competitions and they are authentic.

Pavel Pegov, a Soviet student, whose build – almost 6ft tall and weighing 12½ stone (180cm; 80kg) – seems perfect, broke the 500m record on consecutive days in 1983 at Medeo. That same year he broke the 1000m record with a time of 1:12.58.
Pegov did not compete in the Olympic 500 at Sarajevo, 1984 (and was only 13th in the 1000m). The Olympic record, set by Eric Heiden (USA) in Lake Placid, 1980 – 38.03 seconds – was not broken. The Sarajevo winner was Sergei Fokitchev (URS) in a time of 38.19 seconds.

Clas Thunberg (Finland), who set the record at Davos, Switzerland in 1929 and beat it in 1931, is one of the legendary figures of the 500, winning the world title in 1923, '24, '25, '27, '29 and '31. He won the 1500m title seven times.

The men's 500m title goes back to 1893, when it was won by Jaap Eden (Holland). The women's title goes back to 1936, when it was won by Kit Klein (USA).

Speed Skating (500m Men)

Time	Competitor	Venue	Dat
50.5	Oscar Grunden (SWE)	Stockholm	28/2/9
50.2	Einar Halvorsen (NOR)	Hamar	28/2/9
49.4	Alfred Naess (NOR)	Hamar	5/2/9
48.0	Einar Halvorsen (NOR)	Hamar	26/2/9
48.0	Alfred Naess (NOR)	Hamar	26/2/9
47.8	Oscar Fredriksen (NOR)	Kristiania	21/1/9
47.0	Einar Halvorsen (NOR)	Hamar	24/2/9
47.0	Alfred Naess (NOR)	Hamar	24/2/9
46.8	Wilhelm Mauseth (NOR)	Trondheim	3/2/9
46.6	Peder Ostlund (NOR)	Trondheim	7/2/9
45.2	Peder Ostlund (NOR)	Davos	10/2/0
44.8	Rudolf Gundersen (NOR)	Davos	27/1/0
44.4	Johan Wikander (FIN)	Davos	9/2/0
44.4	Sigurd Mathisen (NOR)	Davos	9/2/0
44.2	Oscar Mathisen (NOR)	Kristiania	17/2/1
44.0	Oscar Mathisen (NOR)	Hamar	16/3/1
43.7	Oscar Mathisen (NOR)	Kristiania	10/1/1
43.4	Oscar Mathisen (NOR)	Davos	17/1/1
43.1	Roald Larsen (NOR)	Davos	4/2/2
42.8	Clas Thunberg (FIN)	Davos	19/1/2
42.6	Clas Thunberg (FIN)	St Moritz	13/1/3
42.5	Hans Engnestangen (NOR)	Davos	21/1/3
42.4	Allan Potts (USA)	Oslo	18/1/3
42.3	Hans Engnestangen (NOR)	Davos	30/1/3
41.8	Hans Engnestangen (NOR)	Davos	5/2/38
41.7	Yuri Sergeyev (URS)	Medeo	6/1/5
41.2	Yuri Sergeyev (URS)	Medeo	19/1/5
40.9	Yuri Sergeyev (URS)	Medeo	25/1/5
40.8	Yuri Sergeyev (URS)	Medeo	19/1/55
40.2	Yevgeny Grishin (URS)	Misurina	22/1/56
40.2	Yevgeny Grishin (URS)	Misurina	28/1/5
39.6	Yevgeny Grishin (URS)	Medeo	27/1/6
39.5	Yevgeny Grishin (URS)	Medeo	28/1/6
39.2	Erhard Keller (FRG)	Inzell	28/1/6
39.2	Keiichi Suzuki (JPN)	Inzell	1/3/69
39.09	Valeriy Muratov (URS)	Medeo	9/1/7
39.03	Boris Guliayev (URS)	Medeo	13/1/7
38.99	Valeriy Muratov (URS)	Medeo	24/1/7
38.87	Hasse Borjes (SWE)	Medeo	25/1/7
38.73	Valeriy Muratov (URS)	Medeo	29/1/7
38.71	Keiichi Suzuki (JPN)	Inzell	7/3/7
38.46	Hasse Borjes (SWE)	Inzell	8/3/7
38.42	Erhard Keller (FRG)	Inzell	14/3/7
38.30	Erhard Keller (FRG)	Inzell	2/1/7
38.0	Leo Linkovesi (FIN)	Davos	8/1/72
38.0	Erhard Keller (FRG)	Inzell	4/3/7
38.0	Hasse Borjes (SWE)	Inzell	4/3/7
38.0	Lasse Efskind (NOR)	Davos	13/1/7
37.99	Yevgeny Kulikov (URS)	Medeo	15/3/7
37.97	Yevgeny Kulikov (URS)	Medeo	16/3/7
37.85	Valeriy Muratov (URS)	Medeo	18/3/7
37.20	Yevgeny Kulikov (URS)	Medeo	28/3/7
37.00	Yevgeny Kulikov (URS)	Medeo	29/3/7
36.91	Yevgeny Kulikov (URS)	Medeo	28/3/8
36.68	Pavel Pegov (URS)	Medeo	25/3/8
36.57	Pavel Pegov (URS)	Medeo	26/3/8
36.49*	Igor Zhelezovsky (URS)	Medeo	21/12/85

Represents an average speed of 49.32km/h (30.65mph)

● Eric Heiden (USA) shows the powerful style of the speed skater during the 1980 Olympics

Yevgeny Grishin (URS), the 500 record holder between 1956 and 1968, won the Olympic gold medals in 1956 and 1960. He deadheated for the 1500 gold in 1956 with another Soviet.

● Former world record holder Pavel Pegov (URS)

Leonhard Stock (Austria) was perhaps the luckiest gold medal winner. Largely unknown, he went to Lake Placid in 1980 as reserve, but was so fast in training he forced reigning world champion, Josef Walcher, out of the team. Stock had not even won a World Cup race when he became Olympic champion.

Rosi Mittermaier (West Germany) could have taken all three gold medals at Innsbruck in 1976, but she was second in the giant slalom. She won the downhill by a comparatively comfortable margin — 1:46.16 against Brigitte Totschnigg (Austria) who had 1:46.68.

DOWNHILL SKIING

The downhill is the centrepiece of any Winter Olympic Games: the majesty of a man against a mountain with but a single chance. There is only one run in the downhill, and the winner takes all.

It began, at Garmisch in southern Germany, in 1936 when the Winter Games were almost quaint, with a total of 755 competitors from 28 countries. These figures would be comfortably doubled by Sarajevo, 1984. But in 1936, after Hitler had opened the Games, a Norwegian, Birger Ruud, achieved something astonishing, taking both the downhill and the ski jumping.

Despite Norway's traditional suspicion of Alpine events like the downhill — they were more adept at cross country skiing — another Norwegian, Laila Schou Nilsen, then only 16, took the women's race. She was better known as a speed skater and tennis player.

The next Games had been scheduled for Sapporo, Japan, but by 1940 the world was at war. After it, racing became more and more specialised. At St. Moritz in 1948, there were separate downhill and slalom events, plus another set of medals for a combination of the two. From Oslo 1952, there were separate medals for the three disciplines, downhill, slalom and giant slalom. Jean-Claude Killy (France) was the last great all-rounder, taking all three at Grenoble in 1968. From that moment onwards the downhill belonged to downhill experts, at least in the men's competition.

The technology of ski manufacture, fuelled by so many winter holiday-makers buying their own pairs that it became an important industry, improved. The wax coated onto racing skis to make them go faster became an art form. Year round training became commonplace and necessary. Technicians roved over the courses clutching walkie-talkies sending precise information back to their racers waiting to go.

It ensured that times kept coming down — witness the 11mph increase between 1972 and 1976; but, times aside, exact comparisons are impossible. Weather changes. No two mountains are alike. No two courses are alike, either.

Any men's course must be between two and three miles long, the women's one and a half miles. The vertical drop will be between 800m and 1000m for men, 500m to 700m for women. In the really fast sections, the course must be at least 30m wide.

Within these margins, there is no constancy. The Innsbruck course in 1976, where Klammer broke through the 100kmh barrier, was 3020m long with a drop of 870; at Sarajevo in 1984, the course was 3066m, the drop 803. In Lake Placid, 1980, artificial snow had to be made by cannons firing water into the air because of lack of natural snow.

But if direct comparisons cannot be made one fact is certain: the times do keep coming down.

• Bill Johnson

Two men have won Olympic gold medals in all three disciplines, Killy and Toni Sailer. At Cortina in 1956, Sailer took the downhill by 3.5 seconds, a staggering margin. At Sarajevo in 1984, it would have encompassed the first 28 finishers.

At Sarajevo in 1984, Bill Johnson became the first North American to win an Olympic downhill. His time of 1:45.59 beat that of Peter Mueller (Switzerland), who had 1:45.86.

Skiing – Speed Record (Men)

Speed	Name	Venue	Year
105km/h (65.24mph)	Gustav Lantschner (AUT)	St Moritz	1930
136km/h (84.50mph)	Leo Gasperl (AUT)	St Moritz	1932
159km/h (98.79mph)	Zeno Colo (ITA)	Cervinia	1947
160km/h (99.41mph)	Edoardo Agreiter (ITA)	Cervinia	1959
163km/h (101.28mph)	Luigi di Marco (ITA)	Cervinia	1960
172km/h (106.87mph)	Ludwig Leitner (FRG)	Cervinia	1965
184km/h (114.33mph)	Alessandro Casse (ITA)	Cervinia	1973
189km/h (117.43mph)	Steve McKinney (USA)	Cervinia	1974
194.384km/h (120.78mph)	Pino Meynet (FRA)	Cervinia	1975
194.489km/h (120.84mph)	Tom Simons (USA)	Cervinia	1976
198.020km/h (123.04mph)	Steve McKinney (USA)	Cervinia	1978
200.222km/h (124.41mph)	Steve McKinney (USA)	Portillo	1978
201.230km/h (125.03mph)	Steve McKinney (USA)	Les Arcs	1982
203.16km/h (126.23mph)	Franz Weber (AUT)	Silverton	1982
208.092km/h (129.30mph)	Franz Weber (AUT)	Silverton	1983
208.936km/h (129.82mph)	Franz Weber (AUT)	Les Arcs	1984

Skiing Speed Record (Women)

Speed	Name	Venue	Year
165.898km/h (103.08mph)	Catherine Breyton (FRA)	Portillo	1978
169.332km/h (105.21mph)	Catherine Breyton (FRA)	Silverton	1981
175.353km/h (108.95mph)	Catherine Breyton (FRA)	Les Arcs	1982
179.103km/h (111.28mph)	Marty Martin-Kuntz (USA)	Silverton	1982
190.375km/h (118.29mph)	Marty Martin-Kuntz (USA)	Les Arcs	1983
194.384km/h (120.78mph)	Kirsten Culver (USA)	Silverton	1983
200.780km/h (124.75mph)	Melissa Dimino (USA)	Les Arcs	1984

Franz Klammer (Austria) was the greatest downhill racer. Between 1974 and 1978, he won 22 races, six of them in a row to beat Jean-Claude Killy's record. He was World Cup downhill champion in 1975, '76, '77, '78 and '83. After winning the gold at the 1976 Olympics, he was dropped for Lake Placid, he came back at Sarajevo — but was only tenth.

• Fastest man on skiis . . . Franz Weber

Skiing
(Average speeds in Olympic Downhill races)

Men

Speed	Name	Date
47.599km/h (29.576mph)	Birger Ruud (NOR)	1936
66.034km/h (41.031mph)	Henri Oreiller (FRA)	1948
57.629km/h (35.808mph)	Zeno Colo (ITA)	1952
72.356km/h (44.959mph)	Toni Sailer (AUT)	1956
88.429km/h (54.947mph)	Jean Vuarnet (FRA)	1960
81.297km/h (50.515mph)	Egon Zimmermann (AUT)	1964
86.808km/h (53.939mph)	Jean-Claude Killy (FRA)	1968
85.291km/h (52.997mph)	Bernhard Russi (SWI)	1972
102.828km/h (63.894mph)	Franz Klammer (AUT)	1976
102.677km/h (63.800mph)	Leonhard Stock (AUT)	1980
104.532km/h (64.953mph)	Bill Johnson (USA)	1984

Women

Speed	Name	Date
39.031km/h (24.252mph)	Laila Schou Nilsen (NOR)	1936
43.695km/h (27.150mph)	Hedy Schlunegger (SWI)	1948
50.420km/h (31.329mph)	Trude Jochum-Beiser (AUT)	1952
55.484km/h (34.476mph)	Madeleine Berthod (SWI)	1956
67.426km/h (41.896mph)	Heidi Biebl (GER)	1960
74.496km/h (46.289mph)	Christl Haas (AUT)	1964
77.080km/h (47.895mph)	Olga Pall (AUT)	1968
78.568km/h (48.819mph)	Marie-Thérèse Nadig (SWI)	1972
85.286km/h (52.994mph)	Rosi Mittermaier (FRG)	1976
99.598km/h (61.887mph)	Annemarie Moser-Pröll (AUT)	1980
96.428km/h (59.917mph)	Michela Figini (SWI)	1984

SKI JUMPING

The longest jump achieved in Olympic Games jumping was 119m by Matti Nykaenen (FIN) at Sarajevo in 1984, on the 90m hill.

• Innauer on his way to the top

Former World Cup ski jumping champion Armin Kogler of Austria says the closest sport to his own is golf. In both sports according to Kogler, a fledgling duffer, "the swing is every thing."

The home owners of southern Norway's Telemark region may have had different clubs in mind when thrill-seeking skiers launched the sport by leaping off their snow-laden roof in the late 1800s.

Serious ski jumping began at the Chamonix Olympics of 1924 and Norwegians dominated from the outset, winning every Olympic gold medal in jumping until a Finn broke the

Ski-Jumping — World Cup
(instituted in 1980)

Date	Winner
1980	Hubert Neuper (AUT)
1981	Armin Kogler (AUT)
1982	Armin Kogler (AUT)
1983	Matti Nykaenen (FIN)
1984	Jens Weissflog (GDR)
1985	Matti Nykaenen (FIN)
1986	Matti Nykaenen (FIN)

string in 1956. Birger Ruud was the preeminent pre-war jumper. The short, jolly Ruud won two Olympics (1932 and 1936) and three championships in the Thirties. The longest jump by Ruud, a world record in 1934, was 92m (301ft).

Since Ruud's day, distances have changed greatly but equipment has not. The skiis now are fibreglass not wood. (At 11.5cm wide, and as long as 255cm, they are the biggest of all types of skiis. But bindings and boots unlike high-tech, alpine ski gear, remain simple affairs. A metal cable holds a lace boot to a steel toeplate but leaves the heel free to lift. Roof tops have been replaced by two standard sizes for international and Olympic jumping – 70m and 90m jumps. Since 1979, a winterlong World Cup season takes the best jumpers to the continent, North America, Japan, and Scandinavia, climaxing annually in March at the mecca of Nordic skiing, the Holmenkollen mountain above Oslo. Upwards of 100,000 spectators have filled the immense landing bowl below the 90m Holmenkollen jump, including, every year without fail, King Olav V of Norway, himself a former jumper.

In competition, distance counts most, but jumpers are also scored by judges for the style of their crouched in-run, the steadiness of their form in the air and the sureness of their one-foot forward, "Telemark" landing.

Jumping style, however, has changed much recently. In short, competitors no longer simply jump, now they fly. And as with any flight, take-off is critical.

"It's the timing of what you do right at the take-off – the swing – that is now the most important thing in jumping," says Kogler, who won the World Cup in 1981 and 1982.

The robust Kogler, however, was more jumper than flyer. As technique changed, Kogler's type gave way to the likes of Canada's native Indian jumper, Steve Collins (who set a 90m hill record of 124m that still stands in Lahti, Finland, as a 15-year-old), and to Finland's mercurial Matti Nykaenen. Both are light-boned and eye-blink quick, like birds.

Despite a troubled private life, the immensely talented Nykaenen won the 90m Sarajevo Olympic jumping in 1984 and the World Cup title three times, most recently in 1986. Sweeping down at 90km/h, Nykaenen springs forward at the lip with exquisite timing, extending flat out over his skiis to form an airfoil. Gloved hands trail behind to steer and steady the flight. Nykaenen's flying has taken him to the limits of safety in this relatively injury-free sport. In 1985, practising at Planica, Yugoslavia, Nykaenen set an unofficial world record for ski flying (simply ski jumping on a bigger hill: ski flying meets are held once or twice a year). From lip to landing, Nykaenen flew 191m – practically the length of two football pitches, and further than many men can hit a golf ball.

Ski-Jumping – Olympic Champions

Date	70m hill Winner	90m hill* Winner
1924	Jacob Tullin Thams (NOR)	–
1928	Alf Andersen (NOR)	–
1932	Birger Ruud (NOR)	–
1936	Birger Ruud (NOR)	–
1948	Petter Hugsted (NOR)	–
1952	Arnfinn Bergmann (NOR)	–
1956	Antti Hyvaerinen (FIN)	–
1960	Helmut Recknagel (GER)	–
1964	Veikko Kankkonen (FIN)	Toralf Engan (NOR)
1968	Jiri Raska (CZ)	Vladimir Belousov (URS)
1972	Yukio Kasaya (JAN)	Wojciech Fortuna (POL)
1976	Hans-Georg Aschenbach (GDR)	Karl Schnabl (AUT)
1980	Toni Innauer (AUT)	Jouko Tormaenen (FIN)
1984	Jens Weissflog (GDR)	Matti Nykaenen (FIN)

*Not held until 1964

The remarkable Birger Ruud, who won two gold medals in the 1932 and 1936 events, also won a silver medal in 1948 when aged over 36, making him the oldest ever Olympic jumping medallist. Former world record holder Sepp Bradl of Austria was two years older when he competed in the 1956 Games.

• The ski jumps at Lake Placid

• Matti Nykaenen the Finland flyer

In the 1924 Olympic Games, the first time ski jumping was included, the bronze medal was awarded to Thorleif Haug of Norway. Some fifty years later an error was discovered in the addition of the points and it was realised that third place should have been awarded to another Norwegian, Anders Haugen, who was competing for his adopted country, America. Happily Haugen was still alive, and Haug's daughter presented the bronze medal to 86-year-old Haugen in 1974. Her late father would not have minded as he (Haug) had already won three gold medals in other Nordic Skiing events.

Progressive Ski-Jumping Records

Metres	Ft/In	Name	Venue	Year
73	239.6	N Nelson (USA)	Revelstoke	1924
75	246.1	R Badrutt (SWI)	Bernina	1930
76.5	251.0	Birger Ruud (NOR)	Oddnes	1931
81.5	267.5	Sigmund Ruud (NOR)	Davos	1931
82.5	270.6	R Lymburne (CAN)	Revelstoke	1932
84	275.7	Sigmund Ruud (NOR)	Villars	1933
86	282.2	Sigmund Ruud (NOR)	Villars	1933
87	285.5	H Ruchet (SWI)	Villars	1933
92	301.10	Birger Ruud (NOR)	Planica	1934
93	305.1	Reidar Anderson (NOR)	Planica	1935
97	318.3	Stanislaw Marusarz (POL)	Planica	1935
99	324.10	Reidar Andersen (NOR)	Planica	1935
99.5	326.5	F Kainersdorfer (SUI)	Ponte di Legno	1935
101	331.5	Josef Bradl (AUT)	Planica	1936
107	351.1	Josef Bradl (AUT)	Planica	1938
118	387.2	R Gehring (FRG)	Planica	1941
120	393.9	Fritz Tshannen (SUI)	Planica	1948
124	406.10	W Gantschnigg (AUT)	Oberstdorf	1950
127	416.8	Josef Weiler (FRG)	Oberstdorf	1950
135	442.11	Dan Netzell (SWE)	Oberstdorf	1950
139	456.1	Tauno Luiro (FIN)	Oberstdorf	1951
141	462.7	Josef Slibar (YUG)	Oberstdorf	1961
141	462.7	Peter Lesser (GDR)	Mitterndorf-Kulm	1962
142	465.11	Dalibor Motejlek (TCH)	Oberstdorf	1964
144	472.6	Ninr Zandanel (ITA)	Oberstdorf	1964
145	475.9	Peter Lesser (GDR)	Mitterndorf-Kulm	1965
146	479.0	Bjorn Wirkola (NOR)	Vikersund	1966
147	482.4	Lars Grini (NOR)	Oberstdorf	1967
148	485.7	Kjell Sjoeberg (SWE)	Oberstdorf	1967
150	492.2	Lars Grini (NOR)	Oberstdorf	1967
154	505.3	Reinhold Bachler (AUS)	Vikersund	1967
156	511.10	Bjorn Wirkola (NOR)	Planica	1969
156	511.10	Jiri Raska (TCH)	Planica	1969
160	524.11	Bjorn Wirkola (NOR)	Planica	1969
164	538.1	Jiri Raska (TCH)	Planica	1969
165	541.4	Manfred Wolf (GDR)	Planica	1969
169	554.6	Heinz Wossipiwo (GDR)	Oberstdorf	1973
170	557.9	Uwe Berg (NOR)	Oberstdorf	1976
174	570.11	Anton Innauer (AUT)	Oberstdorf	1976
176	577.5	Anton Innauer (AUT)	Oberstdorf	1976
176	577.5	Klaus Ostwald (GDR)	Planica	1979
176	577.5	Armin Kogler (AUT)	Harrachov	1980
180	590.6	Armin Kogler (AUT)	Oberstdorf	1981
181	593.10	Pavel Ploc (TCH)	Harrachov	1983
185	606.11	Matti Nykaenen (FIN)	Oberstdorf	1984
186	610.3	Matti Nykaenen (FIN)	Planica	1985

MOTOR RACING

The first Grand Prix was organised by the Automobile Club of France in 1906. It was over 1239km (769 miles) and lasted two days. Motor racing blossomed with the motor car itself. The famous Le Mans 24-hour endurance race was first run in 1923.

In 1926, the first German Grand Prix was held at the Avus circuit outside Berlin. The Thirties was a decade of aero-dynamic cars which were averaging the Nurburgring at over eighty miles an hour. The Mercedes, for example, produced a 5.6 litre engine which gave 646 brake horse power.

But Grand Prix racing as we know it did not begin until 1950, and it was intended to be a proper world championship. Normally aspirated engines could be of 4500cc, super-charged 1500cc. That first year, five teams – Alfa Romeo, Fer-rari, Maserati, Talbot and Gordini – competed. Juan Manuel Fangio was beaten by three points for the championship by Giuseppe Farina. Both drove Alfa Romeos.

But in the 1950s, Fangio dominated, although there were superb drivers around – Stirling Moss and Mike Hawthorn among them. But it was an engine which altered Formula One. In 1965, the Ford Motor Company sanctioned an English designer, Keith Duckworth, to build an engine. It would be called the Cosworth. It would win 155 races – but contribute much more. Because it was reliable and relatively inexpen-sive a lot of teams could go motor racing. And did.

It was the era of Lotus and the master technician Colin Chapman; the era of Ken Tyrrell and his master driver, Jackie Stewart; of Graham Hill and Jim Clark and Jack Brabham. And the cars were going faster, ever faster.

Despite elaborate rear wings and such passing phases as six-wheeled cars (a phase which passed very quickly indeed)

• Racing at Brooklands in 1936

the next decisive step came from Renault. It came at the Brit-ish Grand Prix at Silverstone in July 1977. They introduced a 1.5 litre turbo-charged engine. It was a novelty and it didn't last beyond lap 17.

By 1982, turbo engines had been refined to the point where everybody began a scramble to get them. When they were added to the skirts – strips along the flanks of the cars which made the air passing under the car suck it to the ground – the results were extraordinary. By 1985, every team had a turbo, despite the horrific cost at between £60,000 and £90,000 an engine. And the cars were going faster, ever faster.

• The great Fangio in 1951

It had become an odd world, with teams needing budgets of five million dollars to run two cars; a world of computer technology, of space age kevlar material for bodywork, of tyre technology so intense that one company regarded it as a good proving ground for Jumbo jet tyres as they landed; of drivers earning a million dollars and more, much more.

The cars had become so fast the skirts were taken off. The cornering ability with them was too awesome. People feared a catastrophe if a car lost control. Fuel consumption was limited to 220 litres a race.

And still the cars went faster and faster.

The summit came in 1985 when Keke Rosberg – albeit in qualifying – averaged more than 160 miles an hour round Sil-verstone. He covered the circuit, plus chicane to slow cars down, in one minute 5.591 seconds. In 1950, also at Silver-stone, Farina had set the fastest lap: one minute 50.6 sec-onds. Rosberg was almost twice as fast. That captures every-thing about the rate of progress in Formula One.

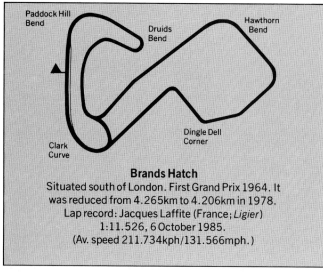

Brands Hatch
Situated south of London. First Grand Prix 1964. It was reduced from 4.265km to 4.206km in 1978.
Lap record: Jacques Laffite (France; *Ligier*)
1:11.526, 6 October 1985.
(Av. speed 211.734kph/131.566mph.)

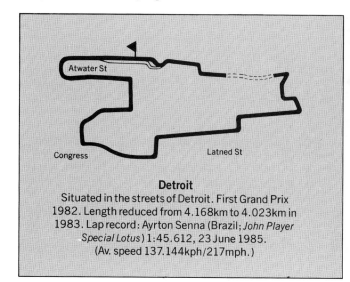

Detroit
Situated in the streets of Detroit. First Grand Prix 1982. Length reduced from 4.168km to 4.023km in 1983. Lap record: Ayrton Senna (Brazil; *John Player Special Lotus*) 1:45.612, 23 June 1985.
(Av. speed 137.144kph/217mph.)

Stirling Moss, one of the best remembered drivers, won 16 Grands Prix – but was never world champion. He was second in 1955, '56, '57 and '58, third in 1959, '60, '61.

Danger is inherent in all forms of motor sport.

The worst accident was at Le Mans, France, in 1955 during the 24 Hour race, when Pierre Levegh's Mercedes crashed and the engine was thrown into the crowd. Levegh and 81 spectators were killed.

In Formula One there have been 26 occasions with fatalities. The worst was at Monza in 1961 when Wolfgang Von Trips's Ferrari killed 13 spectators.

In Grand Prix races, or practices for them, 22 drivers have lost their lives.

This list does not include Jim Clark, killed in 1968 in a Formula Two race at Hockenheim, West Germany, Peter Revson (USA) who was killed in 1974 during private practices at Kyalami, South Africa, nor Elio De Angelis who died in practice in France in 1986.

In recent years, the system of qualifying for the starting grid – a timed flat out lap, often driven among cars going much more slowly – has provoked questions.

Gilles Villeneuve (Canada) was killed in this way in Belgium in 1982. The same year Riccardo Paletti (Italy) was killed in Canada when his car ran into the back of a stalled Ferrari on the starting grid.

Imola
Situated in northern central Italy, south of Bologna. Called the Autodromo Dino Ferrari. First Grand Prix 1980 (but since 1981 this has been called the San Marino Grand Prix). Length 5.040km. Lap record: Michele Alboreto (Italy; *Ferrari*) 1:30.961, 5 May 1985. (Av. speed 199.47kph/123.945mph.)

Monte Carlo
Situated in the Principality of Monaco. First Grand Prix 1950. It has changed in length seven times. Present length 3.312km. Lap record: Michele Alboreto (Italy; *Ferrari*) 1:22.637, 19 May 1985. (Av. speed 144.284kph/89.654mph.)

FORMULA ONE: THE GREAT DRIVERS

Who was the greatest racing driver? It's a tantalising and pro-vocative question, because motor sport – and particularly Formula One – is governed by statistics, an endless sub-culture of them. Every lap is recorded in practice, qualifying and the races. Every average speed is carefully noted. There's an Italian journalist who specialises in drawings of engines and knows the dimensions of every nut and bolt on every Formula One engine. There's a man from Longines who will patiently explain how they have three systems (one secretive and attached to each car; but tamper-proof) to get the timing right.

But nowhere among all these statistics is the answer to the only really pressing question: who was the greatest driver? It is tantalising because you can assemble the endless statistics and make them prove what you want. It is provocative because the fellow next to you might make them prove what he wants. There are too many factors in the equation: the ever increasing sophistication of the cars, the ever increasing safety of the tracks, and a theme which runs through all sport: ever increasing professionalism.

Statistics certainly do tell us that Jackie Stewart (Scot-land) was the most successful driver to sit behind the wheel of a Formula One car. He won 27 times in 99 Grands Prix. They also tell us that Jim Clark won 25 from 72. Niki Lauda (Austria) scored the most points, 420½ from 171 races. Graham Hill (England) drove the most races, 176.

In the list of the most points scored, Juan Fangio (Argen-tina) is seventh. But he drove in only 51 races – between 1950 and 1958 – and won 24 of them. He was ruthless in his con-ceptions of which team to join which season because, then as now, you absolutely must have a car at the forefront. His movements are worth charting: 1950, 1951, Alfa Romeo; 1953, Maserati; 1954, Maserati and Mercedes; 1955, Mer-cedes; 1956, Ferrari; 1957, Maserati; 1958, Maserati. His statistics are overwhelming. 28 pole positions, 23 fastest laps and in the the world championship second, first, second, first, first, first, first, 14th.

Fangio was of a generation which loved to drive; it didn't have to be Formula One. In the great Le Mans crash of 1955,

he went through a gap between the cars in front of him so pre-cisely that he was completely unscathed but his Mercedes bore the green bodypaint of a car he had touched. Even in the sudden chaos of cars veering in front of him, he was as pre-cise as that. And he was 44 then.

Stirling Moss, a contemporary of Fangio and, in legend, associated with him in the matter of undiluted speed, was paradoxically never world champion. In Formula One he drove between 1951 and 1961, won 16 races. His world championship positions: 12th, second, second, second, sec-ond, third, third, third. Like Fangio, he could drive all kinds of fast cars and his victory in the Mille Miglia in Italy in 1955 (ordinary roads, huge speeds) – has become a legend all by itself.

Lauda was perhaps the most clinical driver of all. He sur-vived a crash at the Nurburgring and was given the Last Rites, but when he heard the priest mouthing them he made up his mind to recover, drove again and was world champion in 1984. In testing he could tell you what was right with a car – and what was wrong – so exactly that he spoke as a statisti-cian.

While Lauda bore the burn-marks of his crash at the Nur-burgring, Stewart was unmarked at the end of his career. He had two priceless gifts: the ability to get a car round faster than anybody else, and then to explain it was possible to do that. After his retirement, he earned a fortune explaining.

There was a time roughly between mid Fifties and mid Six-ties, when Britain had people who ought to have been fighter pilots but were just a generation too late and found cars instead: Hill, buoyant hero of Monaco (five wins there); Clark with all the instinctive control of a spitfire pilot; Moss dealing in speed, real speed and that inexplicable touch which allows a man to harness it to his will.

James Hunt (England) was the last of that breed. Tall, angular, well educated, always carrying with him the air of the inspired amateur, he won the world championship in 1976. But beneath the public schoolboy – who might have drifted into racing because it was a bit of a lark – was a hell of a driver. World champions always are. The course – an average of 16 races spread over four continents – is too long, involves too many statistics, to allow anyone else but the best to achieve the summit.

Now, it belongs to the technicians: to Alain Prost (France) who was beaten by Lauda by half a point in 1984 and won it in

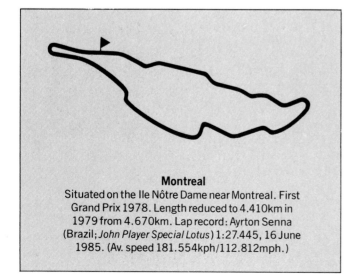

Montreal
Situated on the Ile Nôtre Dame near Montreal. First Grand Prix 1978. Length reduced to 4.410km in 1979 from 4.670km. Lap record: Ayrton Senna (Brazil; *John Player Special Lotus*) 1:27.445, 16 June 1985. (Av. speed 181.554kph/112.812mph.)

Monza
Situated near Milan. First Grand Prix 1950. It has changed in length nine times. Present length 5.800km. Lap record: Nigel Mansell (Britain; *Williams Honda*) 1:28.283, 8 September 1985. (Av. speed: 236.512kph/146.961mph.)

ickie Stewart • Jim Clark

iki Lauda • Keke Rosberg

The first Grand Prix of modern times was run at Silverstone on 13 May 1950. It was won by Giuseppe Farina (Italy; Alfa Romeo).

Graham Hill (Britain) drove in the most races – 176. He is followed by Niki Lauda (Austria) with 171. Jim Clark (Britain) had the most pole positions – 33. Juan Fangio (Argentina) had 28, Lauda 24.

Motor Racing – World Championships

	Drivers' Championship		Constructors' Championship
1950	Giuseppe Farina (ITA)	Alfa Romeo	–
1951	Juan Manuel Fangio (ARG)	Alfa Romeo	–
1952	Alberto Ascari (ITA)	Ferrari	–
1953	Alberto Ascari (ITA)	Ferrari	–
1954	Juan Manuel Fangio (ARG)	Maserati	–
1955	Juan Manuel Fangio (ARG)	Mercedes	–
1956	Juan Manuel Fangio (ARG)	Ferrari	–
1957	Juan Manuel Fangio (ARG)	Maserati	–
1958	Mike Hawthorn (GBR)	Ferrari	Vanwall
1959	Jack Brabham (AUS)	Cooper-Climax	Cooper-Climax
1960	Jack Brabham (AUS)	Cooper-Climax	Cooper-Climax
1961	Phil Hill (USA)	Ferrari	Ferrari
1962	Graham Hill (GBR)	BRM	BRM
1963	Jim Clark (GBR)	Lotus-Climax	Lotus-Climax
1964	John Surtees (GBR)	Ferrari	Ferrari
1965	Jim Clark (GBR)	Lotus-Climax	Lotus-Climax
1966	Jack Brabham (AUS)	Repco-Brabham	Repco-Brabham
1967	Denny Hulme (NZL)	Repco-Brabham	Repco-Brabham
1968	Graham Hill (GBR)	Lotus-Ford	Lotus-Ford
1969	Jackie Stewart (GBR)	Matra-Ford	Matra-Ford
1970	Jochen Rindt (FRG)	Lotus-Ford	Lotus-Ford
1971	Jackie Stewart (GBR)	Tyrrell-Ford	Tyrrell-Ford
1972	Emerson Fittipaldi (BRA)	JPS-Lotus-Ford	JPS-Lotus-Ford
1973	Jackie Stewart (GBR)	Tyrrell-Ford	JPS-Lotus-Ford
1974	Emerson Fittipaldi (BRA)	McLaren-Ford	McLaren-Ford
1975	Niki Lauda (AUT)	Ferrari	Ferrari
1976	James Hunt (GBR)	McLaren-Ford	Ferrari
1977	Niki Lauda (AUT)	Ferrari	Ferrari
1978	Mario Andretti (USA)	Lotus-Ford	Lotus-Ford
1979	Jody Scheckter (SAF)	Ferrari	Ferrari
1980	Alan Jones (AUS)	Williams-Ford	Williams-Ford
1981	Nelson Piquet (BRA)	Brabham-Cosworth	Williams-Ford
1982	Keke Rosberg (FIN)	Williams-Cosworth	Ferrari
1983	Nelson Piquet (BRA)	Brabham-BMW	Ferrari
1984	Niki Lauda (AUT)	McLaren-TAG-Porsche	McLaren-TAG-Porsche
1985	Alain Prost (FRA)	McLaren-TAG-Porsche	McLaren-TAG-Porsche

1985; to Nelson Piquet, languid, laid very far back, who goes o his native Brazil, where he's not even on the telephone, to ish between races; and to Keke Rosberg (Finland), a street ighter who can make a motor car go as fast as any man who has ever lived (Silverstone, 1985, first-ever lap averaging 160mph).

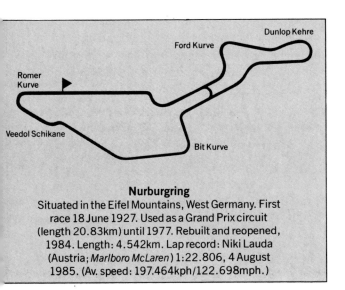

Nurburgring
Situated in the Eifel Mountains, West Germany. First race 18 June 1927. Used as a Grand Prix circuit (length 20.83km) until 1977. Rebuilt and reopened, 1984. Length: 4.542km. Lap record: Niki Lauda (Austria; *Marlboro McLaren*) 1:22.806, 4 August 1985. (Av. speed: 197.464kph/122.698mph.)

Osterreichring
Situated in central Austria. First Grand Prix 1970. It was increased from 5.911km to 5.942km in 1977. Lap record: Alain Prost (France; *Marlboro McLaren*) 1:29.241, 18 August 1985. (Av. speed 239.701kph/148.943mph.)

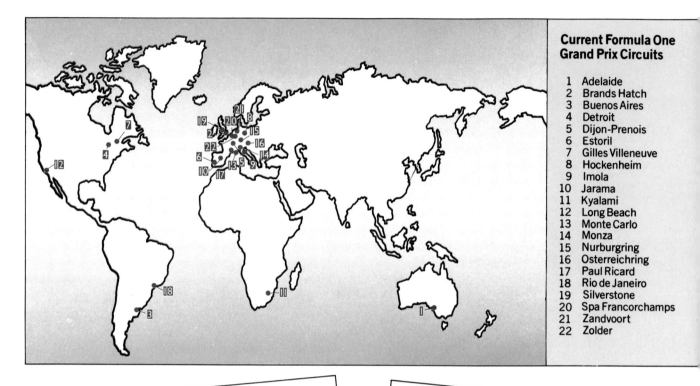

Current Formula One Grand Prix Circuits

1 Adelaide
2 Brands Hatch
3 Buenos Aires
4 Detroit
5 Dijon-Prenois
6 Estoril
7 Gilles Villeneuve
8 Hockenheim
9 Imola
10 Jarama
11 Kyalami
12 Long Beach
13 Monte Carlo
14 Monza
15 Nurburgring
16 Osterreichring
17 Paul Ricard
18 Rio de Janeiro
19 Silverstone
20 Spa Francorchamps
21 Zandvoort
22 Zolder

THE FASTEST LAPS:

There is an argument between the purists and the rest. The purists insist that a lap record can be set only during a race. The rest insist a lap record ought to belong to the man who got round fastest, whether he did it in practice, in qualifying or in a race. The fastest lap of modern times was set in qualifying by Keke Rosberg at the Marlboro British Grand Prix, Silverstone on 20 July 1985, when he covered 2.932 miles in 1 minute 5.5691 seconds — breaking the barrier of averaging 160mph (160.925mph/258.984kph). The difficulty of comparing fastest laps is that circuits are different — Austria is fast, Monaco round the streets isn't; and in the pursuit of safety, circuits have had chicanes added to slow the cars. Silverstone demonstrates this. In 1950, the winner's fastest lap averaged 151.278kph (94mph). By 1973 this had risen to 215.750kph (134mph). With the chicane, it fell to 209.948kph (130mph) in 1975 — even with the chicane Alain Prost had 243.066kph (151mph) in the Grand Prix in 1985.

THE HORSE POWER:

There are secrets about this, as in most other aspects of Grand Prix racing. The Cosworth engine which dominated racing until 1983 (and won 155 races) was giving 510 brake horse power at 11,200 revs. Turbo engines have made that slow. At about the same time as Cosworth were being outpaced, Renault, who first introduced turbo engines, were getting 640bhp at 11,000 revs — a staggering difference. Porsche produced a reliable engine for Marlboro McLaren which — they don't announce these things — must be giving around 800bhp in race trim. And in qualifying, where the engine can be "wound up" for a flying lap, the Brabham is freely rumoured to have 1,000bhp. What does this mean? The Williams Honda does 0-60mph (96kph) in three seconds, 60-120mph (96-193kph) in another three seconds. McLaren estimate their car will do: 80mph (128kph) in first gear, 115mph (185kph) in second, 140mph (225kph) in third, 170mph (273kph) in fourth, 205mph (329kph) in fifth.

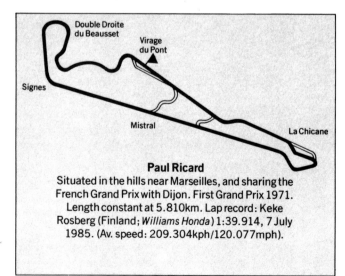

Paul Ricard
Situated in the hills near Marseilles, and sharing the French Grand Prix with Dijon. First Grand Prix 1971. Length constant at 5.810km. Lap record: Keke Rosberg (Finland; *Williams Honda*) 1:39.914, 7 July 1985. (Av. speed: 209.304kph/120.077mph).

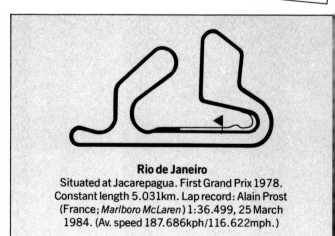

Rio de Janeiro
Situated at Jacarepagua. First Grand Prix 1978. Constant length 5.031km. Lap record: Alain Prost (France; *Marlboro McLaren*) 1:36.499, 25 March 1984. (Av. speed 187.686kph/116.622mph.)

THE GREAT RACES

• James Hunt

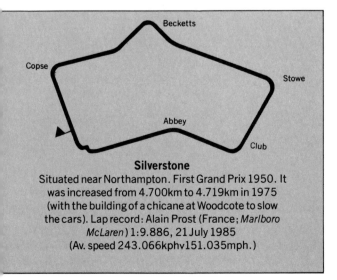

• Jackie Stewart

Between 1950 and 1985, there have been 420 Grand Prix races. Arguably the most amazing finish was at Monza in 1969 when Jackie Stewart (Matra Ford) won. The drivers behind him were Jochen Rindt (Lotus Ford) at 0.08 seconds, Jean-Pierre Beltoise (Matra Ford) at 0.17 seconds and Bruce McLaren (McLaren Ford) at 0.19 seconds.

A year earlier, Stewart won the German Grand Prix at the feared and fearsome Nurburgring in a violent storm. He started on the third row of the grid and, with visibility dreadful, charged into the lead. At the end of the first lap, he had ten seconds over Graham Hill. Incredibly, he began to lap people — and that over a course 14.7 miles long. "The visibility was so bad I didn't know when I was getting to the cars in front." He won the race by four minutes.

Juan Fangio, perhaps the greatest driver of all, had his greatest race at the Nurburgring, too. He had been world champion in 1954, '55 and '56, but he was aged 46 in 1957. He drove a Maserati. Lap after lap he smashed the record, bringing it down to 9 minutes 29.5 seconds. Then he had a disastrous pit stop for new tyres and lost 52 seconds. In pur-

suit of Mike Hawthorn he went round the Ring in a staggering 9 minutes 17.4 seconds. He overtook Hawthorn with a lap to go and won by 3.6 seconds.

James Hunt (McLaren) won the World Championship in 1976 in bizarre circumstances. The final race, at Fuji, Japan, was run in bad weather and Hunt needed only to finish fourth to take the title. But as the track dried and cars came in for dry tyres, nobody was really sure who was running where.

Hunt pitted on lap 67. It took only 27 seconds to change all four tyres. When he got back out on the track, he got pit signals telling him he was sixth. He drove superbly but at the end was convinced he'd lost the title. It wasn't until he reached the pits, in a rage, that they told him he'd been third — and was world champion.

> The closest Grand Prix finish was almost certainly in the Spanish race of 1986 when Ayrton Senna (BRA) beat Nigel Mansell (GBR). The times: Senna — one hour 48 minutes 47.735 seconds; Mansell — one hour 48 minutes 47.749 seconds. In real distance, perhaps a foot.

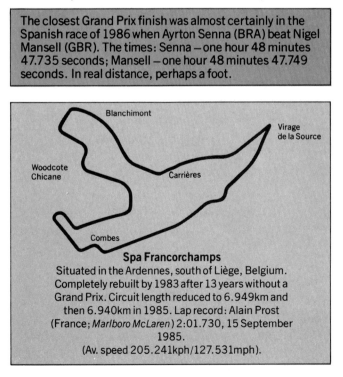

Silverstone
Situated near Northampton. First Grand Prix 1950. It was increased from 4.700km to 4.719km in 1975 (with the building of a chicane at Woodcote to slow the cars). Lap record: Alain Prost (France; *Marlboro McLaren*) 1:9.886, 21 July 1985
(Av. speed 243.066kphv151.035mph.)

Spa Francorchamps
Situated in the Ardennes, south of Liège, Belgium. Completely rebuilt by 1983 after 13 years without a Grand Prix. Circuit length reduced to 6.949km and then 6.940km in 1985. Lap record: Alain Prost (France; *Marlboro McLaren*) 2:01.730, 15 September 1985.
(Av. speed 205.241kph/127.531mph).

INDIANAPOLIS 500

Of all the motor races in the world, three are so famous that they overspill the confines of the sport itself and are known to a wider public: The Monaco Grand Prix at Monte Carlo, the Indianapolis 500 mile thriller – that word is used accurately, not loosely – in Indiana, and the Le Mans 24 hours endurance race at a circuit on the very outskirts of Le Mans, a provincial town in (roughly) the middle of France.

Curiously, Monaco is not loved by as many people as you might think. The track, contorting through the streets and round the harbour, makes overtaking extremely difficult and all too frequently there is wreckage marking the precise point where drivers tried.

The Indy is quite different. There is a symmetry about its arrangements: exactly 200 laps of a 2½ mile (4.023km) circuit making exactly 500 miles. Almost all the cars are powered by the British Cosworth engine – the firm which used to dominate Grand Prix racing (and thus Monaco, too). They give enormous, stark, startling power and average speeds in excess of 160mph. They reach over 200mph. This is possible because the circuit consists of four corners which are the same – all lefthanders – making the whole track into a sort of oblong shape. At such speeds, crashes are extremely spectacular and as dangerous as they look.

Although Graham Hill once won the race, the recent heroes of the Indy have been Americans.

• The *Indy* trophy

A.J. Foyt won four times between 1961 and 1977; Al Unser won three times between 1970 and 1978.

Indy was never easy. Emerson Fittipaldi, a Brazilian who competed in 144 Grands Prix before going there, said, "When you look at the design of the track, four corners exactly the same, it should be easy. But the setting-up of the car is completely different to anything I've done in Formula One. You know you are turning left all the time so you have to have cross-weight, different tyre stagger, different toe-ins and toe-outs, different wheel caster one side to the other . . ."

The circuit (called The Brickyard because it was originally made of bricks) is banked and has a solid wall at the top of the banking to stop the car going into the crowd. This wall has the effect of deflecting the cars who stray into it back into the fray. Hence those spectacular crashes. And that average speed of over 160mph includes pit stops . . .

• A.J. Foyt at Brands in 1978

LE MANS

At Le Mans, film star, Paul Newman, competed in 1979 and finished second. He was 54 then. "Even my mother says I'm no longer a spring chicken," he said.

Indianapolis 500 Winners

Date	Winner	Car	Speed
1911	Ray Harroun	Marmon	74.59mph
1912	Joe Dawson	Nationa	78.72mph
1913	Jules Goux	Peugot	75.93mph
1914	Rene Thomas	Delage	82.47mph
1915	Ralph De Palma	Mercedes	89.84mph
1916	Dario Resta	Peugeot	84.00mph
1919	Howard Wilcox	Peugeot	88.05mph
1920	Gaston Chevrolet	Monroe	88.62mph
1921	Tommy Milton	Frontenac	89.62mph
1922	James Murphy	Murphy Spl	94.48mph
1923	Tommy Milton	H.C.S. Spl	90.95mph
1924	L. Corum/J. Boyer	Duesenberg Spl	98.23mph
1925	Peter De Paolo	Duesenberg Spl	101.13mph
1926	Frank Lockhart	Miller Spl	95.91mph
1927	Gorge Sounders	Duesenberg	97.55mph
1928	Louis Meyer	Miller Spl	99.48mph
1929	Ray Keech	Simplex Piston Ring Spl	97.58mph
1930	Billy Arnold	Miller Hartz Spl	10.45mph
1931	Louis Schneider	Bowes Seal Fast Spl	96.63mph
1932	Fred Frame	Miiler Hartz Spl	101.14mph
1933	Louis Meyer	Tydol Spl	104.16mph
1934	Bill Cummings	Boyle Products Spl	104.86mph
1935	Kelly Petillo	Glimore Speedway Spl	106.24mph
1936	Louis Meyer	Ring Free Spl	109.07mph
1937	Wilbur Shaw	Shaw Gilmore Spl	113.58mph
1938	Floyd Roberts	Burd Piston Ring Spl	117.20mph
1939	Wilbur Shaw	Boyle Spl	115.03mph
1940	Wilbur Shaw	Boyle Spl	114.27mph
1941	F. Davis/M. Rose	Noc-Out House Clamp	115.12mph
1946	George Robson	Thorne Engineering Spl	114.82mph
1947	Mauri Rose	Blue Crown Spark Plug Spl	116.34mph
1948	Mauri Rose	Blue Crown Spark Plug Spl	119.81mph
1949	Bill Holland	Blue Crown Spark Plug Spl	121.33mph
1950	Johnny Parsons	Wynn's Friction Proofing	124.00mph
1951	Lee Wallard	Belanger Spl	126.24mph
1952	Troy Ruttmann	Agajanian Spl	128.92mph
1953	Bill Vukovich	Fuel Injection Spl	128.74mph
1954	Bill Vukovich	Fuel Injection Spl	130.84mph
1955	Bob Sweikert	John Zink Spl	128.21mph
1956	Pat Flaherty	John Zink Spl	128.49mph
1957	Sam Hanks	Belond Exhaust Spl	135.60mph
1958	Jimmy Bryan	Belond AP Spl	133.79mph
1959	Rodger Ward	Leader Card 500	135.86mph
1960	Jim Rathmann	Ken-Paul Spl	138.77mph
1961	A.J. Foyt	Bowes Seal Fast Spl	139.13mph
1962	Rodger Ward	Leader Card 500	140.29mph
1963	Parnelli Jones	Agajanian Willard Battery	143.14mph
1964	A.J. Foyt	Sheraton Thompson Spl	147.35mph
1965	Jimmy Clark	Lotus powered by Ford	150.69mph
1966	Graham Hill	American Red Ball Spl	144.32mph
1967	A.J. Foyt	Sheraton Thompson Spl	151.21mph
1968	Bobby Unser	Rislone Spl	152.88mph
1969	Mario Andretti	STP Oil Treatment Spl	156.87mph
1970	Al Unser	Johnny Lightning Spl	155.75mph
1971	Al Unser	Johnny Lightning Spl	157.73mph
1972	Mark Donohue	Sunoco McLaren	162.96mph
1973	Gordon Johncock	STP Double Oil Filter Spl	159.04mph
1974	Johnny Rutherford	Gulf McLaren	158.59mph
1975	Bobby Unser	Jorgensen Eagle	149.21mph
1976	Johnny Rutherford	Hy-Gain McLaren	148.72mph
1977	A.J. Foyt	Gilmore Coyote	161.33mph
1978	Al Unser	First National Lola	161.36mph
1979	Rick Mears	Gould Penske	158.89mph
1980	Johnny Rutherford	Pennzoil Chaparral	142.86mph
1981	Bobby Unser	Norton Penske	139.08mph
1982	Gordon Johncock	STP Wildcat	162.02mph
1983	Tom Sneva	Texaco March	162.11mph
1984	Rick Mears	Penzoil March	163.61mph
1985	Danny Sullivan	March 85C-Cosworth DFX	152.98mph

• The Porsche 962 of Ickx, Mass, Bell in 1985

Le Mans is the pinnacle of the World Endurance Championship and, because it is spread over 24 hours, stands as a true test of endurance for a man, the machine he drives and the team who support him. The circuit is 8.467 miles long (13.626km), speeds along the Mulsanne Straight are over 200mph and the total distance covered in the 24 hours can be as much as 3,000 miles (approx 4,800km).

In recent years it has been dominated by the German team Porsche, who have managed to build into their cars almost super-human reliability and found two drivers – Jacky Ickx (Belgium) and Derek Bell (England) – who complement that precisely. Part of the attraction (and danger) of Le Mans is that a lot of inexperienced drivers seem to find their way in; and the difference in speeds between the front-runners and the rest is enormous. To take but one example: in 1984 the winner completed 359 laps, the last car to cross the line had completed only 255.

One of the problems can be that this part of France gets extremely hot, turning the cockpits into pressure cookers, exhausting the drivers – a team consists of two or three – who have to try and snatch an hour's sleep in nearby motorhomes while their partner takes over. At the end, extreme dehydration is not unknown and Bell himself, a very strong man, almost passed out one year, before a litre and a half of Evian water revived him.

Small wonder. Most ordinary motorists never achieve 130mph even for a fleeting moment in their lives, never mind doing it all the time for 24 hours.

RALLYING

Rallying was dreamed up as a way of convincing the public that the motor car was a reliable and worthwhile means of transport. That was at the turn of the century.

Today, we don't need assurances about something which forms an everyday part of our lives. And yet rallying has become one of the most popular and spectacular forms of international motor sport. Today, rallying is the great technical forcing house for the cars of tomorrow.

Rallying is, arguably, the oldest form of motoring competition. The London to Brighton run in 1896 saw the birth of the rally in its simplest form; a procession from A to B. Things became more serious in 1900 with the Thousand Miles Trial; a long and arduous series of road sections which included special tests. The aim was to show potential motorists that the automobile could do everything the manufacturers said it could.

In 1911 came the first Monte Carlo Rally. The RAC saw the potential in this and organised their first rally in March 1932. Over 350 car owners responded to the slogan "Enter the Rally and see Britain", an appropriate summary of the 1000-mile event which finished in Torquay. Along the way, there were speed hillclimbs and driving tests but, by and large, it was a jolly, social affair. At least five Earls had entered, along with a host of well-heeled socialites and motoring experts with names such as Fotheringham Parker and Scrap Thistlethwayte.

The next year, motorists were invited to take part in the Awfully Big Adventure . Many did and the RAC Rally became an annual event. But, while rallying in Europe became faster and faster, the British events were constricted by law. Speeds on the public roads were severely curtailed.

It became obvious that the rally would have to move off the roads if drivers were to continue racing against the clock. In 1960, the format of the RAC Rally changed dramatically.

Forest tracks were introduced and the Special Stage was born. Here, the cars would start singly and at regular intervals to drive flat out along rutted, gravel roads. These stages were linked by road sections which did not require a high average speed and the same basic principles apply today.

Now, rallies run for around 2,000 miles and the emphasis is on endurance for both the car and its crew. The co-driver's job is to navigate and generally help out. He often takes the wheel for the sections between stages, thus allowing the driver to snatch some sleep since rallies can often run for more than 24 hours at a stretch.

The kudos of winning a major international rally was not lost on manufacturers. Factory teams soon became common place and, by the mid Sixties, it was essential to send your crews to practice and prepare notes. This reconnaissance is not permitted on the RAC Rally but is a vital part of European events, most of which are held on fast, tarmac roads, closed to the public.

The increased competitiveness has led to cars specially prepared for rallying, a far cry from 30 years ago when you could enter a family saloon and stand a chance of winning.

Today's rally cars are the thoroughbreds which have paved the way for technological advances such as turbocharging and four-wheel drive. The investment costs manufacturers millions. The payoff is increased sales brought by success. Rallying may have changed greatly but the original idea of proving a car's durability still holds.

The first rally to catch the public imagination was from Peking to Paris in 1907 organised by *Le Matin* over a distance of 12,000km (7,500 miles). There were five starters, and the race was won by Prince Scipione Borghese of Italy driving an Itala. He took 61 days.

● The late Henri Toivonen

RAC Rally

Date	Driver	Car
1951	Ian Appleyard (GBR)	Jaguar
1952	Goff Imhof (GBR)	Cadillac-Allard
1953	Ian Appleyard (GBR)	Jaguar
1954	John Wallwork (GBR)	Triumph
1955	Jim Ray (GBR)	Standard
1956	Lyndon Sims (GBR)	Aston Martin
1957	Not held	
1958	Pete Harper (GBR)	Sunbeam Rapier
1959	Gerry Burgess (GBR)	Ford Zephyr
1960	Erik Carlsson (SWE)	Saab
1961	Erik Carlsson (SWE)	Saab
1962	Erik Carlsson (SWE)	Saab
1963	Tom Trana (SWE)	Volvo
1964	Tom Trana (SWE)	Volvo
1965	Rauno Aaltonen (FIN)	Mini Cooper
1966	Bengt Soderstrom (SWE)	Ford Cortina
1967	Not held	
1968	Simo Lampinen (FIN)	Saab
1969	Harry Kallstrom (FIN)	Lancia Fulvia
1970	Harry Kallstrom (FIN)	Lancia Fulvia
1971	Stig Blomqvist (SWE)	Saab
1972	Roger Clark (GBR)	Ford Escort
1973	Timo Makinen (FIN)	Ford Escort
1974	Timo Makinen (FIN)	Ford Escort
1975	Timo Makinen (FIN)	Ford Escort
1976	Roger Clark (GBR)	Ford Escort
1977	Bjorn Waldegaard (SWE)	Ford Escort
1978	Hannu Mikkola (FIN)	Ford Escort
1979	Hannu Mikkola (FIN)	Ford Escort
1980	Henri Toivonen (FIN)	Talbot Sunbeam Lotus
1981	Hannu Mikkola (FIN)	Audi Quattro
1982	Hannu Mikkola (FIN)	Audi Quattro
1983	Stig Blomqvist (SWE)	Audi Quattro
1984	Ari Vatanen (FIN)	Peugeot
1985	Henri Toivonen (FIN)	Lancia Delta

Pauli Toivonen, of Finland, won the 1966 Monte Carlo Rally in a Citroen. Exactly 20 years on, his son, Henri, dominated the event for Lancia, before tragically dying in an accident in the Corsican Rally in 1986.

• Hannu Mikkola on the Alps in 1973

MONTE CARLO RALLY

The Monte Carlo Rally is probably the most famous rally, if not the most famous motoring event in the world. The most successful partnership has been that of Walter Rohrl and Christian Geistdorfer, who have won the event on four occasions. Sandro Munari has also won four times, but not always with the same partner.

The Monte Carlo Rally, the classic Alpine event loathed by competitors because of the ever-changing weather conditions that can be encountered on the tortuous route, is arguably the most well known of all international motorsport events.

From being a rich man's "macho" proving test, the Monte captured the attention of ordinary folk in the Sixties when the beloved Mini trounced the opposition. And following a hesitant spell during the Seventies when a fuel crisis was rife, the rally's interest is on the up, with the world's leading car manufacturers once again bidding for glory.

The first Monte took place in 1911, attracting 23 crews who started from various points around Europe. The competitors were, in the main, well-off amateur drivers, who needed to average the now laughable speed of 15mph as they headed for the Principality.

The event was originally a commercial exercise to attract visitors to Monaco in the winter months – and it seemed to work. For the following year, the starting figure had quadrupled with cars being despatched from St. Petersburg, Turin and Le Havre.

After a brief experiment with a March date in 1924, the organisers reverted to the original January fixture, hoping the weather would provide a greater challenge. But crews needed a sterner test yet, and so a 50-mile loop over the mountains above Monaco was introduced.

Five years later, the French added a series of driving tests on the actual promenade, although complex regulations still discouraged "factory" teams. This, coupled with varying weather which could be encountered on the different routes, still made the rally something of a lottery.

But after the Second World War, the first post-war Monte in 1949 became much more popular, attracting hundreds of cars. This in turn created more interest for the general public, while the world's press were also forced to sit up and take notice – which of course tempted the "works" teams into action.

BMC and the Rootes Group, from Britain, and the French Citroen and Renault organisations roared onto the scene in the mid Fifties, and were joined by West Germany's Mercedes Benz when the advantages or disadvantages of one starting point, compared to another, were quashed. The organisers directed cars to a particular point from where they followed a "common" route south to Monte Carlo.

A decade later, with the number of starting towns reduced still further, drivers were now tested to the full. The route, starting from Chambery, consisted of a tough drive over snow covered mountains to Monte. They were then required to drive at speed along narrow ice covered tracks in a series of loops from Monte, and it was in this format that the Monte Carlo Rally began to hit the headlines.

In 1964, Ulsterman Paddy Hopkirk scored a superb win for BMC. His Mini Cooper 'S' – which had started from the Soviet Union – hardly missed a beat, while Finland's Timo Makinen dominated the following season's contest, which attracted nearly 250 cars.

• Walter Rohrl/Audi Quattro

• Henri Toivonen/Lancia Delta (54)

The biggest scandal in rallying occurred on the 1966 Monte when four British cars, three Minis and a Lotus Cortina were disqualified. They had, incidentally, finished in the first four positions.

Five times Formula One French GP winner, Louis Chiron who, although a Monegasque from Monte Carlo, was of French parentage, claimed victory in the 1954 Monte Carlo Rally for Lancia.

The region suffered a dismal winter, and all manner of weather was thrown at the competitors ranging from rain, snow and ice to blinding blizzards. But through it all emerged Makinen, benefitting from "studded" tyres which produced superb adhesion in the treacherous conditions, allowing the Finn to put on a faultless display.

The British team also "won" in 1966, until that is the French scrutineers disqualified the winning Mini for an insignificant lighting infringement which conveniently handed victory to Citroen – repeating the nation's dubious victory of 1961 when a Panhard again inherited the laurels following a rival's disqualification. Undeterred, the Brits returned to claim a hat trick of "official" Monte victories when Rauno Aaltonen triumphed in 1967.

The Seventies was very much the domain of the Italian Lancias, the prestige event now one for the big, well-financed "works" teams, whose budgets could afford numerous service vehicles and unlimited special tyres. Sandro Munari scored three consecutive victories in the raucous sounding Stratos in 1975, 1976 and 1977, having opened his Monte account in 1972.

More recently, Walter Rohrl has become the undisputed "Monte Meister", the 39-year-old West German netting wins in 1980, 1982, 1983 and 1984, the cars having been transformed into immensely powerful "supercars" offering phenomenal grip and traction on the route's slippery roads.

The first manufacturer to adopt the four-wheel-drive, turbocharged theme was Audi. Their trend-setting Quattro triumphed in Rohrl's hands in 1984, while Peugeot later took over the mantle of the car to beat with the 205 TI6 – Ari Vatanen scoring his one and only Monte success to date in 1985.

Lancia quickly followed suit with their unique super and turbocharged Delta S4. Henri Toivonen, having scored a debut win on the Lombard RAC Rally – the British forest event which unlike the Monte, does not permit prior practicing on the stages – followed it up by snatching the 1986 laurels.

The event that year was a total of 3,984km, which included 36 special stages of 881km, while 160 cars departed from six European locations (Bad Homburg, Barcelona, Lausanne, Paris, Sestriere and Monte itself). All headed for Aix-les-Bains on the Concentration (common) leg before starting the rally proper, which threaded its way to Monte via Vienne, Grospierres, and Gap. The third and final leg consisted of a 831km loop north of Monte Carlo which included the infamous Col de Turini, made so by the huge volume of vociferous Italians who camp in their thousands for the whole weekend.

Austin Rover also returned to the World Championship fray, and it's surely a sign of the times that the Cowley-based team had over 20 support vehicles – plus an aeroplane – all in radio contact with the two competing MG Metro 6R4's. As for tyres on the "tarmac" event, Michelin offered up to 20 different compounds to choose from – for each of the 36 stages – while rivals Pirelli transported almost 3,000 covers, including Grand Prix Formula One qualifying "slicks", over for the near 2,500 mile test.

The 1986 rally was the 54th running of the famous Monte Carlo Rally, an event which has changed beyond all proportions since its humble beginnings.

Monte Carlo Rally

Date	Drivers	Car
1960	Walter Schock – R. Moll	Mercedes Benz
1961	Maurice Martin – Robert Bateau	Panhard
1962	Erik Carlsson – Gunnar Haggbom	Saab (96)
1963	Erik Carlsson – Gunnar Palm	Saab (96)
1964	Paddy Hopkirk – Henry Liddon	BMC Mini-Cooper (S)
1965	Timo Makinen – Paul Easter	BMC Mini-Cooper (S)
1966	Pauli Toivonen – Ensio Mikander	Citroen
1967	Rauno Aaltonen – Henry Liddon	BMC Mini-Cooper (S)
1968	Vic Elford – David Stone	Porsche (911)
1969	Bjorn Waldegaard – Lars Helmer	Porsche (911)
1970	Bjorn Waldegaard – Lars Helmer	Porsche (911)
1971	Ove Andersson – David Stone	Alpine Renault (A110)
1972	Sandro Munari – Mario Mannucci	Lancia Fulvia
1973	Jean-Claude Andruet – "Biche"	Alpine Renault (A110)
1974	Not held	
1975	Sandro Munari – Mario Mannucci	Lancia Stratos
1976	Sandro Munari – Silvio Maiga	Lancia Stratos
1977	Sandro Munari – Silvio Maiga	Lancia Stratos
1978	Jean-Pierre Nicolas – Vincent Laverne	Porsche Carrera (911)
1979	Bernard Darniche – Alain Mahe	Lancia Stratos
1980	Walter Rohrl – Christian Geistdorfer	Fiat Abarth (131)
1981	Jean Ragnotti – Jean-Marc Andrié	Renault 5 Turbo
1982	Walter Rohrl – Christian Geistdorfer	Opel Ascona (400)
1983	Walter Rohrl – Christian Geistdorfer	Lancia Rally
1984	Walter Rohrl – Christian Geistdorfer	Audi Quattro
1985	Ari Vatanen – Terry Harryman	Peugeot 205 Turbo (T16)
1986	Henri Toivonen – Sergio Cresto	Lancia Delta (S4)

MOTOR BIKE RACING

all the motor bike world speed record-breakers a slim, iet German stands apart: Ernst Henne, who, on his BMWs, most single-handedly carried the sport away from the brute ce of huge engines bolted inside slender chassis and into e more subtle field of aerodynamics.

For eight years, between 1929-37, Henne was supreme, eaking the record six times and raising it from 137.58mph 21.540km/h) to 173.57mph (279.503km/h). That last cord, thanks to the Second World War, was to endure until 51.

Henne joined BMW in 1928 and soon afterwards they oduced for him the first machine with overhead valves. It is supercharged, too, which more than compensated for e engine's modest displacement of 735cc. Henne, in tight ite leathers with an aerodynamic conical infill on his back-le, crouched behind it to set his opening record on a stretch the Autobahn between Munich and Ingolstadt on 19 Sep-mber 1929.

A new era had begun, far removed from 16 June 1909 en Englishman Will Cook established the first world record th 75.92mph (122.16km/h) at Brooklands on his NLG orth London Garages) powered by a 944cc Peugeot V-twin gine. Later that year on an NLG boasting a massive 2713cc P engine, Cook went over 90mph (144.8km/h); but the run is not ratified.

By 1920 men were knocking loudly on the door of the Omph (160km/h) barrier and on 14 April 1920 American Ed alker was credited with 104.12mph (167.5km/h) on a 994cc dian at Daytona.

In one incredible day of speed at Arpajon, France, on 25 igust 1929, the record fell four times in front of 20,000 pic-cking spectators. Britain's reigning record holder Oliver aldwin was there. So were his great rivals, Herbert Le Vack, bert Denley, Freddie Hicks, Joe Wright and Bill Lacey.

Wright was the first to succeed, recording 126.12mph 02.931km/h) on his 996cc Zenith JAP. Then Le Vack was a cimal point faster on his 998cc Brough Superior JAP. right edged him again ... but Le Vack finished with

● Brooklands 1936

128.86mph (207.30km/h). Two years later he was killed in a road accident.

By then Ernst Henne had made his exciting appearance and seemed set to dominate. Joe Wright, though, had other ideas and at Cork, Ireland, in 1930 added a mighty 13mph to the world record to go through the 150mph barrier with 150.65mph (242.590km/h). It was two years before Henne reclaimed the mark with 151.77mph (244.4km/h) to begin four years of supremacy.

Everything that Henne had previously achieved, however, palled on 12 October 1936 when he unveiled his new, compact wonderbike. In place of the 735cc engine, BMW had introduced a highly supercharged 495cc version and instead of streamlining himself with cones on his backside, Henne was now totally enclosed by a fairing. Crouched inside, Henne recorded 168.92mph (272.006km/h) along the Frankfurt-Darmstadt Autobahn.

Briefly, Henne's record was usurped by Italian Piero Taruffi and his "flying pillar box", a 492cc Gilera enclosed in a stubby, yet ludicrously tall, red fairing. On 21 October 1937, at dawn, Taruffi clocked 170.27mph (274.181km/h) on the Autostrada between Brescia and Bergamo in Italy. His reign lasted three weeks. Then Henne wheeled the BMW onto the Frankfurt-Munich Autobahn to record 173.57mph (279.503km/h).

It was not until 12 April 1951 that the now retired Henne watched his record beaten as countryman Wilhelm Hertz aimed his 499cc NSU up and down the Munich Autobahn for an average 180.29mph (290.322km/h).

Four years later on an ordinary wet road at Swannanoa in New Zealand a 25-year-old Kiwi rider, Russell Wright, rode a standard 998cc Vincent Black Lightning complete with streamline shell to 184.83mph (297.640km/h). It was the last record to be set by a conventional motor bike on a conventional road. From now on all future attempts would take place at Bonneville Salt Flats in Utah, a hard, smooth eight miles (13km) by 15 miles (24km) stretch of white land.

Hertz, now 44, was the first to make his official mark there, simultaneously booming through the 200mph and 300km/h barriers on his 499cc NSU on 4 August 1956. His speed: 211.40mph (338.092km/h).

The 250mph barrier followed 14 years later. Californian Don Vesco, a Yamaha dealer, became his own best advert when he bolted two twin cylinder 350cc 2-stroke Yamaha engines together to bomb through Bonneville's measured mile at 251.66mph (405.25km/h) on 17 September 1970.

Vesco's monster ran on pump petrol. Not so Calvin Rayborn's contraption, a Harley-Davidson 1480cc which used nitromethane fuel and twice in 1970 raised the record, finishing with 265.49mph (426.40km/h).

Vesco was back on the salt in 1975 in his 1496cc Yamaha-powered Silver Bird and became, on 28 September, the first to exceed 300mph with 302.92mph (487.515km/h).

● Vesco's "Lightning Bolt"

And that after he had crashed during practice at 270mph.

Still it was not enough, Vesco wanted to go faster. And on Monday 28 August 1978 Vesco returned to Bonneville with 'Lightning Bolt', a streamlined, torpedo-shaped machine measuring 6.4m (21ft) long, a mere 533mm (21in) wide and 813mm (32in) high. Total weight was 545kg (1200lb) and the two Kawasaki KZ 1000 engines were turbo-charged and ran on methanol fuel. The frame was of welded tubular steel encased in a body of sheet aluminium 1.65mm (0.065in) thick. The wheels were of cast aluminium. A disc brake sys-tem was backed up by two parachutes.

On his first run Vesco entered the measured mile at 314.286mph (505.794km/h) and exited at 322.696mph (519.328km/h) for an average speed of 318.330mph (512.302km/h). Within the hour, as stipulated by the *Fédéra-tion Internationale Motocycliste*, Vesco notched another average speed of 318.866mph (513.165km/h) on his second run to give him an overall average of 318.598mph (512.733km/h). He had become the first man on two wheels to surpass 500km/h.

MOTOR CYCLING
500cc WORLD CHAMPIONSHIPS

The 500cc class of the World Road Racing Championships is the equivalent of car racing's Formula One. It is the ultimate in two-wheeled power and the peak of rider-challenge. A fully factory-supported works 500 machine represents the seat of costly and unlimited development. Such mounts are rare and priceless, and to become a highly-paid works rider like the current Rothmans Honda world champion, Freddie Spencer, is an Everest achievement.

This is the Grand Prix class which has created pages of history and legend through past winners like Geoff Duke (Norton-Gilera), John Surtees (MV-Agusta), Mike Hailwood (MV-Agusta), Giacomo Agostini and Phil Read (MV-Agusta), Barry Sheene (Suzuki), Kenny Roberts (Yamaha) and Freddie Spencer (Honda).

These greats of the sport are the eye-catching answer to an enthusiast's speed dream. Their stage is an exacting Grand Prix Circus with multi-cylinder machines now capable of reaching around 190 mph-plus. The showpiece dates back to 1949, when Britain's Les Graham won the first World 500cc Championship on his AJS.

A British-built challenger has long disappeared. For the past 11 years the progressive Japanese factories of Suzuki, Yamaha and Honda have dominated the 500 series.

They can continue to do so in 1986, when the series will be contested over 11 rounds in Spain, Italy, West Germany, Austria, Yugoslavia, Holland, Belgium, France, Britain, Swe-den and San Marino.

Britain, although lacking the competitive machinery, has continued to provide many leading stars of the sport. Immor-tals like Mike Hailwood, whose nine world championship vic-tories included four 500 titles on the renowned and depend-able Italian MV (Meccanica Verghera) Agusta and four 250 and 350 crowns with Honda during 1966-67, when he also raced in the 500 class. It was a unique and exhausting Grand Prix attempt, both physically and mentally. It included the sport's most costly development plan, aimed, unsuccessfully at winning the 500 title on a power-packed, hard-to-handle mount.

The Union Jack parade has seen world beaters like John Surtees, the only man to win world championships on two and four wheels (MV and Ferrari) and brilliant Barry Sheene, the courageous Cockney and double champion, who earned Suzuki their first crown in 1976.

Now the Stars and Stripes flies high, with the 23-year-old Freddie Spencer, from California, defending his second world title alongside the factory's Australian recruit, 26-year-old Wayne Gardner, fourth in last season's World 500 champion-ship.

Spencer followed the supreme Kenny Roberts, who sparked off the American invasion with Yamaha by winning the 500 championship in 1978, 1979 and 1980. Then came California's Yamaha-Marlboro 1984 winner Eddie Lawson, second to Spencer last season.

Italy's Giacomo Agostini, who won a record 15 world championships, eight in the 500 class, is manager of the Yamaha-Marlboro Team Agostini. He has signed Britain's Rob McElnea to partner Lawson in the 1986 series.

Big McElnea, from South Humberside, won the 1983 and 1984 Classic events and the 1984 Senior race at the Isle of Man TT. On an underpowered Suzuki he finished ninth in the 1985 World 500 Championship. He has the skill, courage and determination to join that elite band of riders who have cap-tured the sport's most coveted crown.

Kenny Roberts (2) leads Barry Sheene (7)

World Champions — 500cc Class

ate	Rider	Machine
49	Leslie Graham (GBR)	AJS
50	Umberto Masetti (ITA)	Gilera
51	Geoff Duke (GBR)	Norton
52	Umberto Masetti (ITA)	Gilera
53	Geoff Duke (GBR)	Gilera
54	Geoff Duke (GBR)	Gilera
55	Geoff Duke (GBR)	Gilera
56	John Surtees (GBR)	MV
57	Libero Liberati (ITA)	Gilera
58	John Surtees (GBR)	MV
59	John Surtees (GBR)	MV
60	John Surtees (GBR)	MV
61	Gary Hocking (RHO)	MV
62	Mike Hailwood (GBR)	MV
63	Mike Hailwood (GBR)	MV
64	Mike Hailwood (GBR)	MV
65	Mike Hailwood (GBR)	MV
66	Giacomo Agostini (ITA)	MV
67	Giacomo Agostini (ITA)	MV
68	Giacomo Agostini (ITA)	MV
69	Giacomo Agostini (ITA)	MV
70	Giacomo Agostini (ITA)	MV
71	Giacomo Agostini (ITA)	MV
72	Giacomo Agostini (ITA)	MV
73	Phil Read (GBR)	MV
74	Phil Read (GBR)	MV
75	Giacomo Agostini (ITA)	Yamaha
76	Barry Sheene (GBR)	Suzuki
77	Barry Sheene (GBR)	Suzuki
78	Kenny Roberts (USA)	Yamaha
79	Kenny Roberts (USA)	Yamaha
80	Kenny Roberts (USA)	Yamaha
81	Marco Luccinelli (ITA)	Suzuki
82	Franco Uncini (ITA)	Suzuki
83	Freddie Spencer (USA)	Honda
84	Eddie Lawson (USA)	Yamaha
85	Freddie Spencer (USA)	Honda

• Geoff Duke

• Giacomo Agostini

• Kenny Roberts

• Freddie Spencer

ISLE OF MAN TT's

Through the Isle of Man, just off the coast of England, there threads the most famous 37.733 miles (60.712km) in motor bike history. It includes 265 corners and bends, some of them gentle, sweeping curves, others vicious chicanes. This is the Mountain Circuit, annual test for TT (Tourist Trophy) riders and along the route are dotted the names of those who came to grief. There is Handley's Cottage, named after Walter Handley who crashed during the 1932 race. There is Doran's Bend, named after Bill Doran who broke his leg in a pile up at the left-handed corner in the Fifties.

There is Birkin's Bend after the tragic Archie Birkin who collided with a van during practice for the 1927 race and was killed. The roads have been closed to private traffic ever since.

There is Brandish Corner after Walter Brandish, who came off at the lefthander during practice in 1923 and injured his thigh so badly he never raced again. There is the Graham Memorial for Les Graham who was killed at the foot of Bray Hill in the 1953 TT. And the highest point on the Mountain Circuit has been re-christened Hailwood Heights after the incomparable Mike Hailwood, undisputed king of the island with 14 TT victories, who died so tragically in a car accident after his retirement.

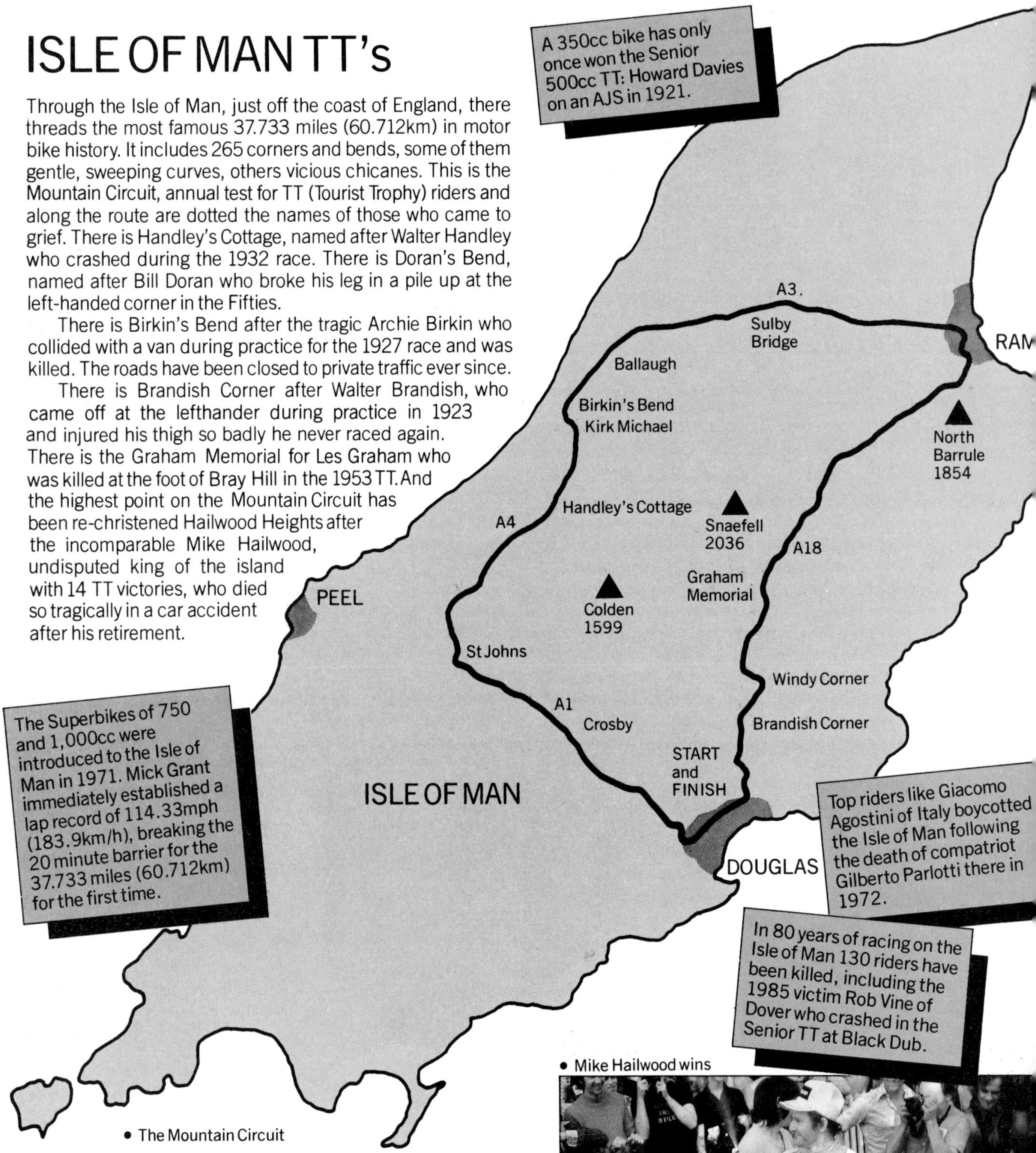

A 350cc bike has only once won the Senior 500cc TT: Howard Davies on an AJS in 1921.

The Superbikes of 750 and 1,000cc were introduced to the Isle of Man in 1971. Mick Grant immediately established a lap record of 114.33mph (183.9km/h), breaking the 20 minute barrier for the 37.733 miles (60.712km) for the first time.

Top riders like Giacomo Agostini of Italy boycotted the Isle of Man following the death of compatriot Gilberto Parlotti there in 1972.

In 80 years of racing on the Isle of Man 130 riders have been killed, including the 1985 victim Rob Vine of Dover who crashed in the Senior TT at Black Dub.

A3.
Sulby Bridge
RAM
Ballaugh
Birkin's Bend
Kirk Michael
North Barrule 1854
Handley's Cottage
A4
Snaefell 2036
A18
PEEL
Graham Memorial
Colden 1599
St Johns
Windy Corner
A1
Crosby
Brandish Corner
START and FINISH
ISLE OF MAN
DOUGLAS

• The Mountain Circuit

• Mike Hailwood wins

The Mountain Circuit was first used in 1911 and gradually modified until taking its present form in 1922. Before 1911 the St John's Circuit had been raced over from 1907 with a lap of 15 miles 1430 yd (25.442km).

The first 60mph (96km/h) lap over the Mountain Course came in 1924 from Jimmy Simpson on a 350cc AJS. In 1926 Simpson was first through 70mph (112km/h) on a 500cc AJS and in 1931 went beyond 80mph (128km/h) on a 500cc Norton. The 90mph (144km/h) came from a Norton too, ridden by Freddie Frith in 1937. But after such rapid advancement it was to be another two decades before Bob McIntyre beat the ton, when he sent his works-entered Gilera racing round for a

• John Surtees on a Vincent Grey Flash

ew lap record of 101.12mph (162.7km/h).

Now came the golden era for British motor bike racers on he Isle of Man. First Geoff Duke, then John Surtees, then like Hailwood . . . all of them giants of their time.

Duke, a Lancastrian, had learned to ride as a motorcycle spatch messenger during the Second World War. After working briefly in the BSA workshop he joined Norton and in 1949 laimed his first TT success in the Senior Clubman's race. he following year he was back in the Isle of Man to set a new p record while winning the Senior TT. In 1951 he won almost very competition he began in the world championship eries, including the Junior and Senior TT's, with lap records nd race records in both. In 1955 his lap record in the Senior T was announced as 99.97mph (160.88km/h), although nofficial timing recorded him at over 100mph (160km/h),

two years before McIntyre's official "ton-up".

John Surtees took up the high speed baton from Duke, joining MV Augusta in 1956 because Norton were winding up their racing programme. Surtees won six TTs and in 1960 became the first man to win the Senior TT three years running.

After Surtees came the greatest Manx rider of them all . . . Mike Hailwood. In a decade of motorbike racing that began in 1957 the Oxford-born Hailwood captured 12 TTs. At the age of 28 he retired to try his luck on four wheels, but returned ten years later in 1978 to win the Formula 1 TT on a Ducati. And in 1979, his farewell year, he took the Senior TT on a Suzuki RG 500A at a record-breaking 111.75mph (179.84km/h). On the way he set a new 500cc lap record of 114.02mph (183.49km/h).

• Kenny Roberts

The most consistent competitor in the Isle of Man was C.W. Johnston who started in 32 TT races over a 30 year period from 1922-1951, finishing in 13 of them and winning one, the 1926 Lightweight TT.

TRACK CYCLING

One of the most popular and fastest growing sports in Japan is track cycling, which draws vast crowds to the purpose-built indoor tracks and the performers are some of the highest earners in Japan.

Richest of them all is Koichi Nakano who won his first world sprint title in 1977 and has not lost it since. His nine consecutive wins are a record for any event at the world cycling championships.

Track racing dates back to 1880 when the first tracks were constructed in London (Paddington and Herne Hill), Manchester, Bristol and Coventry. The materials have varied over the years but present day velodromes are usually made of wood. The track, between 200m-300m long, is oval-shaped with prominent banking up to 55 degrees at either end.

When cyclists leave that banking and head for the line they can be reaching speeds well in excess of 40 mph (64km/h).

In sprint racing, competitors race over 1000m but their times are recorded only for the final 200m. By contrast to the fast speeds in the final sprint, the rest of the race is a cat and mouse affair with both riders jockeying for the best positions.

It is advantageous to be behind your opponent until the wind-up for the sprint finish, so sprint cyclists are expert at stopping dead on their bikes in order to let their opponent pass. But for sheer determination Giovanni Pettenella of Italy and Pierre Trentin of France take some beating. In their semi-final meeting during the 1964 Olympics they both stood still for 21min 57sec.

Sprint racing has produced some excellent champions over the years. France's Daniel Morelon must rank as the greatest amateur sprinter of all time. He won three Olympic golds, a silver and a bronze between 1964-76 and also seven world titles between 1966-75.

Jef Scherens (Belgium) and Antonio Maspes (Italy) each won the professional sprint title seven times, and rank second only to Nakano.

Britain, too, has produced a champion in the shape of Reg Harris, the former baker's assistant from Manchester. He was the man who put British cycling on the map after the last war – thanks to a somewhat charmed life. A tank he was travelling in blew up, nearly killing him, but he managed to come back and win the world amateur sprint title in 1947. Then, after breaking his neck in a car accident, he went on to win four professional world titles.

• Eddy Merckx

• Mark Gorski current Olympic champion

• The start in 1908

Cycling – Progressive 1 Hour Record

Km	Competitor	Venue	Dat
35.325	Henri Desranges (FRA)	Paris	11/5/9
38.220	Jules Dubois (FRA)	Paris	31/10/9
39.240	Van Den Eynde (BEL)	Vincennes	30/7/9
40.781	Hamilton (USA)	Denver	9/7/9
41.110	Lucien Petit-Breton (FRA)	Paris	24/8/C
41.520	Marcel Berthet (FRA)	Paris	20/6/0
42.360	Oscar Egg (SUI)	Paris	22/8/1
42.741	Marcel Berthet (FRA)	Paris	7/8/1
43.525	Oscar Egg (SUI)	Paris	21/8/1
43.775	Marcel Berthet (FRA)	Paris	20/9/1
44.247	Oscar Egg (SUI)	Paris	18/6/1
44.777	Maurice Richard (FRA)	St. Trond	29/8/3
45.090	Guiseppe Olmo (ITA)	Milan	31/10/3
45.325	Maurice Richard (FRA)	Milan	14/10/3
45.485	Frans Slaats (HOL)	Milan	29/9/3
45.796	Maurice Archambaud (FRA)	Milan	3/11/3
45.848	Fausto Coppi (ITA)	Milan	7/11/4
46.159	Jacques Anquetil (FRA)	Milan	29/6/5
46.394	Ercole Baldini (ITA)	Milan	19/9/5
46.923	Roger Riviere (FRA)	Milan	18/9/5
47.346	Roger Riviere (FRA)	Milan	23/9/5
48.093	Ferdinand Bracke (BEL)	Rome	30/10/6
48.653	Ole Ritter (DEN)	Mexico City	10/10/6
49.431	Eddy Merckx (BEL)	Mexico City	25/10/7
50.809	Francesco Moser (ITA)	Mexico City	19/1/8

Cycling — World Sprint Championships

Year	Amateur	Professional	Year	Amateur	Professional
93	Arthur Zimmermann (USA)	—	1946	Oscar Plattner (SUI)	Jan Derksen (HOL)
94	August Lehr (GER)	—	1947	Reg Harris (GBR)	Jef Scherens (BEL)
95	Jaap Eden (HOL)	Robert Protin (BEL)	1948	Mario Ghella (ITA)	Arie Van Vliet (HOL)
96	Harry Reynolds (IRL)	Paul Bourrilon (FRA)	1949	Sid Patterson (AUS)	Reg Harris (GBR)
97	Edwin Schrader (DEN)	Willy Arend (GER)	1950	Maruice Verdeun (FRA)	Reg Harris (GBR)
98	Paul Albert (GER)	G. Banker (USA)	1951	Enzo Sacchi (ITA)	Reg Harris (GBR)
99	Tommy Summersgill (GBR)	Major Taylor (USA)	1952	Enzo Sacchi (ITA)	Oscar Plattner (SUI)
00	A. Didier-Nauts (BEL)	E. Jacquelin (FRA)	1953	Marino Morettini (ITA)	Arie Van Vliet (HOL)
01	Emile Maitrot (FRA)	Thorwald Ellegaard (DEN)	1954	Cyril Peacock (GBR)	Reg Harris (GBR)
02	Chalres Piard (FRA)	Thorwald Ellegaard (DEN)	1955	Guiseppe Ogna (ITA)	Antonio Maspes (ITA)
03	Arthur Reed (GBR)	Thorward Ellegaard (DEN)	1956	Michael Rousseau (FRA)	Antonio Maspes (ITA)
04	Marcus Hurley (USA)	Ivar Lawson (USA)	1957	Michael Rousseau (FRA)	Jan Derksen (HOL)
05	Jimmy Benyon (GBR)	Gabriel Poulain (FRA)	1958	Valentino Gasparella (ITA)	Michael Rousseau (FRA)
06	Francesco Verri (ITA)	Thorwald Ellegaard (DEN)	1959	Valentino Gasparella (ITA)	Antonio Maspes (ITA)
07	Jean Devoissoux (FRA)	Emile Friol (ITA)	1960	Sante Gaiardoni (ITA)	Antonio Maspes (ITA)
08	Vic Johnson (GBR)	Thorwald Ellegaard (DEN)	1961	Hendrick Nijdam (HOL)	Antonio Maspes (ITA)
09	Bill Bailey (GBR)	Victor Dupre (FRA)	1962	Sergio Bianchetto (ITA)	Antonio Maspes (ITA)
10	Bill Bailey (GBR)	Emile Friole (FRA)	1963	Patrick Sercu (BEL	Sante Gaiardoni (ITA)
11	Bill Bailey (GBR)	Thorwald Ellegaard (DEN)	1964	Pierre Trentin (FRA)	Antonio Maspes (ITA)
12	Donald MacDougall (USA)	Frank Kramer (USA)	1965	Omari Phakadze (URS)	Giuseppe Beghetto (ITA)
13	Bill Bailey (GBR)	Walter Rutt (GER)	1966	Daniel Morelon (FRA)	Guiseppe Beghetto (ITA)
20	Maurice Peeters (HOL)	Bob Spears (AUS)	1967	Daniel Morelon (FRA)	Patrick Sercu (BEL)
21	Brask Andersen (DEN)	Piet Moeskops (HOL)	1968	Luigi Borghetti (ITA)	Guiseppe Beghetto (ITA)
22	Thomas Johnson (GBR)	Piet Moeskops (HOL)	1969	Daniel Morelon (FRA)	Patrick Sercu (BEL)
23	Lucien Michard (FRA)	Piet Moeskops (HOL)	1970	Daniel Morelon (FRA)	Gordon Johnson (AUS)
24	Lucvien Michard (FRA)	Piet Moeskops (HOL)	1971	Daniel Morelon (FRA)	Leijin Loeveseijn (HOL)
25	Jaap Meyer (HOL)	Ernest Kaufmann (SUI)	1972	*Daniel Morelon (FRA)	Robert van Lancker (BEL)
26	Avanti Martinetti (ITA)	Piet Moeskops (HOL)	1973	Daniel Morelon (FRA)	Robert van Lancker (BEL)
27	Mathias Engel (GER)	Lucien Michard (FRA)	1974	Anton Tkac (TCH)	Peder Pedersen (DEN)
28	Willy Falk Hansen (DEN)	Lucien Michard (FRA)	1975	Daniel Morelon (FRA)	John Nicholson (AUS)
29	Antoine Mazairac (HOL)	Lucien Michard (FRA)	1976	*Anton Tkac (TCH)	John Nicholson (AUS)
30	Louis Gerardin (FRA)	Lucien Michard (FRA)	1977	Hans-Jurgen Geschke (GDR)	Koichi Nakano (JPN)
31	Helger Harder (DEN)	Willy Falck Hansen (DEN)	1978	Anton Tkac (TCH)	Koichi Nakano (JPN)
32	Albert Richter (GER)	Jef Scherens (BEL)	1979	Lutz Hesslich (GDR)	Koichi Nakano (JPN)
33	Jacobus Van Egmond (HOL)	Jef Scherens (BEL)	1980	*Lutz Hesslich (GDR)	Koichi Nakano (JPN)
34	Benedetto Pola (ITA)	Jef Scherens (BEL)	1981	Sergei Koyplov (URS)	Koichi Nakano (JPN)
35	Toni Merkens (GER)	Jef Scherens (BEL)	1982	Sergei Kopylov (URS)	Koichi Nakano (JPN)
36	Arie Van Vliet (HOL)	Jef Scherens (BEL)	1983	Luts Hesslich (GDR)	Koichi Nakano (JPN)
37	Johan Van der Vijver (HOL)	Jef Scherens (BEL)	1984	*Mark Gorski (USA)	Koichi Nakano (JPN)
38	Johan Van der Vijver (HOL)	Arie Van Vliet (HOL)	1985	Lutz Hesslich (GDR)	Koichi Nakano (JPN)
39	Jan Derksen (HOL)	—			

Olympic titles

...ain's Reg Harris, in ...7, was the first man to officially clocked at ...der 11 seconds for the ...al 200m of a sprint. ...rris also won the 1974 ...itish professional sprint ...le at the age of 54 – 30 ...ars after winning his first ...ritish title.

CYCLING: TOUR DE FRANCE

For three weeks in June – July each year the French people turn out in their millions to watch the world's greatest cycle race, the Tour de France.

Even though the television companies give peak viewing time to live coverage of the race an estimated 10 million still line the 4,000km (in 1986) route to make it the biggest attended event in the world of sport. Those fans may only see a glimpse of the 150 or so riders for a few seconds but the Tour de France offers more than that.

It is an institution and the cavalcade and razzmatazz before the arrival of the riders is a carnival atmosphere loved by the race followers.

To have the Tour pass through a town, village or region is of the highest prestige and costly. Plumelec, in the Moribihan region, paid £350,000 ($525,000) for the privilege of staging the prologue to the 1985 race. "The cheapest way of publicising the region" said the mayor.

The race is spread over 23 days and covers a wide variety of French terrain. It passes through the vineyards of Bordeaux, the industrial area of the Nord, the plains of Normandy, the mountain regions in the Pyrenees and crosses the frontiers into many adjacent European neighbours. The 1974 Tour came to England for a special stage at Plymouth.

The starting point for the Tour varies from year to year, and has in recent summers been started outside France. But the race always finishes in Paris, on the Champs Elysées.

Financial rewards for Tour winners are great. It is not only the prize money from the race that will secure a rider's financial future, but the endorsements that follow. A winner of the race can expect to earn about £250,000 ($375,000) the year after his success. Even stage winners are regarded as heroes in France and can command around £3,000 ($4,500) appearance money per race, just for being billed as a "Tour de France stage winner". But any Tour winner will tell you he could not do it without the back up of his team who provide protection for their stars. All prizewinnings are shared among the squad of riders and the army of backroom boys such as mechanics.

The first Tour de France, held in 1903, was the idea of Henri Desgrange. It covered just 2428km in six stages and involved a great deal of night riding – something today's Tour riders do not have to endure.

Maurice Garin was the first in the long line of Tour de France winners. The host country dominated the event in the early years, and provided the first double winner in Lucien Petit-Breton.

Belgium broke France's domination just before and after the First World War, and Phillippe Thys was their outstanding rider. In the inter-war period France, Italy, Belgium and Luxembourg shared the honours but the post-war era saw the arrival of a succession of truly great champions.

The first was Italian Gino Barteli. He had won the 1938 Tour and, ten years later, became the only man to win the race both sides of the war. He was followed by Fausto Coppi, another Italian, who won the Tour in 1949 and 1952.

Coppi, who also claimed his native Tour of Italy five times, died at the age of 41 in 1960. Many believe he was the greatest of them all.

Frenchman Louison Bobet, who became the first man to win the Tour in three successive years – 1953-55 – succeeded Coppi. Then his compatriot Jacques Anquetil went one better

The longest race was in 1926 when the Tour covered 5745km (3569 miles)

Romain Maes, in 1935, is the only man to have won the Tour having worn the leader's yellow jersey from start to finish.

• Bernard Hinau

by winning the race four years in succession – 1961-64. I had also triumphed in 1957.

The 1965 champion was Felice Gimondi, the first Italia since Coppi to get among the world class cyclists. Had he n been racing in the same era as Belgium's Eddy Merck Gimondi could well have added to his list of honours, whic included wins in the other two gruelling tours, of Italy ar Spain.

Merckx arrived on the scene with his first Tour win in 196 and dominated the early Seventies, winning five times ar claiming a record 96 yellow jerseys. His five success equalled the record of Anquetil and in 1985 Frenchman Be nard Hinault joined them when he won the title for the fif time to add to his 1978, 79, 81 and 1982 triumphs.

Up to 1985 there had not been an English speakir winner of the Tour de France. Ireland's Shay Elliott and En land's Tommy Simpson both came close in the 1960 Simpson gave his life in the quest in 1967 when he collapse on the 13th stage from a combination of drugs and exhau tion. His final words " Put me back on my bike" became pa of the Tour de France legend.

Australia's Phil Anderson, America's Greg LeMond, Sco land's Robert Millar and Irish pair Sean Kelly and Stephe Roche are all vying for the honour of being the first Englis speaking winner of the race. Their rewards would immense.

The closest race was in 1968 when, after 25 days racing and 4665km (2899 miles) Holland's Jan Jansen beat Belgium's Herman van Springel by just 38 seconds. Jansen also became the first winner not to have worn the leader's yellow jersey.

When Bernard Hinault won the race in 1981 he won with the fastest ever average speed — 23.51 mph. (37.84km/h)

Tour de France

Date	Competitor	Date	Competitor
1903	Maurice Garin (FRA)	1965	Felice Gimondi (ITA)
1904	Henri Cornet (FRA)	1966	Lucien Aimar (FRA)
1905	Louis Trousselier (FRA)	1967	Roger Pingeon (FRA)
1906	Rene Pottier (FRA)	1968	Jan Janssen (HOL)
1907	Lucien Petit-Breton (FRA)	1969	Eddy Merckx (BEL)
1908	Lucien Petit-Breton (FRA)	1970	Eddy Merckx (BEL)
1909	Francois Faber (LUX)	1971	Eddy Merckx (BEL)
1910	Octave Lapize (FRA)	1972	Eddy Merckx (BEL)
1911	Gustave Garrigou (FRA)	1973	Luis Ocana (SPA)
1912	Odile Defraye (BEL)	1974	Eddy Merckx (BEL)
1913	Philippe Thys (BEL)	1975	Bernard Thevenet (FRA)
1914	Philippe Thys (BEL)	1976	Luxien van Impe (BEL)
1919	Firmin Lambot (BEL)	1977	Bernhard Thevenet (FRA)
1920	Philippe Thys (BEL)	1978	Bernard Hinault (FRA)
1921	Leon Scieur (BEL)	1979	Bernard Hinault (FRA)
1922	Firmin Lambot (BEL)	1980	Joop Zoetemelk (HOL)
1923	Henri Pelissier (FRA)	1981	Bernard Hinault (FRA)
1924	Ottavio Bottecchia (ITA)	1982	Bernard Hinault (FRA)
1925	Ottavio Bottecchia (ITA)	1983	Laurent Fignon (FRA)
1926	Lucien Buysse (BEL)	1984	Laurent Fignon (FRA)
1927	Nicholas Frantz (LUX)	1985	Bernard Hinault (FRA)
1928	Nicholas Frantz (LUX)		
1929	Maurice Dewaele (BEL)		
1930	André Leducq (FRA)		
1931	Antonin Magne (FRA)		
1932	André Leducq (FRA)		
1933	Georges Speicher (FRA)		
1934	Antonin Magne (FRA)		
1935	Romain Maes (BEL)		
1936	Sylvere Maes (BEL)		
1937	Roger Lapebie (FRA)		
1938	Gino Bartali (ITA)		
1939	Sylvere Maes (BEL)		
1947	Jean Robic (FRA)		
1948	Gino Bartali (ITA)		
1949	Fausto Coppi (ITA)		
1950	Ferdinand Kubler (SUI)		
1951	Hugo Koblet (SUI)		
1952	Fausto Coppi (ITA)		
1953	Louison Bobet (FRA)		
1954	Louison Bobet (FRA)		
1955	Louison Bobet (FRA)		
1956	Roger Walkowiak (FRA)		
1957	Jacques Anquetil (FRA)		
1958	Charly Gaul (LUX)		
1959	Federico Bahamontes (SPA)		
1960	Gastone Nencini (ITA)		
1961	Jacques Anquetil (FRA)		
1962	Jacques Anquetil (FRA)		
1963	Jacques Anquetil (FRA)		
1964	Jacques Anquetil (FRA)		

The 1983 Tour de France was the first for 11 years not to go out of France.

• Jacques Anquetil

• Sean Kelly — an English speaking winner at last?

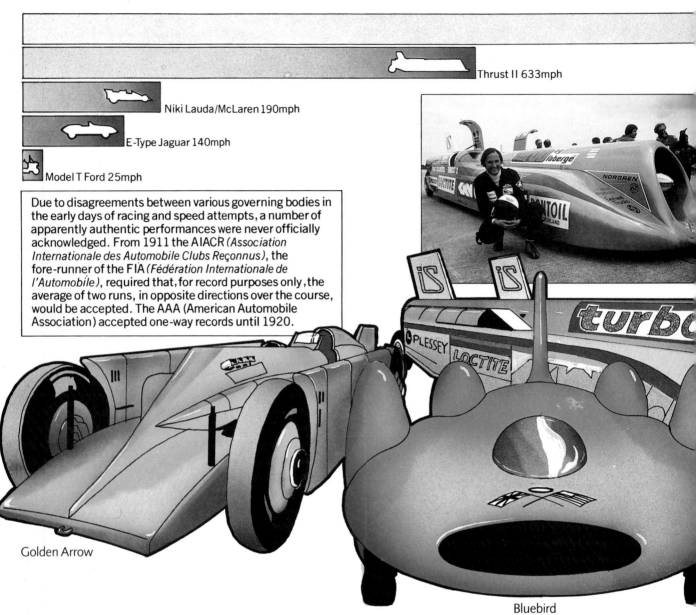

Thrust II 633mph

Niki Lauda/McLaren 190mph

E-Type Jaguar 140mph

Model T Ford 25mph

Due to disagreements between various governing bodies in the early days of racing and speed attempts, a number of apparently authentic performances were never officially acknowledged. From 1911 the AIACR *(Association Internationale des Automobile Clubs Reçonnus)*, the fore-runner of the FIA *(Fédération Internationale de l'Automobile)*, required that, for record purposes only, the average of two runs, in opposite directions over the course, would be accepted. The AAA (American Automobile Association) accepted one-way records until 1920.

Golden Arrow

Bluebird

LAND SPEED RECORD

The lure of speed has proved a fatal fascination for man since the appearance of the first horseless carriage. Like moths to a flame they have been drawn by the challenge of thrusting back the frontiers of power and pace.

Their names are now part of Britain's heritage: Sir Henry Segrave, John Cobb, Sir Malcolm Campbell and his son Donald. But all were surpassed on 4 October 1983, when Richard Noble, an eccentric Englishman, aimed his four and a half ton jet-propelled juggernaut across Nevada's Black Rock desert at an average speed of 633.468mph – thus increasing by more than 10mph the land speed record set by America's Gary "Gabalot" Gabelich 13 years earlier.

Noble's achievement ended nine years of glorious struggle when bankruptcy stared him, and his seemingly impossible dream, in the face on countless occasions. He talked his way to £1.75 million in sponsorship money and – more crucially – he persuaded the Ministry of Defence to part with a Lightning Fighter's Rolls-Royce Avon engine for £500. He called his project Thrust II, partly because of the jet jargon, but mainly because "it had a nice sexy ring".

Noble now has one more ambition . . . to stick wheels on a Concorde engine and send it booming through the sound barrier. "A supersonic racer is just around the corner," he says. "We have only scratched the surface of man's potential for speed on land. There is no reason why we should not travel at up to 2,000 miles an hour."

Two limiting factors determine the ultimate – the length of a flat surface capable of sustaining such velocity (Black Rock is 15 miles) – and the ability of the human body to withstand acceleration. Says Noble: "Tracks can be found, or even man-made. As for the bag of blood and bones to steer such a contraption, the human body is capable of withstanding far greater stresses than you would imagine." Back in the pioneer days of motor racing, doctors insisted humans would be unable to breathe at speeds of more than 60mph. Then scientists claimed friction would cause wheels to drop off at more than 200mph. Since then controlled tests at US air bases show man could withstand a force of 30Gs. If you consider that 20Gs is equivalent to accelerating from 0-440mph in *one second* you can see how much faster we are capable of going.

Concorde engine with wheels 2000mph?

- John Cobb
- Richard Noble

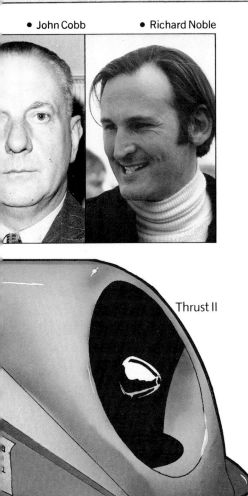

Thrust II

Richard Noble's wife Sally smashed a mirror on the morning of his attempt on the land speed record. Not perhaps the best omen on a day so fraught with danger, but Noble felt a strange sense of calm when he strapped himself into the cockpit and adjusted his oxygen mask at 3.19pm on 4 October 1983.

His first leg through the measured mile came up at 624.241mph. Within an hour he was in position for the second, crucial leg. He remembers: "The engine ran for just 59 seconds, but every tick of the clock was like an hour. Time expanded. As I reached optimum acceleration I was acutely aware of minute details like tyre tracks. Everything came and went in slow motion. All the time I was holding the steering wheel between finger and thumb. Any white knuckle stuff takes away the minute feeling that is so essential. As we came out of the mile markers I hit the parachute button and felt the familiar tug, bruising my ribs. As they opened the cockpit when we stopped, the usual cloud of dust swirled free and I could see everyone dancing about in celebration."

Progressive Land Speed Record

km/h	mph	Car	Driver	Venue	Year
63.16	39.24	Jeantaud	Comte Gaston de Chasseloup-Laubat	Achères	1898
66.66	41.42	Jenatzy	Camille Jenatzy	Achères	1899
70.31	43.69	Jeantaud	Comte Gaston de Chasseloup-Laubat	Achères	1899
89.34	49.62	Jenatzy	Camille Jenatzy	Achères	1899
92.78	57.65	Jeantaud	Comte Gaston de Chasseloup-Laubat	Achères	1899
105.88	65.79	Jenatzy	Camille Jenatzy	Achères	1899
120.80	75.06	Serpollet	Leon Serpollet	Nice	1902
122.44	76.08	Mors	William Vanderbilt jnr	Ablis	1902
123.28	76.60	Mors	Henri Fournier	Dourdan	1902
124.13	77.13	Mors	M. Augieres	Dourdan	1902
134.33	83.47	Gobron-Brillié	Arthur Duray	Ostend	1903
136.36	84.73	Gobron-Brillié	Arthur Duray	Dourdan	1903
147.03	91.37	Ford Arrow	Henry Ford	Lake St Clair	1904
148.52	92.30	Mercedes	William Vanderbilt jnr	Daytona	1904
152.54	94.78	Gobron-Brillié	Louis Rigolly	Nice	1904
156.25	97.25	Mercedes	Baron de Caters	Ostend	1904
166.65	103.55	Gobron-Brillié	Louis Rigolly	Ostend	1904
168.21	104.52	Darracq	Paul Baras	Ostend	1904
168.42	104.65	Napier	A. Macdonald	Daytona	1905
174.46	109.65	Darracq	Victor Hémery	Arles	1905
195.65	121.57	Stanley Steamer	Fred Marriott	Daytona	1906
202.69	125.95	Benz	Victor Hémery	Brooklands	1909
211.98	131.72	Benz	Barney Oldfield	Daytona	1910
199.72*	124.10	Benz	L. Hornsted	Brooklands	1914
215.25	133.75	Sunbeam	Lee Guinness	Brooklands	1922
230.64	143.31	Delage	Rene Thomas	Arpajon	1924
234.98	146.01	Fiat	Ernest Eldridge	Arpajon	1924
235.22	146.16	Sunbeam	Malcolm Campbell	Pendine	1924
242.80	150.87	Sunbeam	Malcolm Campbell	Pendine	1925
245.15	152.33	Sunbeam	Henry Segrave	Southport	1926
272.46	169.30	Thomas Special	Parry Thomas	Pendine	1926
275.23	171.02	Thomas Special	Parry Thomas	Pendine	1926
281.45	174.88	Napier-Campbell	Malcolm Campbell	Pendine	1927
327.97	203.79	Sunbeam	Henry Segrave	Daytona	1927
330.06	206.96	Napier-Campbell	Malcolm Campbell	Daytona	1928
334.02	207.55	White-Triplex	Ray Keech	Daytona	1928
372.48	231.44	Irving-Napier	Henry Segrave	Daytona	1929
396.04	246.09	Napier-Campbell	Malcolm Campbell	Daytona	1931
408.73	253.97	Napier-Campbell	Sir Malcolm Campbell	Daytona	1932
438.48	272.46	Campbell Special	Sir Malcolm Campbell	Daytona	1933
445.49	276.82	Campbell Special	Sir Malcolm Campbell	Daytona	1935
484.62	301.13	Campbell Special	Sir Malcolm Campbell	Bonneville	1935
502.12	312.00	Thunderbolt	George Eyston	Bonneville	1937
556.01	345.49	Thunderbolt	George Eyston	Bonneville	1938
563.59	350.20	Railton	John Cobb	Bonneville	1938
575.34	357.50	Thunderbolt	George Eyston	Bonneville	1938
595.04	369.74	Railton	John Cobb	Bonneville	1939
634.39	394.20	Railton-Mobil	John Cobb	Bonneville	1947
648.73**	403.10	Bluebird-Proteus	Donald Campbell	Lake Eyre	1964
664.98	413.20	Wingfoot Express	Tom Green	Bonneville	1964
698.49	434.02	Green Monster	Art Arfons	Bonneville	1964
754.33	468.72	Spirit of America	Craig Breedlove	Bonneille	1964
846.97	526.28	Spirit of America	Craig Breedlove	Bonneville	1964
863.75	536.71	Green Monster	Art Arfons	Bonneville	1964
893.96	555.48	Spirit of America -Sonic I	Craig Breedlove	Bonneville	1965
927.87	576.55	Green Monster	Art Arfons	Bonnville	1965
966.67	600.60	Spirit of America -Sonic I	Craig Breedlove	Bonneville	1965
1014.51	630.38	The Blue Flame	Gary Gabelich	Bonneville	1970
1019.46***	633.46	Thrust	Richard Noble	Black Rock Desert	1983

*The first official two-way run record.
**The last time that a wheel-driven car has held the record. The current best by such a car is 658.67km/h (409.27mph) by Robert Summers in *Goldenrod* at Bonneville in 1965. However in 1964 at Lake Eyre, Donald Campbell in *Bluebird* attained a speed of 690.90km/h (429.31mph).
***In 1979 at Rogers Dry Lake, USA, Stan Barrett in *The Budweiser Special* reached a speed of 1190.37km/h (739.66mph) over a short distance.

AIR SPEED

● Take off for powered flight – the Wright brothers 'Flyer' heralds a new era

● The Lockheed SR-71A

Can it really be only a little more than 80 years since those celebrated cycle-makers from Dayton, Ohio, the Wright Brothers were constructing their 30mph (45km/h) *Flyer* which achieved an undulating flight of 120ft (36.5m) in North Carolina on 17 December 1903?

Quite a leap from there to the 2,000 plus mph of the modern fighter or the 4,500mph of the American rocket-powered X-15A-2. Two World Wars have helped more than somewhat, of course.

The inaugural, ratified air speed record (recognised by the *Fédération Aéronautique Internationale*) came six years after *Flyer's* historic hop when, in 1909 Frenchman Paul Tissandier piloted a more sophisticated Wright biplane at 34.03mph (54.77km/h).

In these early, pioneer days dominated by French pilots, the emphasis was more on distance than speed. But in August 1909 both elements came together as Englishman Hubert Latham set the first world speed record over 100km during the Reims International Meeting. Flying an Antoinette he covered the distance in 1hr 28 min 17 sec for an average speed of 42mph (67km/h).

The first specifications for a military plane had been laid down by Brigadier-General James Allen, Chief Signal Officer of the US Army, in 1907. These included the stipulation that it must have a speed of at least 40mph in still air. Seven years later, at the onset of the First World War, speeds of more than 100mph were already commonplace.

The British S.E. 4, built at the Royal Aircraft Establishment just before the war was claimed to have a top speed of 131mph, although no figures were officially released for obvious security reasons. The most widely used military plane at the start of hostilities was the Etrich Taube monoplane, designed in Austria-Hungary with a maximum speed of 72mph (116km/h).

The first plane to be built specifically for aerial fighting was the Vickers FB5 Gunbus, powered by a 100hp Gnôme rotary engine in "pusher" configuration (i.e. rear propeller) and with a top speed of 70mph (113km/h). But this was clearly outsped by the German Fokker Eindecker with 87mph (140km/h) which created such havoc between 1915-16 that the period was named the "Fokker Scourge".

By 1916, however, the 93mph (150km/h) Airco de Havilland DH2 had appeared and the Fokker threat diminished. Then in 1917 came the two-seater Bristol Fighter powered by a 280hp Rolls-Royce Falcon 11 engine and capable of 125mph (201km/h). The most successful fighter of them all, however, was the Sopwith Camel with a maximum speed of 115mph (185km/h).

The war had brought the greatest minds in the world to focus on the importance of air supremacy. By the time it had ended in 1918 aviation had been revolutionised.

A far greater leap was to come in preparation for, and during, the Second World War two decades later. Most significantly of all, this war saw the introduction of the first crude turbojet engines in the shape of the Messerschmitt Me 262A which supplied a top speed of 536mph (868km/h).

At the war's end the allies were able to integrate the Germans' advance research into their own findings and the results were startling. In just ten years, from 1946 to 1956 the world record doubled – from the 615.65mph (990.79km/h) of Group Captain E. M. Donaldson in a Gloster Meteor to the staggering 1132mph (1822km/h) of Lt. Peter Twiss in the airey Delta 2 which established the first over 1000mph 600km/h) record. In between planes had gone supersonic, ooming through the Mach 1 barrier of 762mph (1,226km/h).

Twiss' Fairey Delta had been originally built to investigate he problems of transition from subsonic to supersonic speed. was powered by a Rolls Royce Avon turbojet. The data ained by the aircraft was later used in the development of the oncorde.

The SR-71A 'Blackbird' strategic reconnaissance aircraft f the United States Air Force set a world record air speed of 193.17mph (3529.56km/h) in July 1976.

But the fastest manned flight ever made had come almost n years earlier in the American X-15 series which were unched at altitude from a mother plane, the Boeing B-52. he X-15 was made of titanium and stainless steel with an airame covered with nickel alloy steel to withstand temperaures of between minus 184° Centigrade to plus 650° Centirade (−300° to +1200° Farenheit).

The following speeds were attained by the North American X-15 and X-15A-2, powered by rocket engines and carried to altitude under a Boeing B-52.

mph	km/h	Mach No	Pilot	Year
2111	3397	3.19	Joseph Walker (USA)	1960
2196	3534	3.31	Joseph Walker (USA)	1960
2275	3661	3.50	Capt. Robert White (USA)	1961
2905	4675	4.43	Capt. Robert White (USA)	1961
3074	4947	4.62	Maj. Robert White (USA)	1961
3300	5311	4.90	Joseph Walker (USA)	1961
3603	5798	5.27	Maj. Robert White (USA)	1961
3614	5816	5.25	Joseph Walker (USA)	1961
3620	5826	5.25	Cdr. Forrest Petersen (USA)	1961
3647	5869	5.21	Maj. Robert White (USA)	1961
3900	6276	5.74	Joseph Walker (USA)	1961
4093	6587	6.04	Maj. Robert White (USA)	1961
4104	6605	5.92	Joseph Walker (USA)	1962
4250	6840	6.33	William Knight (USA)	1966
4534**	7297**	6.72	William Knight (USA)	1967

**This speed is unlikely ever to be exceeded by another aeroplane*

Air Speed Record
(Recognised by the Fédération Aéronautique Internationale)

ph	km/h	Craft	Pilot	Year	mph	km/h	Craft	Pilot	Year
4.03	54.77	Wright biplane	Paul Tissandier (FRA)	1909	406.94	654.90	Supermarine S6B	Flt. Lt. G. Stainforth (GBR)	1931
3.34	69.75	Herring-Curtiss biplane	Glenn Curtiss (USA)	1909	423.76	681.97	Macchi-Castoldi 72	W/O. Francesco Agello (ITA)	1934
5.17	74.30	Blériot monoplane	Louis Blériot (FRA)	1909	440.60	709.07	Macchi-Castoldi 72	Lt. Francesco Agello (ITA)	1934
7.84	76.99	Blériot monoplane	Louis Blériot (FRA)	1909	463.82	746.45	Heinkel He 100V-8	Fl. Hans Dieterle (GER)	1939
8.20	77.57	Antoinette monoplane	Hubert Latham (FRA)	1910	469.17	754.97	Messerschmitt Bf 109R	Fl. Fritz Wendel (GER)	1939
6.18	106.50	Blériot monoplane	Leon Morane (FRA)	1910			— Second World War —		
8.18	109.73	Blériot monoplane	Alfred Leblanc (FRA)	1910	606.25	975.67	Gloster Meteor F4	Grp. Capt. H. Wilson (GBR)	1945
9.46	111.79	Blériot monoplane	Alfred Leblanc (FRA)	1911	615.65	990.79	Gloster Meteor F4	Grp. Capt. E. Donaldson (GBR)	1946
4.40	119.74	Nieuport biplane	Édouard Nieuport (FRA)	1911	623.61	1003.60	Lockheed P-80R	Col. Albert Boyd (USA)	1947
7.67	124.99	Blériot monoplane	Alfred Leblanc (FRA)	1911	640.60	1030.95	Douglas Skystreak D-558	Cdr. Turner Caldwell (USA)	1947
0.80	130.04	Nieuport biplane	Édouard Nieuport (FRA)	1911	650.78	1047.33	Douglas Skystreak D-558	Maj. Marion Carl (USA)	1947
2.71	133.11	Nieuport biplane	Édouard Nieuport (FRA)	1911	670.84	1079.61	North American Sabre F-86A	Maj. Richard Johnson (USA)	1948
0.18	145.13	Deperdussin monoplane	Jules Védrines (FRA)	1912	698.35	1123.89	North American Sabre F-86D	Capt. Slade Nash (USA)	1952
00.21	161.27	Deperdussin monoplane	Jules Védrines (FRA)	1912	715.60	1151.64	North American Sabre F-86D	Lt. Col. William Barnes (USA)	1953
00.99	162.53	Deperdussin monoplane	Jules Védrines (FRA)	1912	727.48	1170.76	Hawker Hunter 3	Sq. Ldr. Neville Duke (GBR)	1953
03.64	166.79	Deperdussin monoplane	Jules Védrines (FRA)	1912	735.54	1183.74	Supermarine Swift 4	Lt. Cdr. Mike Lithgow (GBR)	1953
04.32	167.88	Deperdussin monoplane	Jules Védrines (FRA)	1912	752.78	1211.48	Douglas Skyray F4D-1	Lt. Cdr. James Verdin (USA)	1953
06.10	170.75	Deperdussin monoplane	Jules Védrines (FRA)	1912	754.99	1215.04	North American Super Sabre YF-100A	Lt. Col. Frank Everest (USA)	1953
08.16	174.06	Deperdussin monoplane	Jules Védrines (FRA)	1912	822.09	1323.03	North American Super Sabre F-100C	Col. Horace Haines (USA)	1955
11.72	179.79	Deperdussin monoplane	Maurice Prévost (FRA)	1913	1131.76	1821.39	Fairey Delta 2	Lt. Peter Twiss (GBR)	1956
19.22	191.87	Deperdussin monoplane	Maurice Prévost (FRA)	1913	1207.34	1943.03	McDonnell Voodoo F-101A	Maj. Adrian Drew (USA)	1957
26.64	203.81	Deperdussin monoplane	Maurice Prévost (FRA)	1913	1403.79	2259.18	Lockheed Starfighter F-104A	Capt. Walter (USA)	1958
		— First World War —			1483.51	2387.48	Mikoyan Type E-66	Col. Georgi Mosolov (URS)	1959
71.01	275.22	Nieuport-Delage 29	Sadi Lecointe (FRA)	1920	1525.93	2455.74	Convair Delta Dart F-106A	Maj. J. Rogers (USA)	1959
76.12	283.43	Blériot monoplane	Jean Casale (FRA)	1920	1606.51	2585.43	McDonnell Phantom II F4H-1F	Lt. Col. Robert Robinson (USA)	1961
81.83	292.63	Spad biplane	Baron de Romanet (FRA)	1920	1665.89	2681.00	Mikoyan Type E-166	Col. Georgi Mosolov (URS)	1962
84.51	296.94	Nieuport-Delage 29	Sadi Lecointe (FRA)	1920	2070.10	3331.51	Lockheed YF-12A	Col. Robert Stephens (USA)	1965
87.95	302.48	Nieuport-Delage 29	Sadi Lecointe (FRA)	1920	2193.16*	3529.56	Lockheed SR-71A	Capt. Eldon Joersz & Maj. George Morgan (USA)	1976
91.98	308.96	Spad biplane	Baron de Romanet (FRA)	1920					
94.49	313.00	Nieuport-Delage 29	Sadi Lecointe (FRA)	1920					
05.20	330.23	Nieuport-Delage 29	Sadi Lecointe (FRA)	1922					
11.89	341.00	Nieuport-Delage 29	Sadi Lecointe (FRA)	1922					
22.93	358.77	Curtiss HS D-12	Brig-Gen Billy Mitchell (USA)	1922					
33.00	374.95	Nieuport-Delage 29	Sadi Lecointe (FRA)	1923					
36.54	380.67	Curtiss R-6	Lt. Russell Maughan (USA)	1923					
55.40	411.04	Curtiss HS D-12	Lt. A. Brown (USA)	1923					
67.16	429.96	Curtiss R-2 C-1	Lt. Alford Williams (USA)	1923					
78.47	448.15	Ferbois V-2	Adj Chef A. Bonnet (FRA)	1924					
97.83	479.21	Macchi M-52	Maj. Mario de Bernardi (ITA)	1927					
18.57	512.69	Macchi M-52bis	Maj. Mario de Bernardi (ITA)	1928					
57.67	575.62	Supermarine S6	Sq. Ldr. A. Orlebar (GBR)	1929					

This is the highest ratified speed attained by an aircraft which has taken off under its own power.

HORSE RACING

THE DERBY

Whether one regards the Epsom Derby course as the supreme test of the thoroughbred or as the *Illustrated London News* of 1864 would have it, "The worst and most dangerous course we have", there is no denying that this unique race run on the first Wednesday in June for three-year-old colts and fillies makes unusual demands on both horse and jockey.

It is fitting, therefore, that no man has shown a greater mastery of the idiosyncratic Epsom switchback track than Lester Piggott, the greatest jockey of his – or perhaps any – era.

Piggott's record breaking nine victories in the race have covered the whole spectrum of a jockey's art from the motionless grace with which he steered home the great champion *Nijinsky* in 1970 to the brute strength required to snatch a last stride win on *Roberto* in 1972. Piggott's record in the Derby will surely never be surpassed.

In marked contrast, the "Knight of the Turf" Gordon Richards, won the Derby on *Pinza* at his 28th and final attempt.

The concept for the world's most prestigious and influential race was hatched by two men – Edward Stanley, the 12th Earl of Derby and Sir Charles Bunbury. And the race name was decided on the toss of a coin during a rip-roaring party at Derby's home near Epsom.

Bunbury had the consolation of winning the inaugural one mile event in 1780 with *Diomed*. Four years later the current distance of one and a half miles was established.

But it was over a century before the 1886 Derby produced a winner with genuine claims to be hailed the greatest racehorse of all time – *Ormonde*. In the hands of the immortal Fred Archer, *Ormonde* easily defeated another champion *The Bard*, and was never extended in any of his 16 races. He is one of only eight Derby winners who remained unbeaten – the three this century being *Bahram* (1935), *Morston* (1973) and *Golden Fleece* (1982).

Records in other areas of athletic ability have been broken regularly in the post-war period, but the best time for the Derby remains that of *Mahmoud* (2m 33.8) in 1936. *Bustino* managed to shave nearly half a second off that in the electrically-timed Coronation Cup, over the same course and distance in 1975, but the point remains that racehorses have apparently stood still in the last 50 years. Whether that's because trainers are rooted to old-fashioned training methods or that we have come to a plateau in the physiological development of the thoroughbred remains to be seen.

Some claim it is simply that courses are more regularly watered these days to prevent jarring. When *Mahmoud* ran the dust was flying.

Certainly, despite the greater competition of racing in the modern age, we are going through a period where one horse is able to totally dominate his Derby rivals. *Sea-Bird's* two length victory over *Meadow Court* in the 1965 race in no way reflects his superiority, but the seven-length wins of *Troy* (1979), *Slip Anchor* (1985) and the record-breaking 10 length success of *Shergar* in 1981 satisfactorily mirror their dominance over contemporaries.

The narrow margins between victory and defeat can make a difference of millions to a stallion's value. In addition wherever vast sums of money are gambled the breath of scandal is never far away. Perhaps the most infamous case in he Derby was the 1844 'victory' of *Running Rein*. Six weeks ater the horse was exposed as a four-year-old called *Macabeus* and duly disqualified.

More regrettably, the 1961 race was marred when ante-ost favourite *Pinturischio*, reputedly the best horse Noel Murless ever trained, was twice doped and had to be with-Irawn three days before the event.

Fastest time: 2min 33.8sec Mahmoud (1936).

Biggest winning margin: 10 lengths: Shergar (1981).

Longest priced winners: Jeddah (1898); Signorinetta (1908); Aboyeur (1913).

Top Trainer: Robert Robson, John Porter, Fred Darling (7 wins).

Top jockey: Lester Piggott (9 wins).

● Steve Cauthen on *Slip Anchor*

DERBY

Year	Horse	Jockey	Year	Horse	Jockey	Year	Horse	Jockey
1918	Gainsborough	J. Childs	1941	Owen Tudor	W. Nevett	1964	Santa Claus	S. Breasley
1919	Grand Parade	F. Templeman	1942	Watling Street	H. Wragg	1965	Sea Bird II	P. Glennon
1920	Spion Kop	F. O'Neill	1943	Straight Deal	T. Carey	1966	Charlottown	S. Breasley
1921	Humorist	S. Donoghue	1944	Ocean Swell	W. Nevett	1967	Royal Palace	G. Moore
1922	Captain Cuttle	S. Donoghue	1945	Dante	W. Nevett	1968	Sir Ivor	L. Piggott
1923	Papyrus	S. Donoghue	1946	Airborne	T. Lowrey	1969	Blakeney	E. Johnson
1924	Sansovino	T. Weston	1947	Pearl Diver	G. Bridgland	1970	Nijinsky	L. Piggott
1925	Manna	S. Donoghue	1948	My Love	R. Johnstone	1971	Mill Reef	G. Lewis
1926	Coronach	J. Childs	1949	Nimbus	C. Elliott	1972	Roberto	L. Piggott
1927	Call Boy	C. Elliott	1950	Galcador	R. Johnstone	1973	Morston	E. Hide
1928	Felstead	H. Wragg	1951	Arctic Prince	C. Spares	1974	Snow Knight	B. Taylor
1929	Trigo	J. Marshall	1952	Tulyar	C. Smirke	1975	Grundy	P. Eddery
1930	Blenheim	H. Wragg	1953	Pinza	G. Richards	1976	Empery	L. Piggott
1931	Cameronian	F. Fox	1954	Never Say Die	L. Piggott	1977	The Minstrel	L. Piggott
1932	April the Fifth	F. Lane	1955	Phil Drake	F. Palmer	1978	Shirley Heights	G. Starkey
1933	Hyperion	T. Weston	1956	Lavandin	R. Johnstone	1979	Troy	W. Carson
1934	Windsor Lad	C. Smirke	1957	Crepello	L. Piggott	1980	Henbit	W. Carson
1935	Bahram	F. Fox	1958	Hard Ridden	C. Smirke	1981	Shergar	W. Swinburn
1936	Mahmoud	C. Smirke	1959	Parthia	H. Carr	1982	Golden Fleece	P. Eddery
1937	Mid-day Sun	M. Beary	1960	St Paddy	L. Piggott	1983	Teenoso	L. Piggott
1938	Bois Roussel	C. Elliott	1961	Psidium	R. Poincelet	1984	Secreto	C. Roche
1939	Blue Peter	E. Smith	1962	Larkspur	N. Sellwood	1985	Slip Anchor	S. Cauthen
1940	Pont l'Eveque	S. Wragg	1963	Relko	Y. Saint-Martin			

PRIX DE L'ARC DE TRIOMPHE

The Prix de l'Arc de Triomphe was introduced at Longchamp in the Bois de Boulogne, Paris, in October 1920 as a celebration of the return to peace after the First World War.

The concept of providing a genuinely international, all-aged, end-of-season test over the Classic distance of one and a half miles made a promising start and two of the early runnings were won by British-trained horses – Comrade (1920) and Parth (1923). But it was not until after the Second World War when the growing popularity of the new Tiercé bet made increased revenue available for French prize money that the Arc was elevated into the European race with the greatest international prestige.

The creation of a world championship for horses remains an unfulfilled dream but the Arc is the nearest thing we have, a fact which was never better demonstrated than in 1965 when Sea-Bird contemptuously brushed aside his unbeaten French comrade Reliance by six lengths, with the great Russian horse Anilin in fifth place and American champion Tom Rolfe sixth. That performance remains the most devasting victory in a top class event ever seen on a European racetrack since the Second World War.

A decade earlier, the Italian champion Ribot, who was never beaten in 16 races, had become only the fifth horse to win the race for a second time when trouncing Talgo and Tanerko. Ribot was the best horse bred by Federico Tesio, a remarkable man who as owner, breeder and trainer had dominated Italian racing for 50 years.

Ironically, Tesio was unable to see the crowning glory of a lifetime's work since he died before Ribot set foot on a racecourse.

Ribot went on to sire two subsequent Arc winners, Molvedo (1961) and Prince Royal (1964) but neither bear comparison with Sea-Bird's daughter Allez France, who won the race in 1974 and is arguably the best middle distance race mare trained in France this century.

Least lauded of all recent dual winners was Alleged, who represented the formidable combination of trainer Vincent O'Brien and jockey Lester Piggott. He easily justified favouritism in both 1977 and 1978 and yet has never really commanded the respect that tremendous feat deserves.

Fastest time: 2min 28.0sec Detroit (1980).

Biggest winning margin: 6 lengths: Ribot (1956); Sea-Bird (1965).

Longest priced winner: StarAppeal (1975) at 119-1.

Top trainer: Charles Semblat, Alec Head, François Mathet (4 wins).

Top jockey: Jacko Doyasbère, Freddy Head, Yves Saint-Martin (4 wins).

● 1984 winners Yves Saint-Martin and Sagace

● Rainbow Quest (right) about to beat Sagace in 1985

PRIX DE L'ARC DE TRIOMPHE

Year	Horse	Jockey	Year	Horse	Jockey	Year	Horse	Jockey
1920	Comrade	F. Bullock	1943	Verso	G. Duforez	1965	Sea-Bird	P. Glennon
1921	Ksar	G. Stern	1944	Ardan	J. Doyasbere	1966	Bon Mot	F. Head
1922	Ksar	F. Bullock	1945	Nikellora	R. Johnstone	1967	Topyo	W. Pyers
1923	Parth	F. O'Neill	1946	Caracalla	C. Elliott	1968	Vaguely Noble	W. Williamson
1924	Massine	F. Sharp	1947	Le Paillon	F. Rochetti	1969	Levmoss	W. Williamson
1925	Priori	M. Allemand	1948	Migoli	C. Smirke	1970	Sassafras	Y. Saint-Martin
1926	Biribi	D. Torterolo	1949	Coronation	R. Poincelet	1971	Mill Reef	G. Lewis
1927	Mon Talisman	C. Semblat	1950	Tantieme	J. Doyasbere	1972	San San	F. Head
1928	Kantar	A. Esling	1951	Tantieme	J. Doyasbere	1973	Rheingold	L. Piggott
1929	Ortello	P. Caprioli	1952	Nuccio	R. Poincelet	1974	Allez France	Y. Saint-Martin
1930	Motrico	M. Fruhinsholtz	1953	La Sorellina	M. Larraun	1975	Star Appeal	G. Starkey
1931	Pearl Cap	C. Semblat	1954	Sica Boy	R. Johnstone	1976	Ivanjica	F. Head
1932	Motrico	C. Semblat	1955	Ribot	E. Camici	1977	Alleged	L. Piggott
1933	Crapom	P. Caprioli	1956	Ribot	E. Camici	1978	Alleged	L. Piggott
1934	Brantome	C. Bouillon	1957	Oroso	S. Boullenger	1979	Three Troikas	F. Head
1935	Samos	W. Sibbritt	1958	Ballymoss	S. Breasley	1980	Detroit	P. Eddery
1936	Corrida	C. Elliott	1959	Saint Crespin	G. Moore	1981	Gold River	G. Moore
1937	Corrida	C. Elliott	1960	Puissant Chef	M. Garcia	1982	Akiyda	Y. Saint-Martin
1938	Eclair au Chocolat	C. Bouillon	1961	Molvedo	E. Camici	1983	All Along	W. Swinburn
1939-40	Not held		1962	Soltikoff	M. Depalmas	1984	Sagace	Y. Saint-Martin
1941	Le Pacha	P. Francolon	1963	Exbury	J. Deforge	1985	Rainbow Quest	P. Eddery
1942	Djebel	J. Doyasbere	1964	Prince Royal	R. Poincelet			

HE OAKS

he Oaks Stakes, named after the 12th Earl of Derby's home ear Epsom, was first run in 1779, a year before the inaugural erby.

The most prestigious race for fillies, the mile and a half lassic over the Epsom Downs has seen victories this century y the five most famous racemares ever seen on a British acetrack – *Sceptre*, *Pretty Polly*, *Sun Chariot*, *Meld* and *etite Etoile*.

Almost unbelievably, just two years separated the suc- esses of *Sceptre* (1902) and *Pretty Polly* (1904) in the race. *ceptre* won four of the five British Classics whereas *Pretty olly* "settled for" the fillies' triple crown of the 1,000 Guineas,)aks and St Leger, all of which she won easily. Her reputation aused only three opponents to take her on at Epsom and at 00/8 on she remains the shortest-priced favourite ever to in a Classic.

Not until 1942, when *Sun Chariot* dominated her con- emporaries, did a filly come along who could be mentioned in he same breath as *Sceptre* and *Pretty Polly*. *Sun Chariot* had bility and temperament in equal measures and never was his better demonstrated than in the wartime substitute Oaks vhich she won at Newmarket. Her mulish behaviour ruined hree possible starts before, at the fourth attempt, she umped off the best part of 100 yds behind the others. At that tage, those who had backed her at 4/1 on must have been hredding their betting tickets, but under Gordon Richards he came through in the final furlong to win by a length.

There was no early evidence that *Petite Etoile* would ecome one of the truly great fillies. Indeed, on her first public ppearance she was beaten eight lengths in a two-horse race! ven in the 1,000 Guineas (1959), when one of five runners rom the Murless yard, stable jockey Lester Piggott overlooked er in favour of *Collyria*. It was one of the most costly mistakes f Lester's career. Doug Smith steered *Petite Etoile* to victory vhile *Collyria* was unplaced.

Piggott, with four to choose from in the Oaks, did not make he same mistake, and nursed her beautifully to stay the one nd a half miles, winning in a canter. From then the partner- hip hardly looked back. *Petite Etoile* became the idol of the

● *Oh So Sharp*

racing public as she and Piggott toyed with top class opposi- tion, often leaving their devastating final thrust until the last 50 yds.

'Four years before *Petite Etoile's* Classic season, *Meld* had written her way into the history books by following up wins in the Guineas and the Oaks by taking the St Leger, despite coughing on the morning of the race and running below her brilliant best. Her Leger victory enabled trainer Cecil Boyd-Rochfort to become the first man to win £1 million for his own- ers.

Boyd-Rochfort's stepson, Henry Cecil, skilfully guided the most recent triple crown heroine *Oh So Sharp* to her great achievement in 1985.

Fastest time: 2min 34.21sec Time Charter (1982).

Biggest winning margin: 12 lengths – Sun Princess (1983).

Longest priced winner: Vespa (1833) at 50/1.

Top trainer: Robert Robson (12 wins).

Top jockey: Frank Buckle (9 wins).

OAKS

Year	Horse	Jockey	Year	Horse	Jockey	Year	Horse	Jockey
918	My Dear	S. Donoghue	1941	Commotion	H. Wragg	1964	Homeward Bound	G. Starkey
919	Bayuda	J. Childs	1942	Sun Chariot	G. Richards	1965	Long Look	J. Purtell
920	Charlebelle	A. Whalley	1943	Why Hurry	C. Elliott	1966	Valoris	L. Piggott
921	Love in Idleness	J. Childs	1944	Hycilla	G. Bridgland	1967	Pia	E. Hide
922	Pogrom	E. Gardner	1945	Sun Stream	H. Wragg	1968	La Lagune	G. Thiboeuf
923	Brownhylda	V. Smyth	1946	Steady Aim	H. Wragg	1969	Sleeping Partner	J. Gorton
924	Straitlace	F. O'Neill	1947	Imprudence	R. Johnstone	1970	Lupe	S. Barclay
925	Saucy Sue	F. Bullock	1948	Masaka	W. Nevett	1971	Altesse Royale	G. Lewis
926	Short Story	R. Jones	1949	Musidora	E. Britt	1972	Ginevra	A. Murray
927	Beam	T. Weston	1950	Asmena	R. Johnstone	1973	Mysterious	G. Lewis
928	Toboggan	T. Weston	1951	Neasham Belle	S. Clayton	1974	Polygamy	P. Eddery
929	Pennycomequick	H. Jelliss	1952	Frieze	E. Britt	1975	Juliette Marny	L. Piggott
930	Rose of England	G. Richards	1953	Ambiguity	J. Mercer	1976	Pawneese	Y. Saint-Martin
931	Brulette	C. Elliott	1954	Sun Cap	R. Johnstone	1977	Dunfermline	W. Carson
932	Udaipur	M. Beary	1955	Meld	H. Carr	1978	Fair Salinia	G. Starkey
933	Chatelaine	S. Wragg	1956	Sicarelle	F. Palmer	1979	Scintillate	P. Eddery
934	Light Brocade	B. Carslake	1957	Carrozza	L. Piggott	1980	Bireme	W. Carson
935	Quashed	H. Jelliss	1958	Bella Paola	M. Garcia	1981	Blue Wind	L. Piggott
936	Lovely Rosa	T. Weston	1959	Petite Etoile	L. Piggott	1982	Time Charter	W. Newnes
937	Exhibitionist	S. Donoghue	1960	Never Too Late	R. Poincelet	1983	Sun Princess	W. Carson
938	Rockfel	H. Wragg	1961	Sweet Solera	W. Rickaby	1984	Circus Plume	L. Piggott
939	Galatea	R. Jones	1962	Monade	Y. Saint-Martin	1985	Oh So Sharp	S. Cauthen
940	Godiva	D. Marks	1963	Noblesse	G. Bougoure			

THE KENTUCKY DERBY

Seattle Slew

Steve Cauthen on *Affirmed*

The Kentucky Derby is more than just a race, it is part of America's heritage and legend. Also called "The Run for the Roses" – the winning three-year-old is draped with a blanket of roses – the Kentucky Derby is staged at Churchill Downs in Louisville, Kentucky on the first Saturday in May.

First run in 1875, it gained prestige thanks to the promotional flair of Colonel Matt J Winn in the early years of the 20th century and rapidly became the showcase of US racing. However, the most famous American horse of all time, *Man O'War*, never took part in the 1920 renewal, his owner Samuel Riddle considering that the 10 furlong test came too early in the season for his colt.

Man O'War or "Big Red" as he was affectionately known, won 20 of his 21 races, his only defeat occurring in most unlikely circumstances when he was boxed on the rails. *Man O'War's* reputation was such that he started odds-on for every race and he set a standard by which even contemporary American horses are judged.

Perhaps the most famous of *Man O'War's* victories came in a celebrated match with the first Triple Crown winner, *Sir Barton*. It was the first time *Man O'War* had faced an older opponent, but he cantered in.

The term 'Triple Crown' first gained currency in the States in the 1930s and referred to the Kentucky Derby, the Preakness Stakes (1m 1½f) and the Belmont Stakes (1½m). Despite the fact that these races are run within a space of six weeks and do not demand the versatility required to succeed in the British equivalent, to complete the US Triple Crown is still considered one of the greatest achievements in American sport.

The first horse who drew comparison with *Man O'War* was *Citation*, who took all three jewels in the Triple Crown during 1948. Citation was kept in training after a leg injury with the specific purpose of becoming the first equine millionaire, a title earned in July 1951 when he lifted the Hollywood Gold Cup.

Canadian-bred *Northern Dancer*, currently the most famous stallion in the world, failed to stay the mile and a half trip of the Belmont Stakes, having won the '64 Derby and Preakness. It was therefore 25 years before *Citation's* Triple Crown feat was repeated by *Secretariat,* who registered the most phenomenal victory ever seen in a Classic when winning the 1973 Belmont Stakes by 31 lengths.

Willie Shoemaker, the most successful jockey in the world, has never found the Kentucky Derby a particularly lucky race until 1986. In a record which parallels Gordon Richards' lack of success in England, "The Shoe" has won only four Derbys in 25 attempts and in 1957 committed the cardinal sin of easing up before the line on *Gallant Man* and being touched off by Bill Hartack-ridden *Iron Liege.*

Eddie Arcaro shares with Hartack the record number of wins for a jockey (five) in the race and provides an inspiration for all slow starters in sport. On retirement Arcaro had ridden 4,779 winners, but his first 250 riders were losers.

Fastest time: 1min 59.4sec Secretariat (1973).

Biggest winning margin: 8 lengths: Old Rosebud (1914), Johnstown (1939), Whirlaway (1941), Assault (1946).

Longest priced winner: Donerail (1913) at 91½/1.

Top trainer: Ben Jones (6 wins).

Top jockeys: Eddie Arcaro and Bill Hartack (5 wins).

KENTUCKY DERBY

Year	Horse	Jockey	Year	Horse	Jockey	Year	Horse	Jockey
1918	Exterminator	W. Knapp	1941	Whirlaway	E. Arcaro	1964	Northern Dancer	W. Hartack
1919	Sir Barton	J. Loftus	1942	Shut Out	W. Wright	1965	Lucky Debonair	W. Shoemaker
1920	Paul Jones	T. Rice	1943	Count Fleet	J. Longden	1966	Kauai King	D. Brumfield
1921	Behave Yourself	C. Thompson	1944	Pensive	C. McCreary	1967	Proud Clarion	R. Ussery
1922	Morvich	A. Johnson	1945	Hoop Jnr	E. Arcaro	1968	Forward Pass	I. Valenzuela
1923	Zev	E. Sande	1946	Assault	W. Mehrtens	1969	Majestic Prince	W. Hartack
1924	Black Gold	J. Mooney	1947	Jet Pilot	E. Guerin	1970	Dust Commander	M. Manganello
1925	Flying Ebony	E. Sande	1948	Citation	E. Arcaro	1971	Canonero	G. Avila
1926	Bubbling Over	A. Johnson	1949	Ponder	S. Brooks	1972	Riva Ridge	R. Turcotte
1927	Whiskery	L. McAtee	1950	Middleground	W. Boland	1973	Secretariat	R. Turcotte
1928	Reigh Count	C. Lang	1951	Count Turf	C. McCreary	1974	Cannonade	A. Cordero Jnr
1929	Clyde Van Dusen	L. McAtee	1952	Hill Gail	E. Arcaro	1975	Foolish Pleasure	J. Vasquez
1930	Gallant Fox	E. Sande	1953	Dark Star	H. Moreno	1976	Bolf Forbes	A. Cordero Jnr
1931	Twenty Grand	C. Kurtsinger	1954	Determine	R. York	1977	Seattle Slew	J. Cruguet
1932	Burgoo King	E. James	1955	Swaps	W. Shoemaker	1978	Affirmed	S. Cauthen
1933	Brokers Tip	D. Meade	1956	Needles	D. Erb	1979	Spectacular Bid	R. Franklin
1934	Cavalcade	M. Garner	1957	Iron Liege	W. Hartack	1980	Genuine Risk	J. Vasquez
1935	Omaha	W. Saunders	1958	Tim Tam	I. Valenzuela	1981	Pleasant Colony	J. Velasquez
1936	Bold Venture	I. Hanford	1959	Tomy Lee	W. Shoemaker	1982	Gato Del Sol	E. Delahoussaye
1937	War Admiral	C. Kurtsinger	1960	Venetian Way	W. Hartack	1983	Sunny's Halo	E. Delahoussaye
1938	Lawrin	E. Arcaro	1961	Carry Back	J. Sellers	1984	Swale	L. Pincay Jnr
1939	Johnstown	J. Stout	1962	Decidedly	W. Hartack	1985	Spend A Buck	A. Cordero Jnr
1940	Gallahadion	C. Bierman	1963	Chateaugay	B. Baeza			

THE CHELTENHAM GOLD CUP

Who was the greatest ever steeplechaser – *Golden Miller* or *Arkle*? Despite the fact that *Golden Miller* won five consecutive Cheltenham Gold Cups from 1932 to 1936 while *Arkle* notched a hat-trick of victories ('64-6), the body of opinion comes down in favour of the immortal Irish horse, *Arkle*.

Golden Miller's record around Cheltenham might have been better, since the opportunity to make it six straight wins in 1937 was lost when there was no race. When he returned as an 11-year-old in 1938 he was narrowly beaten by *Morse Code*.

However, in *Golden Miller's* day the Cheltenham Gold Cup did not enjoy its current status. When Dorothy Paget's great chaser won for the first time in 1936 the first prize was just £670 whereas, in the same year, *Reynoldstown's* connections took home £7,095 for his second Grand National win.

Today prize money for the two races is almost identical but by the time *Arkle* came along the Gold Cup had already usurped the National's position as the championship race for chasers, even if there was still no prize money parity.

Mr F H Cathcart and the rest of the Cheltenham executive probably had no idea that the weight-for-age steeplechase over three and a quarter miles, which they introduced in 1924 at Prestbury Park, Cheltenham, Gloucestershire, would become the most coveted prize in the jumping calendar and the centrepiece of the finest three days in National Hunt racing, the Cheltenham Festival in March. Nor that their race would create an idol in *Arkle*, whose affection in public hearts has never been matched, not even by *Red Rum*.

Arkle was trained by the great Tom Dreaper and ridden in all 26 races over fences by Pat Taaffe.

He won 22 of them, meeting defeat as a young horse against the formidable *Mill House*, when giving away crippling amounts of weight in handicaps or, as in his final race, when fracturing a pedal bone in his off-fore hoof and finishing lame. At the relatively young age of nine he had run his last race.

Arkle recorded two of the most emphatic victories in the Gold Cup and twice easily defeated *Mill House* in the race. A measure of his ability is that *Mill House* had been talked of as

● *Dawn Run*

another *Golden Miller* but *Arkle* handsomely beat him on the last four occasions they met.

The Vincent O'Brien-trained triple winner *Cottage Rake* (1948-50) and the dual scorer *L'Escargot* (1970-1) who also went on to win a National, deserve honourable mention, as does the current Cup holder *Dawn Run* (1986), who won the coveted prize in her novice year.

The debate as to who was the greatest chaser will never be resolved, but few would argue as to the finest training feat in the history of the Cheltenham Gold Cup – 33-year-old Michael Dickinson's saddling of the first five home in 1985.

Fastest time: 6min 23.4sec Silver Fame (1951).

Biggest winning margin: 30 lengths: Arkle (1966).

Longest priced winner: Gay Donald (1955); L'Escargot (1970) at 33/1.

Top trainer: Tom Dreaper (5 wins).

Top jockey: Pat Taaffe (4 wins).

CHELTENHAM GOLD CUP

Year	Horse	Jockey	Year	Horse	Jockey	Year	Horse	Jockey
1924	Red Splash	F. Rees	1946	Prince Regent	T. Hyde	1967	Woodland Venture	T. Biddlecombe
1925	Ballinode	T. Leader	1947	Fortina	R. Black	1968	Fort Leney	P. Taaffe
1926	Koko	J. Hamey	1948	Cottage Rake	A. Brabazon	1969	What a Myth	P. Kelleway
1927	Thrown In	H. Grosvenor	1949	Cottage Rake	A. Brabazon	1970	L'Escargot	T. Carberry
1928	Patron Saint	F. Rees	1950	Cottage Rake	A. Brabazon	1971	L'Escargot	T. Carberry
1929	Easter Hero	F. Rees	1951	Silver Frame	M. Molony	1972	Glencaraig Lady	F. Berry
1930	Easter Hero	T. Cullinan	1952	Mont Tremblant	D. Dick	1973	The Dikler	R. Barry
1931	*Not held*		1953	Knock Hard	T. Molony	1974	Captain Christy	B. Beasley
1932	Golden Miller	T. Leader	1954	Four Ten	T. Cusack	1975	Ten Up	T. Carberry
1933	Golden Miller	W. Stott	1955	Gay Donald	A. Grantham	1976	Royal Frolic	J. Burke
1934	Golden Miller	G. Wilson	1956	Limber Hill	J. Power	1977	Davy Lad	D. Hughes
1935	Golden Miller	G. Wilson	1957	Linwell	M. Scudamore	1978	Midnight Court	J. Francome
1936	Golden Miller	E. Williams	1958	Kerstin	S. Hayhurst	1979	Alverton	J. O'Neill
1937	*Not held*		1959	Roddy Owen	B. Beasley	1980	Master Smudge	R. Hoare
1938	Morse Code	D. Morgan	1960	Pas Seul	W. Rees	1981	Little Owl	J. Wilson
1939	Brendan's Cottage	G. Owen	1961	Saffron Tarton	F. Winter	1982	Silver Buck	R. Earnshaw
1940	Roman Hackle	E. Williams	1962	Mandarin	F. Winter	1983	Bregawn	G. Bradley
1941	Poet Prince	R. Burford	1963	Mill House	W. Robinson	1984	Burrough Hill Lad	P. Tuck
1942	Medoc II	H. Nicholson	1964	Arkle	P. Taaffe	1985	Forgive 'n Forget	M. Dwyer
1943-44	*Not held*		1965	Arkle	P. Taaffe	1986	Dawn Run	J. O'Neill
1945	Red Rower	D. Jones	1966	Arkle	P. Taaffe			

THE CHAMPION HURDLE

Encouraged by the response to their new steeplechase, the Gold Cup, the Cheltenham executive repeated the level weights race experiment and inaugurated the Champion Hurdle Challenge Cup in 1927.

The early runnings were bedevilled by poor fields – only twice before the Second World War did more than 10 go to post – but the race steadily assumed its role as England's championship and now invariably decides the best hurdler in training.

The electrifying manner in which *See You Then* swept to his second successive seven length victory in 1986 bore the hallmark of greatness. Can he join the trio of all-time heroes – *Hatton's Grace*, *Sir Ken* and *Persian War*, who all won the race on three consecutive occasions?

Intriguingly, the three great triple Champions all failed to win the race at their fourth attempt.

Bought by Vincent O'Brien for 18 guineas, *Hatton's Grace* was turned into the first triple Champion Hurdler when taking advantage of *National Spirit's* last flight fall in 1951.

Tim Malony, who rode *Hatton's Grace* to the third and final win, then completed an unprecedented run of four successes in the race by partnering the legendary *Sir Ken* to victory in the next three runnings. During his time as Champion *Sir Ken* ran up an unbeaten sequence (Flat and National Hunt) of 17 wins.

It was 14 years before hurdling's next superstar emerged. *Persian War* had been only a modest maiden race winner on the Flat for Dick Hern, but was transformed by eight flights of hurdles and the care of Chepstow trainer Colin Davies into taking three consecutive 'Champions' from 1968 to 1970.

It was another 14 years before the great Irish mare *Dawn Run* won her Champion Hurdle (1984) en route to carving her own special niche in jumping's hall of fame by becoming the first horse to win the Cheltenham Gold Cup (1986) as well.

Fastest time: 3min 51.7sec See You Then (1985).

Biggest winning margin: 12 lengths: Insurance (1932).

Longest priced winner: Kirriemuir (1965) at 50/1.

Top trainer: Peter Easterby (5 wins).

Top jockey: Tim Malony (4 wins).

THE GRAND NATIONAL

Becher's Brook, Canal Turn, The Chair – even individual fences on the Grand National course have become part of everyday language as the race has developed into not only the most famous steeplechase in the world, but also one of the great annual sporting spectacles.

Four and a half miles over 30 fir-dressed, thorn obstacles and a heart-breaking 494 yd run-in from the last fence make the Grand National at Aintree the most forbidding test a steeplechaser can face.

Champions rarely win the race. *Golden Miller*, arguably the greatest chaser seen this century, won the 1934 running but failed to complete the course in four other attempts. Whereas lesser horses sometimes relish the unique demands on jumping, courage and stamina which Aintree makes. One thing is for certain, every winner is a hero.

Two horses, in particular, have left their mark on the race: *Manifesto* at the turn of the century and, in the modern era, the only triple winner, *Red Rum*.

Manifesto's record of eight appearances in the race is unlikely to be surpassed. He won it in 1897 and 1899 – sadly missing the 1898 race through injury when still in his prime – and made the frame on four other occasions. His final attempt came as a 16-year-old in 1904 and only once did he fail to get round.

Red Rum not only won the race in 1973, '74 and '77, but was runner-up on his other two tries – a record which turned him into a public idol. Quite rightly a full-scale bronze statue of *Red Rum* by the former jockey Philip Blacker is to be erected at Aintree in 1988 to celebrate the 150th anniversary of the race there.

Who would have thought back in 1839 when the appropriately-named *Lottery* won the inaugural running at Aintree that this marathon would develop such global appeal.

William Lynn, a Liverpool hotel owner instigated the race we know today as the Grand National. He organised precursors of the great event at Maghull just outside Liverpool, before the venue moved in 1839 to Aintree, a course skirted by the Leeds/Liverpool canal.

In 1843 the race became a handicap and was presided over by new Clerk of the Course Edward Topham, forging a family connection with the track which was to continue unbroken for 130 years. The title Grand National Steep-

---

CHAMPION HURDLE

Year	Horse	Jockey	Year	Horse	Jockey	Year	Horse	Jockey
1927	Blaris	G. Duller	1948	National Spirit	R. Smyth	1968	Persian War	J. Uttley
1928	Brown Jack	F. Rees	1949	Hatton's Grace	A. Brabazon	1969	Persian War	J. Uttley
1929	Royal Falcon	F. Rees	1950	Hatton's Grace	A. Brabazon	1970	Persian War	J. Uttley
1930	Brown Tony	T. Cullinan	1951	Hatton's Grace	T. Molony	1971	Bula	P. Kellaway
1931	*Not held*		1952	Sir Ken	T. Molony	1972	Bula	P. Kellaway
1932	Insurance	T. Leader	1953	Sir Ken	T. Molony	1973	Comedy of Errors	W. Smith
1933	Insurance	W. Stott	1954	Sir Ken	T. Molony	1974	Lanzarote	R. Pitman
1934	Chenango	D. Morgan	1955	Clair Soleil	F. Winter	1975	Comedy of Errors	K. White
1935	Lion Courage	G. Wilson	1956	Doorknocker	H. Sprague	1976	Night Nurse	P. Broderick
1936	Victor Norman	H. Nicholson	1957	Merry Deal	G. Underwood	1977	Night Nurse	P. Broderick
1937	Free Fare	G. Pellerin	1958	Bandalore	G. Slack	1978	Monksfield	T. Kinane
1938	Our Hope	R. Harding	1959	Fare Time	F. Winter	1979	Monksfield	D. Hughes
1939	African Sister	K. Piggott	1960	Another Flash	R. Beasley	1980	Sea Pigeon	J. O'Neill
1940	Solford	S. Magee	1961	Eborneezer	F. Winter	1981	Sea Pigeon	J. Francome
1941	Seneca	R. Smyth	1962	Anzio	W. Robinson	1982	For Auction	C. Magnier
1942	Forestation	R. Smyth	1963	Winning Fair	A. Lillington	1983	Gaye Brief	R. Linley
1943-44	*Not held*		1964	Magic Court	P. McCarron	1984	Dawn Run	J. O'Neill
1945	Brains Trust	T. Rimell	1965	Kirriemuir	W. Robinson	1985	See You Then	S. Smith Eccles
1946	Distel	R. O'Ryan	1966	Salmon Spray	J. Haine	1986	See You Then	S. Smith Eccles
1947	National Spirit	D. Morgan	1967	Saucy Kit	R. Edwards			

chase was adopted for the first time in 1847.

The economics of running the race proved too much for course owner Mrs Mirabel Topham and in 1965 began a sad series of the "last" Grand Nationals. Even after Mrs Topham sold the course in 1973, the place continued to decay and the threat of closure loomed large. And it was not until the course was bought by the Jockey Club in 1984 with marvellous financial support coming from the public that the future of the race was assured.

Outstanding Aintree achievements include: jockey George Stevens, who won five Nationals and completed the course on all 15 rides; Reynoldstown's two victories in the race from his only appearances; Vincent O'Brien's extraordinary feat of winning three consecutive Grand Nationals with three different horses – *Early Mist* (1953), *Royal Tan* (1954) and *Quare Times* (1955) – and Fred Rimell's record-breaking four victories even if the first of them, E.S.B. in 1956, profited from the inexplicable collapse of the Queen Mother's *Devon Loch* on the run-in.

Ironically, though, it has been during the period when the race was under greatest threat that some of the most romantic tales have arisen, broadening, if anything, its unbelievable appeal.

• The most famous steeplechase in the world

There was *Foinavon* taking advantage of an extraordinary pile-up at the 23rd to win in 1967 at Tote odds of 441/1; the era of *Red Rum* and the gallant attempt by *Crisp* to concede him 23lb in 1973; Bob Champion's 1981 victory on the twice broken down *Aldaniti*, having himself recovered from cancer and Dick Saunders becoming, at 48, the oldest jockey to win the race in 1982.

The Grand National refused to die; long may it continue.

Fastest time: 9min 1.90sec Red Rum (1973).

Biggest winning margin: Distance – Covertcoat (1913); Shaun Spadah (1921); Tipperary Tim (1928).

Longest priced winners: Tipperary Tim (1928); Gregalach (1929); Caughoo (1947); Foinavon (1967) all at 100/1.

Top trainer: Fred Rimell (4 wins).

Top jockey: George Stevens (5 wins).

*Only one jockey has been killed at Aintree. James Wynne O'Connell suffered fatal injuries when falling at The Chair in 1862.

• *West Tip* (No 8), 1986 winner

GRAND NATIONAL

Year	Horse	Jockey	Year	Horse	Jockey	Year	Horse	Jockey
1918	Poethlyn	E. Piggott	1940	Bogskar	M. Jones	1966	Anglo	T. Norman
1919	Poethlyn	E. Piggott	1941-45	Not held		1967	Foinavon	J. Buckingham
1920	Troytown	J. Anthony	1946	Lovely Cottage	R. Petre	1968	Red Alligator	B. Fletcher
1921	Shaun Spadah	F. Rees	1947	Caughoo	E. Dempsey	1969	Highland Wedding	E. Harty
1922	Music Hall	L. Rees	1948	Sheila's Cottage	A. Thompson	1970	Gay Trip	P. Taaffe
1923	Sergeant Murphy	G. Bennett	1949	Russian Hero	L. McMorrow	1971	Specify	J. Cook
1924	Master Robert	R. Trudgill	1950	Freebooter	J. Power	1972	Well To Do	G. Thorner
1925	Double Chance	J. Wilson	1951	Nickel Coin	J. Bullock	1973	Red Rum	B. Fletcher
1926	Jack Horner	W. Watkinson	1952	Teal	A. Thompson	1974	Red Rum	B. Fletcher
1927	Sprig	T.E. Leader	1953	Early Mist	B. Marshall	1975	L'Escargot	T. Carberry
1928	Tipperary Tim	W.P. Dutton	1954	Royal Tan	B. Marshall	1976	Rag Trade	J. Burke
1929	Gregalach	R. Everett	1955	Quare Times	P. Taaffe	1977	Red Rum	T. Stack
1930	Shaun Goilin	T. Cullinan	1956	E.S.B.	D. Dick	1978	Lucius	R. Davies
1931	Grakle	R. Lyall	1957	Sundew	F. Winter	1979	Rubstic	M. Barnes
1932	Forbra	J. Hamey	1958	Mr What	A. Freeman	1980	Ben Nevis	C. Fenwick
1933	Kellsbro' Jack	D. Williams	1959	Oxo	M. Scudamore	1981	Aldaniti	R. Champion
1934	Golden Miller	G. Wilson	1960	Merryman II	G. Scott	1982	Grittar	R. Saunders
1935	Reynoldstown	F. Furlong	1961	Nicolaus Silver	H. Beasley	1983	Corbiere	B. De Haan
1936	Reynoldstown	F. Walwyn	1962	Kilmore	F. Winter	1984	Hallo Dandy	N. Doughty
1937	Royal Mail	E. Williams	1963	Ayala	P. Buckley	1985	Last Suspect	H. Davies
1938	Battleship	B. Hobbs	1964	Team Spirit	W. Robinson	1986	West Tip	R. Dunwoody
1939	Workman	T. Hyde	1965	Jay Trump	C. Smith			

SHOW JUMPING

Britain's Houses of Parliament are responsible for the birth of show jumping with the passing of the Enclosure Act in the 18th century, when it no longer became possible to cross the country without clearing obstacles.

The transition from a simple means of transport to a form of entertainment was a slow and painful process. When horse and rider first appeared in the ring at a harness or agricultural show, it was only to parade before the public. They were then sent out into the nearby countryside to jump a few natural obstacles, out of view of the disappointed spectators. Show jumping was all jump and nothing to show! The public complained, with the result that a series of simple fences were built in the arena and the world was given a new sport.

The contests for "wide" and "high" leaps staged in Dublin in 1865 were among the earliest show jumping competitions ever staged. Jumping was to become popular in a number of countries in the late 19th century, though it bore little resemblance to today's sport. Rules were non-existent when agricultural shows in England began to include "lepping"

in their programmes during the 1870s. The rules that were introduced when show jumping became an Olympic event in 1912 were far more complex than today. Thin strips of wood, known as "slats", were placed on top of each fence and horses were penalised for "touching" an obstacle and thereby dislodging the slat. Lowering the actual fence was twice as costly if the impact came from the horse's fore (rather than hind) legs. This put a great deal of reliance on the eyesight of the and led to judges frequent controversy.

• Harvey Smith

At the second modern Olympics in Paris in 1900 three jumping classes were included, but it was not until after another 12 years that equestrian sports became accepted as a regular part of the Games.

Nick Skelton, one of Britain's leading professional riders, soared to prominence in 1978 when he broke the high jump record at Olympia in London which had stood for 41 years. Riding the German-bred *Lastic*, he cleared 7ft 7¼in (2.32m) in the puissance, the competition which tests jumping ability alone.

Col. Harry Llewellyn and *Foxhunter* in the 1952 Olympics

• Pat Smythe with *Tosca*

Slats, though abolished from Olympic jumping in time for the 1920 Games, continued to be used in Britain and some other countries until the late 1940s. Meanwhile the *Fédération Équestre Internationale* had been founded in 1921 to become the ruling body for all equestrian sport except racing, and it produced the complete set of rules for international show jumping contests that had been so urgently needed.

International jumping was almost entirely confined to army officers but after the 1948 Olympics in London, when all 44 show jumping competitors were military men, things changed. As the number of cavalry regiments declined the sport was opened up.

However, three notable military men, Britain's Lt. Col. Harry Llewellyn on his legendary *Foxhunter* and the stylish d'Inzeo brothers of the Italian cavalry, were to be leading lights after the civilians had moved in. During the post-war years show jumping literally took a major leap forward, especially as a spectator sport. Courses, hitherto very dull, became far more imaginative; time was used as the deciding factor in most jump-offs so that an outright winner emerged. Pat Smythe gave an added impetus by providing the sport with a talented leading lady.

Already popular on television in the 1950s, (Britain won Olympic gold in Helsinki in 1952), show jumping received greatly increased coverage – and some would say eventual over-exposure – during the next two decades. More money came into it as a result, with big prizes and the sponsorship of

Britain staged her first international horse show at Olympia in 1907 and seven overseas countries were represented. The Dutch and the Belgians rode off with most of the prize money. Two years later international classes were held at Lucerne and Madison Square Garden, New York, where the national horse show had been in existence since 1883.

Baron de Coubertin, who was responsible for reviving the Olympic Games, played a leading role in the birth of the *Fédération Équestre Internationale*, the sport's ruling body. There was an urgent need for a complete set of international rules and regulations and the Baron instigated a meeting of the leading nations. The FEI was founded in 1921 and it was not until two years later that the British Show Jumping Association was formed.

individual riders. Britain's two main beneficiaries, David Broome and Harvey Smith, turned professional.

In the early 1970s many Britons were pushed, in some cases unwillingly, into the professional ranks. Prince Philip, in his role as President of the International Federation, had asked all the member countries to "put their houses in order" by eliminating "shamateurism". Having done so, the British found themselves out on a limb when other countries failed to follow suit.

Sponsorship of professional riders in Britain, and of the few elsewhere who had voluntarily changed their status, was to saddle some of the horses with extended commercial names – *Sanyo Olympic Video* and *Willora Carpets* are just two examples.

The burgeoning success of the excellent Whitaker brothers, both still amateurs, brought a glimmer of hope back to Britain's Olympic aspirations that seemed to have been obliterated by the switch to professionalism. When the United States won the 1984 Olympic team event, Britain's amateurs gave the sport at home a tremendous boost by finishing second, above the powerful Germans.

In this immensely skilful sport, which uses distance problems as well as the height and width of fences to sort the chaff from the wheat, Britain, Germany and America have long been dominant. By the end of 1985, professional Nick Skelton had a massive lead in the British computer rankings, but there were already heartening signs of new amateur blood emerging.

• David Broome

EVENTING

The testing and training of horses by means of athletic exercises has probably existed ever since man discovered the benefits of horsepower 3,000 years ago. It barely seemed feasible, however, that a routine devised by French cavalry officers for their chargers in 1902 could evolve into the major sport of three-day eventing. Variations on this French theme which comprised dressage, steeplechase, a gruelling long distance ride and show jumping, soon spread to other countries – notably Sweden, whose Count Clarence von Rosen was largely responsible for introducing equestrian events into the Olympic Games in 1912. The sport was then known as the "Military" or "Pentathlon on horseback."

British cavalry officers showed little interest, regarding the dressage phase as a bit of Continental nonsense. In their eyes the much older pursuits of hunting and polo were infinitely superior. Sweden won the 1912 Olympic Military, while all four of the British officers who took part were eliminated.

Though the rules allowed civilians to compete from 1924, the Olympic three-day event was to remain a military bastion until after the Games in London in 1948. That year the Olympic three-day event was staged at Aldershot where the Duke of Beaufort was among the spectators. Intrigued by the sport and dismayed by the poor showing of the eliminated British team, he decided to introduce eventing to his estate at Badminton. The inaugural contest took place in 1949 and it was an instant success.

Both competitors and public saw the new sport as a marvellous all-round test of horse and rider, with its three separate phases – dressage to test the horses' obedience in a series of gymnastic exercises, then speed, endurance and cross-country, followed by the final show jumping.

The cross-country was (as it rightly remains) the thrilling ingredient, with brave horses and riders tackling the most awesomely solid fences that most people had ever seen. Though the show jumping seemed comparatively tame, it was soon realised how nail-bitingly exciting this final phase could be when the marks were close. Badminton has since grown into the biggest equestrian occasion on the British calendar and the greatest annual three-day event in the world. On the Saturday alone, a quarter of a million people annually make the pilgrimage.

Once Badminton was established, British riders were quick to capitalise on their experience in the hunting field by proving their superiority across country. Their dressage was often weak but, in the Fifties and Sixties, it was still possible to win after a mediocre dressage if you could achieve a bold and faultless performance across country. For two decades, Britain was by far and away the most successful nation.

British women, though barred from the Olympics until 1968, made a valiant contribution to that success and did their best to refute the prevailing view that the sport was too tough for girls. But the controversy about selecting women to

Badminton

Year	Winner	Horse
1949	John Shedden (GBR)	Golden Willow
1950	Tony Collings (GBR)	Remus
1951	Hans Schwarzenbach (SUI)	Vae Victus
1952	Mark Darley (IRL)	Emily Little
1953	Lawrence Rook (GBR)	Starlight
1954	Margaret Hough (GBR)	Bambi
1955	Francis Weldon (GBR)	Kilbarry
1956	Francis Weldon (GBR)	Kilbarry
1957	Sheila Wilcox (GBR)	High and Mighty
1958	Sheila Wilcox (GBR)	High and Mighty
1959	Sheila Waddington (née Wilcox) (GBR)	Airs and Graces
1960	William Roycroft (AUS)	Our Solo
1961	Lawrence Morgan (AUS)	Salad Days
1962	Anneli Drummond-Hay (GBR)	Merely-A-Monarch
1963	*Not held*	
1964	James Templar (GBR)	M'Lord Connolly
1965	Eddie Boylan (IRL)	Durlas Eile
1966	*Not held*	
1967	Celia Ross-Taylor (GBR)	Jonathan
1968	Jane Bullen (GBR)	Our Nobby
1969	Richard Walker (GBR)	Pasha
1970	Richard Meade (GBR)	The Poacher
1971	Mark Phillips (GBR)	Great Ovation
1972	Mark Phillips (GBR)	Great Ovation
1973	Lucinda Prior-Palmer (GBR)	Be Fair
1974	Mark Phillips (GBR)	Columbus
1975	*Not held*	
1976	Lucinda Prior-Palmer (GBR)	Wideawake
1977	Lucinda Prior-Palmer (GBR)	George
1978	Jane Holderness-Roddam (née Bullen) (GBR)	Warrior
1979	Lucinda Prior-Palmer (GBR)	Killaire
1980	Mark Todd (NZL)	Southern Comfort
1981	Mark Phillips (GBR)	Lincoln
1982	Richard Meade (GBR)	Spectator III
1983	Lucinda Green (née Prior-Palmer) (GBR)	Regal Realm
1984	Lucinda Green (GBR)	Beagle Bay
1985	Virginia Holgate (GBR)	Priceless

• Dressage   • Cross-country   • Show jumping

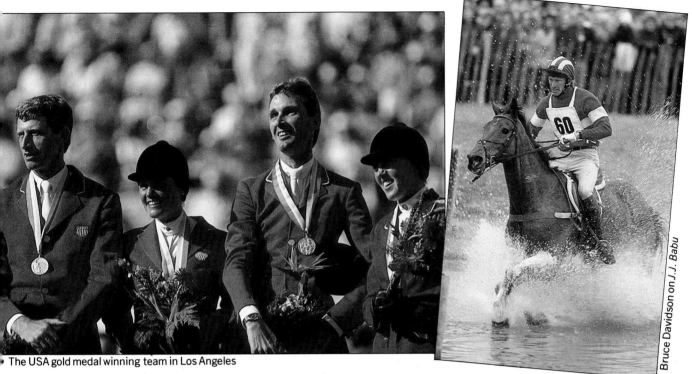

The USA gold medal winning team in Los Angeles

Bruce Davidson on *J.J. Babu*

compete against teams that were nearly always exclusively male was to persist through the 1970s. It continued long after Princess Anne had won the 1971 European Championship and Lucinda Prior-Palmer (now Mrs Green) had emerged as the world's most thrilling cross-country rider, before it finally petered out.

Despite Lucinda's brilliance and her many individual triumphs (which by 1984 included a World Championship, two European titles and six Badmintons), the eight years from 1973 to 1980 were comparatively lean for Britain. An increasing number of good dressage riders in other countries had begun to get their cross-country act together. The United States, strong in all departments, moved ahead – with Bruce Davidson twice winning the World title. Responding to the challenge the British selectors looked for new blood among the younger horses and the British riders took a more profound interest in dressage.

A great new partnership emerged in Ginny Holgate (now Mrs Leng) and *Priceless*. Ginny pursued perfection in all phases and became as exciting to watch across country as Lucinda Green. The same is true of New Zealand's Mark Todd, who is based in England, and the nimble *Charisma* with whom he won his Olympic gold medal in 1984.

By then there was little to choose between the two most powerful nations in the sport, the United States and Britain, the respective winners of gold and silver team medals in the Los Angeles Olympics with less than five penalties between them at the finish. In this thrillingly close contest, there was still that marvellous sense of sportsmanship that is eventing's special hallmark.

The three-day event developed from cavalry endurance tests which took the form of long distance rides. One such event, from Brussels to Ostend in 1902, was particularly disastrous. It resulted in the death of 16 of the 29 horses that took part.

Major Derek Allhusen represented Britain in the Winter Olympic Games of 1948 and, 20 years later at the age of 54, competed as a horseman in the 1968 Games. There he won a team gold medal and the individual silver.

• Virginia Holgate (Mrs Leng)

World Championships (introduced in 1966)

Year	Individual	Horse	Team
1966	Carlos Moratorio (ITA)	*Chalon*	IRL
1970	Mary Gordon-Watson (GBR)	*Cornishman V*	GBR
1974	Bruce Davidson (USA)	*Irish Cap*	USA
1978	Bruce Davidson (USA)	*Might Tango*	CAN
1982	Lucinda Green (GBR)	*Regal Realm*	GBR

MOUNTAINEERING

One of the most obvious human challenges is to stand on the summit of the world's highest mountain. Everest was first observed by Westerners in 1849, but it was a further 72 years before the first attempt to climb it was made. After many attempts it was finally scaled in 1953. Since then over 160 people have been to the summit. At 29,028ft (8848m) the lack of oxygen is right on the limit of human tolerance and until recently the use of bottled oxygen was considered essential for survival.

Everest lies on the Nepalese-Tibetan frontier and like other big mountains has acquired different names from different viewpoints. From Nepal it has been known as Sagarmatha but from the Tibetan side it is known as Chomolungma. Before 1949 all approaches were made from the North or Tibetan side because Nepal was closed to foreigners. This entailed a month's walk from Darjeeling across the barren Tibetan plateau. (Nowadays the Chinese have built a road nearly to Base Camp on the North side of the mountain, although it still takes a week to walk to Everest from the Nepalese side).

The first reconnaissance expedition took place in 1921, reaching the North Col at 6990m. The following year Granville Bruce led a British expedition to the North Ridge, reaching the remarkable height of 8320m. Captain Bruce and Captain Finch reached the high point by making use of oxygen, although Mallory, Norton and Somervell reached 8225m without using oxygen on the same climb.

The third British expedition took place in 1924 and their high point of about 8575m was not bettered for nearly 30 years. In one of mountaineering's most famous incidents Mallory and Irvine set off towards the summit on 8 June from Camp Six at 8160m. They were never seen again, although Noel Odell, who was at 7950m, believed he saw them at about 8600m. It is possible that they reached the summit and then died on the descent, but probably no one will ever know what really happened. Tantalising pieces of later evidence have turned up but nothing concrete has been added to the story, despite endless speculation as to whether this pair of brave climbers actually reached the summit some thirty years before Hillary and Tenzing.

During the Thirties several British expeditions attempted Everest but got no higher than the 1924 expedition. In 1949 Nepal opened its doors to foreign climbers and in 1951 a British reconnaissance expedition explored the approach to the Western Cwm and the South Col, which subsequently became the *voie normale* of Everest. In 1952 the Swiss came in the pre-monsoon and the post-monsoon seasons to make the first attempts from the South. Lambert and Tenzing reached 8600m on 28 May before turning back.

Finally in 1953 John Hunt led the expedition which was successful in reaching the summit of the world's highest mountain. Edmund Hillary and Sherpa Tenzing reached the summit on 29 May and with perfect timing the news was released on the Coronation Day of Queen Elizabeth II. They used bottled oxygen and the ascent went smoothly. As far as the public was concerned the conquest of Everest was finished, but of course the climbers remained and have continued to seek out even greater challenges on Everest and the other thousands of difficult mountains in the Himalayas.

An obvious challenge was to climb Everest without oxygen and this was finally achieved in the spring of 1978 by Tyrolean Reinhold Messner and Austrian Peter Habeler. Even in the 1920s climbers believed that Everest without oxygen was perfectly feasible. It is amazing that over fifty years elapsed before it was done.

Because mountaineering achievements are not directly measurable, and therefore comparable, they tend to be rather incomprehensible to the general public. Climbers aspire to climb harder and harder new routes on steeper and more difficult faces. The initial peak bagging stage of mountaineering was more or less complete by the end of the Sixties and climbers turned their attention to putting up hard new climbs on the highest mountains.

In 1971 Dougal Haston and Don Whillans reached the summit of Annapurna (8091m) by the very steep South Face and ushered in a new era of Himalayan climbing. The Face had ten thousand vertical feet of a standard of difficulty until then encountered nearer to home only on routes like the North Face of the Eiger. In the same year Yannick Seigneur and Bernard Mellet climbed the equally difficult West Pillar of Makalu (8481m).

Inevitably climbers turned their attention to climbing the steepest face on Everest and in 1975 Chris Bonington led an expedition to the South-west Face. Doug Scott and Dougal Haston reached the summit, but had an enforced bivouac on the South Summit at 8765m. The weather was kind and they spent the highest night out that man has survived. They had no sleeping bags or supplies and had run out of oxygen.

In total 11 distinctly different routes have been climbed on Everest and only one ridge, the ENE, remains unclimbed. Two of Britain's best climbers, Pete Boardman and Joe Tasker, disappeared high onto the unclimbed ridge in 1982 near to the point where they would have joined the North ridge. By a twist of fate it was similar to the disappearance of Mallory and Irvine nearly fifty years earlier. No one knows what happened to them.

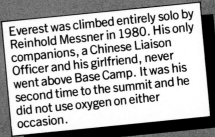

Everest was climbed entirely solo by Reinhold Messner in 1980. His only companions, a Chinese Liaison Officer and his girlfriend, never went above Base Camp. It was his second time to the summit and he did not use oxygen on either occasion.

● Sherpa Tenzing

● Edmund Hillary

Who will be the first climber to scale all the 8000m peaks in the world? There are 14 of them and by 1986 Messner had completed 12, with just Makalu and Lhotse left to climb. His nearest rival is the Polish climber Jerzy Kakukcza, who has done 10 so far.

● John Evans on the Khumbu ice-fall, mt. Everest

153

K2

K2 (8611m) is the world's second highest mountain, but it is generally regarded as the hardest mountain in the world to climb by its easiest route. Although first climbed by an Italian team in 1954 it has been climbed only ten times since. "The Savage Mountain", as it is often called, is the mountaineer's mountain. Elegant, inaccessible, beautiful and harsh. So far four ridges have been climbed but that still leaves two ridges and six faces unclimbed. It lies on the Chinese-Pakistani frontier in the great Karakorum chain. The mountain has never been climbed in Alpine style.

Broad Peak (8047m) was climbed in just one day by Polish climber Krzysztof Wielicki. He set off from Base Camp at twenty past midnight and reached the summit 3000m higher at four o'clock in the afternoon.

CERRO TORRE

Not all the hardest mountains lie in the Himalayas. Cerro Torre (3128m) is near the tip of Patagonia, at the southern extremity of the Andes. Completely sheer on all sides it is battered by the worst weather in the world. It was first climbed by Maestri and Egger in 1958, but Egger died on the descent. Subsequently this ascent was doubted by mountaineers and generally discredited, although there was never any proof either way. Maestri later returned and did climb the mountain by a different route, but this time he used a compressed air drill to place numerous bolts in the rock and this ascent became as controversial as his first effort. Technically speaking this mountain is undoubtedly one of the hardest in the world to climb. It is almost certainly the world's most dramatic mountain.

THOSE WHO DIED

MOUNTAINEERING (Progressive heights attained)

Metres	Feet	Climber(s)	Mountain/Range	Year
6784	22,260	A. & R. Schlagintweit	On Abi Gamin, Garwhal Himalaya	1855
6890	22,606	William Conway & Matthias Zurbriggen	On Baltoro Kangri, Karakoram	1892
6960	22,834	Matthias Zurbriggen	Aconcagua, Andes	1897
7130	23,394	William Workman & others	On Pyramis Peak, Karakoram	1903
7250	23,787	Thomas Longstaff & others	On Gurla Mandhata, Tibetan Himalaya	1905
c7285	c23,900	Carl Rubenson & Monrad Aas	On Kabru, Sikkim Himalaya	1907
7500	24,607	Duke of Abruzzi & others	On Chogolisa, Karakoram	1909
c7590	c24,900	George Mallory, Edward Norton & others	On Everest, Himalaya	1922
8225	26,986	George Mallory, Edward Norton & others	On Everest, Himalaya	1922
c8320	c27,300	George Finch & Granville Bruce	On Everest, Himalaya	1922
8575	28,133	Edward Norton & Howard Somervell	On Everest, Himalaya	1924
8575	28,133	Wynn Harris & Lawrence Wager	On Everest, Himalaya	1933
8575	28,133	Francis Smythe	On Everest, Himalaya	1933
8599	28,215	Raymond Lambert & Tenzing Norgay	On Everest, Himalaya	1952
8754	28,721	Thomas Bourdillon & Robert Evant	On Everest, Himalaya	1953
8848	29,028	Edmund Hillary & Tenzing Norgay	Everest, Himalaya	1953

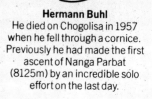

Hermann Buhl
He died on Chogolisa in 1957 when he fell through a cornice. Previously he had made the first ascent of Nanga Parbat (8125m) by an incredible solo effort on the last day.

MODERN STYLES OF CLIMBING

Traditional climbing expeditions require a sophisticated level of organisation and a great deal of expenditure. The army style model of a logistical pyramid, developed in the Twenties with the idea of placing two men on the summit, has been used with great success on all the world's mountains. Recently, though, climbers have increasingly questioned the validity of this method. It seems possible to climb anything given enough money, people and organisation.

Alpine style climbing has evolved as the most satisfying method of climbing big mountains. A few climbers arrive at the base of a mountain and climb up it without any prior preparation, fixed ropes, assistance from sherpas or oxygen. Generally the whole team reaches the top or the whole team retreats. The rules have changed to keep the challenge within the sport.

The high water mark of the old style was the British ascent of the South-west Face of Everest: lots of people, lots of money. British climbers have been to the fore in pushing new standards of Alpine style climbing. In 1978 a young British team, Rab Carrington, Roger Baxter Jones, Brian Hall and Al Rouse, surprised the climbing world by climbing the very difficult Jannu (7710m) in pure Alpine style. Previous ascents had taken months of preparation, but they climbed the route with little fuss in just five days. Messner, with Habeler, had previously climbed Hidden Peak (8068m) by a technically easy route in only two days. Of course Alpine style climbs are much cheaper than expedition style climbs and therefore bring top standard Himalayan climbing within reach of anyone with sufficient determination and ability.

In 1985 the hardest face yet climbed at high altitude was conquered for the first time: the West Face of Gasherbrum 4 (7925m). This was climbed by the two man team of Robert Schauer and Wojiech Kurtyka who took seven days, climbing in pure Alpine style. This has effectively demonstrated that old style expeditions are now outdated for climbers pushing the frontiers of the possible.

THE DANGER

Mountaineering in the Himalayas is one of the most dangerous peacetime activities in which people willingly participate.

John Evans on the Khumbu ice-fall, Mt. Everest

Many dangers are objective like avalanches, stonefall or bad weather, but a particular feature of climbing at high altitude is the extreme lack of oxygen which can lead to impaired judgements or the fatal conditions of pulmonary or cerebral oedema. In order to climb safely in these extreme conditions the mountaineer must be thoroughly conditioned mentally to the environment by many years of climbing. Once the sharp edge of judgement has gone your instinctive feelings are crucial. Discomfort must be endured for days on end, with little sleep, minimal food and cold conditions, throughout which the climber must perform to a high level in order to survive. A primeval struggle.

There is no rescue service at high altitude so you are on your own. Technology is irrelevant. In recent years nearly half of Britain's leading young Himalayan climbers have died on the big mountains.

Dougal Haston
He died in a skiing accident at his home in Leysin in 1978. He had made the first ascent of the South Face of Annapurna and the South-west Face of Everest.

Alex McIntyre
He was hit by stonefall on the South Face of Annapurna in 1982. He had already climbed the East Face of Dhaulagiri (8167m) and the South Face of Shisma Pangma (8046m).

Pete Boardman
Disappeared high on the East-north-east Ridge of Everest in 1982 with Joe Tasker. He had climbed the North Ridge of Kangchenjunga (8586m) and the South-west Face of Everest.

BALLOONING

Ballooning has come a long way since Father Bartolomeu de Gusmao flew the first hot-air balloon indoors in Portugal in 1709. More than 5,000 miles in distance and 20 miles in height to be exact.

For the current world record in distance travelled by a balloon is the 5208.68 miles (8382.54km) recorded by the helium-filled Double Eagle V which flew from Nagashima, Japan, to Covello, California, on 9-12 November 1981 with a crew of four.

The greatest altitude reached is the 21.54 miles (34,668m) attained by Commander Malcolm Ross and Lieutenant Commander Victor Prother in an ascent over the Gulf of Mexico in 1961. Unofficially another American, Nicholas Piantanida, reached 23.45 miles (37,735m) over Sioux Falls, South Dakota, in 1966. But he died during the attempt.

The record altitude in an open basket is the ten miles (16,150m) attained by Chauncey Dunn of America in 1979. He wore a pressure suit.

The first free flight in a balloon was by Jean François Pilâtre de Rozier and the Marquis d'Arlandes (FRA) in their hot-air balloon over Paris in November 1783, when they ascended to a height of approximately 330ft (100m) during a 22 minute flight. The previous month de Rozier had reached a height of 80ft (24m) in a tethered balloon.

Professor Auguste Piccard (SUI) became the first man to reach the stratosphere when with a companion he reached a then record 51,961ft (15837m) in a balloon over Augsburg, Germany, in May 1931. Twenty-two years later, at the age of 69 he descended in a bathyscaphe of his own design to an ocean depth of nearly two miles. His son, Jacques Piccard, reached the current record depth of 35,820ft (10,917m).

• A balloon convention in America

The first known person to parachute from an aircraft was an American exhibition flyer, Albert Berry, in Missouri in 1912. However, a number of Frenchmen had used parachute-like apparatus to descend from towers and balloons in the late 18th century.

DEEP DIVING

The Pearl divers of the South Pacific work daily in depths of up to 30ft (9.14m), but they do not even begin to compare with Frenchman Jacques Mayol who set a breath-held diving record of 344ft (105m) off Elba, Italy, in December 1983. Mayol used a sled for the descent which took 104 seconds. He came up in 92 seconds.

The women's world record is 147ft 6in (45m) set by Italian Guiliana Treleani off Cuba, in September 1967.

The deepest dive with self-contained under-water breathing apparatus (Scuba) is 437ft (133m) by John Gruener and Neal Watson, both USA, off Freeport, Grand Bahama, in October 1968.

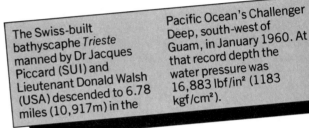

The Swiss-built bathyscaphe *Trieste* manned by Dr Jacques Piccard (SUI) and Lieutenant Donald Walsh (USA) descended to 6.78 miles (10,917m) in the Pacific Ocean's Challenger Deep, south-west of Guam, in January 1960. At that record depth the water pressure was 16,883 lbf/in² (1183 kgf/cm²).

PARACHUTING

Parachuting became a recognised sport in 1951 with the staging of the first world championships, but many of the important records are held by military personnel, partly because of their access to essential equipment like high-flying planes, and also because of necessity through war or accident.

Thus the highest escape ever made is credited to Flight Lieutenant J. de Salis and Flying Officer P. Lowe of the Royal Air Force, who were forced to bail out at a height of 10.6 miles (56,000ft/17,068m) over Monyash, Derbyshire, in April 1958. And the lowest escape was by Squadron Leader Terence Spencer, also RAF, who jumped 40ft (12m) into the Baltic's Wismar Bay in April 1945.

The longest delayed drop is by Captain Joseph Kittinger (USA) who touched speeds of more than 600mph (960km/h), when jumping from a balloon at 19.46 miles (102,800ft/31,333m) over New Mexico in August 1960.

Since the world championships were inaugurated, the Soviet Union have dominated the competition. A team title was introduced in 1954 and the Soviets won it in 1954, 1958, 1960, 1966, 1972, 1976 and 1980. They won the women's team title in 1956, 1958, 1966, 1968, 1972 and 1976. And the outstanding individual parachutist of recent times has also been a Soviet, Nikolai Ushamyev, who won the world championship in 1974 and 1980.

But it is a British woman, Jacqueline Smith who holds the record for accuracy. She scored ten consecutive dead centre landings into a 4in (10cm) circle during the 1978 World Championships in Zagreb. American Dwight Reynolds holds the men's all time best with 105 dead centres at Yuma, Arizona, also in 1978.

In parascending, the longest distance covered in free flight is the 2.8 miles (4500m) completed by Paul Truelove (GBR) at Humberside in 1985. The longest duration of free flight was the 16min 1sec of Lee Clements (GBR) at Elvington, England, in June 1984.

LONG DISTANCE WALKING AND RUNNING

For many athletes the Marathon is merely the beginning. They run one in training each day . . . and further. These are the ultra-distance athletes, wonders of cardio-vascular physiology who can maintain slow, constant speeds for hours on end.

Many of these exceptional runners are British, displaying the Anglo-Saxon characteristic of dogged determination. The most celebrated of them all is Bruce Tulloh, the barefooted European 5,000m champion of 1962, who ran across America from Los Angeles to New York in 1969, covering the 2876 miles in 65 days.

But Tulloh himself, 5ft 7in (1.70m) and 8st 3lb (52.27kg) in his prime, believes he does not hold a candle to the Tarahumara Indians, part of the Apache nation who live 6000ft up in a remote mountain region in Mexico. Tulloh spent three weeks with the tribe in 1971, where he witnessed them running non-stop for up to 48 hours. "After a day's work ordinary lads would have a six hour race for a bet," he says.

In the official ultra-distance world records, Britain's Donald Ritchie stands supreme. Born 6 July 1944, Ritchie still holds the best marks for 40 miles (3:48:35), 50 miles (4:51:49) and 100 miles (11:30:51).

Another Briton, David Dowdie, held the 24 hour best of 170 miles 974 yds (274,480km) set in 1982. And Dowdie also held the 48 hour best of 238 miles 1122 yds (384,050km) set the following year.

But in late 1984 he was overtaken by a Greek sensation, Yiannis Kouros, who in the space of five months smashed eight ultra-distance world records. He began in November 1984 with four simultaneously in Kolac, Australia: the 500km (60:23:00), 500 miles (105:42:09), 1000km (136:17:00) and the six days (1023.2km). Then in March 1985 at Montauban, France, he broke four more: the 200km (15:11:10), 200 miles (27:48:35), 24 hours (283.6km) and 48 hours (452.27km).

The longest official foot race in the world is the Paris-Colmar walking competition of 322 miles (518km). Until 1980 this was the Strasbourg-Paris race and the fastest time for that 315 miles (507km) is the 60 hr 1 min 10 sec of Belgium's Robert Pietquin. This does not include four hours of compulsory stops and represents an average speed of 5.25mph (8.45km/h).

In April 1910, 20-year-old Rumanian Dumitru Dan attempted to walk 100,000km (62.137 miles) in a competition organised by the Touring Club de Paris. He managed 96,000km (59.651 miles) up to 24 March 1916, an average over those six years of 43.85km (27.24 miles) a day.

The longest known race ever was the 1929 New York – Los Angeles run over 3,665 miles (5898km). The winner was Johnny Salo, born in Finland but living in America, who took an overall time of 79 days. His actual running time was 525 hours 57 min 29 sec, and he beat the runner-up, Pete Gavuzzi (GBR) by only 2 min 47 sec. In financial straits, the race organizer was unable to pay any prize money.

Kelvin Bowers (GBR) ran from England to Australia, a distance of 10,289 miles (16,558km), in 522 days between April 1974 and September 1975. He averaged just under 20 miles (32km) per day.

The best-known long distance walk in Britain is the London-Brighton, 53 miles (85km), the record for which is held by the 1960 Olympic 50km champion Don Thompson (GBR) with 7 hr 35 min 12 sec in 1957.

• Bruce Tulloh

The longest non-stop walk is the 412.08 miles (663.17km) by Malcolm Barnish (GBR) of the British Army in 6 days 10 hr 32 min at Dortmund West Germany on 12-18 May 1985.

American George Schilling is reported to have walked around the world from 3 August 1897 to June 1904. It was officially achieved by another American, David Kunst, from 10 June 1970 to 5 October 1974.

• Ian Botham discovers the delights of long distance walking

CHANNEL SWIMMING

Women's higher percentage of body fat makes them more efficient at long distance swimming, both through flotation and insulation. So it is no surprise to find that the fastest cross Channel swim was posted by a woman, America's Penny Dean, who in June 1978, at the age of 23, swam the 21 miles from Shakespeare Beach, Dover, to Cap Gris Nez, France in 7 hrs 40 mins.

Indeed, the first woman to succeed in crossing the Channel, one of the most famous strips of water in the world, Gertrude Ederle, a one time child sensation from America, achieved it in a then world record time of 14 hrs 39 mins in August 1926.

Penny Dean's world record time compares well with the fastest ever crossing by a relay team . . . the 7 hrs 17 mins set by six Dover lifeguards swimming from England to France in August 1981.

The first person to swim the Channel was Merchant Navy Captain Matthew Webb who, at the age of 27, swam breaststroke from Dover to Calais Sands in 21 hrs 45 mins in August 1875. Webb is thought to have swum 31 miles in all.

The first official records were kept after the formation of the Channel Swimming Association in 1927. Since then hundreds have achieved the feat, including Britain's Michael Read who made 31 crossings – including six in one year – between 1969 and 1984. The most by a woman is Cindy Nicholas' 19 between 1975 and 1982.

The first double crossing came from Antonio Abertondo of Argentina in 1961. Aged 41, he swam from England to France in 18 hrs 50 mins, took four minutes rest and then made the return trip in 24 hrs 16 mins. The fastest double crossing is the 18 hrs 15 mins by Dutchwoman Irene van der Laan in 1983. The first triple crossing was by Jon Erikson (USA) who took 38 hrs 27 mins in 1981.

The youngest cross Channel swimmer is Britain's Marcus Hooper who went from Dover to Sangatte in 14 hrs 37 mins at the age of 12 years and 53 days in 1979. Samantha Druce of Britain was 12 years and 119 days, when she swam from Dover to Cape Gris Nez in 15 hrs 27 mins in 1983. The oldest is Ashby Harper, who was 65 years and 332 days when he crossed from Dover to Cap Blanc Nez in 13 hrs 52 mins in 1982.

But even the Channel pales into insignificance when placed alongside the furthest ever endurance swims. Ricardo Hoffman swam a non-stop 299 miles (481.5km) in the River Parana, Argentina, in 84 hrs 37 mins in 1981.

● Abla Khairy aged 13 about to enter the water

Due to winds and tides the length of Channel swims and the time taken can vary enormously. The most extreme recorded was that by Henry Sullivan (USA) in 1923, when he covered an estimated distance of 56 miles (90km) taking nearly 27 hours – but he did it.

● Kevin Murphy

WEIGHTLIFTING

Men have always had a desire to show off their strength. The Chinese are reputed to have practised weightlifting around 3500 BC. And in the 17th and 18th centuries, feats of strength were regular features at fairgrounds.

But weightlifting did not become a competitive sport until 1891 when the first world championships were held at London's Cafe Monico in Piccadilly on 28 March. That first title was won by Englishman Lawrence Levy.

At the 1896 Olympics there were no weight categories and only two gold medals were contested, one for the double handed lift and one for the single handed lift. Englishman Launceston Elliot won the latter and remains Britain's only weightlifting gold medallist.

It was not until 1920 that other weight divisions were added to the Olympic programme and from then until the Second World War Italy, Austria, France and Egypt dominated the events.

In the early post-war years the United States were dominent. But, since 1960, the Communist countries have monopolised the Olympic weightlifting events, particularly the Soviets with almost 500,000 registered lifters in their massive Socialist Republic.

Between 1960-80 USSR, Poland and Bulgaria won 38 of the 49 Olympic titles.

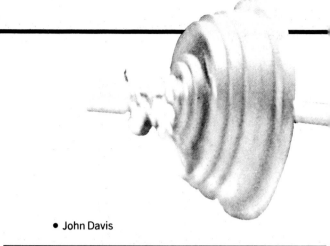

● John Davis

A 36 egg omelette for breakfast, followed by six steaks for lunch and 20 pints of beer was just a routine morning's diet for the first of the great superheavyweight weightlifters, Vasili Alexeyev of the Soviet Union. By dinner time he was really hungry.

But by maintaining his huge body weight of some 364lb (165kg) Alexeyev was able to break 80 world records between 1972-80, the most for any competitor in any sport. He also collected eight world titles, two Olympic golds, and nine European Championships.

His last clean and jerk record in 1977 – lifting over his head from the ground – was 256kg (5649lb) or the equivalent of a grand piano. His massive countryman Anatoli Pisarenko has since raised that to an incredible 265kg (584 lb).

Superheavyweight Clean and Jerk Progressive World Record

Kg	Competitor	Venue	Date
147.5	Charles Rigoulot (FRA)	Paris	24
152.5	Charles Rigoulot (FRA)	Paris	24
157.5	Charles Rigoulot (FRA)	Paris	25
160.5	Charles Rigoulot (FRA)	Paris	25
161.5	Charles Rigoulot (FRA)	Paris	28/6/25
167.0	El Sayed Noseir (EG)	Luxembourg	1/3/31
167.5	Arnold Luhaäär (EST)	Revel	8/8/37
170.5	Ahmed Geissa (EG)		9/4/45
171.0	Jakov Kucenko (URS)		25/10/46
173.0	Jakov Kucenko (URS)		8/5/47
174.0	Jakov Kucenko (URS)		20/7/47
174.5	John Davis (USA)		27/9/47
177.5	John Davis (USA)	London	11/8/48
180.0	John Davis (USA)	Buenos Aires	11/3/51
182.0	John Davis (USA)	Los Angeles	16/6/51
185.0	Norbert Schemansky (USA)		52
187.5	Norbert Schemansky (USA)		15/2/53
188.5	Norbert Schemansky (USA)	Vienna	26/2/54
189.0	Norbert Schemansky (USA)		54
190.0	Norbert Schemansky (USA)	Copenhagen	54
192.5	Norbert Schemansky (USA)	Lille	17/10/54
196.5	Paul Anderson (USA)	Cleveland	24/4/55
197.0	Paul Anderson (USA)		1/9/55
197.5	Juri Vlasov (URS)	Leningrad	22/4/59
202.0	Juri Vlasov (URS)	Rome	10/9/60
205.0	Juri Vlasov (URS)	Kislovodsk	27/6/61
206.0	Juri Vlasov (URS)	London	29/7/61
208.0	Juri Vlasov (URS)	Vienna	28/9/61
210.5	Juri Vlasov (URS)	Dnepropetrovsk	22/12/61
211.0	Juri Vlasov (URS)	Hämeenlinna	30/5/62
212.5	Juri Vlasov (URS)	Stockholm	13/9/63
213.0	Leonid Zhabotinsky (URS)	Moscow	22/3/64
215.5	Juri Vlasov (URS)	Podolsk	3/8/64
217.5	Leonid Zhabotinsky (URS)	Tokyo	18/10/64
218.0	Leonid Zhabotinsky (URS)	Berlin	21/10/66
218.5	Leonid Zhabotinsky (URS)	Sofia	18/6/67
219.0	Leonid Zhabotinsky (URS)	Moscow	3/8/67
220.0	Leonid Zhabotinsky (URS)	Lugansk	19/5/68
220.5	Robert Bednarski (USA)	York	9/6/68
221.5	Vasili Alexeyev (URS)	Velikie Luki	24/1/70
222.0	Serge Reding (BEL)	Herbeumont	18/4/70
223.5	Vasili Alexeyev (URS)	Vilnius	26/4/70
225.5	Vasili Alexeyev (URS)	Szombathely	28/6/70
226.5	Serge Reding (BEL)	La Roche	28/8/70
227.5	Vasili Alexeyev (URS)	Columbus	20/9/70
228.0	Vasili Alexeyev (URS)	Volgograd	17/11/70
228.5	Vasili Alexeyev (URS)	Shakhti	4/12/70
229.5	Vasili Alexeyev (URS)	Dnepropetrovsk	26/12/70
230.0	Vasili Alexeyev (URS)	Paris	14/2/71
230.5	Vasili Alexeyev (URS)	Taganrog	18/4/71
231.0	Vasili Alexeyev (URS)	Sofia	27/6/71
232.5	Vasili Alexeyev (URS)	Sofia	27/6/71
233.0	Vasili Alexeyev (URS)	Moscow	24/7/71
235.0	Vasili Alexeyev (URS)	Moscow	24/7/71
235.5	Vasili Alexeyev (URS)	Lima	26/9/71
236.0	Vasili Alexeyev (URS)	Tallinn	15/4/72
237.5	Vasili Alexeyev (URS)	Tallinn	15/4/72
238.0	Vasili Alexeyev (URS)	Donetsk	29/4/73
240.0	Vasili Alexeyev (URS)	Madrid	18/6/73
240.5	Vasili Alexeyev (URS)	Erivan	20/3/74
241.0	Vasili Alexeyev (URS)	Tbilisi	28/4/74
241.5	Vasili Alexeyev (URS)	Manila	29/9/74
242.0	Vasili Alexeyev (URS)	Glazov	3/11/74
242.5	Vasili Alexeyev (URS)	London	27/11/74
243.0	Vasili Alexeyev (URS)	Zaporozhe	15/12/74
243.5	Vasili Alexeyev (URS)	Lipetsk	29/12/74
245.0	Vasili Alexeyev (URS)	Vilnius	11/7/75
245.5	Vasili Alexeyev (URS)	Moscow	23/9/75
246.5	Gerd Bonk (GDR)	Karl-Marx-Stadt	28/11/75
247.5	Vasili Alexeyev (URS)	Montreal	7/12/75
252.5	Gerd Bonk (GDR)	Berlin	11/4/76
255.0	Vasili Alexeyev (URS)	Montreal	27/7/76
255.5	Vasili Alexeyev (URS)	Moscow	1/9/77
256.0	Vasili Alexeyev (URS)	Moscow	1/11/77
257.5	Vladimir Marchuk (URS)	Lvov	22/3/81
258.0	Anatoli Pisarenko (URS)	France	7/3/82
258.5	Anatoli Pisarenko (URS)	Onsepropetrovsk	23/5/82
260	Vladimir Marchuk (URS)	Moscow	19/12/82
261	Sergei Didyk (URS)	Moscow	31/7/83
265	Anatoli Pisarenko (URS)	Vienna	16/9/84

China's first day back in Olympic competition in 1984, after a 32-year absence, saw them win their first ever Olympic gold medal, in the flyweight weightlifting class, through Zeng Guoiang. They ended up as weightlifting's top nation in Los Angeles with four golds.

The silver medallist in the 1948 Olympic light-heavyweight class was American Harold Sakata — better known later as 'Oddjob' in the James Bond film, *Goldfinger*.

The leading-medal winning nations at the Olympics are:

	Gold	Silver	Bronze	Total
USSR	33	19	2	54
USA	15	16	10	41
Poland	4	2	15	21
Bulgaria	7	10	3	20
France	9	2	4	15
Italy	5	5	15	15
France	5	3	7	15

● Vasili Alexeyev

● Anatoli Pisarenko

BOXING

In 100 years of heavyweight boxing, from 1886-1986, 39 men could lay claim to having held the so-called greatest prize in sport. Of those 32 have been American. And of those 32, 21 have been black.

In recent years, of course, the famous crown has lost some of its glitter with the plethora of titles – World Boxing Association, World Boxing Council and International Boxing Federation – which has handed the championship to such as John Tate, Mike Weaver, Michael Dokes, Gerrie Coetzee, Greg Page, Tim Witherspoon, Pinklon Thomas and Tony Tubbs, at a time when every fight fan was happy to recognise Larry Holmes as the one true champion.

The complications really began when Muhammad Ali retired on 15 September 1978 after winning the title for the third time in his return bout with Leon Spinks. And they grew worse in December 1983, when Larry Holmes resigned his WBC title and launched his own IBF championship. At the start of 1986 there were three champions – Tim Witherspoon for the WBC, Trevor Berbick for the WBC and Michael Spinks for the IBF. Berbick, for one, had announced his intention of unifying the title.

Not that the promoters were complaining; three world champions gave them three times as many chances of building multi million dollar programmes. But it had all been far, far easier to follow back in 1885 when John L. Sullivan, the 'Boston Strong Boy' took the first recognised world title despite a training regime based mainly on wine and women.

Sullivan, who stood only 5ft 10½in (1.79m) was champion during the transition from bare knuckle to gloved fighting and on 7 September 1892 in New Orleans fought the first world title bout held under the Marquis of Queensberry rules. After 21 rounds the 37-year-old Sullivan was battered to defeat by the scientific style of James J. Corbett.

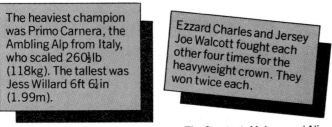

The heaviest champion was Primo Carnera, the Ambling Alp from Italy, who scaled 260½lb (118kg). The tallest was Jess Willard 6ft 6¼in (1.99m).

Ezzard Charles and Jersey Joe Walcott fought each other four times for the heavyweight crown. They won twice each.

• The Greatest, Muhammad Ali

THE HEAVYWEIGHT CHAMPIONSHIP
Boxers are American unless otherwise stated

Date		Winner	Result	Loser
1885	29 Aug	John L. Sullivan	w.pts. 6	Dominick McCaffrey
1886	13 Nov	John L. Sullivan	w.ko. 3	Paddy Ryan (IRL)
1888	10 Mar	§ John L. Sullivan	drew 39	Charlie Mitchell (GBR)
1889	8 July	§ John L. Sullivan	w.ko. 75	Jake Kilrain
1892	7 Sept	James J. Corbett	w.ko. 21	John L. Sullivan
1894	25 Jan	James J. Corbett	w.ko. 3	Charlie Mitchell (GBR)
1896	21 Feb	Bob Fitzsimmons (GBR)	w.ko. 1	Peter Maher (IRL)
1897	17 Mar	Bob Fitzsimmons (GBR)	w.ko. 14	James J. Corbett
1899	9 June	James J. Jeffries	w.ko. 11	Bob Fitzsimmons (GBR)
	3 Nov	James J. Jeffries	w.pts. 25	Tom Sharkey (IRL)
1900	11 May	James J. Jeffries	w.ko. 23	James J. Corbett
1901	15 Nov	James J. Jeffries	w.ret. 5	Gus Ruhlin
1902	25 Jul	James J. Jeffries	w.ko. 8	Bob Fitzsimmons (GBR)
1903	14 Aug	James J. Jeffries	w.ko. 10	James J. Corbett
1904	26 Aug	James J. Jeffries	w.ko. 2	Jack Munro
		Jeffries retired undefeated as champion		
1905	3 July	Marvin Hart	w.rsf. 12	Jack Root
1906	23 Feb	Tommy Burns (CAN)	w.pts. 20	Marvin Hart
	2 Oct	Tommy Burns (CAN)	w.ko. 15	Jim Flynn
	28 Nov	Tommy Burns (CAN)	drew 20	Philadelphia Jack O' Br
1907	8 May	Tommy Burns (CAN)	w.pts. 20	Philadelphia Jack O'Br
	4 July	Tommy Burns (CAN)	w.ko. 1	Bill Squires (AUS)
	2 Dec	Tommy Burns (CAN)	w.ko. 10	Gunner James Moir (G
1908	10 Feb	Tommy Burns (CAN)	w.ko. 4	Jack Palmer (GBR)
	17 Mar	Tommy Burns (CAN)	w.ko. 1	Jem Roche (IRL)
	18 April	Tommy Burns (CAN)	w.ko. 5	Jewey Smith (GBR)
	13 June	Tommy Burns (CAN)	w.ko. 8	Bill Squires (AUS)
	24 Aug	Tommy Burns (CAN)	w.ko. 13	Bill Squires (AUS)
	2 Sept	Tommy Burns (CAN)	w.ko. 6	Bill Lang (AUS)
	26 Dec	Jack Johnson	w.rsf. 14	Tommy Burns (CAN)
1909	9 Sept	Jack Johnson	ND 10	Al Kaufman
	16 Oct	Jack Johnson	w.ko. 12	Stanley Ketchel
1910	4 July	Jack Johnson	w.rsf. 15	James J. Jeffries
1912	4 Jul	Jack Johnson	w.ko. 9	Jim Flynn
1913	19 Dec	Jack Johnson	drew 10	Jim Johnson
1914	27 June	Jack Johnson	w.pts. 20	Frank Moran
	15 Dec	Jack Johnson	w.ko. 3	Jack Murray
1915	5 Apr	Jess Willard	w.ko. 26	Jack Johnson
1916	25 Mar	Jes Willard	ND 10	Frank Moran
1919	4 July	Jack Dempsey	w.ret. 3	Jess Willard
1920	6 Sept	Jack Dempsey	w.ko. 3	Billy Miske
	14 Dec	Jack Dempsey	w.ko. 12	Bill Brennan
1921	2 July	Jack Dempsey	w.ko. 4	Georges Carpentier (FF
1923	4 July	Jack Dempsey	w.pts. 15	Tom Gibbons
	14 Sept	Jack Dempsey	w.ko. 2	Luis Firpo (ARG)
1926	23 Sept	Gene Tunney	w.pts. 10	Jack Dempsey
1927	22 Sept	Gene Tunney	w.pts. 10	Jack Dempsey
1928	23 July	Gene Tunney	w.rsf. 11	Tom Heeney (NZ)
		Tunney retired undefeated as champion		
1930	12 June	Max Schmeling (GER)	w.dis. 4	Jack Sharkey
1931	3 July	Max Schmeling (GER)	w.rsf. 15	Young Stribling
1932	21 June	Jack Sharkey	w.pts. 15	Max Schmeling (GER)
1933	29 June	Primo Carnera (ITA)	w.ko. 6	Jack Sharkey
	22 Oct	Primo Carnera (ITA)	w.pts. 15	Paulino Uzcudun (ESF
1934	1 Mar	Primo Carnera (ITA)	w.pts. 15	Tommy Loughran
	14 Jun	Max Baer	w.ko. 11	Primo Carnera (ITA)
1935	13 June	James J. Braddock	w.pts. 15	Max Baer
1937	22 June	Joe Louis	w.ko. 8	James J. Braddock
	30 Aug	Joe Louis	w.pts. 15	Tommy Farr (GBR)
1938	23 Feb	Joe Louis	w.ko. 3	Nathan Mann
	1 Apr	Joe Louis	w.ko. 5	Harry Thomas
	22 June	Joe Louis	w.ko. 1	Max Schmeling (GER)
1939	25 Jan	Joe Louis	w.rsf. 1	John Henry Lewis
	17 Apr	Joe Louis	w.ko. 1	Jack Roper
	28 June	Joe Louis	w.rsf. 4	Tony Galento
	20 Sept	Joe Louis	w.ko. 11	Bob Pastor
1940	9 Feb	Joe Louis	w.pts. 15	Arturo Godoy (CHI)
	29 Mar	Joe Louis	w.ko. 2	Johnny Paycheck
	20 June	Joe Louis	w.rsf. 8	Arturo Godoy (CHI)
	16 Dec	Joe Louis	w.ret. 6	Al McCoy (CAN)

THE HEAVYWEIGHT CHAMPIONSHIP
Boxers are American unless otherwise stated

Date	Winner	Result	Loser
1941 1 Jan	Joe Louis	w.ko. 5	Red Burman
17 Feb	Joe Louis	w.ko. 2	Gus Dorazio
21 Mar	Joe Louis	w.ko. 13	Abe Simon
8 Apr	Joe Louis	w.ko. 9	Tony Musto
23 May	Joe Louis	w.dis. 7	Buddy Baer
18 June	Joe Louis	w.ko. 13	Billy Conn
29 Sept	Joe Louis	w.rsf. 6	Lou Nova
1942 9 Jan	Joe Louis	w.o. 1	Buddy Baer
27 Mar	Joe Louis	w.ko. 6	Abe Simon
1946 19 Jun	Joe Louis	w.ko. 8	Billy Conn
18 Sept	Joe Louis	w.ko. 1	Tami Mauriello
1947 5 Dec	Joe Louis	w.pts. 15	Jersey Joe Walcott
1948 25 June	Joe Louis	w.ko. 11	Jersey Joe Walcott
	Louis retired undefeated as champion		
1949 22 June	Ezzard Charles	w.pts. 15	Jersey Joe Walcott
10 Aug	Ezzard Charles	w.rsf. 7	Gus Lesnevich
14 Oct	Ezzard Charles	w.ko. 8	Pat Valentino
1950 15 Aug	Ezzard Charles	w.rsf. 14	Freddy Beshore
27 Sept	Ezzard Charles	w.pts. 15	Joe Louis
5 Dec	Ezzard Charles	w.ko. 11	Nick Barone
1951 12 Jan	Ezzard Charles	w.rsf. 10	Lee Oma
7 Mar	Ezzard Charles	w.pts. 15	Jersey Joe Walcott
30 May	Ezzard Charles	w.pts. 15	Joey Maxim
18 July	Jersey Joe Walcott	w.ko. 7	Ezzard Charles
1952 5 June	Jersey Joe Walcott	w.pts. 15	Ezzard Charles
23 Sept	Rocky Marciano	w.ko. 13	Jersey Joe Walcott
1953 15 May	Rocky Marciano	w.ko. 1	Jersey Joe Walcott
24 Sept	Rocky Marciano	w.rsf. 11	Roland LaStarza
1954 17 June	Rocky Marciano	w.pts. 15	Ezzard Charles
17 Sept	Rocky Marciano	w.ko. 8	Ezzard Charles
1955 16 May	Rocky Marciano	w.rsf. 9	Don Cockell (GBR)
21 Sept	Rocky Marciano	w.ko. 9	Archie Moore
	Marciano retired undefeated as champion.		
1956 30 Nov	Floyd Patterson	w.ko. 5	Archie Moore
1957 29 July	Floyd Patterson	w.rsf. 10	Tommy Jackson
22 Aug	Floyd Patterson	w.ko. 6	Pete Rademacher
1958 18 Aug	Floyd Patterson	w.ret. 12	Roy Harris
1959 1 May	Floyd Patterson	w.ko. 11	Brian London (GBR)
26 June	Ingemar Johansson (SWE)	w.rsf. 3	Floyd Patterson
1960 20 June	Floyd Patterson	w.ko. 5	Ingemar Johansson (SWE)
1961 13 Mar	Floyd Patterson	w.ko. 6	Ingemar Johansson (SWE)
4 Dec	Floyd Patterson	w.ko. 4	Tom McNeeley
1962 25 Sept	Sonny Liston	w.ko. 1	Floyd Patterson
1963 22 July	Sonny Liston	w.ko. 1	Floyd Patterson
1964 25 Feb	Cassius Clay	w.ret. 6	Sonny Liston
	Clay changed his name to Muhammad Ali. WBA withdrew recognition of Ali as champion		
1965 5 Mar	*Ernie Terrell	w.pts. 15	Eddie Machen
25 May	Muhammad Ali	w.ko. 1	Sonny Liston
1 Nov	*Ernie Terrell	w.pts. 15	George Chuvalo (CAN)
22 Nov	Muhammad Ali	w.rsf. 12	Floyd Patterson
1966 29 Mar	Muhammad Ali	w.pts. 15	George Chuvalo (CAN)
21 May	Muhammad Ali	w.rsf. 6	Henry Cooper (GBR)
28 June	*Ernie Terrell	w.pts. 15	Doug Jones
6 Aug	Muhammad Ali	w.ko. 3	Brian London (GBR)
19 Sept	Muhammad Ali	w.rsf. 12	Karl Mildenberger (FRG)
14 Nov	Muhammad Ali	w.rsf. 3	Cleveland Williams
1967 6 Feb	Muhammad Ali	w.pts. 15	Ernie Terrell
22 Mar	Muhammad Ali	w.ko. 7	Zora Folley
28 Apr	*Ali stripped of title by WBA and New York State Athletic Commission for ignoring US army draft.*		
1968 4 Mar	†Joe Frazier	w.rsf. 11	Buster Mathis
27 Apr	*Jimmy Ellis	w.pts. 15	Jerry Quarry
24 June	†Joe Frazier	w.ret. 2	Manuel Ramos (MEX)
14 Sept	*Jimmy Ellis	w.pts. 15	Floyd Patterson
10 Dec	†Joe Frazier	w.pts. 15	Oscar Bonavena (ARG)
1969 22 Apr	†Joe Frazier	w.ko. 1	Dav Zyglewicz
23 June	†Joe Frazier	w.rsf. 7	Jerry Quarry
1970 16 Feb	Joe Frazier	w.ret. 4	Jimmy Ellis
18 Nov	Joe Frazier	w.ko. 2	Bob Foster
1971 8 Mar	Joe Frazier	w.pts. 15	Muhammad Ali

Date	Winner	Result	Loser
1972 15 Jan	Joe Frazier	w.rsf. 4	Terry Daniels
25 May	Joe Frazier	w.rsf. 4	Ron Stander
1973 22 Jan	George Foreman	w.rsf. 2	Joe Frazier
1 Sept	George Foreman	w.ko. 1	Jose 'King' Roman
1974 26 Mar	George Foreman	w.rsf. 2	Ken Norton
30 Oct	Muhammad Ali	w.ko. 8	George Foreman
1975 24 Mar	Muhammad Ali	w.rsf. 15	Chuck Wepner
16 May	Muhammad Ali	w.rsf. 11	Ron Lyle
1 July	Muhammad Ali	w.pts. 15	Joe Bugner (GBR)
1 Oct	Muhammad Ali	w.ret. 14	Joe Frazier
1976 20 Feb	Muhammad Ali	w.ko. 5	Jean-Pierre Coopman (BEL)
30 Apr	Muhammad Ali	w.pts. 15	Jimmy Young
24 May	Muhammad Ali	w.ko. 5	Richard Dunn (GBR)
28 Sept	Muhammad Ali	w.pts. 15	Ken Norton
1977 16 May	Muhammad Ali	w.pts. 15	Alfredo Evangelista (ITA)
29 Sept	Muhammad Ali	w.pts. 15	Earnie Shavers
1978 15 Feb	Leon Spinks	w.pts. 15	Muhammad Ali
15 Sept	*Muhammad Ali	w.pts. 15	Leon Spinks

§Bare-knuckle *WBA †WBC KO Knock out PTS Points
RET Retired DIS Disqualified RSF Referee stopped fight

WORLD BOXING COUNCIL 1978/1985

Leon Spinks stripped of world title for refusing to defend against Norton.

1978 10 June	Larry Holmes	w.pts. 15	Ken Norton
10 Nov	Larry Holmes	w.ko. 7	Alfredo Evangelista (ITA)
1979 24 Mar	Larry Holmes	w.rsf. 7	Osvaldo Ocasio (PR)
22 June	Larry Holmes	w.rsf. 12	Mike Weaver
28 Sept	Larry Holmes	w.rsf. 11	Earnie Shavers
1980 3 Feb	Larry Holmes	w.ko. 6	Lorenzo Zanon (ITA)
31 Mar	Larry Holmes	w.rsf. 8	Leroy Jones
7 July	Larry Holmes	w.rsf. 7	Scott Le Doux
2 Oct	Larry Holmes	w.ret. 10	Muhammad Ali
1981 11 Apr	Larry Holmes	w.pts. 15	Trevor Berbick (CAN)
12 Jun	Larry Holmes	w.ret. 3	Leon Spinks
6 Nov	Larry Holmes	w.rsf. 11	Renaldo Snipes
1982 12 June	Larry Holmes	w.rsf. 13	Gerry Cooney
25 Nov	Larry Holmes	w.pts. 15	Randall 'Tex' Cobb
1983 27 Mar	Larry Holmes	w.pts. 12	Lucien Rodriguez (FRA)
20 May	Larry Holmes	drew 15	Tim Witherspoon
10 Sept	Larry Holmes	w.rsf. 5	Scott Frank
11 Dec	*Larry Holmes resigned title. Boxed under IBF banner*		
1984 9 Mar	Tim Witherspoon	w.pts. 12	Greg Page
31 Aug	Pinklon Thomas	w.pts. 12	Tim Witherspoon
1985 15 June	Pinklon Thomas	w.rsf. 8	Mike Weaver
1986 22 Mar	Trevor Berbick (CAN)	w.pts. 12	Pinklon Thomas

INTERNATIONAL BOXING FEDERATION 1983/1985

1983 25 Nov	Larry Holmes	w.rsf. 1	Marvis Frazier
1984 9 Nov	Larry Holmes	w.rsf. 12	James 'Bonecrusher' Smith
1985 15 Mar	Larry Holmes	w.rsf. 10	David Bey
1985 20 May	Larry Holmes	w.pts. 15	Carl Williams
20 Sept	Michael Spinks	w.pts. 15	Larry Holmes
1986 19 April	Michael Spinks	w.pts. 15	Larry Holmes

WORLD BOXING ASSOCIATION 1979/1985

1979 20 Oct	John Tate	w.pts. 15	Gerrie Coetzee (SA)
1980 31 Mar	Mike Weaver	w.ko. 15	John Tate
25 Oct	Mike Weaver	w.ko. 13	Gerrie Coetzee (SA)
1981 3 Oct	Mike Weaver	w.pts. 15	James Tillis
1982 10 Dec	Michael Dokes	w.rsf. 1	Mike Weaver
1983 20 May	Michael Dokes	drew 15	Mike Weaver
23 Sept	Gerrie Coetzee (SA)	w.ko. 10	Michael Dokes
1984 1 Dec	Greg Page	w.ko. 8	Gerrie Coetzee (SA)
1985 29 Apr	Tony Tubbs	w.pts. 15	Greg Page
1986 17 Jan	Tim Witherspoon	w.pts. 15	Tony Tubbs

Modern day boxing had arrived and since then there have been five men the experts rate as the greatest of all time. In alphabetical order they are: Muhammad Ali, Jack Dempsey, Jack Johnson, Joe Louis and Rocky Marciano. All Americans, all driven by poverty to fight their way from the ghettos to the richest prize in sport.

Of those five, two stand apart. Ali and Louis. Who was the greatest? Ali, with his lightning combinations, his unbelievable durability, his speed of foot? Or Louis with his more methodical skill and a knockout punch in either hand?

Suffice to say they towered above their contemporaries. As did the other three in our top five. Here, man by man is the analysis of those outstanding careers in chronological order:

Jack Johnson

The first two black boxers to fight for the world heavyweight title were Jack Johnson and Battling Jim Johnson in Paris in 1913. It ended in a draw.

Height 6ft 1¼ in (1.86m).
Weight 192lb (87kg).

Johnson, the first black champion, was 30 when he won the title in 1908, having been denied an earlier challenge purely on the grounds of his colour. Like Ali 60 years later he was ballet-dancer light on his feet and a master of defence, blocking punches with elbows and gloves or slipping them effortlessly with a sway of his shoulders. His left jab was fierce and fast and his right held sledgehammer power. One of six children fathered by an illiterate labourer in Galveston, Texas, Johnson was of the first generation of blacks to be born free.

He was to become the most famous and the most hated black American of his day; a battle cry for his own race, a figure inspiring hostility and fear from the whites. Johnson made them pay for their insults by abusing their women and humiliating their men.

He finally earned his shot at the title after eight years of trying by pursuing Canadian Tommy Burns across the world to Australia. A purse offer of 30,000 dollars to Burns from Australian Hugh "Huge Deal" McIntosh ended the chase and the colour bar. Burns would fight . . . the white world waited aghast.

Johnson mocked Burns throughout the one-sided 14 rounds, knocking him down twice in the first round and chiding him "Now then, Tahmy, be careful," any time the champion connected. Clearly Johnson was determined to prolong Burns' agony, punishing him just enough each round to allow him to continue. Then, in the 14th, as Burns sank to his knees again the ringside doctor called enough.

Johnson toyed similarly with Stanley Ketchel, the world middleweight champion, before dispatching him with a 12th round uppercut so powerful that three of Ketchel's teeth were found embedded in Johnson's glove when he returned to the dressing room.

By now all of white America was concerned only with beating "the nigger", who boasted he was the best lover in the world, especially with white women. Accordingly Jim Jeffries who had reigned as champion for five years before retiring i 1904 was persuaded to return at the age of 35 and after a si year absence. It was a mistake.

More than 25,000 gathered in Reno, Nevada, for the con test. The blacks prayed openly in the streets for a Johnson vic tory. Johnson did not disappoint them, taunting the lumberin Jeffries, skipping away one moment and then dancing in t thrash him around the head with that mighty right hand. On hook to the jaw had Jeffries staggering and he jigged a little t pretend he had not been hurt. "Gee, that's funny," sneere Johnson, "Do it again Mistah Jeff." Finally the brave Jeffrie succumbed in the 15th, counted out as he tried to haul him self up with the bottom rope.

It took two years for another white hope to be produced then Johnson KO'd Jim Flynn, a railroad fireman, with a nint round uppercut. But now Johnson, increasingly arrogan made his mistake and his enemies pounced. He was arreste on a trumped up charge of taking a white prostitute, Bell Schreiber, across a State Line for immoral purposes in contra vention of the Mann Act. He was sentenced to a year's impris onment, released on bail and escaped to Canada and then t Europe.

He was a celebrity wherever he went, twice defendin his world title in Paris before the outbreak of the First Worl War ended his livelihood and he sailed to Buenos Aires wher he knocked out Jack Murray in three rounds.

Meanwhile, back in America, the search for the whit hope had centred on Jess Willard, the giant cowboy who stoo 6ft 6¼ in (1.99m) and had a reach of 83 in (2.11m). At 33 Wi lard was hardly in the flush of youth, but he had lost only fou of 30 fights . . . and he had powerful allies. In his subseque biography Johnson maintained he was bribed into throwin the fight on the promise of a Federal pardon and re-entry int the United States. Little in the ensuing clash at Havar racecourse in Cuba contradicted that assertion. Johnson, b now 37 and his beautiful body carrying some excess poun age, was still far too spry and sharp for Willard in the first te rounds, punishing him fiercely. But in round 26, with 19 still go, Johnson walked into a right uppercut, went down an shielded his eyes from the sun as the referee counted him ou

Johnson's pardon was not forthcoming, but he st returned to the States – to serve his sentence at Leavenwor Prison, Kansas.

Jack Dempsey

The oldest heavyweight champion was Jersey Joe Walcott at 37 years and six months.

The youngest heavyweight champion was Floyd Patterson at 21 years and ten months.

Height: 6ft 0¾ in (1.85m
Weight: 187lb (85kg

Willard was to hold the title for four years, although defendin it successfully only once before he ran into Jack Dempsey, th two-fisted all action lumberjack from Manassa, Colorad whose early record showed 21 first round knock outs.

He was born William Harrison Dempsey, but took his first name from the hard-hitting former middleweight champion Jack Dempsey. By 1919 he had established himself as the front line contender for Willard's crown – except that Willard was due to meet Fred Fulton, another massive man of 6ft 4½in (1.94m). Dempsey's manager Jack Kearns talked promoter Tex Rickard into letting Dempsey tackle Fulton first. He agreed and Dempsey destroyed him inside a round to earn his crack at the world title on Independence Day 1919 at Bay View Park, Toledo.

There was a delay to the opening round because Willard objected to the ring canvas, which had been stained with blood from a supporting bout. By the end of the first round, the new one was in an even worse state as Willard hauled himself off the deck seven times with immense courage against the bobbing, weaving whirlwind with the sledgehammer punches. By round three, with Willard a walking nightmare, everyone had had enough except for the referee. One of Willard's handlers reached for the towel and Dempsey was world champion at the age of 24.

Billy Miske (round three) and Bill Brennan (round 12) quickly became victims of Dempsey's flying fists and Dempsey's box office appeal grew as fast as they fell.

In 1921 Frenchman Georges Carpentier, a light heavyweight, was lured to an open air arena at Jersey City and 91,000 fans bought every seat to give a gross take of $1,789,238 – the first million dollar gate. Carpentier came as a knock out specialist, but found Dempsey could walk through his hardest punches while delivering a terrible beating to the body. In the second round the Frenchman broke his right thumb on Dempsey's jaw and in the fourth he curled up quietly as they counted him out.

Dempsey's following defence was an anti-climax, a 15 round points victory over Tom Gibbons. To restore his sagging prestige and garner another million dollar jackpot, promoter Rickard searched the world and came up with Argentinian Luis Firpo, 6ft 3in (1.90m) and 216lb (98kg). This Wild Bull of the Pampas had proved a KO specialist in his admittedly short fighting life. But he was ready, Rickard decided, to face Dempsey at New York's Polo Grounds.

This time 82,000 spectators paid over a million dollars. And they weren't disappointed. In one of the most exciting title fights ever seen, Dempsey floored Firpo seven times in the opening round and was once dumped completely outside the ring himself by a haymaking right from the Argentinian. In the second round, though, a left and right combination ended Firpo's brave challenge.

Dempsey had run out of opponents. Except for one man ... Harry Wills, the Black Panther, an athletic hard-punching negro who had lost only five of his 84 contests. But it was a fight foiled by politicians who could remember only too clearly the furore over Jack Johnson. They wanted no black heavyweight champion. So instead Dempsey, after three years' inactivity, was signed to meet James Joseph "Gene" Tunney, a stylish ex-marine from Greenwich Village, New York.

Almost 121,000 fans packed the Sesquicentennial Stadium in Philadelphia on 23 September 1926 for the match. Dempsey was expected to win easily. But in a ring made slippery by a downpour, Tunney glided gracefully round avoiding Dempsey's killing hooks and scoring incessantly with a copy book jab for a decisive points victory.

The return followed a year later at Soldiers' Field, Chicago. The gate was worth two and a half million dollars and Tunney, in his first defence, got a million of it.

The contest turned on the controversial seventh round, and the immortalised "long count". Dempsey floored Tunney with a lightning four-punch combination. Tunney seemed helpless but the referee refused to take up the count until Dempsey had retired to a neutral corner. The delay gave Tunney the chance to recover. By the time he had struggled to his feet ringsiders had clocked his stay on the canvas at 14 seconds.

He held off Dempsey's frenzied attack and then skilfully boxed out the remaining three rounds to take a unanimous points victory after himself dropping Dempsey for a count of eight.

Joe Louis

Max and Buddy Baer are the only brothers to have fought for the world heavyweight title. Max held it for one fight. Buddy was beaten twice by Joe Louis.

Height: 6ft 1½in (1.86m).
Weight: 197¼lb (89.5kg).

As Europe waited in the shadow of the Nazi invasion, so the United States found their own warlike figure ... The Brown Bomber. Joseph Louis Barrow, whose mother wanted him to be a violinist but discovered he was spending the money on boxing lessons. He learned well. At the end of his superb reign he had been king of the heavyweights for 11 years and defended his title, a record 25 times.

Louis was methodical, but chillingly efficient. Rarely did he throw a wild punch: he could take the hardest and come back. He was exciting.

At the age of 21 he was considered ready to battle with Primo Carnera, The Ambling Alp from Italy who had been world champion 12 months earlier and had made a fortune for the mobsters who controlled him.

Louis stopped him in the sixth after administering a terrible beating. Next he stopped another former world champion, Max Baer, in the fourth. But a third ex-champion, Germany's Max Schmeling ended the sequence, knocking Louis out in the 12th for his first defeat. Schmeling thus became the logical contender for the championship crown held by James Braddock. But promoter Mike Jacobs offered Braddock an irresistible deal to face Louis instead: ten per cent of all Louis' earnings for all the time he was champion if he beat Braddock.

Accordingly, Louis and Braddock met in Chicago and Louis knocked out the 34-year-old champion in round eight with one of the fiercest, cleanest right hands ever seen. Louis became the second black man to hold the title. It was the start of the longest reign of any world heavyweight champion – 11 years and nine months, from 22 June 1937 to 1 March 1949.

In truth, some of his opponents scarcely merited their chance at the championship, especially in 1941 when Louis' "Bum of the Month" campaign really took off with six opponents in the first six months. All were knocked out.

There were, though, some wars to be fought and some scores to be settled. Welshman Tommy Farr came into the first category, in Louis' first defence of his title on 30 August 1937. For 15 rounds the gallant Farr stood toe to toe with Louis refusing to be intimidated by the power of his punching and although justifiably losing a close decision restored some much needed pride to British heavyweight boxing. It was, Louis admitted later, his toughest fight.

The revenge came against German Max Schmeling, now 33. Louis floored him with almost the first punch of the fight and then thrashed him with a merciless combination. Ringsiders say Schmelling screamed with pain as one body punch cracked his ribs. He was quickly down again, the contest over in 1 min 24 secs.

A year later Louis had the unusual experience of being dumped on his illustrious backside by Two Ton Tony Galento, the barrel-shaped barman from New Jersey, who had promised to "moider da bum". Galento's left hook caught Louis in the third. The startled champ scampered to his feet at the count of two and proceeded to roll out the barrel in round four.

Louis showed his powers of recovery again in his 1941 fight with Buddy Baer, brother of former champion Max Baer. A swinging left hook sent him through the ropes and he needed all his agility to haul himself back in and all his resilience to weather Baer's storm of punches. The contest ended amid even more drama in the sixth. Louis, now clearly on top, poleaxed Baer with a punch that was programmed just as the bell sounded to end the round. Baer was unable to start the seventh and his corner demanded a disqualification. They got it . . . but it was Baer who was thrown out for refusing to restart.

Light heavyweight Billy Conn gave Louis problems of a different kind with his dancing feet and lightning jab. By the end of round 12 of their 15 round match, Conn had built a useful lead. But now he became overconfident and Louis, who had predicted beforehand "He can run but he can't hide", drilled him with a short, explosive right to the chin to set up the 13th round KO.

A return with Buddy Baer was next and this time Baer lasted only 2 mins 56 secs. Louis donated his purse to the Naval Relief Fund. From the defence against Abe Simon, Louis donated his purse to the Army Relief Fund, and then joined up himself and spent the next three years entertaining the troops with exhibition matches at army camps.

By the time the war was over Louis was 31 and it was another year before he resumed his world title career, halting a faded Billy Conn in eight rounds on 19 June 1946 in New York. The 45,266 spectators paid almost two million dollars. A seemingly simple contest against the four months older Jersey Joe Walcott turned into Louis' hardest battle since Tommy Farr. The champion prevailed by a narrow points margin and then, in the inevitable return, knocked out Walcott in the 11th. Eight months later The Brown Bomber announced his retirement, rated as the greatest champion yet seen. And so it should have remained, but income tax problems brought the ageing Bomber back . . . to a points defeat by new champion Ezzard Charles and a humiliating eighth round knock out by the new white sensation, Rocky Marciano.

John L. Sullivan and Jake Kilrain fought the last bare knuckle heavyweight fight at Richburg, Mississippi, on 8 July 1889. Sullivan won with a 75th round KO.

The shortest reign of an undisputed world heavyweight champion is the 235 days of Marvin Hart (USA) from 3 July 1905 to 23 February 1906

Rocky Marciano

Five world heavyweight champions retired while still holding the title: James J. Jeffries, Gene Tunney, Joe Louis, Rocky Marciano and Muhammad Ali. Only Marciano retired undefeated. Ali was beaten in his second and third spells as champion.

Height: 5ft 10¼ in (1.78m)
Weight: 184lb (83.6kg)

Marciano had begun his fighting career in a Cardiff pub brawl when one mighty right hander put a large Australian spark out and persuaded The Rock to take up amateur boxing. Back in Brockton, Massachusetts, Marciano had 27 bouts, won all but three inside the distance and lost only one, to Coley Wallace, in the final of the AAU tournament. It was to be his only defeat in a career hallmarked by relentless aggression, superhuman durability and a careless regard for the rules. If the Rock could hit them with his elbow or his head, he did. For him the ring was a place for fighting, not etiquette.

Within 16 months of turning pro the rough, tough, Rocco Francis Marchegiano had scored 21 victories. He was ready for New York where he dispatched the well-rated Rex Layne in six rounds and the 37-year-old Louis in eight. The unbeaten run grew to 41 and the public clamour demanded that champion Jersey Joe Walcott, at 38 nine years older than Marciano, should face the Italian Stallion.

Walcott was confident Marciano's wide open style would suit his powerful left hook . . . and so it looked as the clubbing weapon dumped Marciano down for the first time in his career after only one minute. For three seconds The Rock lay prone. Then he climbed up and waded straight back into Walcott. By round 13, Marciano was a mess with blood pouring from his face and his body covered in bruises. But less than a minute into the round Wallcott offered his first serious opening and Marciano's bludgeoning right hand thundered through to grab the title. The rematch eight months later lasted 2 min 25 secs.

It was a pattern continued with Ezzard Charles. The former champion gave Marciano a hard time in a 15 round points defeat in New York, but was then comprehensively knocked out in a return three months later.

Marciano seemed set to reign for years. But the champion himself carried a shrewd brain inside that bullet head. He knew his style of boxing opened him up for serious injuries and there was pressure, too, from his wife Barbara.

So he planned two last contests in 1955. First he destroyed the challenge of Britain's brave, overblown light heavyweight Don Cockell in eight rounds; then he overpowered the veteran Archie Moore in nine. But Moore had succeeded in decking Rocky with a right hander. At the age of 32 Marciano decided it was time to go, unbeaten in 49 pro bouts of which 43 had ended inside the distance. Unlike so many others he stuck to his decision refusing huge offers for a comeback. Tragically, the seemingly indestructable Rock was killed in a plane crash in Iowa one day short of his 46th birthday.

uhammad Ali

eight: 6ft 3in (1.90m). Weight: 210½lb (95.6kg).

e arrived as Cassius Clay, retired as Muhammad Ali and ong the way his admirers unhesitatingly renamed him ain. Simply as The Greatest. Like Louis, the world never w the best of Ali. Louis' prime years were spent in the army, i's enforced absence of three and three-quarter years came cause he refused to join up. When he was stripped of his le, Ali had made ten successful title defences.

In the beginning, though, it was almost all too easy for the ung Cassius Clay. An Olympic gold medal at light heavy- eight in the 1960 Games was followed by a pro contract with group of Louisville businessmen and the signing up with anager Angelo Dundee.

After his first eight bouts Clay began calling the round in hich he would defeat his opponent, and then he started to ess up his prediction in doggerel verse. Britain's Henry ooper came closest to gagging the Louisville Lip with his otorious left hook which spreadeagled Clay at Wembley. But ay had time to recover and cut Cooper to pieces in the fifth.

At the age of 22 Clay was ready to fight for the world le . . . against the awesome Sonny Liston, the powerful -convict who had lost only one of 36 fights – and then cause he had a broken arm – and who had destroyed Floyd atterson twice in round one. Liston was 7-1 ON favourite.

In the event the bout was tainted by controversy. Liston, eemingly unmarked after six rounds of largely long range oxing, retired on his stool complaining of a shoulder injury. he return 15 months later – by which time Clay had changed s name to the Muslim Muhammad Ali – was even more sus- cious, Liston collapsing after only one minute, hit by a right nd punch no-one else saw.

But Ali now showed his true worth, putting up his title ven times in 12 months between November 1965 and ovember 1966. Six of the challengers did not make the dis- nce. Only George Chuvalo lasted the course.

The rival WBA (World Boxing Association) had meanwhile stated Ernie Terrell as their supposed world champion and a ontest was arranged to unify the title. Terrell refused to refer his opponent as Ali, calling him Clay. The infuriated Ali sub- cted Terrell to a brutal humiliation, demanding "What's my ame?" as he systematically cut Terrell's face to pieces. Ter- ll, to his credit, lasted the full 15 rounds, along with Chuvalo, e only man to do so. Six weeks later Ali was at Madison quare Garden to obliterate Zora Folley in seven rounds. Ali as unbeaten in 29 contests. Where was there an opponent test him? Sadly, one loomed in the shape of the US Army raft Board. Ali, because of his religious beliefs, refused to ght outside the ring and was stripped of his title.

By the time he returned the world stage was dominated by Smokin' Joe Frazier. Could Ali possibly regain that old speed of foot and hand necessary to defeat such a powerful oppo- nent? On 26 October 1970 Ali suggested he could, with a three round comeback defeat of Jerry Quarry. Then he scored a 15 round stoppage over the rugged Argentinian Oscar Bonavena. Now Ali-Frazier had to be on . . . it was, fixed for 8 March 1971 at Madison Square Garden. The purse offer was a staggering five million dollars, shared equally between the two men. Frazier, shorter by 3½in (8.8cm) and lighter by 5lb (2.3kg), was made a fractional favourite. The fight was worthy of the occasion, with Frazier stomping forward throwing his crunching hooks and Ali, up on his toes, jabbing and floating.

The floating ended abruptly in the 11th as Frazier caught him flush with a fearsome left hook. Ali clung on desperately until the 15th, then another crushing left took him on the point of the chin and Ali was down for the first time in his life, for a count of three. Within seconds of rising to his feet the bell sig- nalled the end. Frazier had won on points and was undis- puted champion of the world.

It was a title he was to lose in stunning fashion two years later in Kingston, Jamaica, against the giant black American George Foreman. Three times Frazier was battered to the canvas in the first round; and three times more in the second. "Stay down Joe," pleaded Foreman but Frazier dragged him- self to his feet before the referee called a halt.

Ali was now 32, six years older than Foreman, who had since disposed of Ken Norton in just two rounds. For once Ali was the complete underdog as they stepped into the ring at Kinshasa, Zaire, on 30 October 1974. But the backers recko- ned without Ali's brilliant boxing brain and ability to soak up punishment. In the debilitating humidity, Ali ducked and weaved, blocked and wrestled, draining away the champion's strength. By round eight Foreman, the supposedly unbeat- able, was a spent force, lumbering after the taunting shadow. Ali stepped in for the kill . . . a right hand to the jaw which sent him pitching headlong onto the canvas.

Ali embarked upon his second great reign, with ten more defences which included the third decisive meeting with Frazier, the Thriller in Manilla, which Ali won when Frazier was forced to retire through cuts at the end of the 14th. "The next thing to death," Ali called his feeling of exhaustion at the end. There was also another points defeat of Norton before Ali met Leon Spinks in Las Vegas on 15 February 1978.

Suspicion will always surround this fight. Ali had claimed he wanted to become the first to win the heavyweight title three times. So far he had done it twice the same as Floyd Patterson. To achieve his goal, he needed to lose the title. And that is just what he did with a 15 rounds points defeat.

Precisely seven months later Spinks was on the receiving end of a similar 15 rounds points defeat by Ali in New Orleans. The Greatest had achieved his ambition and announced his retirement. Unlike Marciano but the same as Louis, Ali failed to keep his word. During the debacle of his fights with Spinks, the WBC (World Boxing Council) had announced Norton as champion, a position he quickly relinquished to Larry Holmes.

Holmes' continued success aroused Ali's indignation. He was also financially embarrassed despite grossing some 50 million dollars in his magical career. Against all advice, Ali agreed to meet Holmes at Las Vegas on 2 October 1980. His dream: to win the title for the fourth time. But he was 38 and had been out of action for two years. He was forced to retire after ten rounds, the first time he had been stopped in his life.

FENCING

A carving in the temple of Medinet-Habu, near Luxor in upper Egypt, depicts two of the world's earliest fencers. Their swords are shown with tips on and the duellists are wearing masks in the carving, dated around 1190 BC.

But it was two and a half thousand years later in Germany that fencing became an organised sport with the setting up of the Marxbruder Fencing Guild in Frankfurt around 1450. Such organisations soon spread throughout Europe and one

of them, the Acadamie d'Armes, was established in Paris the 16th century. By the following century fencing was t supreme sport of the court in France and the country was produce a host of fencing masters over the years.

The first Modern Olympic Games at Athens in 189 included fencing and it has been part of every subseque

The fencing competition at the first Olympics in 1896 was a farce. Many of the judges had never officiated at a fencing contest before and thought the fencer received points if *he* was hit.

The Italians were the pioneers at using the point of the sword rather than the blade as an effective weapon. In the 16th century Castiglione's famous book *Il Cortegiano* was translated into English, explaining intricate strategies that were new to the sport and Italian masters became the most sought after throughout Europe.

Olympic programme. France and Italy dominated early O mpic competitions, but in recent years the Eastern Bloc, no ably Hungary and the Soviet Union, have produced many fir Olympic champions.

The most outstanding fencer of the 20th century has bee Frenchman Christian d'Oriola. He won four individual wor titles – in 1947, 1949, 1953 and 1954. He also won the inc vidual foil titles at the 1952 and 1956 Olympics.

But the record for most Olympic medals is held by Italia Eduardo Mangiarotti with 13. And Hungarian Aladar Gerevic has won a record seven Olympic gold medals. Six came successive Games from 1932-60, which make him the or competitor, in any sport, to win gold medals at six consecuti celebrations.

Olympic fencing has produced some notable fam achievements. Mangiarotti's brother Dario won three meda in 1948 and 1952. And another pair of Italian brothers, Nec and Aldo Nadi, hold the distinction of winning the most meda at one celebration—in any sport—by members of one fami They won nine medals, eight golds and one silver, in 1920.

Boris Onischenko

● Jim Fox at Montreal in 1976

● Riccardi (ITA) scores a hit in the 1936 Olympic final of the individual epée

Fencing is one of the five disciplines included in the modern pentathlon programme and it was during the fencing section of the pentathlon at the 1976 Olympics that one of the Games' most controversial incidents occurred.

Following Soviet Army Major Boris Onischenko's bout with Britain's Jim Fox, the British team lodged an appeal as Onischenko's sword was registering "hits" when Fox was adamant he was not making contact. The Soviet's sword was examined and found to contain a switch that Onischenko could activate so as to indicate a "hit".

The three types of sword in competitive use are: the *foil* which was introduced in the 17th century, the *epée*, established in the mid-19th century and the *sabre* which was introduced in the late 19th century.

Olympic Fencing Medal Table

	Gold	Silver	Bronze	Total
France	32	31	26	89
Italy	31	32	20	83
Hungary	30	17	22	69
USSR	17	13	13	43
W. Germany	8	10	5	23
Poland	4	5	7	16
Cuba	6	4	3	13
Belgium	5	3	5	13
United States	–	4	8	12
Great Britain	1	9	–	10
Greece	3	3	3	9
Rumania	1	2	5	8
Netherlands	–	1	7	8
Sweden	2	3	2	7
Austria	1	1	5	7
Denmark	1	2	3	6
Switzerland	–	2	3	5
Czechoslovakia	–	–	2	2
China	1	–	–	1
Mexico	–	1	–	1
Argentina	–	–	1	1
Portugal	–	–	1	1

YACHTING

From Perth in Western Australia, to Earls Court ("Kangaroo Valley") in West London, the celebrations were joyous, unending and raucously Australian. As they were on every other continent that had seen, via satellite TV, the America's Cup finally wrested away from the United States after 132 years and 25 challenges.

The Hundred Guinea Cup, which became the greatest prize in yachting, was finally unbolted from its resting place in the New York Yacht Club and handed over to Australia's Alan Bond together with the four foot long bolt that had held it secure for more than a century . . . and for what the Americans believed would be forever.

The ceremony in one of Newport, Rhode Island's, famous mansions, the Vanderbilt's Marble House, was simple and, for members of the New York Yacht Club and, for that matter, the entire nation, heartbreaking.

The unthinkable had happened. The oldest trophy to be raced for and held in the longest sequence of wins by a single nation was bound for a new home, Down Under.

America, winner of every series since 1870 had lost only eight of the 85 races sailed. They were invincible. At least they *were* until Alan Bond's *Australia II*, steered by John Bertrand, came back from 3-1 down to win the last three races against American defender, *Liberty*, helmed by Dennis Conner.

Australian Prime Minister, Bob Hawke, and the entire nation, watched the victory on TV and then jubilantly pronounced: "It isn't often a Prime Minister can say he is speaking for everybody, but I know I am speaking for every Australian when I say this is the proudest day in our lives."

The Aussies had to win eliminating races against Britain, France, Canada and Italy to emerge as rightful challengers. It was their seventh attempt and, for the first time in the long history of the challenges, the first time the series went to all seven races.

In the end the final race was won by a mere 41 seconds. The date: 26 September 1983, now written indelibly into every Australian history book and forever to be recalled by all those bleary eyed Australians, half a world away, who had watched the TV pictures of Bertrand whittling down Conner's 57 second lead and then, perilously close to the finish, passing him to secure yachting's most improbable victory.

If any one man could be named as responsible for starting what was to become the blue riband event not just for yachting but for sports lovers everywhere, that man was John Cox Stevens, son of an army colonel who, with his brothers, owned a highly profitable steamship company which operated on the Hudson river.

John, immensely wealthy, was a dedicated gambler and totally enraptured by the mechanics and the challenge of sailing. With a handful of friends who shared his passion for the sea Stevens founded the New York Yacht Club in 1844 and six years later decided to build a yacht and sail her to England for the Great Exhibition of 1851.

It was to be a sort of "Showing the flag" expedition to underline Steven's firmly held belief that America was dominant in ship building. Certainly the American clippers were winning the trade route races from China and beyond.

Inevitably the Stevens' yacht, roughly 102ft overall and carrying more than 5,000 square ft of sail, was named *America*. She arrived at Cowes, on the Isle of Wight, head-

quarters of the Royal Yacht Squadron, about six weeks aft setting sail from New York, having laid up in Le Havre for while for a good wash and brush up.

At first the Squadron yachtsmen refused to race again *America*. She looked, as The Times reported "a hawk amor a flock of pigeons." Even an outrageous challenge by Steve "to race any yacht for a £10,000 wager" failed to produce response.

But in the end the newspapers, impressed by Stevens ar his daring, goaded the Squadron into inviting America to s in their annual Round the Island race.

The price would be a 27in high silver ewer weighing 8 6oz and named the Hundred Guinea Cup (because that w what Garrard, the London jewellers, charged to make it).

The race, on 22 August, over a 53 mile course, was virt ally all over for the 14 British yachts at the halfway mar *America*, despite a slow start, had sailed through the field lead by two and a half miles at halfway. She was never heade and at one time was seven miles in front.

Ten days later, having first won a 40-mile race by an ho to collect a 500 dollar bet, Stevens sold *America* to an Iri peer and returned to New York with his bottomless silver u and a profit of nearly 2,000 dollars.

Stevens died on 10 June 1857, and the following mon the Hundred Guinea Cup was handed over to the New Yo Yacht Club with instructions that it should become a perpetu challenge cup for competition between yacht clubs from for ign countries. Neither individual nor government challeng would be entertained. Only those from yacht clubs.

Thus was born the America's Cup with the New York Yac Club as its custodian and perpetual defender, until such tin as the cup might be lost to some foreign challenger.

The American Civil War, among other things, held up ar challenges until 1870 when Britain's James Ashbury, a gre social climber with his eye to a parliamentary career, enter his schooner, *Cambria*.

She raced against 17 New York YC schooners through th Narrows off Staten Island but was never in contention, finis ing 10th and almost 40 minutes adrift of the winner, *Magic*.

Ashbury returned the following year with an even bigg schooner – *Livonia* – 20ft longer than *Cambria* and with th greatest spread of sail – 18,000 square feet – ever seen on cup yacht.

Livonia lost the first two races to *Columbia* but when sh won the third the Americans replaced *Columbia* with *Sap pho. Sappho* won the next two and an embittered Ashbu returned home beaten 4-1 but insisting that but for the "cu ning, unfair and unsportsmanlike proceedings" he wou have won 4-3.

Two Canadian challenges – *Countess of Dufferin* (187 and *Atalanta* (1881) – were seen off without the America defenders, *Madeleine* and *Mischief*, losing a race.

Sir Richard Sutton's *Genesta* took up the gauntlet in 188 and also failed to win a race. Next to go, *Galatea* (1886), the *Thistle* (1887).

It was getting boringly monotonous. Three wins in con secutive years without losing a race. The Americans real were invincible and so much so that for a while it wa rumoured they would finance a challenge against themselve to make a real race of it for the Cup.

Valkyrie II came in 1893 and again in 1895 but like before her returned empty handed. Was it ever to change?

The grocer thought so. For the next 31 years, from 189 until 1930, Sir Thomas Lipton tried five times .

Sir Thomas, born in Glasgow of Irish parents, was very much a self-made man. He spent a few years in America before returning to Scotland as a 19-year-old to open a grocery store, forerunner to what was to become an international chain.

He made millions and spent quite a few of them in his quest for the America's Cup. Eighteen times his *Shamrocks* raced – but won only twice.

Sir Thomas was 80 when he made his final bid to lift what he fondly referred to as "The auld mug." He failed but a generous American nation had a public whip round to present him with a gold cup as the world's best loser!

Thomas Sopwith, who made his fortune from building aircraft, made the challenges in 1934 and 1937 with *Endeavour* and *Endeavour II*. There were high hopes when Sopwith won the first two races but he was beaten in the next four by the narrowest of margins. Still, it was worth another try. So back he came, only to be "whitewashed" by the Burgess-Stephens designed *Ranger*.

The Australians appeared on the scene in 1962 with *Gretel*. Their challenge, fronted by newspaper and TV tycoon, Sir Frank Packer, infuriated, among others, the Royal Yacht Squadron.

"What right had these upstarts to encroach on what had always been a predominantly American-British affair?" fumed Squadron members.

To which Packer replied: "I just reckon it's about time a younger member of the family took a hand."

And they did. After six challenges that had yielded only three wins they collared sport's greatest and most cherished prize.

They may not hold it as long as the Americans did. No-one ever will again. But it is the sort of game the Australians like best where nobody ever comes second and only the winner counts.

All races for the America's Cup were held off New York until 1920. They then moved to the course off Newport, Rhode Island.

The 1937 challenge by Tommy Sopwith's *Endeavour II* saw the last of the great J Boats. When the series resumed in 1958 the races were disputed by the smaller, sleeker, faster and much more thoroughbred 12m yachts.

Under the International Rule which classifies racing yachts, classes range from 6m (about 35ft) to 23m (130ft). The 12m is around 60ft overall, with 45ft on the water.

THE AMERICA'S CUP

Year	Defender	Challenger
1870	*Magic* (1)	*Cambria,* GBR (10th)
1871	*Columbia /Sappho* (4)	*Livonia,* GBR (1)
1876	*Madeleine* (2)	*Countess of Dufferin,* CAN (0)
1881	*Mischief* (2)	*Atalanta,* CAN (0)
1885	*Puritan* (2)	*Genesta,* GBR (0)
1886	*Mayflower* (2)	*Galatea,* GBR (0)
1887	*Volunteer* (2)	*Thistle,* GBR (0)
1893	*Vigilant* (3)	*Valkyrie II,* GBR (0)
1895	*Defender* (3)	*Valkyrie III,* GBR (0)
1899	*Columbia* (3)	*Shamrock I,* GBR (0)
1901	*Columbia* (3)	*Shamrock II,* GBR (0)
1903	*Reliance* (3)	*Shamrock III,* GBR (0)
1920	*Resolute* (3)	*Shamrock IV,* GBR (2)
1930	*Enterprise* (4)	*Shamrock V,* GBR (0)
1934	*Rainbow* (4)	*Endeavour,* GBR (2)
1937	*Ranger* (4)	*Endeavour II,* GBR (0)
1958	*Columbia* (4)	*Sceptre,* GBR (0)
1962	*Weatherly* (4)	*Gretel,* AUS (1)
1964	*Constellation* (4)	*Sovereign,* GBR (0)
1967	*Intrepid* (4)	*Dame Pattie,* AUS (0)
1970	*Intrepid* (4)	*Gretel II,* AUS (1)
1974	*Courageous* (4)	*Southern Cross,* AUS (0)
1977	*Courageous* (4)	*Australia,* AUS (0)
1980	*Freedom* (4)	*Australia,* AUS (1)
1983	*Liberty* (3)	*Australia II,* AUS (4)

In 1870 Cambria raced against 17 American defenders; in 1871 America was represented by both Columbia and Sappho; in 1930 the present best-of-seven race system was introduced.

• The America's Cup

• *Australia II*

WATER SPEED

The pursuit of the world water speed record has claimed the lives of enough distinguished men to fill a small Who's Who. Daredevils who survived repeated attempts on the land speed record came to their doom with tragic monotony when they tried to repeat their exploits on water.

Sir Henry Segrave, John Cobb and Donald Campbell, all drivers who held the land speed record, died when they moved onto water with its surface variations and natural hazards such as driftwood.

Segrave was the first to come to grief over such vagaries on Lake Windemere in 1930, when his *Miss England II* hit a submerged log at some 120mph (193km/h) and cartwheeled. Minutes earlier the boat had been timed on a two-way run at a world record average of 98.76mph (158.94km/h).

Segrave, who had served as a soldier on the Western Front, then joined the Royal Flying Corps and been shot down three times, who had become the first man to drive on land at more than 200mph (322km/h), was carried from the water to a private house where he died from a punctured lung after three hours of conscious pain. He was 34.

The next great racing knight to take to the water was Sir Malcolm Campbell, a legendary racer who had nine times raised the world land speed record, taking it from 146.16mph (235.22km/h) in 1924 to 301.13mph (484.62km/h) in 1935. He stood only 5ft 6in (1.68m) tall, but had an upright, military bearing, piercing blue eyes and a quick high-pitched voice. Like his cars, all his boats were named *Bluebird*, after the play *The Blue Bird* written by his great friend Maurice Maeterlinck. Unlike so many others, Campbell would survive his switch to water.

In 1937, at the age of 54, Campbell piloted the Rolls Royce powered *Bluebird K3* to an average 126.33mph (203.31km/h) at Lake Maggiore, a huge stretch of water between Italy and Switzerland.

The following day *Bluebird K3* pushed that record to 129.5mph (208.4km/h).

A year later Campbell found himself another stretch of water, Lake Hallwilersee near Geneva and raised his record a third time, to 130.84mph (210.73km/h). But he was concerned that the hydroplane was unstable and set about building *Bluebird K4*. Or *Bluebird II* as she was popularly known. She was 27ft (8.23m) long and 11ft 2in (3.40m) wide. The all-timber hull was christened by Sir Malcolm's son, Donald, and six days later, on 19 August 1939 his father clocked his fourth world record with 141.74mph (228.10km/h). "The most marvellous boat I've ever driven," he reported. "Steady as a rock. What can she achieve?" Sir Malcolm never found out. Three weeks later Britain declared war on Germany and although he returned to the water in 1947 he was frailer and suffering failing eyesight. He died the next year after a stroke.

His son Donald, who had been discouraged from racing on water while Sir Malcolm was alive, now decided to take up the challenge. But as he was preparing *Bluebird* in 1950, so he heard that American Stanley Sayres, a 53-year-old Chrysler dealer from Seattle had aimed his *Slo-Mo-Shun IV*, powered by a 2,000 hp Allison aero-engine, to 160.32mph (258.01km/h).

Campbell was confident he could regain the record for Britain, and his sureness was seemingly well founded as the reconstructed *Bluebird K4* reached 170mph (273km/h) in

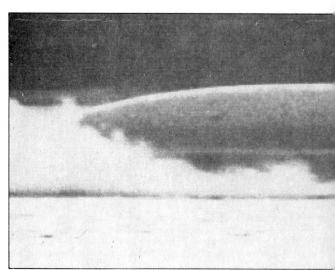

● The record breaking run of Bluebird K7 on Lake Coniston in 1956

trials. But a collision with a submerged railway sleeper sent her to the bottom of Lake Coniston. She was recovered, but Campbell's financial resources were at an end. For now.

Into the breech stepped the powerful, gentlemanly John Cobb, three times breaker of the world land speed record in his Napier-Railtons. Now the genius of Reid Railton was set to designing a boat which would recapture the water record. He came up with *Crusader*, a boat capable of 200mph (322km/h). Built of birch plywood, reinforced by a high tensile alloy, the 31ft (9.45m) *Crusader* was a three-pointer: a small seaplane hull with two floats mounted on outriggers. "A tricycle with one wheel in front," said Railton.

Cobb decided to test his pride and joy at Loch Ness in Scotland. Carefully he ran her through speeds of 100mph, 130mph, 150mph. He had never driven a speedboat before. "It's like driving a London omnibus without tyres on," he said. By September he was ready to attack the record.

But conditions change rapidly in the Highlands in September and it was not until the 29th that the weather report was considered good enough to attempt a record run. Even then Cobb had three false starts before, at 10.30am, the water flattened and the wind passed. On the way to the start line, however, Cobb met his support boat, the *Maureen,* which for some inexplicable reason had decided to return to base rather than wait by the measured mile. At 40ft (12.19m), the *Maureen* created a sizeable wash when she moved, a wash which might rebound in and out across the loch for some time. Cobb waited only ten minutes after the *Maureen* had returned to her station before firing his de Haviland Ghost engine. *Crusader* sped like a bullet, well over 200mph . . . and then hit three swells rolling out broadside from the shores of the loch. *Crusader* bucked, flooded and then exploded into a thousand fragments. Cobb died from shock. And Railton was so distressed by his death that he pulled out completely from a design field in which he stood supreme.

A similar fate awaited Italy's Mario Verga. In 1953 the Italian Motornautical Federation offered a prize of five million lire for an Italian to beat Stanley Sayres' record (which he had now raised to 178.49mph; 287.26km/h) using a boat, and engine produced in Italy. Verga produced the *Laura III* powered by two 159 Alfetta engines and on 9 October 1954 decided he was ready to accept the challenge. At a speed of well over 190mph (305km/h) *Laura III* lifted backwards in the water, catapulted Verga out of his cockpit and barrel-rolled back into the water. Like Cobb, Verga died from shock.

By now people were beginning to suspect that the 00mph (322km/h) barrier might prove impassable on water. Donald Campbell did not agree. He estimated that, using a propeller for thrust, he would need an engine developing ,500hp. The old boy network was invoked and Donald found wo Rolls-Royce Griffin engines placed at his disposal. Although still short of funds, Campbell had been spurred into ction by Cobb's death and teamed up with the Norris Brothers, consulting engineers at Burgess Hill, Sussex. ogether they set about designing an all metal craft, the Bluebird K7.

But tests quickly showed that no propeller would give the propulsion they wanted. Campbell made the revolutionary decision to switch to jet power.

Now he needed an engine that would give about 4,500lb of thrust. It came in the shape of a Metropolitan-Vickers unit

known as the "Beryl". It weighed 1,780lb and consumed 650 gallons of fuel an hour and three tons of air a minute. The craft itself was 26ft (7.92m) long with a 10ft 6in (3.20m) beam and a height of 4ft 9in (1.45m). The alloy hull was held in place by 70,000 rivets. At Ullswater on 23 July 1955 Campbell and his *Bluebird* howled over the calm surface to record 202.32mph (325.60km/h). The dreaded barrier had fallen.

Campbell took *Bluebird* on a promotional trip to the United States for the Lake Mead Regatta in Nevada in 1955 and while there raised the record to 216.2mph (347.9km/h). Campbell's own reading showed he had touched 280mph (450km/h) on one of the runs, but deteriorating water conditions slowed down his return leg. Now he was dreaming about 300mph (483km/h)!

It was never to be, even though Campbell and *Bluebird* were to raise the record five more times between 1956 and 1964, finishing with 276.33mph (444.71km/h) at Lake Dumbleyung in Western Australia. In search of more power he ditched the Beryl and installed a Bristol Sydney Orpheus jet engine which developed almost 5,000lb of thrust. But *Bluebird* was growing old and had already far outreached her design potential. Campbell was warned he was taking terrible risks . . . especially as he chose to race his new engine on Lake Coniston in winter, a poor time for water conditions.

On January 4 1967 Campbell steered *Bluebird* out to his starting point. He had been playing cards the night before and drawn the ace and queen of spades, the same combination as Mary Queen of Scots the day before her execution. "I have this awful premonition that I'm going to get the chop," he said.

Bluebird's first run was timed at 297mph (480km/h). But instead of waiting to refuel and so allow his own wash to subside, Campbell inexplicably began his second run straight away. He was travelling at an estimated 328mph (528km/h) – yes, over that 300mph target – when the bows rose and *Bluebird* turned crazy cartwheels across the lake.

Progressive Water Speed Record
(as homologated by the Union Internationale Motonautique)

.m/h	mph	Boat	Pilot	Venue	Year
49.40	92.83	Miss America VII	George Wood	Detroit	1928
49.86	93.12	Miss America VII	Gar Wood	Indian Creek	1929
58.94	98.76	Miss England II	Sir Henry Segrave	Lake Windemere	1930
64.56	102.25	Miss America IX	Gar Wood	Indian Creek	1931
66.55	103.49	Miss England II	Kaye Don	Parana River	1931
77.38	110.22	Miss England II	Kaye Don	Lake Garda	1931
79.78	111.71	Miss America IX	Gar Wood	Indian Creek	1932
88.98	117.43	Miss England III	Kaye Don	Lock Lomond	1932
92.81	119.81	Miss England III	Kaye Don	Lock Lomond	1932
201.02	124.91	Miss America X	Gar Wood	Revier Canal	1932
203.31	126.33	Bluebird K3	Sir Malcolm Campbell	Lake Maggiore	1937
208.4	129.5	Bluebird K3	Sir Malcolm Campbell	Lake Maggiore	1937
210.73	130.94	Bluebird K3	Sir Malcolm Campbell	Lake Hallwyl	1938
228.10	141.74	Bluebird K4	Sir Malcolm Campbell	Coniston Water	1939
258.01	160.32	Slo-Mo-Shun IV	Stan Sayres	Lake Washington	1950
287.26	178.49	Slo-Mo-Shun IV	Stan Sayres	Lake Washington	1952
325.60	202.32	Bluebird K7	Donald Campbell	Ullswater	1955
347.9	216.2	Bluebird K7	Donald Campbell	Lake Mead	1955
363.12	225.63	Bluebird K7	Donald Campbell	Coniston Water	1956
384.75	239.07	Bluebird K7	Donald Campbell	Coniston Water	1957
400.12	248.62	Bluebird K7	Donald Campbell	Coniston Water	1958
418.99	260.35	Bluebird K7	Donald Campbell	Coniston Water	1959
444.71*	276.33	Bluebird K7	Donald Campbell	Lake Dumbleyung	1964
459.00	285.21	Hustler	Lee Taylor Jr	Lake Guntersville	1967
464.45**	288.60	Spirit of Australia	Ken Warby	Blowering Dam	1977
514.39	319.627	Spirit of Australia	Ken Warby	Blowering Dam	1978

● Donald Campbell

Campbell's last words showed how he kept his nerve until the end: "Nose up . . . pitching a bit down here, probably from my own wash . . . getting straightened up now on track . . . passing close to Peel Island and we're tramping like mad . . . full power . . . tramping like hell here . . . I can't see much and the water's very bad indeed . . . I can't get over the top . . . I'm getting a lot of bloody row in here . . . I can't see anything . . . I've got the bows up . . . I've gone . . . Oh." Campbell's body was never found.

*Prior to his fatal crash on Coniston Water in 1967 Donald Campbell reached 528km/h (328mph). Warby reached an estimated speed of 555.9km/h (345.4mph) on one run.

WATER SKIING

Mention water skiing and the mind immediately conjures up pictures of golden beaches, endless sun and flat, placid seas. And indeed, countries blessed by such conditions like the United States and Australia have ruled the waves in impressive fashion ever since the sport became a world championship event just after the Second World War in 1949.

But in recent years a growing challenge to that supremacy has come from the cold water babes of Britain and the awakening might of the Soviet Union.

America still ride supreme, however, in a sport they can justifiably claim to have pioneered back in 1922 when Ralph Samuelson negotiated Lake Pepin, Minnesota, on two curved pine boards. Since then they have dominated the record lists, winning the team gold medal at every world championship since 1949 . . . 19 in all.

In 1985 their Sammy Duvall became the first male skier to claim three successive overall world titles and Bob La Point the first to claim four world slalom titles. In earlier years the elegant Liz Allan Shetter, three times the women's world overall champion, had become the only person to win all four individual world titles – slalom, jumps, tricks and overall – in one year (1969).

The great Canadian George Athans and the powerful Englishman Mike Hazelwood challenged that USA might during the Seventies and early Eighties. Athans took the overall title in 1971 and 1973; Hazelwood the overall title in 1977 and the jumps championship in both 1979 and 1981.

There were also occasional outbreaks of brilliance from such as the one-eyed Italian Robbi Zucchi, who won the slalom title in 1975 at Thorpe, England, and tricks specialists

Carlos Suarez (Venezuela) and Patrice Martin (France).

But at the last biennial world championships – in Toulouse, France in 1985 – the Americans were firmly back in charge winning half of the eight titles on offer as well as the team trophy yet again. Their closest challenge came from the revitalised Australians who took the men's jumps (Geof Carrington), and the women's overall (Karen Neville).

Venezuela, who had collected at least one title in seven of the past eight championships through the skills of Suarez and the trick-skiing Carrasco sisters, finished empty-handed.

British skiers such as Paul Seaton, who set a world jumps record before being forced to retire with a crippling knee injury incurred during the 1975 world championships, the outstanding Hazelwood, and the athletic Andy Mapple, who equalled the world slalom record of five buoys on a 11.25m line in September 1985, have proved that climate is not the only criterion for great water skiers.

In part the Soviets have underlined that fact. Of course they have the warm water of the Caspian and Black seas, but much of their preparation, like Britain's, has been carried out on less hospitable stretches of water. The result nonetheless has been an impressive string of skiers, mostly in women's tricks. Natalia Ponomaryeva set a world record of 7850 points twice in 1984, a mark that was overtaken in sensational style by Venezuela's Ana Maria Carrasco with a massive 8350 at McCormick Lake, Florida, on 14 September 1984. Ana's sister Maria Victoria Carrasco had won the world tricks title three times in succession from 1973-77, in the forefront of the great

One of the earliest exponents of the sport in Britain was the late Lord Louis Mountbatten, and in America Errol Flynn and David Niven led the way among movie stars. In the Middle East the Shah of Iran and King Hussein of Jordan were keen water-skiers. Both Prince Philip, the Duke of Edinburgh, and his son Prince Charles have taken up water-skiing, while Prince Bernhard of the Netherlands was one of his country's first aficionados.

Carlos Suarez

● Sammy Duvall

Ana Maria Carrasco

Deena Brush

Venezuelan water skiing surge which saw Suarez set world tricks records and win three world titles.

The Soviets are confidently expected to launch an even greater challenge in following years, now they have tasted a measure of success.

World Water-Skiing Championships

Men

Year	Overall	Slalom	Tricks	Jumping
1949	Christian Jourdan (FRA) Guy de Clerq (BEL)	Christian Jourdan (FRA)	Pierre Gouin (FRA)	Guy de Clerq (BEL)
1950	Dick Pope Jnr (USA)	Dick Pope Jnr (USA)	Jack Andresen (USA)	Guy de Clerq (BEL)
1953	Alfredo Mendoza (USA)	Charles Blackwell (CAN)	Warren Witherall (USA)	Alfredo Mendoza (USA)
1955	Alfredo Mendoza (USA)	Alfredo Mendoza (USA)	Scotty Scott (USA)	Alfredo Mendoza (USA)
1957	Joe Cash (USA)	Joe Cash (USA)	Mike Amsbry (USA)	Joe Mueller (USA)
1959	Chuck Stearns (USA)	Chuck Stearns (USA)	Philippe Logut (FRA)	Buster McCalla (USA)
1961	Bruno Zaccardi (ITA)	Jimmy Jackson (USA)	Jean Marie Muller (FRA)	Larry Penacho (USA)
1963	Billy Spencer (USA)	Billy Spencer (USA)	Billy Spencer (USA)	Jimmy Jackson (USA)
1965	Roland Hillier (USA)	Roland Hillier (USA)	Ken White (USA)	Larry Penacho (USA)
1967	Mike Suyderhoud (USA)	Tito Antunano (MEX)	Alan Kempton (USA)	Alan Kempton (USA)
1969	Mike Suyderhoud (USA)	Bruce Cockburn (AUS)	Victor Palomo (ESP)	Wayne Grimditch (USA)
1971	George Athans (CAN)	Ricky McCormick (USA)	Mike Suyderhoud (USA)	Mike Suyderhoud (USA)
1973	George Athans (CAN)	Wayne Grimditch (USA)	George Athans (CAN)	Ricky McCormick (USA)
1975	Carlos Suarez (VEN)	Wayne Grimditch (USA)	Roby Zucchi (ITA)	Ricky McCormick (USA)
1977	Mike Hazelwood (GBR)	Carlos Suarez (VEN)	Bob LaPoint (USA)	Mike Suyderhoud (USA)
1979	Joel McClintock (USA)	Patrice Martin (FRA)	Bob LaPoint (USA)	Mike Hazelwood (GBR)
1981	Sammy Duvall (USA)	Cory Pickos (USA)	Andy Mapple (GBR)	Mike Hazelwood (GBR)
1983	Sammy Duvall (USA)	Cory Pickos (USA)	Bob LaPoint (USA)	Sammy Duvall (USA)
1985	Sammy Duvall (USA)	Bob LaPoint (USA)	Patrice Martin (FRA)	Geoff Carrington (AUS)

Women

Year	Overall	Slalom	Tricks	Jumping
1949	Willa Worthington (USA)	Willa Worthington (USA)	Madeleine Boutellier (FRA)	Willa Worthington (USA)
1950	Willa Worthington-McGuire (USA)	Evie Wolford (USA)	Willa Worthington-McGuire (USA)	Johnette Kirkpatrick (USA)
1953	Leah Marie Rawls (USA)	Evie Wolford (USA)	Leah Marie Rawls (USA)	Sandra Swaney (USA)
1955	Willa McGuire (USA)	Willa McGuire (USA)	Marina Doria (SUI)	Willa McGuire (USA)
1957	Marina Doria (SUI)	Marina Doria (SUI)	Marina Doria (SUI)	Nancie Rideout (USA)
1959	Vickie Van Hook (USA)	Vickie Van Hook (USA)	Piera Castelvetri (ITA)	Nancie Rideout (USA)
1961	Sylvie Hulsemann (LUX)	Janelle Kirkley (USA)	Sylvie Hulsemann (LUX)	Renate Hansluvka (AUT)
1963	Jeannette Brown (USA)	Jeannette Brown (USA)	Guyonne Dalle (FRA)	Renate Hansluvka (AUT)
1965	Liz Allan (USA)	Barbara Cooper-Clack (USA)	Dany Duflot (FRA)	Liz Allan (USA)
1967	Jeannette Stewart-Wood (GBR)	Liz Allan (USA)	Dany Duflot (FRA)	Jeannette Stewart-Wood (GBR)
1969	Liz Allan (USA)	Liz Allan (USA)	Liz Allan (USA)	Liz Allan (USA)
1971	Christy Weir (USA)	Willi Stahle (HOL)	Christy Freeman (USA)	Christy Weir (USA)
1973	Lisa St John (USA)	Maria Victoria Carrasco (VEN)	Sylvie Maurial (FRA)	Liz Allan-Shetter (USA)
1975	Liz Allan-Shetter (USA)	Maria Victoria Carrasco (VEN)	Liz Allan-Shetter (USA)	Liz Allan-Shetter (USA)
1977	Cindy Todd (USA)	Maria Victoria Carrasco (VEN)	Cindy Todd (USA)	Linda Giddens (USA)
1979	Cinty Todd (USA)	Natalya Rumiantseva (URS)	Pat Messner (CAN)	Cindy Todd (USA)
1981	Karin Roberge (USA)	Ana Maria Carrasco (VEN)	Cindy Todd (USA)	Deena Brush (USA)
1983	Ana Maria Carrasco (VEN)	Natalya Ponomaryeva (URS)	Cindy Todd (USA)	Cindy Todd (USA)
1985	Karen Neville (AUS)	Camille Duvall (USA)	Judy McClintock (CAN)	Deena Brush (USA)

100m FREESTYLE (MEN)

Sprinters from the United States, Australia and East Germany have done most of the record breaking in swimming's blue riband event, the 100m freestyle.

One of the earliest greats, Duke Kahanamoku had royal Hawaiian blood in his veins and could plane on the surface of the water as no man of his size had done before. He was born in Princess Ruth's palace in Honolulu during a visit, in 1890, of the Duke of Edinburgh, second son of Queen Victoria, and got his christian name to celebrate the occasion.

In his 20-year swimming career, Kahanamoku twice broke the 100m record. The second occasion, on his 30th birthday, was at the 1920 Antwerp Olympics. The Duke won easily in 1 min 00.4. There was a protest between two other swimmers and the final had to be reswum. This time the Hawaiian was a second slower though still the victor. But his earlier record stood.

Johnny Weissmuller, the most famous of the film "Tarzans", voted the "Greatest Swimmer of the Half Century" in 1950 and heir to the Duke's swimming kingdom, was the first to shoot through the magic minute barrier with 58.6 sec in 1922.

● Johnny Weismuller (left) shakes hands with Duke Kahanamoku

Jon Henricks, John Devitt and Mike Wenden, all winners of this Olympic event, brought Australia seven records. Then came Mark Spitz in 1970. He started an American record run which – with one particular exception – took the figures from 51.94 sec to 48.95 sec in 15 years.

Along the way, Jim Montgomery became the first to break 50 sec, by one hundredth of a second, in winning the 1976 Olympic title in 49.99 sec.

Unlucky Jonty Skinner stemmed the US flood. The American-trained South African was barred from Montreal because his country had been thrown out of the Olympics due to its apartheid policies. Three weeks after Montgomery's victory, Skinner showed what might have been. He cut the record to 49.44 sec and it was almost five years before Rowdy Gaines got it back for the USA.

Matt Biondi, the latest of a long line of super American sprinters, became the first under 49 sec. His 48.95 in August 1985 was only a day after he had first broken the Gaines record.

Since world records were first recognised in 1908 (when some earlier known marks were also approved) 105 different events have been in (and many out) of the record book. In 1969, a tidy list of 31 metric events (which became 32 in 1982 when the 4 x 200m for women was added) was established.
Of the 32, all but the 800m for men and 1,500m for women make up the programmes for major competitions.

Conditions for world records have changed over the years. In the early days, times could be set in any length pool (from 25 yards upwards) except for 800m and over distances where the minimum length had to be 50m.

Records in "short course" pools (ie. less than 50m) were discontinued on 30 April 1957 when linear distances nearest to metric ones (ie. 110 yds = 100.584m and multiples) were added.

At this time it was possible to break a metric record (in a 55 yd pool) on the way to the longer yards one by taking a mid-bath time as the swimmer passed under a rope or an imaginary eye line.

Imperial records and mid-bath times were discontinued in 1969. Records had to be set in "long course" 50m pools and record-equalling times became recognised for the first time. Listing of world records to 1/100th sec began in 1972.

100m Freestyle (Men)

Time	Competitor	Venue	Date
Early long course bests (some of which were records):			
1:05.6	Charles Daniels (USA)	London	20/7/08
1:01.6	Duke Kahanamoku (USA)	Hamburg	20/7/12
1:00.4	Duke Kahanamoku (USA)	Antwerp	24/8/20
58.6	Johnny Weissmuller (USA)	Alameda	9/7/22
57.2	Peter Fick (USA)	Tokyo	10/8/35
56.2	Alex Jany (FRA)	Monte Carlo	10/9/47
55.8	Jon Henricks (AUS)	Los Angeles	24/6/55
55.4	Jon Henricks (AUS)	Melbourne	30/11/56
55.2	John Devitt (AUS)	Sydney	19/1/57
54.6	John Devitt (AUS)	Brisbane	28/1/57
The progression of the record since 1957 has gone like this:			
54.4	Steve Clark (USA)	Los Angeles	18/8/61
53.6	Manuel dos Santos (BRA)	Rio De Janiero	20/9/61
52.9	Alain Gottvalles (FRA)	Budapest	13/9/64
52.6	Ken Walsh (USA)	Winnipeg	27/7/67
52.2	Mike Wenden (AUS)	Mexico City	19/10/68
51.9	Mark Spitz (USA)	Los Angeles	23/8/70
51.47	Mark Spitz (USA)	Chicago	5/8/72
51.22	Mark Spitz (USA)	Munich	3/9/72
51.12	Jim Montgomery (USA)	Long Beach	21/6/75
51.11	Andy Coan (USA)	Fort Lauderdale	3/8/75
50.59	Jim Montgomery (USA)	Kansas City	23/8/75
50.39	Jim Montgomery (USA)	Montreal	24/7/76
49.99	Jim Montgomery (USA)	Montreal	25/7/76
49.44	Jonty Skinner (SAF)	Philadelphia	14/8/76
49.36	Rowdy Gaines (USA)	Austin	3/4/81
49.24	Matt Biondi (USA)	Mission Viejo	6/8/85
48.95	Matt Biondi (USA)	Mission Viejo	7/8/85

m Montgomery

Each turn in swimming is considered to give a time gain of 0.7 sec. Thus, in the days when records could be set "short course", the time advantage, say, of a 400m swim in a 25m pool (with 15 turns) against one in a "long course" 50m pool (seven turns) was above 5.6 sec (ie. 8 x 0.7).

For this reason, it is unrealistic to try to compare early records set in so many different length pools.

Known early "long course" times, some of which were world records, have been included as "bests" in this book to give some idea of speed advancement.

The lists from 1957 give complete record progressions.

● Dawn Fraser

● Barbara Krause

100m FREESTYLE (WOMEN)

Dawn Fraser from Australia, with 12 marks between 1956 and 1964 and East Germany's Kornelia Ender, an uninterrupted series of 10 in four seasons (1973-76), set between them almost as many records for this event as all the other women in history put together.

Fraser, the only swimmer – man or woman – to win the same titles at three successive Olympics (1956, '60 and '64), brought her times down from 1 min 4.9 sec to 58.9 sec during her remarkable nine years at the top. It was eight years before her last mark was beaten, by Australia's new golden girl, Shane Gould, aged 15.

Ender was 14 when she set her first record of 58.25 in 1973. She quit, at 18, to marry backstroker Roland Matthes, East Germany's greatest male swimmer, having improved her figures by 2.6 sec (equal to about four and a half m) to 55.65 sec.

Barbara Krause, forced out of the 1976 Montreal Games because of illness, carried on the East German tradition with three records. She was the first under 55 sec, with her opening freestyle relay leg of 54.98 sec at the 1980 Moscow Games. The next day she improved to 54.79, winning the individual gold. This record remained still unbeaten in mid-1986.

Fanny Durack of Australia, using old training methods, clocked 1 min 19.8 sec to become the first woman Olympic champion in Stockholm in 1912. Krause, 68 years on, was 45m faster.

100m Freestyle (Women)

Time	Competitor	Venue	Date
Early long course bests (some of which were records):			
1:19.8	Fanny Durack (AUS)	Stockholm	9/7/12
1:16.2	Fanny Durack (AUS)	Sydney	6/2/15
1:13.6	Ethelda Bleibtrey (USA)	Antwerp	25/8/20
1:09.8	Eleanora Garratti (AUS)	Honolulu	7/8/29
1:06.8	Helene Madison (USA)	Los Angeles	9/8/32
1:04.9	Dawn Fraser (AUS)	Melbourne	20/1/56
1:04.5	Dawn Fraser (AUS)	Sydney	21/2/56
1:03.3	Dawn Fraser (AUS)	Townsville	25/8/56
1:03.2	Lorraine Crapp (AUS)	Sydney	20/10/56
1:02.4	Lorraine Crapp (AUS)	Melbourne	25/10/56
1:02.0	Dawn Fraser (AUS)	Melbourne	1/12/56
The progression of the record since 1957 has gone like this:			
1:01.5	Dawn Fraser (AUS)	Melbourne	18/2/58
1:01.4	Dawn Fraser (AUS)	Cardiff	21/7/58
1:01.2	Dawn Fraser (AUS)	Sciedam	10/8/58
1:00.2	Dawn Fraser (AUS)	Sydney	23/2/60
1:00.0	Dawn Fraser (AUS)	Melbourne	23/10/62
59.9	Dawn Fraser (AUS)	Melbourne	27/10/62
59.5	Dawn Fraser (AUS)	Perth	24/11/62
58.9	Dawn Fraser (AUS)	Sydney	29/2/64
58.5	Shane Gould (AUS)	Sydney	8/1/72
58.25	Kornelia Ender (GDR)	E. Berlin	13/7/73
58.12	Kornelia Ender (GDR)	Utrecht	18/8/73
57.61	Kornelia Ender (GDR)	Belgrade	8/9/73
57.54	Kornelia Ender (GDR)	Belgrade	9/9/73
57.51	Kornelia Ender (GDR)	Rostock	4/7/74
56.96	Kornelia Ender (GDR)	Vienna	19/8/74
56.38	Kornelia Ender (GDR)	Dresden	14/3/75
56.22	Kornelia Ender (GDR)	Cali	26/7/75
55.73	Kornelia Ender (GDR)	E. Berlin	1/6/76
55.65	Kornelia Ender (GDR)	Montreal	19/7/76
55.41	Barbara Krause (GDR)	E. Berlin	5/7/78
54.98	Barbara Krause (GDR)	Moscow	20/7/80
54.79	Barbara Krause (GDR)	Moscow	21/7/80

200m FREESTYLE (MEN/WOMEN)

America's Don Schollander, the first swimmer to win four golds at one Olympics (Tokyo 1964), broke the 200m record nine times in six years (1963-68) and was the first to get inside two minutes. His final 1 min 54.33 sec stood for three years and it required a man as great as Mark Spitz to beat it.

Bruce Furniss, the younger and smaller of two record-breaking Furniss brothers (the elder was Steve), opened his record account with two marks in one day. In 1976 he edged towards a sub 1 min 50 sec time but missed by three tenths of a second. Three years on and Sergey Kopliakov, the only Russian to get into this record list, broke through.

Rowdy Gaines, briefly, regained the record for the States. Then it was the turn of West Germany's mighty Michael Gross. His four records in 13 months culminated in his Olympic gold medal-winning 1 min 47.44 sec in Los Angeles.

Between 1958 and 1984 (27 years) the men's figures dropped by 17.4 sec. The women's list, following a parallel graph, was bettered by 20 sec. Dawn Fraser and Lorraine Crapp made dramatic inroads, sharing six marks between them from 1956 to 1960. Six different American girls moved the time down from 2 min 10.5 sec to 2 min 06.9 sec.

Shane Gould from Sydney, who remarkably held all five freestyle records – from 100m to 1,500m – at the same time, opened her score with 2 min 06.5 sec in London in 1971 at the age of 14.

Kornelia Ender was the first under two minutes, emulating the Schollander feat 13 years earlier. The third of Cynthia Woodhead's records, in 1979, stood for five years. Then it was the turn of East Germany's Kristin Otto.

• Michael Gross

• Kornelia Ender

200m Freestyle (Men)

Time	Competitor	Venue	Date
No early 200m long course bests available			
2:04.8	John Konrads (AUS)	Sydney	18/1/58
2:03.2	John Konrads (AUS)	Sydney	5/3/58
2:03.0	Tsuyoshi Yamanaka (JPN)	Osaka	22/8/58
2:02.2	John Konrads (AUS)	Sydney	16/1/59
2:01.5	Tsuyoshi Yamanaka (JPN)	Osaka	26/7/59
2:01.2	Tsuyoshi Yamanaka (JPN)	Osaka	24/6/61
2:01.1	Tsuyoshi Yamanaka (JPN)	Tokyo	6/8/61
2:00.4	Tsuyoshi Yamanaka (JPN)	Los Angeles	20/8/61
2:00.3	Bob Windle (AUS)	Tokyo	21/4/63
1:58.8	Don Schollander (USA)	Los Angeles	27/7/63
1:58.5	Don Schollander (USA)	Tokyo	17/8/63
1:58.4	Don Schollander (USA)	Osaka	24/8/63
1:58.2	Hans-Joachim Klein (FRG)	Dortmund	24/5/64
1:57.6	Don Schollander (USA)	Los Altos	1/8/64
1:57.2	Don Schollander (USA)	Los Angeles	29/7/66
1:56.2	Don Schollander (USA)	Lincoln	19/8/66
1:55.0	Don Schollander (USA)	Winnipeg	29/7/67
1:55.7	Don Schollander (USA)	Oak Park	12/8/67
1:54.3	Don Schollander (USA)	Long Beach	30/8/68
1:54.2	Mark Spitz (USA)	Leipzig	4/9/71
1:53.5	Mark Spitz (USA)	Minsk	10/9/71
1:52.78	Mark Spitz (USA)	Munich	29/8/72
1:51.66	Tim Shaw (USA)	Concord	23/8/74
1:51.41	Bruce Furniss (USA)	Long Beach	18/6/75
1:50.89	Bruce Furniss (USA)	Long Beach	18/6/75
1:50.32	Bruce Furniss (USA)	Kansas City	21/8/75
1:50.29	Bruce Furniss (USA)	Montreal	19/7/76
1:49.83	Sergey Kopliakov (URS)	E. Berlin	7/4/79
1:49.16	Rowdy Gaines (USA)	Austin	12/4/80
1:48.93	Rowdy Gaines (USA)	Mission Viejo	19/7/82
1:48.28	Michael Gross (FRG)	Hanover	21/6/83
1:47.87	Michael Gross (FRG)	Rome	22/8/83
1:47.55	Michael Gross (FRG)	Munich	8/6/84
1:47.44	Michael Gross (FRG)	Los Angeles	29/7/84

200m Freestyle (Women)

Time	Competitor	Venue	Date
Early long course bests (some of which were records):			
2:56.4	Olga Dorfner (USA)	Alameda	21/7/18
2:20.7	Dawn Fraser (AUS)	Sydney	25/2/56
2:19.3	Lorraine Crapp (AUS)	Townsville	25/8/56
2:18.5	Lorraine Crapp (AUS)	Sydney	20/10/56
The progression of the record since 1957 has gone like this:			
2:17.7	Dawn Fraser (AUS)	Adelaide	10/2/58
2:14.7	Dawn Fraser (AUS)	Melbourne	22/2/58
2:11.6	Dawn Fraser (AUS)	Sydney	27/2/60
2:10.5	Pokey Watson (USA)	Lincoln	19/8/66
2:09.7	Pam Kruse (USA)	Philadelphia	19/8/67
2:09.5	Sue Pedersen (USA)	Santa Clara	6/7/68
2:08.8	Edith Wetzel (USA)	Lincoln	2/8/68
2:07.9	Linda Gustavson (USA)	Los Angeles	24/8/68
2:06.9	Debbie Meyer (USA)	Los Angeles	24/8/68
2:06.5	Shane Gould (AUS)	London	1/5/71
2:05.8	Shane Gould (AUS)	Sydney	26/11/71
2:05.21	Shirley Babashoff (USA)	Chicago	4/8/72
2:03.56	Shane Gould (AUS)	Munich	1/9/72
2:03.22	Kornelia Ender (GDR)	Vienna	22/8/74
2:02.94	Shirley Babashoff (USA)	Concord	23/8/74
2:02.94	Shirley Babashoff (USA)	Concord	31/8/74
2:02.27	Kornelia Ender (GDR)	Dresden	15/3/75
1:59.78	Kornelia Ender (GDR)	E. Berlin	2/6/76
1:59.26	Kornelia Ender (GDR)	Montreal	19/7/76
1:59.0	Barbara Krause (GDR)	E. Berlin	2/7/78
1:58.53	Cynthia Woodhead (USA)	W. Berlin	22/8/78
1:58.43	Cynthia Woodhead (USA)	San Juan	3/7/79
1:58.23	Cynthia Woodhead (USA)	Tokyo	3/9/79
1:57.75	Kristin Otto (GDR)	Magdeburg	23/5/84

400/800m FREESTYLE (WOMEN)

In 1956, when Lorraine Crapp, racing "long course", became the first under 5 min for 400m with 4 min 50.8 sec, everyone marvelled. It had been 16 years since Ragnhild Hveger had teetered on the brink of this barrier with 5 min 00.1 sec and she did this in a 25m pool with a time advantage of 5.6 sec because of eight extra turns).

In 1978, Tracey Wickham came within 6.29 sec of a sub 4 min time, winning the World title in 4 min 06.28 sec – 74m faster than Crapp.

Three weeks earlier, Wickham cut her own 800m figures by almost six seconds to 8 min 24.62 sec in taking the Commonwealth Games gold. This was over 1 min 10 sec better than the first record of Debbie Meyer 11 years earlier.

Yet Meyer was the dominating swimmer of the late 1960s. Her three Olympic golds in 1968 (200m, 400m and 800m) and 10 records – five each for 400 and 800 – bear witness to this. Meyer was the first under 4 min 30 sec for 400m. Shane Gould took the record below 4 min 20 sec and Petra Thümer under 4 min 10 sec.

The modern magic mark breakers for 800m were Jane Cederqvist (10 min), Meyer (9 min 30 sec), Ann Simmons (9 min) and Wickham (8 min 30 sec) in just 18 years.

Back in 1919 Ethelda Bleibtrey (6 min 30.2 sec) and Gertrude Ederle (13 min 19.0 sec) became the first record holders. This indicates that these redoubtable ladies, had they raced their modern counterparts, would have finished three and six laps (at least 150m and 298m) behind them. Of course they did not have the advantage of modern training methods.

• Debbie Meyer

• Tracey Wickham

Gertrude Ederle (USA), the first holder of the 800m record, had a second claim to fame. She was the first woman to swim the English Channel. Her 14hr 39min from France to England in 1926 – 51 years after Matthew Webb's famous pioneer crossing – was faster than any man before her.

400m Freestyle (Women)

Time	Competitor	Venue	Date
Early long course bests (some of which were records):			
6:30.2	Ethelda Bleibtrey (USA)	New York	16/8/19
5:53.2	Gertrude Ederle (USA)	Indianapolis	4/8/22
5:42.8	Martha Norelius (USA)	Amsterdam	6/8/28
5:28.5	Helene Madison (USA)	Los Angeles	13/8/32
5:09.0	Ragnhild Hveger (DEN)	London	1/7/38
4:50.8	Lorraine Crapp (AUS)	Townsville	25/8/56
4:47.2	Lorraine Crapp (AUS)	Sydney	20/10/56
The progression of the record since 1957 has gone like this:			
4:45.4	Ilsa Konrads (AUS)	Sydney	9/1/60
4:44.5	Chris von Saltza (USA)	Detroit	5/8/60
4:42.0	Marilyn Ramenofsky (USA)	Los Altos	11/7/64
4:41.7	Marilyn Ramenofsky (USA)	Los Altos	1/8/64
4:39.5	Marilyn Ramenofsky (USA)	New York	31/8/64
4:39.2	Martha Randall (USA)	Maumee	14/8/65
4:38.0	Martha Randall (USA)	Monte Carlo	26/8/65
4:36.8	Pam Kruse (USA)	Fort Lauderdale	30/6/67
4:36.4	Pam Kruse (USA)	Santa Clara	7/7/67
4:32.6	Debbie Meyer (USA)	Winnipeg	27/7/67
4:29.0	Debbie Meyer (USA)	Philadelphia	18/8/67
4:26.7	Debbie Meyer (USA)	Lincoln	1/8/68
4:24.5	Debbie Meyer (USA)	Los Angeles	25/8/68
4:24.3	Debbie Meyer (USA)	Los Angeles	20/8/70
4:22.6	Karen Moras (AUS)	London	30/4/71
4:21.2	Shane Gould (AUS)	Santa Clara	9/7/71
4:19.04	Shane Gould (AUS)	Munich	1/9/72
4:18.07	Keena Rothhammer (USA)	Louisville	22/8/73
4:17.33	Heather Greenwood (USA)	Santa Clara	28/6/74
4:15.77	Shirley Babashoff (USA)	Concord	22/8/74
4:14.76	Shirley Babashoff (USA)	Long Beach	20/6/75
4:11.69	Barbara Krause (GDR)	E. Berlin	3/6/76
4:09.89	Petra Thümer (GDR)	Montreal	20/7/76
4:08.91	Petra Thümer (GDR)	Jönköping	17/8/77
4:07.66	Kim Linehan (USA)	Milwaukee	2/8/78
4:06.28	Tracey Wickham (AUS)	W. Berlin	24/8/78

800m Freestyle (Women)

Time	Competitor	Venue	Date
13.19.0	Gertrude Ederle (USA)	Indianapolis	17/8/19
12:58.2	Ethel McGary (USA)	Detroit	6/8/25
12:56.0	Ethel McGary (USA)	Indianapolis	15/8/25
12:47.2	Martha Norelius (USA)	Philadelphia	7/8/26
12:17.8	Martha Norelius (USA)	Massapaqua	31/7/27
12:03.8	Josephine McKim (USA)	Honolulu	10/8/29
11:41.2	Helene Madison (USA)	Long Beach	6/7/30
11:34.4	Laura Kight (USA)	Manhattan	21/7/35
11:11.7	Ragnhild Hveger (DEN)	Copenhagen	3/7/36
10:52.5	Ragnhild Hveger (DEN)	Copenhagen	13/8/41
10:42.4	Valeria Gyenge (HUN)	Budapest	28/6/53
10:30.9	Lorraine Crapp (AUS)	Sydney	14/1/56
10:27.3	Mary Kok (HOL)	Durban	16/2/57
10:17.7	Ilsa Konrads (AUS)	Sydney	9/1/58
10:16.2	Ilsa Konrads (AUS)	Melbourne	20/2/58
10:11.8	Ilsa Konrads (AUS)	Townsville	13/6/58
10:11.4	Ilsa Konrads (AUS)	Hobart	19/2/59
9:55.6	Jane Cederqvist (SWE)	Uppsala	17/8/60
9:51.6	Carolyn House (USA)	Los Altos	28/8/62
9:47.3	Patty Caretto (USA)	Los Altos	30/7/64
9:36.9	Sharon Finneran (USA)	Los Angeles	28/9/64
9:35.8	Debbie Meyer (USA)	Santa Clara	9/7/67
9:22.9	Debbie Meyer (USA)	Winnipeg	29/7/67
9:19.0	Debbie Meyer (USA)	Los Angeles	21/7/68
9:17.8	Debbie Meyer (USA)	Lincoln	4/8/68
9:10.4	Debbie Meyer (USA)	Los Angeles	28/8/68
9:09.1	Karen Moras (AUS)	Sydney	1/3/70
9:02.4	Karen Moras (AUS)	Edinburgh	18/7/70
8:59.4	Ann Simmons (USA)	Minsk	11/9/71
8:58.1	Shane Gould (AUS)	Sydney	3/12/71
8:53.83	Jo Harshbarger (USA)	Chicago	6/8/72
8:53.68	Keena Rothhammer (USA)	Munich	3/9/72
8:52.97	Novella Calligaris (ITA)	Belgrade	9/9/73
8:50.1	Jenny Turrall (AUS)	Sydney	5/1/74
8:47.66	Jo Harshbarger (USA)	Concord	25/8/74
8:47.59	Jo Harshbarger (USA)	Concord	31/8/74
8:43.48	Jenny Turrall (AUS)	London	31/3/75
8:40.68	Petra Thümer (GDR)	E. Berlin	4/6/76
8:39.63	Shirley Babashoff (USA)	Long Beach	21/6/76
8:37.14	Petra Thümer (GDR)	Montreal	25/7/76
8:35.04	Petra Thümer (GDR)	Leipzig	9/7/77
8:34.86	Michelle Ford (AUS)	Brisbane	6/1/78
8:31.30	Michelle Ford (AUS)	Sydney	21/1/78
8:30.53	Tracey Wickham (AUS)	Brisbane	23/2/78
8:24.62	Tracey Wickham (AUS)	Edmonton	5/8/78

400/1,500m FREESTYLE (MEN)

• Rick DeMont

Henry Taylor of Britain was the first record holder for 400m and 1,500m freestyle with his winning times of 5 min 36.8 sec and 22 min 48.4 sec at the 1908 Olympics in London.

A needy orphan yet the aquatic marvel of his era, Taylor worked in cotton mills at Oldham. He trained during his lunch breaks and the evenings in any water he could find – in canals, streams and in the baths on dirty-water (and cheaper) days.

Swashbuckling happy Henry won four Olympic golds, two silvers and two bronzes at a remarkable span of Games – 1906, '08, '12 and '20 (those of 1916 being cancelled because of the First World War). He was 35 at his last international appearance and was then playing waterpolo for England.

The records have tumbled since Taylor's time. Michael Gross, in an event he seldom races, brought the 400m figures to 3 min 47.80 sec in 1985. Vladimir Salnikov was nearly eight minutes faster than the Briton in 1983 when he clocked 14 min 58.27 sec for 1,500m in Moscow, averaging less than a minute for each 100m. The Russian was also the first under 3 min 50 sec for 400m and 8 min for 800m – 7 min 56.49 in Minsk in 1979.

Rick DeMont was the 4 min breaker in 1973 when he won the first world 400m title in Belgrade. This was just a year after he had touched one hundredth of a second ahead of Brad Cooper in the Munich Olympics and then been dramatically disqualified for failing a dope test. He was found to have minute quantities of a banned substance, ephedrine, which he took to control his asthma, in his body.

The plummeting of the 1,500m record has seen many famed men through magic minute marks. Arne Borg, whose theme song might have been "wine, women and water", improved his figures by 2 min 28.1 sec over four years (1923-27).

• Arne Borg

A great patriot, the Swede still finished in prison when he opted for a holiday in Spain instead of reporting for National service. After all, it was peace time! He was the first under 22 and 20 minutes but Boy Charlton (1926) claimed the first sub 21 min mark.

Tomikatsu Amano was the sub 19 min man (1938), Murray Rose went through the 18 min barrier (1956), Roy Saari 17 min (1965) and John Kinsella 16 min (1970).

Two men became the fastest ever in "cock-a-snoot" circumstances. Hironashin Furuhashi was unable to compete in the 1948 London Olympics because Japan had been suspended from FINA (the international swimming federation) following the Second World War. Peter Szmidt missed the 1980 Olympics as a result of Canada's Moscow boycott.

To make up for not being in London, the Japanese arranged special championships to coincide with the Olympic dates. Furuhashi clocked 4 min 33.0 sec for 400m in Tokyo. Bill Smith (USA) was eight seconds slower in winning his gold. Three days later, the "Flying Fish" swam 1,500m in 18 min 37.0 sec. This was 41.5 sec faster than Wembley winner Jimmy McLane (USA).

The Furuhashi times were 2.2 sec and 21.8 sec better than the respective records of Alex Jany of France (1947) and the 10-year-old mark of his Japanese compatriot, Amano. Neither was ratified because of the suspension.

Canada arranged National championships in the days leading up to the Moscow Games. Szmidt won the 400m in a record 3 min 50.49 sec. This proved to be nearly a second better than the gold medal time of Salnikov.

Steve Holland has a special claim to fame. He swam a mile (1,609.344m) to win his world 1,500m title in record time in Belgrade in 1973 having broken the 800m record on the way.

The Brisbane boy, 15, was on his first trip outside Australia and in his first major race. He had set his mind not to stop swimming until two laps after the whistle had signalled the last 100m. But the officials forgot to blow!

He completed the full distance 5m in front of DeMont with Cooper a further 13m back. The cheers turned to gasps as the fair-haired lad turned and tore up the bath again. The experienced DeMont and Cooper, bemused that their own lap counting was wrong, followed Holland for another 100m. Still the Australian kept swimming. At last frantic officials managed to stop him about 10m up his third extra lap!

Vladimir Salnikov

1500m Freestyle (Men)

Time	Competitor	Venue	Date
22:48.4	Henry Taylor (GBR)	London	25/7/08
22:00.0	George Hodgson (CAN)	Stockholm	10/7/12
21:35.3	Arne Borg (SWE)	Gothenburg	8/7/23
21:15.0	Arne Borg (SWE)	Sydney	30/1/24
21:11.4	Arne Borg (SWE)	Paris	13/7/24
20:06.6	Boy Charlton (AUS)	Paris	15/7/24
20:04.4	Arne Borg (SWE)	Budapest	18/8/26
19:07.2	Arne Borg (SWE)	Bologna	2/9/27
18:58.8	Tomikatsu Amano (JPN)	Tokyo	10/8/38
18:37.0*	Hironashin Furnhashi (JPN)	Tokyo	7/8/48
18:35.7	Shiro Hashizume (JPN)	Los Angeles	16/8/49
18:19.0	Hironashin Furuhashi (JPN)	Los Angeles	16/8/49
18:05.9	George Breen (USA)	New Haven	29/3/56
17:59.5	Murray Rose (AUS)	Melbourne	27/10/56
17:52.9	George Breen (USA)	Melbourne	5/12/56
17:28.7	John Konrads (AUS)	Melbourne	22/2/58
17:11.0	John Konrads (AUS)	Sydney	27/2/60
17:05.5	Roy Saari (USA)	Tokyo	17/8/63
17:01.8	Murray Rose (AUS)	Los Altos	2/8/64
16:58.7	Roy Saari (USA)	New York	2/9/64
16:58.6	Steve Krause (USA)	Maumee	15/8/65
16:41.6	Mike Burton (USA)	Lincoln	21/8/66
16:34.1	Mike Burton (USA)	Oak Park	13/8/67
16:28.1	Guillermo Echevarria (MEX)	Santa Clara	7/7/68
16:08.5	Mike Burton (USA)	Long Beach	3/9/68
16:04.5	Mike Burton (USA)	Louisville	17/8/69
15:57.1	John Kinsella (USA)	Los Angeles	23/8/70
15:52.91	Rick DeMont (USA)	Chicago	6/8/72
15:52.58	Mike Burton (USA)	Munich	4/9/72
15:37.8	Steve Holland (AUS)	Brisbane	5/8/73
15:31.85	Steve Holland (AUS)	Belgrade	8/9/73
15:31.75	Tim Shaw (USA)	Long Beach	21/6/75
15:27.79	Steve Holland (AUS)	Christchurch	25/1/75
15:20.91	Tim Shaw (USA)	Long Beach	21/6/75
15:10.89	Steve Holland (AUS)	Sydney	27/2/76
15:06.66	Brian Goodell (USA)	Long Beach	21/6/76
15:02.40	Brian Goodell (USA)	Montreal	20/7/76
14:58.27	Vladimir Salnikov (URS)	Moscow	22/7/80
14:56.35	Vladimir Salnikov (URS)	Moscow	13/3/82
14:54.76	Vladimir Salnikov (URS)	Moscow	22/2/83

*Never ratified

400m Freestyle (Men)

Time	Competitor	Venue	Date
Early long course bests (some of which were records):			
6:36.8	Henry Taylor (GBR)	London	16/7/08
6:24.4	George Hodgson (CAN)	Stockholm	14/7/12
5:06.6	Johnny Weissmuller (USA)	Honolulu	22/7/22
4:46.4	Shozo Makino (JPN)	Tokyo	14/8/33
4:35.2	Alex Jany (FRA)	Monte Carlo	12/9/47
4:33.0*	Hironashin Furuhashi (JPN)	Tokyo	4/8/48
4:30.7	Jean Boiteaux (FRA)	Helsinki	29/7/52
4:29.2	Murray Rose (AUS)	Brisbane	10/10/56
4:27.0	Murray Rose (AUS)	Melbourne	27/10/56
4:25.9	Murray Rose (AUS)	Sydney	12/1/57
The progression of the record since 1957 has gone like this:			
4:25.9	John Konrads (AUS)	Sydney	15/1/58
4:21.8	John Konrads (AUS)	Melbourne	18/2/58
4:19.0	John Konrads (AUS)	Sydney	7/2/59
4:16.6	Tsuyoshi Yamanaka (JPN)	Osaka	26/7/59
4:15.9	John Konrads (AUS)	Sydney	23/2/60
4:13.4	Murray Rose (AUS)	Chicago	17/8/62
4:12.7	Don Schollander (USA)	Los Altos	31/7/64
4:12.2	Don Schollander (USA)	Tokyo	15/10/64
4:11.8	John Nelson (USA)	Lincoln	18/8/66
4:11.6	Don Schollander (USA)	Lincoln	18/8/66
4:11.1	Frank Wiegand (GDR)	Utrecht	25/8/66
4:10.6	Mark Spitz (USA)	Hayward	25/6/67
4:09.2	Alain Mosconi (FRA)	Monte Carlo	4/7/67
4:08.8	Mark Spitz (USA)	Santa Clara	7/7/67
4:08.2	Greg Charlton (USA)	Tokyo	28/8/67
4:07.7	Mark Spitz (USA)	Hayward	23/6/68
4:06.5	Ralph Hutton (CAN)	Lincoln	1/8/68
4:04.0	Hans Fassnacht (FRG)	Louisville	14/8/69
4:02.8	John Kinsella (USA)	Los Angeles	20/8/70
4:02.6	Gunnar Larsson (SWE)	Barcelona	7/9/70
4:02.1	Tom McBreen (USA)	Houston	25/8/71
4:01.7	Brad Cooper (USA)	Brisbane	12/2/72
4:00.11	Kurt Krumpholtz (USA)	Chicago	4/8/72
3:58.18	Rick DeMont (USA)	Belgrade	6/9/73
3:56.96	Tim Shaw (USA)	Concord	22/8/74
3:54.69	Tim Shaw (USA)	Concord	22/8/74
3:53.95	Tim Shaw (USA)	Long Beach	19/6/75
3:53.31	Tim Shaw (USA)	Kansas City	20/8/75
3:53.08	Brian Goodeii (USA)	Long Beach	18/6/76
3:51.93	Brian Goodell (USA)	Montreal	22/7/76
3:51.56	Brian Goodell (USA)	Berlin	27/8/77
3:51.41	Vladimir Salnikov (URS)	Potsdam	6/4/79
3:51.40	Vladimir Salnikov (URS)	Moscow	19/8/79
3:51.20	Vladimir Salnikov (URS)	Leningrad	24/2/80
3:50.49	Peter Szmidt (CAN)	Etbicoke	16/7/80
3:49.57	Vladimir Salnikov (URS)	Moscow	12/3/82
3:49.57	Vladimir Salnikov (URS)	Kiev	14/7/82
3:48.32	Vladimir Salnikov (URS)	Moscow	19/2/83
3:47.80	Michael Gross (FRG)	Remscheid	27/6/85

*Never ratified

The equivalent speed for a woman is 7.03km/h (4.37mph) achieved by Dara Torres (USA) when she set the female record for 50m freestyle at 25.61 sec at Mission Viejo, California, in July 1984.

When Tom Jager (USA) broke the world record for the 50m freestyle with 22.40 sec at Austin, Texas in December 1985 he averaged a record 8.03km/h (4.99mph) for the distance. That is the greatest speed achieved by a swimmer.

- By comparison with human beings the dolphin has been measured at speeds of over 40km/h (25mph), but the fastest fish known is the swordfish which has been estimated to reach 109km/h (68mph)

100m/200m BACKSTROKE (MEN/WOMEN)

Think of backstroke and the name Roland Matthes is one most likely to come to mind. Often described as the Rolls Royce of swimming, the East German with his deceptively languid stroke and hidden power really was poetry in motion.

He went unbeaten through seven years of major competition – from September 1967 to August 1974 – during which time he broke 16 records, seven for 100m and nine for 200m.

An arch-tactician, he was known to watch the big pool clock as he raced, go into top gear at just the right moment and break a record by the least amount so holding over reserves of speed for other marks in the future.

Matthes, without a break, took the 100m figures from 58.4 to 56.3 in five years. His 200m time span went from 2 min 07.9 sec to 2 min 01.87 between 1967 and 1973, including cutting 2.8 sec at one fell swoop in Leipzig. He was so far ahead of his rivals that it was not until 1976 that another superstar, John Naber, bettered his performances.

Naber, like so many American swimmers, gave his full attention to the sport for just one year. He won both Olympic golds and went through two time barriers with records of 55.49 sec and 1 min 59.19 sec.

Rick Carey, also of the United States, followed Naber into the record book but to his mortification failed to set world figures in winning his two 1984 Olympic titles.

100m Backstroke (Men)

Time	Competitor	Venue	Date
Early long course bests (some of which were records):			
1:14.8	Warren Kealoha (USA)	Antwerp	22/8/20
1:12.4	Warren Kealoha (USA)	Honolulu	13/4/24
1:11.2	Walter Laufer (USA)	Berlin	20/6/26
1:09.0	George Kojac (USA)	Detroit	23/6/28
1:08.2	George Kojac (USA)	Amsterdam	9/8/28
1:07.5	Adolph Kiefer (USA)	Detroit	6/7/35
1:06.5	Adolph Kiefer (USA)	Des Moines	20/6/36
1:05.9	Adolph Kiefer (USA)	Berlin	14/8/36
1:05.4	Yoshinobu Oyakawa (USA)	Helsinki	1/8/52
1:05.1	Gilbert Bozon (FRA)	Turin	9/54
1:02.5	David Thiele (AUS)	Sydney	27/10/56
1:02.2	David Thiele (AUS)	Melbourne	6/12/56
The progression of the record since 1957 has gone like this:			
1:01.5	John Monckton (AUS)	Melbourne	15/2/58
1:01.3	Bob Bennett (USA)	Los Angeles	19/8/61
1:01.0	Tom Stock (USA)	Cuyahoga Falls	11/8/62
1:00.9	Tom Stock (USA)	Cuyahoga Falls	12/8/62
1:00.8	Ernst-Joachim Kuppers (FRG)	Dortmund	28/8/64
1:00.0	Tom Mann (USA)	New York	3/9/64
59.6	Tom Mann (USA)	Tokyo	16/10/64
59.5	Doug Russell (USA)	Tokyo	28/8/67
59.3	Charles Hickox (USA)	Tokyo	28/8/67
59.1	Charles Hickox (USA)	Tokyo	31/8/67
58.4	Roland Matthes (GDR)	Leipzig	21//67
58.0	Roland Matthes (GDR)	Mexico City	26/10/68
57.8	Roland Matthes (GDR)	Wurzburg	23/8/69
56.9	Roland Matthes (GDR)	Barcelona	8/9/70
56.7	Roland Matthes (GDR)	Leipzig	4/9/71
56.6	Roland Matthes (GDR)	Moscow	8/4/72
56.3	Roland Matthes (GDR)	Moscow	9/4/72
56.30	Roland Matthes (GDR)	Munich	4/9/72
56.19	John Naber (USA)	Montreal	18/7/76
55.49	John Naber (USA)	Montreal	19/7/76
55.44	Rick Carey (USA)	Clovis	6/8/83
55.38	Rick Carey (USA)	Clovis	6/8/83
55.19	Rick Carey (USA)	Caracas	21/8/83

200m Backstroke (Men)

Time	Competitor	Venue	Date
Early long course bests (some of which were records):			
3:04.4	Oskar Schiele (GER)	Charlottenburg	27/6/09
2:47.1	Walter Laufer (USA)	Bremen	24/6/26
2:44.9	Walter Laufer (USA)	Nuremberg	13/7/26
2:37.8	Toshio Irie (JPN)	Tamagawa	14/10/28
2:28.6	Adolph Kiefer (USA)	Chicago	5/9/37
2:27.8	Allen Stack (USA)		18/6/48
2:23.0	Frank McKinney (USA)	Indianapolis	13/8/55
2:21.4	John Monckton (AUS)	Brisbane	20/2/56
The progression of the record since 1957 has gone like this:			
2:18.8	John Monckton (AUS)	Sydney	15/1/58
2:18.4	John Monckton (AUS)	Melbourne	18/2/58
2:17.9	Frank McKinney (USA)	Los Altos	12/7/59
2:17.8	Frank McKinney (USA)	Osaka	25/7/59
2:17.6	Charles Bittick (USA)	Los Angeles	26/6/60
2:16.0	Tom Stock (USA)	Toledo	24/7/60
2:13.2	Tom Stock (USA)	Chicago	2/7/61
2:11.5	Tom Stock (USA)	Los Angeles	20/8/61
2:10.9	Tom Stock (USA)	Cuyahoga Falls	10/8/62
2:10.3	Jed Graef (USA)	Tokyo	13/10/84
2:09.4	Charles Hickox (USA)	Tokyo	29/8/67
2:07.9	Roland Matthes (GDR)	Leipzig	8/11/67
2:07.5	Roland Matthes (GDR)	Leipzig	14/8/68
2:07.4	Roland Matthes (GDR)	Santa Clara	12/7/69
2:06.6	Gary Hall (USA)	Louisville	14/8/69
2:06.4	Roland Matthes (GDR)	E. Berlin	29/8/69
2:06.3	Mike Stamm (USA)	Los Angeles	20/8/70
2:06.1	Roland Matthes (GDR)	Barcelona	11/9/70
2:05.6	Roland Matthes (GDR)	Leipzig	3/9/71
2:02.8	Roland Matthes (GDR)	Leipzig	10/7/72
2:02.82	Roland Matthes (GDR)	Munich	2/9/72
2:01.87	Roland Matthes (GDR)	Belgrade	6/9/73
2:00.64	John Naber (USA)	Long Beach	19/6/76
1:59.19	John Naber (USA)	Montreal	24/7/76
1:58.93	Rick Carey (USA)	Clovis	3/8/83
1:58.86	Rick Carey (USA)	Indianapolis	27/6/84
1:58.41	Sergei Zabolotnov (URS)	Moscow	21/8/84
1:58.14	Igor Polianskiy (URS)	Gera	3/3/85

• Roland Matthes   • Igor Poliansky

The Soviet Union's Sergei Zabolotnov and then Igor Polianskiy brought the 200m record back to Europe.

East Germany's women, as they have in so many events, swept up the majority of the backstroke records since 1973. They were led by Ulrike Richter with her nine 100m and two 200m marks. Birgit Trieber, Antje Stille and Rica Reinisch followed. Cornelia Sirch became the first woman under 2 min 10 sec for 200m with 2 min 09.91 sec in 1982 and Ina Kleber, 1 min 00.59 sec in 1984, pointed to a first woman below the minute for 100m very soon.

Satoko Tanaka of Japan and South Africa's Karen Muir are two record breakers who never had a chance to win major medals. Tanaka dominated the 200m between 1959 and 1963 setting 10 records (2 min 37.1 sec down to 2 min 28.2 sec). But this event did not become a championship one for women until 1968.

Muir, of the diamond talent from Kimberley, is the youngest ever record breaker. She was only 12 years and 328 days young on 10 August 1965 when she broke the figures for 110 yards (a distance not recognised after April 1969) with 1

• Ulrike Richter

• Cornelia Sirch

min 8.7 sec in a heat of the English open junior championship at Blackpool.

She set seven metric records just before and after the 1968 Olympics but could not compete in Mexico City because South Africa's apartheid policies caused her country to be barred from the Games.

Doris Hart of Britain, with 1 min 36.7 sec in 1923, was the first 100m record holder. In 1956, Judy Grinham, from Neasden, became Britain's first Olympic swimming champion for 32 years with the first "long course" list record of 1 min 12.9 sec and would have beaten Hart by 25m.

100m Backstroke (Women)

Time	Competitor	Venue	Date
Early long course bests (some of which were records):			
1:36.7	Doris Hart (GBR)	Gothenburg	6/7/23
1:26.6	Sybil Bauer (USA)	Newark	8/8/23
1:21.6	Marie Braun (HOL)	Amsterdam	11/8/28
1:18.2	Eleanor Holm (USA)	Jones Beach	16/7/32
1:14.4	Karen Harup (DEN)	London	5/8/48
1:13.8	Geertje Wielema (HOL)	Helsinki	30/7/52
1:12.9	Judy Grinham (GBR)	Melbourne	5/12/56
The progression of the record since 1957 has gone like this:			
1:12.6	Carin Cone (USA)	Honolulu	13/7/57
1:12.5	Phillipa Gould (NZL)	Auckland	15/3/58
1:12.4	Margaret Edwards (GBR)	Cardiff	19/4/58
1:12.3	Ria van Velsen (HOL)	Nijmegan	20/7/58
1:11.9	Judy Grinham (GBR)	Cardiff	23/7/58
1:11.7	Ria van Velsen (HOL)	Waalwijk	26/7/59
1:11.4	Carin Cone (USA)	Chicago	6/9/59
1:11.0	Ria van Velsen (HOL)	Leipzig	12/6/60
1:10.9	Ria van Velsen (HOL)	Maastricht	10/7/60
1:10.1	Lynn Burke (USA)	Indianapolis	17/7/60
1:10.0	Lynn Burke (USA)	Detroit	4/8/60
1:09.2	Lynn Burke (USA)	Detroit	5/8/60
1:09.0	Lynn Burke (USA)	Rome	2/9/60
1:08.9	Donna de Varona (USA)	Los Angeles	28/7/63
1:08.6	Christine Caron (FRA)	Paris	14/6/64
1:08.3	Ginny Duenkel (USA)	Los Angeles	26/9/64
1:07.7	Cathy Ferguson (USA)	Tokyo	14/10/64
1:07.4	Ann Fairlie (SAF)	Beziers	23/7/66
1:07.3	Elaine Tanner (CAN)	Winnipeg	27/7/67
1:07.1	Elaine Tanner (CAN)	Winnipeg	27/7/67
1:06.7	Karen Muir (SAF)	Kimberley	30/1/68
1:06.4	Karen Muir (SAF)	Paris	6/4/68
1:06.2	Kaye Hall (USA)	Mexico City	23/10/68
1:05.6	Karen Muir (SAF)	Utrecht	6/7/69
1:05.39	Ulrike Richter (GDR)	Utrecht	18/8/73
1:04.99	Ulrike Richter (GDR)	Belgrade	4/9/73
1:04.78	Wendy Cook (CAN)	Christchurch	31/1/74
1:04.43	Ulrike Richter (GDR)	Rostock	7/7/74
1:04.09	Ulrike Richter (GDR)	Vienna	22/8/74
1:03.30	Ulrike Richter (GDR)	Vienna	23/8/74
1:03.08	Ulrike Richter (GDR)	Vienna	24/8/74
1:02.98	Ulrike Richter (GDR)	Concord	1/9/74
1:02.6	Ulrike Richter (GDR)	Tallin	14/3/76
1:01.62	Kornelia Ender (GDR)	E. Berlin	3/6/76
1:01.51	Ulrike Richter (GDR)	E. Berlin	5/6/76
1:01.51	Rica Reinisch (GDR)	Moscow	20/7/80
1:01.50	Rica Reinisch (GDR)	Moscow	22/7/80
1:00.86	Rica Reinisch (GDR)	Moscow	23/7/80
1:00.59	Ina Kleber (GDR)	Moscow	24/8/84

200m Backstroke (Women)

Time	Competitor	Venue	Date
Early long course bests (some of which were records):			
3:06.8	Sybil Bauer (USA)	Brighton Beach	4/7/22
2:39.9	Phillipa Gould (NZL)	Auckland	16/1/57
The progression of the record since 1957 has gone like this:			
2:38.5	Lenie de Nijs (HOL)	Blackpool	17/5/57
2:37.4	Chris von Saltza (USA)	Topeka	1/8/58
2:37.1	Satoko Tanaka (JPN)	Tokyo	12/7/59
2:34.8	Satoko Tanaka (JPN)	Tokyo	2/4/60
2:33.5	Lynn Burke (USA)	Indianapolis	15/7/60
2:33.3	Satoko Tanaka (JPN)	Tokyo	23/7/60
2:33.2	Satoko Tanaka (JPN)	Tokyo	30/7/61
2:32.1	Satoko Tanaka (JPN)	Beppu	3/6/62
2:31.6	Satoko Tanaka (JPN)	Osaka	29/7/62
2:29.6	Satoko Tanaka (JPN)	Sydney	10/2/63
2:28.9	Satoko Tanaka (JPN)	Perth	18/2/63
2:28.5	Satoko Tanaka (JPN)	Perth	21/2/63
2:28.2	Satoko Tanaka (JPN)	Tokyo	4/8/63
2:27.4	Cathy Ferguson (USA)	Los Angeles	26/9/64
2:27.1	Karen Muir (SAF)	Beziers	25/7/66
2:26.4	Karen Muir (SAF)	Lincoln	18/8/66
2:24.4	Elaine Tanner (CAN)	Winnipeg	26/7/67
2:24.1	Karen Muir (SAF)	Kimberley	26/1/68
2:23.8	Karen Muir (SAF)	Los Angeles	21/7/68
2:21.5	Sue Atwood (USA)	Louisville	14/8/69
2:20.64	Melissa Belote (USA)	Chicago	5/8/72
2:20.58	Melissa Belote (USA)	Munich	4/9/72
2:19.19	Melissa Belote (USA)	Munich	4/9/72
2:18.41	Ulrike Richter (GDR)	Leipzig	7/7/74
2:17.35	Ulrike Richter (GDR)	Vienna	25/8/74
2:16.33	Nancy Garapick (CAN)	Brantford	27/4/75
2:16.10	Birgit Trieber (GDR)	Piesteritz	6/6/75
2:15.46	Birgit Trieber (GDR)	Cali	25/7/76
2:14.41	Antje Stille (GDR)	E. Berlin	29/2/76
2:13.5	Antje Stille (GDR)	Tallin	13/3/76
2:12.4	Birgit Trieber (GDR)	E. Berlin	4/6/76
2:11.93	Linda Jezek (USA)	W. Berlin	24/8/78
2:11.77	Rica Reinisch (GDR)	Moscow	27/7/80
2:09.91	Cornelia Sirch (GDR)	Guayaquil	7/8/82

100/200m
BREASTSTROKE (MEN/WOMEN)

The rules for breaststroke, which had undergone many changes, settled down in 1957. Yet there were still a variety of techniques that met the regulations.

Chet Jastremski, of Polish extraction, was a fast and short stroke pioneer. In six weeks, from 2 July to 20 August 1961, the stocky medical student (5ft 9in) – who lived in Giant Street – set six 100m records and two for 200m.

He went through the 1 min 10 sec barrier for the two lap race and under 2 min 30 sec for the longer distance and made amazing improvements in that short time of 3.6 and 5.4 sec.

John Hencken of the United States and Britain's David Wilkie, deadly dissimilar rivals of the 1970s, hardly spoke to each other. Wilkie, dark-haired, long and lean had an elegant gliding stroke with a strong leg kick. The shorter, broader, fair-haired Hencken relied more on his arm power.

The American set seven 100m records between 1973 and 1976. He and Wilkie shared seven 200m marks between them with the Briton's Olympic gold medal 2 min 15.11 sec in 1976 standing for six years – and still not beaten by a European at the end of 1985.

Gerald Mörken took Hencken's 100m and held it for five years. Steve Lundquist followed and on his fifth record became the first man under 1 min 2 sec in winning the Olympic title in Los Angeles. The erratic yet brilliant Victor Davis took over Wilkie's 200m crown.

100m Breaststroke (Men)

Time	Competitor	Venue	Date
1:12.7	Viteslav Svozil (TCH)	Piestany	1/5/57
1:11.6	Chi Lien Yung (PRC)	Canton	1/5/57
1:11.5	Vladimir Minashkin (URS)	Leipzig	15/9/57
1:11.4	Leonid Kolesnikov (URS)	Moscow	5/5/61
1:11.1	Chet Jastremski (USA)	Chicago	2/7/61
1:10.8	Gunter Tittes (GDR)	Berlin	5/7/61
1:10.7	Chet Jastremski (USA)	Tokyo	28/7/61
1:10.0	Chet Jastremski (USA)	Tokyo	30/7/61
1:09.5	Chet Jastremski (USA)	Osaka	3/8/61
1:07.8	Chet Jastremski (USA)	Los Angeles	20/8/61
1:07.5	Chet Jastremski (USA)	Los Angeles	20/8/61
1:07.4	Georgy Prokopenko (URS)	Baku	28/3/64
1:06.9	Georgy Prokopenko (URS)	Moscow	3/9/64
1:06.7	Vladimir Kosinski (URS)	Leningrad	8/11/67
1:06.4	Jose Fiolo (BRA)	Rio de Janeiro	19/2/68
1:06.2	Nicolay Pankin (URS)	Moscow	18/4/68
1:05.8	Nicolay Pankin (URS)	Magdeburg	20/4/69
1:05.68	John Hencken (USA)	Munich	29/8/72
1:05.13	Nobutaka Taguchi (JPN)	Munich	29/8/72
1:04.94	Nobutaka Taguchi (JPN)	Munich	30/8/72
1:04.35	John Hencken (USA)	Belgrade	4/9/73
1:04.02	John Hencken (USA)	Belgrade	4/9/73
1:03.88	John Hencken (USA)	Concord	31/8/74
1:03.88	John Hencken (USA)	Montreal	19/7/76
1:03.62	John Hencken (USA)	Montreal	19/7/76
1:03.11	John Hencken (USA)	Montreal	20/7/76
1:02.86	Gerald Mörken (FRG)	Jönköping	17/8/77
1:02.62	Steve Lundquist (USA)	Mission Viejo	19/7/82
1:02.53	Steve Lundquist (USA)	Indianapolis	21/8/82
1:02.34	Steve Lundquist (USA)	Clovis	6/8/83
1:02.28	Steve Lundquist (USA)	Caracas	17/8/83
1:02.13	John Moffett (USA)	Indianapolis	25/6/84
1:01.65	Steve Lundquist (USA)	Los Angeles	29/7/84

• Steve Lundquist

• David Wilkie

• Victor Da[vis]

Breaststroke has gone through many technical rule changes since it first became a separate racing style in 1904.

Until the early 1930s, the simple rules laid down that the arm and leg actions should be simultaneous and the body always on the breast.

Some bright people realised these rules did not stop the arms being recovered over the water and this could be faster.

Between 1934 and 1952 either style of arm recovery was permitted. Men, in particular, had the power to use the over water style effectively.

To protect the old classic breaststroke, the two styles were separated after the 1952 Olympics, the over water action becoming the butterfly.

Between 1952-56, a loop-hole in the rules allowed those with big lung capacities – especially the Japanese – to swim great distances under water, much faster than on the surface.

This was ruled out after the 1956 Games. The classic breaststroke, with some modern modifications, has been the style since 1957.

200m Breaststroke (Men)

Time	Competitor	Venue	Date
2:36.5	Terry Gathercole (AUS)	Townsville	28/6/58
2:33.6	Chet Jastremski (USA)	Tokyo	28/7/61
2:29.6	Chet Jastremski (USA)	Los Angeles	19/8/61
2:28.2	Chet Jastremski (USA)	New York	30/8/64
2:27.8	Ian O'Brien (AUS)	Tokyo	15/10/64
2:27.4	Vladimir Kosinski (URS)	Tallin	3/4/68
2:26.5	Nicolay Pankin (URS)	Minsk	22/3/69
2:25.4	Nicolay Pankin (URS)	Magdeburg	18/4/69
2:23.5	Brian Job (USA)	Los Angeles	22/8/70
2:22.79	John Hencken (USA)	Chicago	5/8/72
2:21.55	John Hencken (USA)	Munich	2/9/72
2:20.52	John Hencken (USA)	Louisville	24/8/73
2:19.28	David Wilkie (GBR)	Belgrade	6/9/73
2:18.93	John Hencken (USA)	Concord	24/8/74
2:18.21	John Hencken (USA)	Concord	19/9/74
2:15.11	David Wilkie (GBR)	Montreal	24/7/76
2:14.77	Victor Davis (CAN)	Guayaquil	5/8/82
2:14.58	Victor Davis (CAN)	Toronto	19/6/84
2:13.34	Victor Davis (CAN)	Los Angeles	2/8/84

● Sylvia Gerasch (left) and Ute Geweniger of East Germany

Galina Prozumenshikova, the only European to win a swimming title at the 1964 Tokyo Olympics, improved the 200m record by nearly seven seconds in three seasons (1964-66).

The Soviet was followed by Catie Ball, 15 in 1966 when she set the first of her seven records. She was the first under 2 min 40 for 200m. The 2 min 30 sec barrier-breaker was Lina Kachushite and it took six years for Silke Hörner to swim faster.

Ute Geweniger, known as 'Miss Bones' because she was so thin and boney, was a six-times 100m record breaker finally losing this honour to Sylvia Gerasch, her East German countrywoman. Gerasch, the first record breaker of 1986, also took Hörner's 200m mark.

● Anita Lonsbrough

Anita Lonsbrough of Britain had one over-riding thought as she sat behind her block, bathrobe cloaking her shoulders like a queen, waiting for the start of the Olympic 200m breaststroke final in 1960. There was a fly on the water in her lane! Would she swallow it as she dived in? She didn't! But she did win in a world record 2 min 49.5 sec.

100m Breaststroke (Women)

Time	Competitor	Venue	Date
1:21.1	Ada Den Haan (HOL)	Paris	13/7/57
1:20.3	Karin Beyer (GDR)	E. Berlin	20/7/58
1:19.1	Karin Beyer (GDR)	Leipzig	12/9/58
1:19.1	Wiltrud Urselmann (FRG)	Zurich	12/3/60
1:19.0	Ursela Küper (GDR)	Leipzig	14/7/60
1:18.2	Barbara Gobel (GDR)	Rostock	1/7/61
1:17.9	Claudia Kolb (USA)	Los Angeles	11/7/64
1:16.5	Svetlana Babanina (URS)	Tashkent	11/5/65
1:15.7	Galina Prozumenshikova (URS)	Leningrad	17/7/66
1:15.6	Catie Ball (USA)	F. Lauderdale	28/12/66
1:14.8	Catie Ball (USA)	Winnipeg	31/7/67
1:14.6	Catie Ball (USA)	Philadelphia	19/8/67
1:14.2	Catie Ball (USA)	Los Angeles	25/8/68
1:13.58	Cathy Carr (USA)	Munich	2/9/72
1:12.91	Renate Vogel (GDR)	Vienna	22/8/74
1:12.55	Christel Justan	Vienna	23/8/74
1:12.28	Renate Vogel (GDR)	Concord	1/9/74
1:11.93	Carola Nitschke (GDR)	E. Berlin	2/6/76
1:11.11	Hannelore Anke (GDR)	Montreal	22/7/76
1:10.86	Hannelore Anke (GDR)	Montreal	22/7/76
1:10.31	Julia Bogdanova (URS)	E. Berlin	22/8/78
1:10.20	Ute Geweniger (GDR)	Magdeburg	26/5/80
1:10.11	Ute Geweniger (GDR)	Moscow	24/7/80
1:09.52	Ute Geweniger (GDR)	Gera	19/4/81
1:09.39	Ute Geweniger (GDR)	E. Berlin	2/7/81
1:08.60	Ute Geweniger (GDR)	Split	8/9/81
1:08.51	Ute Geweniger (GDR)	Rome	25/8/83
1:08.29	Sylvia Gerasch (GDR)	Moscow	23/8/84

200m Breaststroke (Women)

Time	Competitor	Venue	Date
Early long course bests (some of which were records):			
3:38.2	E. Van de Bogaert (BEL)	Antwerp	7/8/21
3:16.6	Else Jacobsen (DEN)	Oslo	20/8/27
3:11.2	Lotte Muhe (GER)	Berlin	15/7/28
The progression of the record since 1957 has gone like this:			
2:52.5	Ada Den Haan (HOL)	Blackpool	10/5/57
2:51.9	Ada Den Haan (HOL)	Rhenen	3/8/57
2:51.3	Ada Den Haan (HOL)	Rhenen	4/8/57
2:50.3	Anita Lonsborough (GBR)	Waalwijk	25/7/59
2:50.2	Wiltrud Urselmann (FRG)	Aachen	6/6/60
2:49.5	Anita Lonsbrough (GBR)	Rome	27/8/60
2:48.0	Karin Beyer (GDR)	Budapest	5/8/61
2:47.7	Galina Prozumenshikova (URS)	Blackpool	11/4/64
2:45.4	Galina Prozumenshikova (URS)	E. Berlin	18/5/64
2:45.3	Galina Prozumenshikova (URS)	Groningen	12/9/65
2:40.8	Galina Prozumenshikova (URS)	Utrecht	23/8/66
2:40.5	Catie Ball (USA)	Santa Clara	9/7/67
2:39.5	Catie Ball (USA)	Philadelphia	20/8/67
2:38.5	Catie Ball (USA)	Los Angeles	26/8/68
2:37.89	Anne-Katrin Schott (GDR)	Rostock	6/7/74
2:37.44	Karla Linke (GDR)	Vienna	19/8/74
2:34.99	Karla Linke (GDR)	Vienna	19/8/74
2:33.35	Marina Kosheveya (URS)	Montreal	21/7/76
2:33.32	Julia Bogdanova (URS)	Leningrad	7/4/78
2:33.11	Lina Kachushite (URS)	W. Berlin	24/8/78
2:31.42	Lina Kachushite (URS)	W. Berlin	24/8/78
2:31.09	Svetlana Varganova (URS)	Minsk	30/3/79
2:28.36	Lina Kachushite (URS)	Potsdam	6/4/79
2:28.33	Silke Hörner (GDR)	Leipzig	5/6/85
2:28.20	Sylvia Gerasch (GDR)	Leningrad	28/2/86

● Mark Spitz

100/200m BUTTERFLY
(MEN/WOMEN)

Butterfly became the fourth swimming style in 1952 when it was separated from breaststroke. The coordination of the new dolphin flutter kick with the simultaneous over-water arm recovery took a few years to master. Then the records began to tumble.

Takahashi Ishimoto broke the 100m figures five times in a year but failed, by one tenth of a second, to become the first man under the minute. This honour went to Lance Larson, whom many thought had won the Olympic 100m freestyle title in 1960 but only got the silver behind John Devitt (AUS) because of the human judging system at the time.

Ten years after Ishimoto's first world record, Mark Spitz began his run of seven taking his times from 56.3 to 54.27 between July 1967 and August 1972. This last was unchallenged for five years.

In these same years Spitz, whose record seven golds at the Munich Olympics included both butterfly titles, broke the

200m record eight times but just failed to get through the magic two minute barrier. Roger Pyttel did this, in his second world record of the day during the Olympic trials of 1976.

Jon Sieben, 5ft 9in and known as "The Shrimp" was one of the most remarkable record breakers. He trimmed one hundredth of a second from the year-old figures of Michael Gross in beating the 6ft 7in "Albatross" with the 7ft 6in arm span for the 1984 Olympic gold. He turned a 3m deficit with 50m to go to victory by close to a metre.

100m Butterfly (Men)

Time	Competitor	Venue	Date
1:03.4	Gyorgy Tumpek (HUN)	Budapest	26/5/57
1:01.5	Takahashi Ishimoto (JPN)	Kurume	16/6/57
1:01.3	Takahashi Ishimoto (JPN)	Tokyo	7/7/57
1:01.2	Takahashi Ishimoto (JPN)	Tokyo	6/9/57
1:01.0	Takahashi Ishimoto (JPN)	Kochi	14/9/57
1:00.1	Takahashi Ishimoto (JPN)	Los Angeles	29/6/58
59.0	Lance Larson (USA)	Los Angeles	26/6/60
58.7	Lance Larson (USA)	Toledo	24/7/60
58.6	Fred Schmidt (USA)	Los Angeles	20/8/61
58.4	Luis Nicolao (ARG)	Rio de Janeiro	24/4/62
57.0	Luis Nicolao (ARG)	Rio de Janeiro	27/4/62
56.3	Mark Spitz (USA)	Santa Clara	9/7/67
55.7	Mark Spitz (USA)	W. Berlin	7/10/67
55.6	Mark Spitz (USA)	Long Beach	30/8/68
55.0	Mark Spitz (USA)	Houston	25/8/71
54.72	Mark Spitz (USA)	Chicago	4/8/72
54.56	Mark Spitz (USA)	Chicago	4/8/72
54.27	Mark Spitz (USA)	Munich	31/8/72
54.18	Joe Bottom (USA)	E. Berlin	27/8/77
54.15	Pär Arvidsson (SWE)	Austin	11/4/80
53.81	Bill Paulus (USA)	Austin	3/4/81
53.44	Matt Gribble (USA)	Clovis	6/8/83
53.38	Pablo Morales (USA)	Indianapolis	26/6/84
53.08	Michael Gross (FRG)	Los Angeles	30/7/84

200m Butterfly (Men)

Time	Competitor	Venue	Date
Early long course bests (some of which were records):			
2:19.3	Bill Yorzyk (USA)	Melbourne	1/12/56
The progression of the record since 1957 has gone like this:			
2:19.0	Mike Troy (USA)	Los Altos	11/7/59
2:16.4	Mike Troy (USA)	Los Altos	11/7/59
2:15.0	Mike Troy (USA)	Evansville	10/7/60
2:13.4	Mike Troy (USA)	Toledo	23/7/60
2:13.2	Mike Troy (USA)	Detroit	4/8/60
2:12.8	Mike Troy (USA)	Rome	2/9/60
2:12.6	Carl Robie (USA)	Los Angeles	19/8/61
2:12.5	Kevin Berry (AUS)	Melbourne	20/2/62
2:12.4	Carl Robie (USA)	Cuyahoga Falls	11/8/62
2:10.8	Carl Robie (USA)	Cuyahoga Falls	11/8/62
2:09.7	Kevin Berry (AUS)	Sydney	12/1/63
2:08.4	Kevin Berry (AUS)	Sydney	12/1/63
2:08.2	Carl Robie (USA)	Tokyo	18/8/63
2:06.9	Kevin Berry (AUS)	Sydney	29/3/64
2:06.6	Kevin Berry (AUS)	Tokyo	18/10/64
2:06.4	Mark Spitz (USA)	Winnipeg	26/7/67
2:06.0	John Ferris (USA)	Tokyo	30/8/67
2:05.7	Mark Spitz (USA)	W. Berlin	8/10/67
2:05.4	Mark Spitz (USA)	Los Angeles	22/8/70
2:05.0	Gary Hall (USA)	Los Angeles	22/8/70
2:03.9	Mark Spitz (USA)	Houston	27/8/71
2:03.9	Mark Spitz (USA)	Houston	27/8/71
2:03.3	Hans Fassnacht (FRG)	Landskrona	31/8/71
2:01.87	Mark Spitz (USA)	Chicago	2/8/72
2:01.53	Mark Spitz (USA)	Chicago	2/8/72
2:00.70	Mark Spitz (USA)	Munich	28/8/72
2:00.21	Roger Pyttel (GDR)	E. Berlin	3/6/76
1:59.63	Roger Pyttel (GDR)	E. Berlin	3/6/76
1:59.23	Mike Bruner (USA)	Montreal	18/7/76
1:58.21	Craig Beardsley (USA)	Irvine	30/7/80
1:58.01	Craig Beardsley (USA)	Kiev	22/8/81
1:57.05	Michael Gross (FRG)	Rome	26/8/83
1:57.04	Jon Sieben (AUS)	Los Angeles	3/8/84
1:57.01	Michael Gross (FRG)	Remscheid	29/6/85
1:56.65	Michael Gross (FRG)	Sofia	10/8/85

• Jon Sieben

Mary Meagher transformed the butterfly record book with manlike performances when only a teenager. At 14 she swam 200m in 2 min 9.77 sec and in four more bites took the figures down to 2 min 5.96 sec the year after swallowing her disappointment in missing Olympic gold because of the US boycott of the Moscow Games.

Only Cornelia Polit of East Germany, the European record breaker, has come within two seconds – just – of that Meagher time. Over 100m the girl from Louisville has outsprinted her nearest rival by 1.5 seconds and the rest by much more. Her 1981 mark of 57.93 sec would not have left her trailing very far behind Mark Spitz in his early record days.

Kornelia Ender and Rosemarie Kother of East Germany shared nine 100m record performances between 1973 and 1976. Ender's last, record-equalling 1m 00.13 in winning the Olympic title in Montreal in 1976 easily could have been faster and taken her under the minute.

But she could not afford to go out flat because, with barely time to "swim down" Ender had to be back on the block for the start of the 200m freestyle final. The East German completed her record of four golds at a single Games and became the most successful woman swimmer ever by taking this title in another world record.

• Mary Meagher

100m Butterfly (Women)

Time	Competitor	Venue	Date
Early long course bests (some of which were records):			
:16.6	Jutta Langenau (GDR)	Turin	31/8/54
:15.0	Betty Mullen (USA)	Philadelphia	14/8/55
:11.8	Shelley Mann (USA)	Tyler	7/7/56
:11.2	Shelley Mann (USA)	Melbourne	3/12/56
:11.0	Shelley Mann (USA)	Melbourne	5/12/56
The progression of the record since 1957 has gone like this:			
:10.5	Atie Voorbij (HOL)	Rhenen	4/8/57
:09.6	Nancy Ramey (USA)	Los Angeles	28/6/58
:09.1	Nancy Ramey (USA)	Chicago	2/9/59
:08.9	Jan Andrew (AUS)	Tokyo	2/4/61
:08.8	Mary Stewart (CAN)	Philadelphia	12/8/61
:08.2	Susan Doer (USA)	Philadelphia	12/8/61
:07.3	Mary Stewart (CAN)	Vancouver	28/7/62
:06.5	Kathy Ellis (USA)	High Point	16/8/63
:06.1	Ada Kok (HOL)	Soestduinen	1/9/63
:05.1	Ada Kok (HOL)	Blackpool	30/5/64
:04.7	Sharon Stouder (USA)	Tokyo	16/10/64
:04.5	Ada Kok (HOL)	Budapest	14/8/65
:04.1	Alice Jones (USA)	Los Angeles	20/8/70
:03.9	Mayumi Aoki (JAP)	Tokyo	21/7/72
:03.80	Andrea Gyarmati (HUN)	Munchen	31/8/72
:03.34	Mayumi Aoki (JAP)	Munchen	1/9/72
:03.05	Kornelia Ender (GDR)	E. Berlin	14/4/73
:02.31	Kornelia Ender (GDR)	E. Berlin	14/7/73
:02.09	Rosemarie Kother (GDR)	Vienna	21/8/74
:01.99	Rosemarie Kother (GDR)	Vienna	22/8/74
:01.88	Rosemarie Kother (GDR)	Concord	1/9/74
:01.33	Kornelia Ender (GDR)	Piesteritz	9/6/75
:01.24	Kornelia Ender (GDR)	Cali	24/7/75
:00.13	Kornelia Ender (GDR)	E. Berlin	4/6/76
:00.13	Kornelia Ender (GDR)	Montreal	22/7/76
59.78	Christiane Knacke (GDR)	E. Berlin	28/8/77
59.46	Andrea Pollack (GDR)	E. Berlin	3/7/78
59.26	Mary Meagher (USA)	Austin	11/4/80
57.93	Mary Meagher (USA)	Milwaukee	16/8/81

200m Butterfly (Women)

Time	Competitor	Venue	Date
Early long course best:			
2:44.4	Shelley Mann (USA)	Tyler	6/7/56
The progression of the record since 1957 has gone like this:			
2:44.1	Shelley Mann (USA)	Ann Arbor	14/7/57
2:40.5	Nancy Ramey (USA)	Los Angeles	29/6/58
2:38.9	Tinke Lagerberg (HOL)	Naarden	13/9/58
2:37.0	Becky Collins (USA)	Redding	19/7/59
2:34.4	Marianne Heemskerk (HOL)	Leipzig	12/6/60
2:32.8	Becky Collins (USA)	Philadelphia	13/8/61
2:31.2	Sharon Finneran (USA)	Chicago	19/8/62
2:30.7	Sharon Finneran (USA)	Los Altos	25/8/62
2:29.1	Sue Pitt (USA)	Philadelphia	27/7/63
2:28.1	Sharon Stouder (USA)	Los Angeles	12/7/64
2:26.4	Sharon Stouder (USA)	Los Altos	2/8/64
2:26.3	Kendis Moore (USA)	Maumee	15/8/65
2:25.8	Ada Kok (HOL)	Leiden	21/8/65
2:25.3	Ada Kok (HOL)	Groningen	12/9/65
2:22.5	Ada Kok (HOL)	Groningen	2/8/67
2:21.0	Ada Kok (HOL)	Blackpool	25/8/67
2:20.7	Karen Moe (USA)	Santa Clara	11/7/70
2:19.3	Alice Jones (USA)	Los Angeles	22/8/70
2:18.6	Karen Moe (USA)	Los Angeles	7/8/71
2:18.4	Ellie Daniel (USA)	Houston	27/8/71
2:18.4	Ellie Daniel (USA)	Houston	27/8/71
2:18.4	Ellie Daniel (USA)	Minsk	10/9/71
2:16.62	Karen Moe (USA)	Chicago	6/8/72
2:15.57	Karen Moe (USA)	Munich	4/9/72
2:15.45	Rosemarie Kother (GDR)	Belgrade	8/9/73
2:13.76	Rosemarie Kother (GDR)	Belgrade	8/9/73
2:13.6	Rosemarie Kother (GDR)	Tallin	14/3/76
2:12.84	Rosemarie Kother (GDR)	E. Berlin	5/6/76
2:11.22	Rosemarie Kother (GDR)	E. Berlin	5/6/76
2:11.20	Andrea Pollack (GDR)	Leningrad	9/4/78
2:09.87	Andrea Pollack (GDR)	E. Berlin	4/7/78
2:09.87	Tracy Caulkins (USA)	W. Berlin	26/8/78
2:09.77	Mary Meagher (USA)	San Juan	7/7/79
2:08.41	Mary Meagher (USA)	F. Lauderdale	6/8/79
2:07.01	Mary Meagher (USA)	F. Lauderdale	6/8/79
2:06.37	Mary Meagher (USA)	Irvine	30/7/80
2:05.96	Mary Meagher (USA)	Milwaukee	13/8/81

200/400m INDIVIDUAL MEDLEY (MEN/WOMEN)

Although the United States started the idea of individual medley swimming, it was competitors from other countries who took all the 400m records between 1953 and 1957. There were a number of good reasons for this.

Records were still able to be set in short course pools thus giving competitors the time gain of extra turns – 0.7 secs each turn.

America's short course winter season competitions were – and still are – in 25 yd pools. For any single stroke race it was possible to break a metric record in an imperial pool with what was called a "flagged rope" mid-bath time. For medley, with its four precise distance sectors, this was impossible.

Europeans raced over metres, usually 25m, so they had the right conditions – though Britain stuck obstinately to baths of various imperial lengths.

That Frank O'Neill (AUS) became the first 400m medley record breaker on 17 January 1953, swimming in a long course 55yd pool with a time he set for 440yd (402.363m) is not the contradiction it seems.

This was the height of the Australian summer racing season and there was no time target for the first record breaker to beat. Within three months Gusztav Kettesy of Hungary had cut 10 seconds from O'Neill's time. Kettesy set one long course record in mid-summer 1953, but all the others before 1957 were short course, as were the four by women during these years.

The United States, the innovators of individual medley, really took over the record-book in 1957, when all world marks had to be set "long course", in 50m or 55yd pools.

American women claimed 17 400m records without a break from Sylvia Ruuska's 5 min 46.6 sec to the 5 min 4.7 sec by Claudia Kolb, a former 100m breast-

● Shane G

stroke recordholder, in 1968. Kolb's time stood for four years.

Donna da Varona was only 13, in 1960, when she set the first of her seven records during this era. She lost the chance of being the youngest-ever Olympic champion a month later because this event (400m) was not in the Games programme in Rome.

Fair-haired Donna was one of the most photographed of American women athletes. She was a cover girl on *Life, Time, Saturday Evening Post* and, twice, on *Sports Illustrated* and was voted the outstanding sportswoman of the United States in 1964. This was the year she won the 400m medley and a second gold in the freestyle relay at the Tokyo Olympics.

● Butterfly

● Backstroke

● Breaststroke

● Freestyle/crawl

Gary Hall (USA) set his fifth 400m medley record three weeks before the 1972 Olympics yet failed even to win the bronze in Munich. He was 2.5 sec ahead of his nearest rival at half distance on course for another record. He "blew" the breaststroke leg and finished fifth, 11m behind.

● Gary Hall

cy Caulkins

200m Individual Medley (Men)

Time	Competitor	Venue	Date
Early US records before world records were recognised:			
2:30.7	George Harrison (USA)	Los Angeles	24/8/56
2:29.1	Frank Brunel (USA)	Akron	19/7/58
2:26.2	Gary Heinrich (USA)	Los Angeles	27/6/59
2:24.7	Lance Larson (USA)	Santa Clara	11/7/59
2:22.2	John McGill (USA)	Toledo	23/7/60
2:22.1	Ted Stickles (USA)	Toledo	23/7/60
2:21.3	Ted Stickles (USA)	Chicago	2/7/61
2:20.5	Ted Stickles (USA)	Cuyahoga Falls	22/7/61
2:19.6	Ted Stickles (USA)	Los Angeles	19/8/61
2:15.9	Ted Stickles (USA)	Los Angeles	19/8/61
2:15.5	Dick Roth (USA)	Los Altos	2/8/64
2:14.9	Dick Roth (USA)	Maumee	15/8/64
2:13.1*	Greg Buckingham (USA)	Los Altos	24/7/66
The progression of the record since 1966 has gone like this:			
2:12.4	Greg Buckingham (USA)	Lincoln	21/8/66
2:11.3	Greg Buckingham (USA)	Oak Park	23/8/67
2:10.6	Charles Hickcox (USA)	Long Beach	31/8/68
2:09.6	Gary Hall (USA)	Louisville	17/8/69
2:09.5	Gary Hall (USA)	Los Angeles	23/8/70
2:09.3	Gunnar Larsson (SWE)	Barcelona	12/9/70
2:09.30	Gary Hall (USA)	Chicago	6/8/72
2:07.17	Gunnar Larsson (SWE)	Munich	3/9/72
2:06.32	David Wilkie (GBR)	Vienna	24/8/74
2:06.32	Steve Furniss (USA)	Concord	1/9/74
2:06.08	Bruce Furniss (USA)	Kansas City	23/8/75
2:05.31	Graham Smith (CAN)	Montreal	4/8/77
2:05.24	Aleksander Sidorenko (URS)	Moscow	9/7/78
2:04.39	Steve Lundquist (USA)	Milwaukee	2/8/78
2:03.65	Graham Smith (CAN)	W. Berlin	24/8/78
2:03.29	Jesse Vassallo (USA)	San Juan	6/7/79
2:03.24	Bill Barrett (USA)	Irvine	1/8/80
2:02.78	Alex Baumann (CAN)	Heidelberg	29/7/81
2:02.25	Alex Baumann (CAN)	Brisbane	4/10/82
2:01.42	Alex Baumann (CAN)	Los Angeles	4/8/84
2:01.42	Alex Baumann (CAN)	Montreal	4/3/86

*This time was not inside the 2:12.0 minimum standard set for the first World record.

Between 1960 and 1964 she brought the record figures down by 21.6 sec, equivalent to a 36m improvement. Her final 5 min 14.9 sec was not beaten for three years. Donna also set eight US 200m records, which could have been world marks, before this event was recognised.

The men of the United States were almost as dominating. Seven different swimmers broke 16 of the 21 records for 400m between 1967 and 1972. Ian Black of Britain was one of the "odd" five. His 5 min 8.8 sec for 440 yd in Cardiff in 1959 was also a metric mark.

Gary Hall's 4 min 30.81 sec, 13 years later, was 38 sec (about 65m) better than Black.

Ricardo Prado, the American-trained Brazilian, was the first South American to win a world swimming title. This was in Guayaquil, Ecuador, in 1982, when he became the first under 4 min 20 sec for 400m medley. His record 4 min 19.78 sec stood for two years.

America pioneered individual medley racing as the ultimate test of the complete swimmer in the 1930s, long before it became a recognised event. It was not until 1953 that the first world records, for 400m, were ratified. Records for 200m started in 1966.

This most difficult and testing of races consists of equal legs on the four swimming styles. In order, these are butterfly, backstroke, breaststroke and freestyle – which as it must be a stroke other than the first three is invariably front crawl.

The start of medley coincided with the separation of the two techniques of breaststroke. The classic underwater arm action and frog leg kick kept the old title. The overwater arm recovery with a new simultaneous dolphin flutter kick was named butterfly.

At the beginning butterfly, the opening stroke in medley which took a while to master, was the most important style in the repertoire of the medley swimmer. Eventually breaststroke, a style without many of the characteristics of the other three, became the crucial one.

As well as individual medley, there are medley relays. The swimming order of the four team members here is backstroke, breaststroke, butterfly and freestyle.

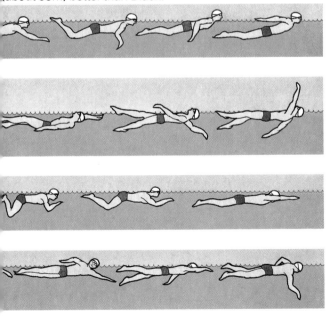

Andras Hargitay of Hungary, a perfect stylist on all four strokes, was the first under 4 min 30 sec with his European title winning time in 1974. His countryman Zoltan Verraszto improved nearly three seconds in the spring of 1976 but his chance of Olympic gold went when he was taken ill in Montreal days before this race.

Alex Baumann, the Czech-born Canadian, illustrated the amazing speed improvements of swimming over the recent years. He won the 1984 Olympic title in a record 4 min 17.41 sec in Los Angeles. This individual time was faster than the combined efforts of a record-breaking Japanese 4 x 100m medley relay quartet in 1957.

Petra Schneider, the greatest of many fine medley women from East Germany, out-did Baumann in 1982. Her 4 min 36.10 sec, winning the world gold in Guayaquil was two seconds faster than the world relay record of the US club Santa Clara just 16 years earlier. The full American Olympic champion squad of 1964 would have beaten Schneider by only 2m (1.5 sec) with their record at the Tokyo Games.

Gail Neall (AUS) spoiled the US record run in 1972 with her Olympic gold performance. Then it was the turn of East Germany.

Gudrun Wegner went under 5 min in 1973. With the exception of the World title performance of Tracy Caulkins (USA) in 1978, it was East Germany all the way with 10 records and a 25 sec (42m) improvement in nine years.

400m Individual Medley (Men)

Time	Competitor	Venue	Date
The early world records set long course were:			
5:48.5	Frank O'Neill (AUS)	Sydney	17/1/53
5:43.0	Frank O'Neill (AUS)	Sydney	24/2/53
5:32.1	Gusztav Kettesy (HUN)	Budapest	26/7/53

The latest of the eight short course records between 1953 and 1957 was 5 min 8.3 sec by Vladimir Stroujanov (URS) on 17/3/57, equivalent to 5:13.9 in a 50m pool.

The progression of the record since 1 May 1957 has gone like this:			
5:12.9	Vladimir Stroujanov (URS)	Moscow	20/10/57
5:08.8	Ian Black (GBR)	Cardiff	6/6/59
5:07.8	George Harrison (USA)	Los Angeles	24/6/60
5:05.3	George Harrison (USA)	Los Angeles	24/6/60
5:04.5	Dennis Rounsavelle (USA)	Toledo	22/7/60
5:04.3	Ted Stickles (USA)	Chicago	1/7/61
4:55.6	Ted Stickles (USA)	Los Angeles	18/8/61
4:53.8	Gerhard Hetz (FRG)	Moscow	24/5/62
4:51.4	Ted Stickles (USA)	Chicago	30/6/62
4:51.0	Ted Stickles (USA)	Louisville	12/7/62
4:50.2	Gerhard Hetz (FRG)	Tokyo	12/10/63
4:48.6	Richard Roth (USA)	Los Altos	31/7/64
4:45.4	Richard Roth (USA)	Tokyo	14/10/64
4:45.3	Andrey Dunaev (URS)	Tallin	3/4/68
4:45.1	Greg Buckingham (USA)	Santa Clara	6/7/68
4:43.4	Gary Hall (USA)	Los Angeles	20/7/68
4:39.0	Charles Hickcox (USA)	Long Beach	30/8/68
4:38.7	Gary Hall (USA)	Santa Clara	12/7/69
4:33.9	Gary Hall (USA)	Louisville	15/8/69
4:31.0	Gary Hall (USA)	Los Angeles	21/8/70
4:30.81	Gary Hall (USA)	Chicago	3/8/72
4:28.89	Andras Hargitay (HUN)	Vienna	20/8/74
4:26.00	Zoltan Verraszto (HUN)	Long Beach	2/4/76
4:23.68	Rod Strachan (USA)	Montreal	25/7/76
4:23.39	Jesse Vassallo (USA)	Milwaukee	4/8/78
4:20.05	Jesse Vassallo (USA)	W. Berlin	22/8/78
4:19.78	Ricardo Prado (BRA)	Guayaquil	2/8/82
4:19.61	Jens-Peter Berndt (GDR)	Magdeburg	23/5/84
4:17.53	Alex Baumann (CAN)	Toronto	17/6/84
4:17.41	Alex Baumann (CAN)	Los Angeles	30/7/84

● Ricardo P

The progression of the 200m, the last individual event to go into the record book, was held up to a degree because this was not an Olympic event in 1976 or 1980.

Kolb opened the women's list with a run of five. Freestyle record breaker Shane Gould (AUS) showed her versatility by trimming Kolb's best four years later, in winning the 1972 Olympic title.

Kornelia Ender (GDR), also better known as a freestyle record-breaker, emulated Gould's medley feat a year later and again in 1976. Only Caulkins, with three records in 1977/78 broke the East German stranglehold since 1973.

Ulrike Tauber claimed six (plus three for 400m) between 1974 and 1977, including being the first under 2 min 20 sec. After Caulkins came Schneider and breaststroke record

na da Varona

reaker Ute Geweniger.

The men's 200m record has swapped hands more often, hough the exchanges, mostly, have been between the North merican nations – the United States and Canada.

The four interlopers included Sweden's Gunnar Larsson nd David Wilkie of Britain. Larsson's times won him golds, at he 1970 European championships and 1972 Olympics.

Wilkie's exclusive record tenure was short-lived. The uture (1976) Olympic 200m breaststroke champion, clocked min 6.32 sec to win the European short medley title on 24 ugust, 1974. Eight days later, Steve Furniss (USA) equalled his time to 1/100th of a second. The following summer, Bruce urniss took the record from his older brother – a remarkable amily double.

200m Individual Medley (Women)

Time	Competitor	Venue	Date
Early US records before world records were recognised:			
2:48.2	Patty Kempner (USA)	Chicago	27/4/57
2:47.7	Becky Collins (USA)	Akron	20/7/58
2:43.2	Sylvia Ruuska (USA)	Fresno	16/8/58
2:40.3	Sylvia Ruuska (USA)	Hobart	14/1/59
2:40.1	Donna de Varona (USA)	Redding	13/5/61
2:37.2	Donna de Varona (USA)	Tenri	9/7/61
2:35.0	Donna de Varona (USA)	Philadelphia	12/8/61
2:33.3	Donna de Varona (USA)	Chicago	18/8/62
2:30.1	Donna de Varona (USA)	Los Angeles	27/7/63
2:29.9	Donna de Varona (USA)	Los Altos	1/8/64
2:29.0*	Lynn Vidali (USA)	Los Altos	22/7/66

*This time was not inside the 2:28.0 minimum standard set for the first World record.

Time	Competitor	Venue	Date
The progression of the record since 1966 has gone like this:			
2:27.8	Claudia Kolb (USA)	Lincoln	21/8/66
2:27.5	Claudia Kolb (USA)	Santa Clara	7/7/67
2:26.1	Claudia Kolb (USA)	Winnipeg	30/7/67
2:25.0	Claudia Kolb (USA)	Philadelphia	18/8/67
2:23.5	Claudia Kolb (USA)	Los Angeles	25/8/68
2:23.07	Shane Gould (AUS)	Munich	28/8/72
2:23.01	Kornelia Ender (GDR)	E. Berlin	13/4/73
2:20.51	Andrea Hubner (GDR)	Belgrade	4/9/73
2:18.97	Ulrike Tauber (GDR)	Vienna	18/8/74
2:18.83	Ulrike Tauber (GDR)	Piesterwitz	10/6/75
2:18.3	Ulrike Tauber (GDR)	Tallinn	12/3/76
2:17.14	Kornelia Ender (GDR)	E. Berlin	5/6/76
2:16.96	Ulrike Tauber (GDR)	Leipzig	10/7/77
2:15.95	Ulrike Tauber (GDR)	Jönköping	20/8/77
2:15.85	Ulrike Tauber (GDR)	E. Berlin	28/8/77
2:15.09	Tracy Caulkins (USA)	Milwaukee	2/8/78
2:14.07	Tracy Caulkins (USA)	W. Berlin	20/8/78
2:13.69	Tracy Caulkins (USA)	Austin	5/1/80
2:13.00	Petra Schneider (GDR)	Magdeburg	24/5/80
2:11.73	Ute Geweniger (GDR)	E. Berlin	4/7/81

400m Individual Medley (Women)

Time	Competitor	Venue	Date
The progression of the record since 1957 has gone like this:			
5:46.6	Sylvia Ruuska (USA)	Los Angeles	27/6/58
5:43.7	Sylvia Ruuska (USA)	Topeka	1/8/58
5:41.1	Sylvia Ruuska (USA)	Melbourne	24/2/59
5:40.2	Sylvia Ruuska (USA)	Redding	17/7/59
5:36.5	Donna de Varona (USA)	Indianapolis	15/7/60
5:34.5	Donna de Varona (USA)	Philadelphia	11/8/61
5:29.7	Donna de Varona (USA)	Los Altos	2/6/62
5:27.4	Sharon Finneran (USA)	Osaka	26/7/62
5:24.7	Donna de Varona (USA)	Osaka	26/7/62
5:21.9	Donna de Varona (USA)	Osaka	28/7/62
5:16.5	Donna de Varona (USA)	Lima	10/3/64
5:14.9	Donna de Varona (USA)	New York	30/8/64
5:11.7	Claudia Kolb (USA)	Santa Clara	8/7/67
5:09.7	Claudia Kolb (USA)	Winnipeg	1/8/67
5:08.2	Claudia Kolb (USA)	Phildelphia	19/8/67
5:05.4	Claudia Kolb (USA)	Santa Clara	6/7/68
5:04.7	Claudia Kolb (USA)	Los Angeles	24/8/68
5:02.97	Gail Neall (AUS)	Munich	31/8/72
5:01.10	Angela Franke (GDR)	Utrecht	13/8/73
4:57.51	Gudrun Wegner (GDR)	Belgrade	6/9/73
4:52.42	Ulrike Tauber (GDR)	Vienna	21/8/74
4:52.20	Ulrike Tauber (GDR)	Piesterwitz	7/6/75
4:48.79	Birgit Trieber (GDR)	E. Berlin	1/6/76
4:42.77	Ulrike Tauber (GDR)	Montreal	24/7/76
4:40.83	Tracy Caulkins (USA)	W. Berlin	23/8/78
4:39.96	Petra Schneider (GDR)	Leningrad	8/3/80
4:38.44	Petra Schneider (GDR)	Magdeburg	27/5/80
4:36.29	Petra Schneider (GDR)	Moscow	26/7/80
4:36.10	Petra Schneider (GDR)	Guayaquil	1/8/82

Acknowledgements

The compilers would like to thank the following for their contributions:

Pat Besford, swimming correspondent Daily Express (swimming)
Tim Glover (show jumping and eventing)
Danny Hall, racing editor Daily Express (horse racing)
Martin Hardy, golf correspondent Daily Express (golf)
Christopher Hilton, senior sports features writer Daily Express (cricket, winter sports, motor racing)
John Morgan, Executive sports editor Daily Express (yachting)
Ian Morrison (darts, snooker, cycling, weightlifting, fencing)
Leslie Nichols motor bike correspondent Daily Express (motor bike racing)
Randall Northam (soccer)
Martin Pass (Monte Carlo rally)
Alan Rouse (mountaineering)
Andy Shaw (ski jumping)
Peter Tozer (squash)

Artwork by
Gerard Browne (pp 22, 29, 34-5, 40-1, 45, 46, 55, 78, 97, 106, 149, 181)
Giorgio Moltoni (pp 87, 93, 116-7, 118-9, 120-1)
Mark Taylor (pp16-7, 24-5, 26, 48-9, 50-1, 66, 70, 72-3, 74-5, 76-7, 104-5, 150)
Woolston Designs (pp10, 12, 17, 18, 22-3, 30-1, 33, 35, 50-1, 52-3, 62-3, 64-5, 117, 130, 133, 134, 136-7, 188-9)

Photo credits
All photography supplied by Allsport except for those pictures listed below.
Chris Bonnington (pp154, 155)
John Cleare Mountain Camera (pp154, 155)
Royal Geographical Society (pp153)
Lockheed Company (pp138)
The Photo Source (pp80, 81, 83, 90, 172, 173)
Quadrant Picture Library (pp138)
S & G Press Agency (pp89, 90, 91, 92, 101, 103, 116, 127, 136)
Doug Scott (pp155)